Encyclopedia of
INSECTS AND
SPIDERS

Encyclopedia of
INSECTS AND
SPIDERS

ROD AND KEN PRESTON-MAFHAM

THUNDER BAY
P·R·E·S·S

San Diego, California

Thunder Bay Press

An imprint of the Advantage Publishers Group
5880 Oberlin Drive, San Diego, CA 92121-4794
www.thunderbaybooks.com

The Brown Reference Group plc
(incorporating Andromeda Oxford Ltd)
8 Chapel Place
Rivington Street
London EC2A 3DQ
England

© 2005 The Brown Reference Group plc

All notations of errors or omissions should be addressed to Thunder Bay Press, Editorial Department, at the above address. All other correspondence (author inquiries, permissions) concerning the content of this book should be addressed to The Brown Reference Group.

ISBN 1-59223-428-3

Library of Congress Cataloging-in-Publication Data available upon request.

Project Directors: Graham Bateman, Lindsey Lowe

Editors: Virginia Carter, Angela Davies

Art Editor and Designer: Steve McCurdy

Main Artists: Denys Ovenden, Richard Lewington

Picture Researcher: Vickie Walters

Production: Alastair Gourlay, Maggie Copeland

Printed in Singapore
1 2 3 4 5 09 08 07 06 05

Title page: **Swallowtail butterfly**
Half title: **Red-kneed tarantula**

Contents

Introduction	6–7
WHAT IS AN INSECT?	8–15
Dragonflies and Damselflies	16–25
Walkingsticks and Leaf Insects	26–31
Termites	32–37
Cockroaches	38–43
Mantids	44–49
Lice	50–51
Fleas	52–55
Crickets	56–59
Grasshoppers	60–67
Mosquitoes and Gnats	68–71
Soldier Flies	72–73
Horseflies and Deerflies	74–77
Hover Flies	78–83
Bot and Warble Flies	84–85
Houseflies and Relatives	86–89
Backswimmers	90–93
Plant Bugs	94–97
Bedbugs	98–99
Assassin Bugs	100–105

Dragonfly

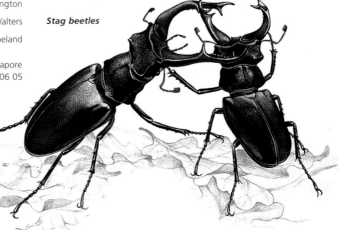

Stag beetles

Stink Bugs 106–115

Aphids 116–121

Ground Beetles 122–125

Diving Beetles 126–127

Fireflies 128–129

Checkered
Beetles 130–131

Ladybugs 132–137

Stag Beetles 138–139

Scarab Beetles 140–153

Weevils 154–161

Swallowtail
Butterflies 162–167

Whites 168–173

Brush–Footed
Butterflies 174–181

Milkweed
Butterflies 182–185

Prominents 186–189

Tiger Moths 190–193

Tussock Moths 194–197

Ermine Moths 198–199

Ants 200–217

Velvet Ants 218–219

Gall Wasps 220–221

Social Wasps 222–235

Honeybees and
Relatives 236–247

WHAT ARE
ARACHNIDS? 248–249

Scorpions 250–253

Mites and Ticks 254–257

Sun Spiders 258–259

*Swallowtail
butterfly*

Tarantulas 260–261

Funnel–Web Spiders 262–263

Net–Casting Spiders 264–265

Crab Spiders 266–271

Sheet–Web
Weavers 272–275

Orb Weavers 276–281

Glossary 282–283

Further Reading/
Websites 284

Index 285–287

Picture Credits 288

Social wasp

*Ground
beetle*

Tarantula

Introduction

LOVE THEM OR HATE THEM, there is no way of avoiding insects and spiders. They are all around us in huge numbers. Not only are there more than 1 million described species, some scientists believe that millions remain to be discovered. It has been estimated that there are 200 million insects for every human on the planet. And in some temperate landscapes there may be as many as 12.5 million spiders per acre (5 million/ha). The statistics are staggering. Approximately 95,000 different insect species and 3,500 species of spiders live in North America north of Mexico.

Insects and their relatives are the most successful animals ever to have evolved. What is more, they have been around for a very long time. They first appeared in the Cambrian period 600 to 500 million years ago. In fact, the earliest fossil arachnid, a scorpion, dates back to the Silurian period, some 400 million years ago.

Why are insects so successful? Along with spiders, crustaceans (lobsters, shrimps, crabs, and so on) they belong to a group called the arthropods. The name "arthropod" is derived from the Greek and literally means "jointed limb." All arthropods have an external skeleton (the exoskeleton). This is the single most important diagnostic feature. The basic chemical component of the insect exoskeleton is chitin, which is a tough and waterproof but pliable substance. It can take all manner of shapes as an insect develops. As the animal grows, it molts its exoskeleton; and after each molt the new cuticle stretches to its new size before hardening.

Insect and Spider Body Plan and Natural History

ALL INSECTS AND SPIDERS have a body that is made up of a number of segments, each covered by the hard plates of the exoskeleton. Between each segment the covering is thinner, allowing the body to be flexible. The segments may bear pairs of appendages, such as antennae, wings, and legs, one arising on each side. The most obvious difference between insects and spiders is that insects have three pairs of legs, while spiders have four pairs. Spiders and their relatives, the scorpions, also lack antennae, wings, and compound eyes. Also, instead of three bodily divisions in insects (the head, thorax, and abdomen), arachnids have only two regions—the anterior cephalothorax (or prosoma) and the posterior abdomen (or opisthosoma).

Arthropods, especially insects, are key components in our planet's survival kit. They have a commanding presence in the dynamic processes that maintain our ecosystems. For example, they dispose of dead vegetation, animal corpses, and dung. They consume huge quantities of vegetation, processing and returning significant amounts of nutrients to the soil as a result. As pollinators of flowers, they provide a vital link in the life cycles of different generations of plants.

The form and the natural history of insects and spiders are more varied than in any other group of animals alive today. The beauty of butterflies, moths, and dragonflies is in marked contrast to the alien appearance of some bugs, scorpions, and spiders. There are hoverflies that look like bees, ants that look like wasps, and even nonpoisonous butterflies that deter predators by resembling unrelated (but poisonous) butterflies. Many insects and spiders resemble their surroundings so closely as to be invisible to predators

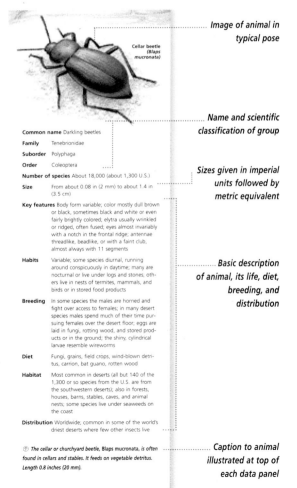

Cellar beetle
(Blaps
mucronata)

Image of animal in typical pose

Common name Darkling beetles

Family Tenebrionidae

Suborder Polyphaga

Order Coleoptera

Number of species About 18,000 (about 1,300 U.S.)

Size From about 0.08 in (2 mm) to about 1.4 in (3.5 cm)

Key features Body form variable; color mostly dull brown or black, sometimes black and white or even fairly brightly colored; elytra usually wrinkled or ridged, often fused; eyes almost invariably with a notch in the frontal ridge; antennae threadlike, beadlike, or with a faint club; almost always with 11 segments

Habits Variable; some species diurnal, running around conspicuously in daytime; many are nocturnal or live under logs and stones; others live in nests of termites, mammals, and birds or in stored food products

Breeding In some species the males are horned and fight over access to females; in many desert species males spend much of their time pursuing females over the desert floor; eggs are laid in fungi, rotting wood, and stored products or in the ground; the shiny, cylindrical larvae resemble wireworms

Diet Fungi, grains, field crops, wind-blown detritus, carrion, bat guano, rotten wood

Habitat Most common in deserts (all but 140 of the 1,300 or so species from the U.S. are from the southwestern deserts); also in forests, houses, barns, stables, caves, and animal nests; some species live under seaweeds on the coast

Distribution Worldwide; common in some of the world's driest deserts where few other insects live

Name and scientific classification of group

Sizes given in imperial units followed by metric equivalent

Basic description of animal, its life, diet, breeding, and distribution

ⓘ *The cellar or churchyard beetle, Blaps mucronata, is often found in cellars and stables. It feeds on vegetable detritus. Length 0.8 inches (20 mm).*

Caption to animal illustrated at top of each data panel

⊖ *Summary panel presents key facts and figures for each animal.*

and prey, while others that are often poisonous are brightly colored as a warning to predators to keep away. American monarch butterflies migrate up to 2,600 miles (4,200km) to their spectacular mass winter roosts in Mexico. These mass hibernation sites are rivaled only by the millions of convergent ladybugs that migrate from the hot lowlands of western North America to cool mountain canyons.

Some insect societies are among the most refined in the animal world, the epitome being the caste systems of termites, ants, and bees. As well as having developed sophisticated social systems, some insects have become master builders. The complex nests of some bees and the intricate webs of many spiders bear testimony to their skill.

Friends or Foes?

MANY INSECTS ARE PESTS OF PEOPLE, their crops, and livestock. At the beginning of the 21st century about 300 million people around the world are affected by malaria, which is transmitted by mosquitoes, and there are 1.5 million deaths annually. Equally devastating in the tropics is sleeping sickness, which is transmitted by tsetse flies. Locusts have decimated crops for thousands of years—according to the Bible, a plague of locusts was sent to punish the Egyptians.

A combination of insect adaptability and modern worldwide trade and communications has enabled many insects to move around the globe, often thriving in their new-found surroundings. The American cockroach, which now occurs throughout the world in association with human habitations, is thought to have originated in Africa. The cabbage white butterfly was accidentally introduced into North America from Europe in 1881 and now occurs across the continent, its caterpillars munching through the same diet of cabbages and related plants. More recently, the soybean aphid, a native of China and a pest of soybean plants, was discovered in the United States, and there is concern about its effects and how quickly it is spreading. The list of such pest introductions is almost endless.

In some cases the tables have been turned by the introduction of alien species to fight other insect pests. The first (highly successful) venture involved the introduction in 1888 of a beetle from Australia to fight the cottony cushion scale, itself an accidental introduction from Australia, that was ravaging California's citrus orchards. The principle of introducing an enemy from the original native home of an introduced species has become the cornerstone of biological control ever since. But it can go wrong! When the European seven-spot ladybug was introduced to "help" the native

American species fight aphids, the foreigner became so successful that it now outnumbers the natives.

For many people insects and spiders are synonymous with bites and stings. Fortunately for most, they only encounter the relatively minor effects of insect and spider bites and stings. Most mosquito bites, for example, produce in the victim an allergic reaction to the insect's saliva that remains in the wound; while the bites of spiders and the stings of bees and wasps produce a reaction to the poisons injected by the animal. The most serious casualties occur when an individual reacts badly to a bite or sting or when he or she is attacked en masse.

Of course there are some exceptionally venomous beasts that should be avoided. The most poisonous spider is the Sydney funnel-web, whose poison, atraxotoxin, is one of the most potent animal poisons. At least 15 people are known to have died after encounters with these amazingly tetchy creatures over the past 60 years, but fortunately an antidote to the venom is now available.

Encyclopedia of Insects and Spiders

IN THIS ENCYCLOPEDIA you will find detailed articles of 51 groups of insects and spiders, all of which are represented in North America. Two introductory articles (What is an Insect? and What is an Arachnid?) describe first the basic body structure, biology, and natural history of insects and spiders respectively. The articles that follow have been selected to give the broadest range of insect types from dragonflies and damselflies to wasps, bees, and ants and from scorpions to orb weaver spiders. For each group there is a detailed summary panel (see left) that gives key facts and figures. There then follows the main article, which describes the most interesting features of representatives from each group. Throughout there are detailed artwork portrayals and dynamic photographs of the animals in the wild.

This encyclopedia can only skim the surface of the amazing lives of the million or more species of insects and spiders, but it is hoped that these pages will inspire your appreciation of their hidden world. As a final thought, while about 7,000 new insect species are described every year, that figure is probably exceeded by the annual losses of unknown species that result from the destruction of habitats, mainly tropical forests. The U.S. Fish and Wildlife Service lists 45 threatened or endangered species of insects that are protected wherever they occur in the United States, while State governments list about 850 species as being under some form of local threat.

What Is an Insect?

SUBCLASS APTERYGOTA	
Thysanura	Silverfish
Archeognatha	Bristletails

SUBCLASS PTERYGOTA	
Ephemeroptera	Mayflies
Odonata	Dragonflies and damselflies
Phasmatodea	Walkingsticks and leaf insects
Dermaptera	Earwigs
Isoptera	Termites
Blattodea	Cockroaches
Mantodea	Mantids
Plecoptera	Stoneflies
Embioptera	Web spinners
Zoraptera	Zorapterans
Thysanoptera	Thrips
Psocoptera	Booklice and barklice
Phthiraptera	Lice
Neuroptera	Lacewings
Megaloptera	Alderflies and dobsonflies
Raphidioptera	Snakeflies
Trichoptera	Caddisflies
Mecoptera	Scorpionflies and hangingflies
Siphonaptera	Fleas
Strepsiptera	Strepsipterans
Hemiptera	True bugs
Coleoptera	Beetles
Diptera	Flies
Orthoptera	Crickets and grasshoppers
Lepidoptera	Butterflies and moths
Hymenoptera	Wasps, ants, bees, and sawflies

Number of species More than 1,000,000 (about 95,000 U.S.)

Size From about 0.01 in (0.2 mm) to 12 in (30 cm)

Key features Segmented body with separate head, thorax, and abdomen; head with exposed biting or sucking mouthparts and a pair of antennae; simple eyes (ocelli) present, but lost in some orders; compound eyes present, but may be absent in cave dwellers; thorax with a pair of legs on each of the 3 segments; wings (when present) on the second and third thoracic segments; abdomen with a maximum of 11 segments; cerci present on more primitive orders; alimentary canal, blood system, nervous system, excretory system, and reproductive system present internally; breathing system of tracheal tubes opening to the outside via spiracles; developmental stages have just nymphs or have larvae and pupae

Habitat All habitats

Distribution Worldwide

There are more different species of insect in existence than any other kind of living organism. They show a great deal of variation both in size and in structure. The smallest insects, for example, are smaller than the largest single-celled animals, while the largest insects are considerably bigger than the smallest vertebrates.

Insect Life Cycles and Development

Newly hatched young of the more primitive groups (such as silverfish) generally resemble miniature adults; but they lack wings, and internally, the sex organs are not developed. These stages are called nymphs. The nymphs feed, grow, and molt several times until a final molt results in a fully developed adult. The period between one nymph and the next following a molt is known as an instar. This type of development is known as ametabolous. In the living world, however, there are exceptions to every generalization. For example, aquatic nymphs of insects such as dragonflies and mayflies tend to be adapted for living in water and therefore do not necessarily closely resemble the adult in appearance.

At the higher end of the primitive groups some plant-sucking bug families such as whiteflies have nymphal stages that do not resemble the adults but look like the developmental stages of the more advanced insects. This is called hemimetabolous development.

Metamorphosis

In the advanced insects such as butterflies, moths, and flies the newly hatched young bears no resemblance to the adult insect and is called a larva. It feeds, grows, and molts through a series of instars until it becomes a pupa

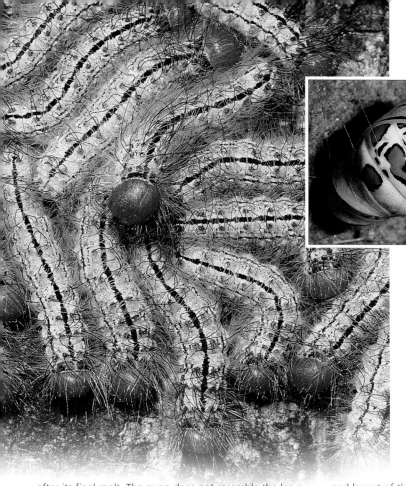

⬅ *Left: These moth caterpillars on a tree in Madagascar belong to one of the advanced insect orders, the Lepidoptera. Inset: This* Papilio *pupa is supported by a silken girdle.*

The Insect Body Plan

The body of all insects is made up of a number of segments, each covered by hard plates. Between each segment the cuticle is thinner, allowing the body to be flexible. The segments may bear pairs of appendages such as antennae and wings, one arising from each side. As a result, they have bilateral symmetry (the right half of the animal is a mirror image of the left half). Occasionally that rule is broken, especially where the structure

after its final molt. The pupa does not resemble the larva. However, in some insect orders (but not all) the vague outline of the adult insect can be seen from the outside. A considerable reorganization of the internal structures takes place inside the pupa to change it from the larval form to the adult form. New structures that are found only in the adult are also formed at this stage. In a final molt the adult insect emerges from the pupa. This is known as holometabolous development.

The final molt from the last nymphal stage to adult or from pupa to adult is referred to as metamorphosis. In the very primitive silverfish (Thysanura) and the bristletails (Archeognatha) there is no metamorphosis. The nymphs grow and molt until they eventually become adult.

One disadvantage of having nymphs rather than larvae is that since the adults and nymphs are so similar physically, they often eat (and so compete for) the same food. Larvae, however, nearly always feed on something different from the adult, and competition is avoided.

and layout of the sex organs are concerned.

At the front end of the body a number of segments are fused together to form the head, which often has a pair of eyes, and behind it there may be further joining of segments to form a thorax. Insects usually have the normal sets of internal organs:

➔ *In primitive insects such as silverfish there is little change between first stage and adult (ametabolous development) (1). Hemimetabolous development occurs in insects such as bugs: The larva resembles a miniature wingless adult (2). More advanced insects go through complete metamorphosis (holometabolous development), including a pupal stage (3).*

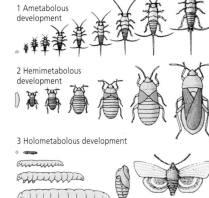

1 Ametabolous development

2 Hemimetabolous development

3 Holometabolous development

9

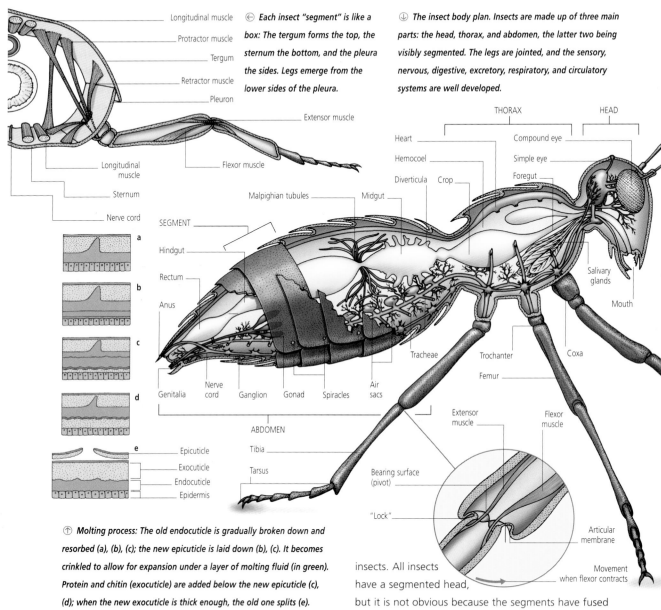

Longitudinal muscle
Protractor muscle
Tergum
Retractor muscle
Pleuron
Extensor muscle
Longitudinal muscle
Flexor muscle
Sternum
Nerve cord

Each insect "segment" is like a box: The tergum forms the top, the sternum the bottom, and the pleura the sides. Legs emerge from the lower sides of the pleura.

The insect body plan. Insects are made up of three main parts: the head, thorax, and abdomen, the latter two being visibly segmented. The legs are jointed, and the sensory, nervous, digestive, excretory, respiratory, and circulatory systems are well developed.

THORAX
HEAD
Heart
Compound eye
Hemocoel
Simple eye
Diverticula   Crop
Foregut
Malpighian tubules
Midgut
Salivary glands
Mouth
SEGMENT
Hindgut
Rectum
Anus
Tracheae
Trochanter
Coxa
Femur
Genitalia   Nerve cord   Ganglion   Gonad   Spiracles   Air sacs
ABDOMEN
Extensor muscle
Flexor muscle
Tibia
Tarsus
Bearing surface (pivot)
"Lock"
Articular membrane
Movement when flexor contracts

a
b
c
d
e
Epicuticle
Exocuticle
Endocuticle
Epidermis

Molting process: The old endocuticle is gradually broken down and resorbed (a), (b), (c); the new epicuticle is laid down (b), (c). It becomes crinkled to allow for expansion under a layer of molting fluid (in green). Protein and chitin (exocuticle) are added below the new epicuticle (c), (d); when the new exocuticle is thick enough, the old one splits (e).

a blood system, a digestive system, a nervous system with a brain in the head, a system for getting rid of waste products, some form of breathing system, and a reproductive system.

Although it is not always clear from the outside, the insect body is divided into separate segments. Segmentation is most easily visible on the abdomen of insects. All insects have a segmented head, but it is not obvious because the segments have fused together to form a head capsule. Some or all of the body segments of insects may have structures, called appendages, protruding from them. They include antennae, mouthparts, legs, and wings.

The two most basic structures making up the mouthparts are the mandibles and the maxillae. Mandibles normally do most of the initial work of killing or cutting up the food item, while the maxillae do the

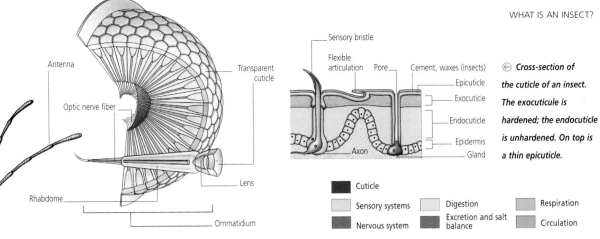

Antenna

Optic nerve fiber

Transparent cuticle

Rhabdome

Lens

Ommatidium

Sensory bristle

Flexible articulation

Pore

Cement, waxes (insects)

Epicuticle

Exocuticle

Endocuticle

Epidermis

Axon

Gland

Cross-section of the cuticle of an insect. The exocuticule is hardened; the endocuticle is unhardened. On top is a thin epicuticle.

Cuticle

Sensory systems

Nervous system

Digestion

Excretion and salt balance

Respiration

Circulation

The compound eyes of insects consist of up to 30,000 individual lenses in visual units called ommatidia. Each ommatidium has a narrow field of vision, but images from adjacent ommatidia overlap.

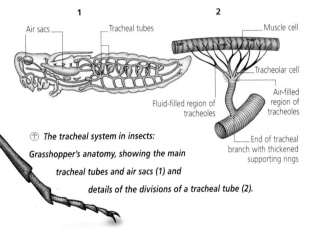

1

Air sacs

Tracheal tubes

Fluid-filled region of tracheoles

2

Muscle cell

Tracheolar cell

Air-filled region of tracheoles

End of tracheal branch with thickened supporting rings

The tracheal system in insects: Grasshopper's anatomy, showing the main tracheal tubes and air sacs (1) and details of the divisions of a tracheal tube (2).

finer slicing and shredding work before the food is swallowed. The basic mouthparts can be highly modified in some insect orders.

Molting

The process of molting, or ecdysis, is important to all insects. Most insects have a tough exoskeleton that cannot expand as they feed and grow. Therefore it has to be replaced at intervals.

When it is ready to molt, the insect stops feeding, and the old exoskeleton begins to separate from the new one that has already developed beneath it. The old exoskeleton splits open along lines of weakness, and the animal wriggles its way out. The new exoskeleton is

wrinkled and has to be stretched to the required new size. In order to do that, the animal takes in air until it is fully expanded.

Animals that live under water, such as some insect larvae, will take in water to expand the exoskeleton. The exoskeleton then hardens and assumes its normal color. In most insects molting usually takes place only during the development from egg to adult.

Pheromones

Pheromones are simply chemical messengers, or scents, that pass through the air to provide information to other members of the same species.

The antennae, like the branching ones of this male giant saturniid moth, Attacus atlas *from Southeast Asia, are used to detect pheromones. They are detected through the olfactory sensillae (below left), cuticular pegs or hairs on the antennae that contain sensory nerve fibers. These fibers transmit impulses to the central nervous system.*

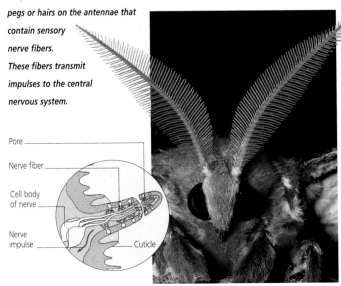

Pore

Nerve fiber

Cell body of nerve

Nerve impulse

Cuticle

Male insects, for example, secrete male pheromones to enable females to identify and locate them. Females often do the same to inform the males. Pheromones can also be used to keep members of the same species together in a group or to indicate pathways to and from a source of food. Alarm pheromones are released when an insect is attacked and may warn other members of the species to take avoiding action or to come to its aid.

Gender Differences

In all the insect orders there are examples of species in which appearances can be deceptive. For example, the males and females may be so different in appearance that they can easily be mistaken for two different species.

There are three ways in which the sexes can differ. To begin with, there can be disparity in size. Males of some species are bigger than females, but more often the females are bigger than the males. Difference in color between males and females also occurs and is called sexual dichromatism. Difference in shape is known as sexual dimorphism—a good example being the stag beetles, in which the female has normal-sized mandibles, but those of the male are greatly increased in size.

Another common difference within species is the degree of development of the adult wings. In many species of bug, for example, adults may lack wings altogether, or the wings may be just a tiny bud. These insects are called apterous forms. Alternatively, the wings may be fully developed. These are the macropterous forms. Finally, there are those individuals with intermediate-sized wings, the brachypterous forms—often referred to as small-winged insects.

⊕ *Many moths have cryptic coloring and often select a suitable matching background. This angle-shade,* Phlogophora meticulosa *from Europe, is effectively camouflaged on a dead leaf.*

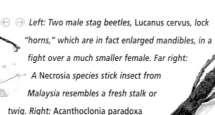

⊖ ⊖ *Left: Two male stag beetles,* Lucanus cervus, *lock "horns," which are in fact enlarged mandibles, in a fight over a much smaller female. Far right: A* Necrosia *species stick insect from Malaysia resembles a fresh stalk or twig. Right:* Acanthoclonia paradoxa *from Trinidad is so sticklike that it can sit safely on a plant in full view.*

Many insects, especially the walkingsticks, resemble twigs. Insect predators do not eat sticks and therefore leave them alone. The same is true of the many insects that resemble living or dead leaves. The important thing for such insects is to remain still, at least during daylight, because if they move, a predator may spot them.

Mimicry in Insects

Protective resemblance can also mean that an insect looks like another type of insect altogether. This is called "mimicry" and is a system that uses color variation in a complex and interesting way.

There are many harmless insects that resemble wasps both in terms of shape, color, and pattern. Wasps are shunned by many birds, which quickly learn that the wasps have an unpleasant sting. As a result, they will usually avoid any insect that looks like a wasp. The imitation of ants is as common as that of wasps, but it is probably more common in the insect's nymphal stages, especially during the early instars.

Insects involved in mimicry fall into three categories. The first level of involvement is as the model (the insect whose color pattern is being mimicked). Second, the insect may be the mimic (the one that is copying the color pattern of the model). Finally, it may simply be the observer (the predator that would like to eat the model or mimic given the chance).

The insect model, which tastes bad and is therefore generally avoided by the predator, is normally very brightly colored and patterned. This is known as aposematic coloration, or warning coloration. The bright colors and patterns enable the predator to remember that the insect

Protective Patterns

A common feature among insects is the variation in color and structure that serves a protective function. This is called "protective resemblance." The insect may have protective coloration that matches the background of its habitat, so that it blends in.

For example, many insects that live on lichen-covered trees have blotches of color, making them look as if they too are covered in lichen. Many species of insect are polymorphic, meaning that they have a number of distinct color or pattern forms— some ladybugs are good examples. There are even some butterflies that have different color forms in the wet and dry seasons. This is called polyphenism.

is either distasteful or capable of biting or stinging. However, the strategy will only work if the predator is intelligent enough to see and recognize the color patterns used. This applies mainly to vertebrates (the system does not work for invertebrate predators since they do not have the intelligence to recognize colors).

The observer, or predator, catches a number of models and finds that they sting or taste very bad, so it lets them go. After a number of such unpleasant encounters it avoids insects with similar colors and patterns. As a result, any mimicking insect, even if it is totally harmless, will also be avoided.

Batesian and Müllerian Mimics

For the mimicry to be successful, however, the predator must meet many more models, in the first instance, than mimics. If it meets more mimics first, it will learn that it is worth going after insects with a particular pattern, because only the occasional one is nasty. This is called Batesian mimicry, in which edible mimics, perhaps from different insect orders, resemble the unpleasant model.

Another form of mimicry is known as Müllerian mimicry. All of the mimics in such a form are themselves unpleasant. Since all the insects in the "mimicry ring" have similar color patterns, protection for one species provides protection for all the others. Such mimicry is quite common in the Lepidoptera, especially in the butterflies.

⬋ *An example of Batesian mimicry in South American butterflies. The nonpoisonous pierid* Dismorphia amphione *(top) successfully mimics the highly poisonous* Heliconius isabella *in the family Nymphalidae.*

The Power of Flight

Flying dominates the adult life of most insects. The ability to fly evolved around 295 to 354 million years ago, but exactly how it came about is not completely known. One theory is that early large insects glided using fixed extensions on the body. Later they became twisted for greater control and eventually were able to be flapped. Another suggestion is that wings evolved from other flappable structures, such as gills. Other adaptations to the body occurred over time to help speed and maneuverability, including a shorter, thicker body and a specialized wing muscle that contracts at much higher rates than other muscles—up to 1,000 times a second in some small flies.

The form of a wing stroke is complex. The leading edge of the wing is tilted down during the downstroke and up during the upstroke. The wing beats are assisted by hinges made of a rubbery protein called resilin and by elasticity in the flight muscles themselves.

Some insects fly at up to 65 feet (20 m) per second. Such high energy output requires the insect to have efficient oxygen supplies to the flight muscles and a high concentration of carbohydrates in the blood.

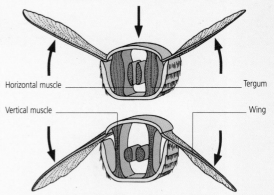

Horizontal muscle — Tergum

Vertical muscle — Wing

⬆ *A basic wing stroke. On the upstroke (top) the vertical muscles pull down the tergum (the dorsal plate on the abdomen), raising the wings. The thorax lengthens, and the horizontal muscles are stretched. When the horizontal muscles contract (bottom), the tergum is moved up, pushing the wings into the downstroke.*

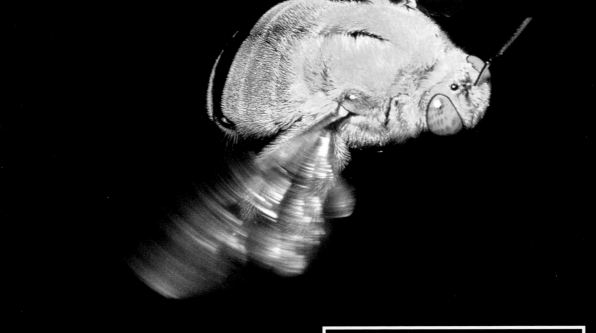

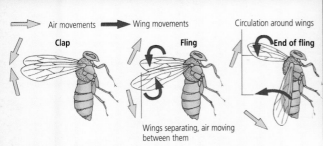

Air movements → Wing movements   Circulation around wings

Clap   **Fling**   **End of fling**

Wings separating, air moving between them

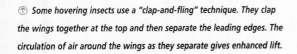

⊕ Some hovering insects use a "clap-and-fling" technique. They clap the wings together at the top and then separate the leading edges. The circulation of air around the wings as they separate gives enhanced lift.

⊕ Top: In Kenya a male carpenter bee, Xylocopa species, puts his aerial skills to good use guarding his territory. Inset: A male cockchafer beetle, Melolontha melolontha, takes flight in England.

♀ **Southern hawker (Aeshna cyanea)**

Common name Dragonflies, damselflies

Order Odonata

Class Insecta

Subphylum Hexapoda

Number of species About 6,500 (438 U.S.)

Size From about 0.7 in (19 mm) to 5 in (13 cm)

Key features Head with large compound eyes and well-developed jaws; antennae very short; 2 pairs of transparent wings almost equal in size; abdomen long and slim in most species; dragonflies hold their wings out to the side, damselflies fold their wings over and along the body; jaws in nymphs can be extended for grabbing prey; damselfly nymphs have 3 external gills, dragonfly nymphs have gills inside the rectum

Habits Damselflies normally found hunting for prey close to water; stronger-flying dragonflies may often be found hunting a long way from water; nymphs mostly aquatic

Breeding Males may grab females in midair or pounce on sitting females; some species have complex courtship routines; eggs laid in or near water

Diet Both adults and nymphs are predators

Habitat Any habitat with suitable still or running water, the latter not too fast; some species can inhabit deserts provided water is available at least for a short time

Distribution Found all over the world except for the North and South Poles

⊕ *A female southern hawker,* Aeshna cyanea, *lays her eggs in a soft, water-logged tree stump. (*Aeshna *means ugly or misshapen and* cyanea *means dark blue, although there is no blue color present in the female of the species.) The southern hawker is widespread throughout Europe. Wingspan up to 3.5 inches (9 cm) and body length up to 2.8 inches (7 cm).*

Dragonflies and Damselflies Odonata

With their large size and often bright colors the dragonflies and damselflies must rank among the most easily recognized insects. Although their size may make some of them seem rather frightening, they are in no way harmful to humans.

THE ODONATA IS SUBDIVIDED into three suborders: the dragonflies in the Anisoptera, the damselflies in the Zygoptera, and finally a very small group (which is almost extinct) called the Anisozygoptera. The latter is known by just two living species from Asia. Dragonflies are heavily built insects and, at rest, can be recognized by the position of their wings—they can only hold them out sideways at roughly right angles to the body. The damselflies have a long, slim body and can both fold the wings up over the body and bring them together vertically, rather like a butterfly.

All-Around Vision

Adult Odonata are normally found close to water. They are predators, mainly catching other insects in flight. The fact that they are skillful fliers helps, but there is another important feature: The dragonflies in particular have very large compound eyes almost meeting on top of the head and giving them excellent all-around vision. The eyes of some dragonflies are made up of as many as 28,000 single units (the ommatidia), each with its own individual lens. In order to help them look around for prey, their neck is very flexible, and their head can be turned from side to side and moved up and down. Some other hunting insects, such as mantids and robber flies, have the same ability.

Dragonflies prey on faster-flying insects such as flies. They can take larger prey—for

⊕ *In the gloom of an approaching thunderstorm a flame skimmer dragonfly,* Libellula saturata, *sits on vegetation close to a pool in Utah. Typical of the dragonfly, it sits with its wings held at roughly 90 degrees from the body.*

example, wasps—and have even been observed to be accidental cannibals, eating members of their own species. Despite their large eyes and strong flying capabilities, they often miss their prey, which can be equally agile in escaping from them. Damselflies, on the other hand, have smaller eyes and a weaker flight, and tend to go after weak-flying, fluttery insects such as small moths.

The legs of both dragonflies and damselflies are poorly adapted for walking, but they are extremely useful for keeping hold of prey items while they are being eaten. Dragonflies in particular can often be found hunting miles away from the nearest stretch of water.

Spider Hunters

A more unusual type of prey is sought by two genera of damselflies from South and Central America. *Megaloprepus* and *Mecistogaster* species include the world's largest damselflies, and *Megaloprepus coerulatus* has the largest wingspan of any of the Odonata. It can sometimes reach 7.5 inches (19 cm). Adults of both genera specialize in spiders as prey, taking them either as they sit at the center of their orb

⬆ *In this face-on view of the southern hawker dragonfly,* Aeshna cyanea *from Europe, the huge compound eyes are very obvious. They are used by the dragonfly in aerial pursuit of prey.*

Masked Killers

Dragonfly and damselfly nymphs, like the adults, are voracious carnivores. They are mostly aquatic and feed on almost any kind of prey that is small enough for them to handle. That includes water insects and their larvae, tadpoles, small frogs, and small fish. The nymphs hunt by stealth, creeping around very slowly on the bottom of the mass of water in which they live or on water vegetation. Just a few species have larvae that live and hunt in marshes, and there is also a handful of species whose nymphs do not live in water at all.

The water dwellers bury themselves beneath loose gravel, mud, vegetation, or other material on the bottom of a lake or pond, effectively concealing themselves from passing prey. When a suitable item of prey comes within range, they employ their killer "mask." The mask is in fact the modified lower lip of the nymph's mouthparts; it gets its name because, when at rest, it covers the other mouthparts like a mask. The labium is long and hinged, with two inward-pointing claws on the end. To catch prey, blood is forced into the labium at high pressure, making it shoot forward very rapidly. The nymph then uses its claws to dig into and trap the prey, which is then pulled to the front of the nymph's face. There it is dealt with by the biting and chewing jaws. Research scientists have found that the mask can be shot out in as little as 25 milliseconds (25 thousandths of a second).

webs or as they sit around on vegetation. Hovering like a helicopter, its transparent wings a blur and its long slim body pointing behind it, the damselfly remains undetected by the spider as it approaches. It then makes a final dart at the spider, grabs it, and with its mandibles cuts off the abdomen from the spider's body. It then lets the rest of the body fall to the ground while it feasts on the juicy abdomen.

Life as a Nymph

In a few families the developmental stages of the Odonata—the nymphs, or stadia—bear some resemblance to wingless adults, but in others there are few similarities. Damselfly nymphs are very slim, while dragonfly nymphs are more heavily built. Some have an abdomen almost as wide as it is long. Apart from the fact that they have a lighter build, damselfly nymphs can be recognized by their three external gills. They are often leaf-shaped structures protruding back from the end of the abdomen.

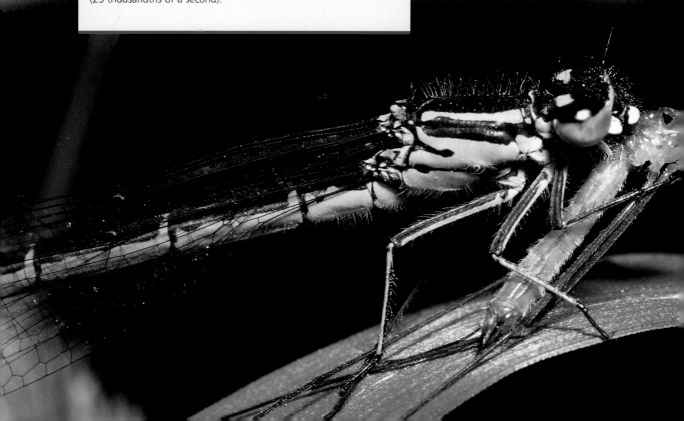

The gills take up oxygen from the water. The oxygen moves from the gills into the nymph's body. Dragonfly nymphs lack these external gills: Instead, they have gills in the rectum, in the rear end of their gut. Water is pumped in and out of the rectum to ventilate the gills.

Although they are proficient killers, the nymphs (especially when they are small) are themselves likely to fall prey to larger predators. They do, however, have one trick that helps them escape. If they are grabbed by a leg, it can break at a weak point at the base of the femur, leaving the predator with just a leg in its mouth and giving the nymph a chance to escape. Dragonfly nymphs have an alternative means of escape. They are able to squirt water under high pressure from the gill chamber in the rectum out of the end of the abdomen. The action shoots them forward in the water and away from possible danger.

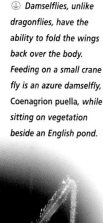

Damselflies, unlike dragonflies, have the ability to fold the wings back over the body. Feeding on a small crane fly is an azure damselfly, Coenagrion puella, *while sitting on vegetation beside an English pond.*

Territorial Skirmishes

The main aim of male Odonata is to find a female and mate with her. That of the female is to find a mate and then lay her eggs. Since the majority of dragonflies and damselflies lay their eggs in water, courtship and mating take place by ponds, lakes, streams, and rivers.

Most male Odonata set up and defend a territory that is suitable as an egg-laying site for a mate. This behavior is often most noticeable around a small pond. It is common to find a single male dragonfly patrolling back and forth across the water, investigating any flying insect that comes near. If it turns out to be another male of his own species, a skirmish may ensue, and the intruder is often chased off. A number of different species often patrol the same pond.

At intervals the defending male may land on a favorite spot and continue his surveillance from there, flying off to investigate any likely intruders. Quite often the male will leave the pond after an hour or so, and his place will be taken by another male, which will stay for a while before he too leaves. They may be leaving to hunt, or they may be moving off to check the availability of a neighboring pond. If a

A male banded demoiselle damselfly, Calopteryx splendens, *claps his wings at another male who is trying to invade his territory. The owner is perched on a yellow water lily.*

receptive female turns up during these patrols, they mate, and the female lays her eggs.

Other species, however, maintain a patrol over their territory during all the hours of daylight throughout their entire short lives, only deserting it if they are driven off by a stronger male. Defending a territory does not guarantee that a male will be the only one to mate with any females that arrive, because the females may have mated before they got there. The females hunt away from water, where they are likely to come across males that are not strong enough to hold a territory but will mate with a passing female.

Males Miss Out

Some dragonflies and damselflies are nonterritorial, in which case there is just a free-for-all. The first male to reach the female is the one that mates with her. Near suitable egg-laying sites males will always outnumber females. The result is that some males never get a chance to mate—perhaps 50 percent, or fewer, succeed. By contrast, all females will mate, some several times.

While courtship in many dragonflies is brief or nonexistent, in damselflies it can be quite complex. A good example is that of the banded

Wheels and Tandems

Members of the Odonata mate in a very unusual way. The structure and position of the sex organs in male Odonata are unique in the insect world. One set of reproductive structures, called the primary genitalia, is in the normal insect position toward the end of the abdomen. There is, however, a set of secondary genitalia on the underside of the second abdominal segment. In addition to that unusual arrangement the males also have a set of special hooks at the tip of the abdomen. Before he is ready to mate, the male releases a spermatophore from the primary genitalia and curves his abdomen around to transfer it into the secondary genitalia. He then looks for a mate.

Having found a female that is happy to receive his advances, he flies above her and grasps her in his legs. He then curves his abdomen forward and holds onto her with the hooks on the tip of his abdomen. In dragonflies the hooks grasp the female by the top of the head, while in damselflies the female is held by the top of the thorax (the pronotum). The arrangement and size of the male's hooks and the shape of the head or thorax of the female vary from species to species, but they are the same for all members within an individual species. Only the hooks of a male from the correct species will fit the shape of the head or thorax of a female of the same species, so cross-mating between different species is avoided. Both insects are able to fly while the male is holding onto the female—this is known as the "tandem" position.

The next stage in the courtship is for the female to bring her abdomen around beneath her body until her reproductive openings make contact with and lock onto the male's secondary genitalia. In this position their bodies form a rough circle, the so-called "wheel" position. The male is then able to pass the spermatophore to the female. The length of time that they remain in the wheel position varies from just a few seconds in some dragonflies to several hours in many damselflies. It is not unusual to find dozens of pairs of damselflies in the wheel position sitting on plants in and around a favored egg-laying pond.

A pair of golden-ringed dragonflies, Cordulegaster boltonii, *sit in the wheel position as they mate. The female is the lower of the two.*

With the bright-red male in front, grasping the female behind the head with his claspers, a pair of ruddy darter dragonflies, Sympetrum sanguineum *from Europe, takes a break between bouts of egg laying.*

demoiselle, *Calopteryx splendens*, a European species. This handsome species, which has closely related species in North America, is found beside canals and slow-moving streams and rivers, especially where there are water lilies on the surface and reeds and rushes growing beside the water. As the female enters the male's territory, she flies in a manner that indicates to him her interest in mating. As he catches sight of her, the male, perched on his favorite water lily leaf, belly-flops into the water. This tells her that he would like to mate with her and that this is a very good place to lay her eggs. The female's response is to fly in a zigzag path over him. Her flight shows that she accepts his invitation to mate and also allows her to memorize exactly where she is to oviposit.

The female then flies to a nearby rush or reed stem and sits there in a manner that indicates to the male that she has accepted him. He performs a short courtship flight, hovering beside her, before they finally mate. If she does not immediately fly to his chosen egg-laying site, he will lead her to it. He shows her the way by using a special wing-whirring flight low over the water. He will also land and float on the water at the chosen place, waggling his tail to encourage her to follow.

Aerial "Dogfights"

In order to lay, she has to make her way beneath the water. During that time she is vulnerable to the attentions of other males. The resident male therefore stands guard close by, chasing off any intruders. If there are too many, he will sit on the female's back to keep them off until she disappears beneath the water. Males defending a territory often have to spend hours at a time defending it against rival males. This involves aerial "dogfights," with one male trying to force his opponent to crash into the water. In years when the area becomes overpopulated with males, the whole courtship system can break down and is replaced by a complete free-for-all. This is not good for the

females, however: They can easily get drowned by the crush of males trying to mate with them.

North American demoiselles also have fairly complex courtships of this kind, but the behavior of one of them—*Hetaerina vulnerata*, the canyon rubyspot—has puzzled scientists. The males normally select and defend a suitable egg-laying site on a fast-flowing stream. Here they mate with visiting females as expected. However, in about one-third of the cases studied, instead of staying to lay, the female somehow persuades the male to leave and go with her, attached in the "tandem" position, to a site of her choice. Most sites are already occupied by other resident males; but if she finds one that is not and she likes it, she stops suddenly in midair. She persuades the male to land with her and to let go of her while she backs into the water to lay her eggs.

Sperm Chambers

The males of some Odonata (both damselflies and dragonflies) have the ability to ensure that most of the eggs laid by the female are fertilized by their own sperm and not by some male with which she has previously mated. That is because the sperm from the spermatophore is stored in a special chamber, the spermatheca, inside the female's body before it is used to

⊕ Dragonflies are often found some distance from water, which they only need to visit for breeding purposes. This eastern amberwing dragonfly, Perithemis tenera *from North America, is hunting in a cemetery some distance from the nearest stretch of water.*

fertilize her eggs. For example, in some damselflies of the family Coenagrionidae the male uses a special structure called a sperm scoop to remove from the female's spermatheca any sperm that have been placed there by another male. Only then will he pass over his spermatophore to the female. A slightly different method is used by some dragonflies of the family Libellulidae. Instead of scraping the sperm out, the male pushes aside any sperm that is already in the spermatheca and places his own sperm on top of it. The result is that most of the eggs will be fertilized by his sperm. This behavior is known as "sperm competition."

Egg-Laying Variations

Dragonflies and damselflies use a number of distinct methods of egg laying (oviposition), although as is so often the case with living things, there are exceptions to the rules. In general, however, most species oviposit in one of the following ways:

Inventive Egg Laying

The females of the giant damselflies of the genus *Mecistogaster* from South and Central America choose an unusual place in which to oviposit—in the water that collects in the rosettes of leaves of members of the plant family Bromeliaceae, such as the pineapple. The water is fairly deep among the leaf bases, which may be why these damselflies have a long, slim body. The nymphs feed on the larvae of other insects living in the so-called "bromeliad tanks." There is evidence from the examination of stomach contents that the larger nymphs eat the smaller ones.

Insects always seem prepared to make use of anything that humans can provide for them in the way of new habitats. That seems to be the case with these damselflies. Sugarcane is grown in large quantities in the region. After the sugarcane has been cut, the remaining hollow stems fill up with water before they eventually decompose. The damselflies have taken to using these stems as alternative egg-laying sites.

One method involves the female making her way into the water until she is completely submerged and then inserting her eggs into the stems of water plants. This method is used by damselflies of the genus *Enallagma* in both North America and Europe. The female, in tandem with her mate, lands on a suitable plant stem sticking up out of the water. The female then backs down the stem and into the water, and the male lets go of her as she becomes completely submerged. She lays her eggs and then rises up to the surface again using air bubbles trapped on her body. Meanwhile the male usually waits for her to reappear and then couples up with her again.

Another common way involves the female sitting and laying her eggs directly into the water or sitting at the surface and laying them into plant tissues below the water. This method is used by many different species of dragonflies and damselflies. A good example occurs in *Aeshna juncea*, known in North America as the sedge darner dragonfly and in Europe as the common hawker dragonfly. Dragonflies that oviposit in this way often accompany the egg laying with a loud rustling of their wings.

In a third method the female oviposits into mud or dead wood, plant debris, or mosses along the water's edge. This is a method favored by some of the *Aeshna* species darner dragonflies from North America and Europe.

⊕ *A female southern hawker dragonfly,* **Aeshna cyanea,** *pushes the tip of her abdomen into a rotten log to lay her eggs.*

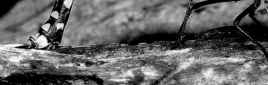

Again, egg laying is often accompanied by a very loud rustling of the wings.

In yet another method the female oviposits directly into sand or mud along the water's edge while in flight. This occurs commonly in the *Sympetrum* species dragonflies, known as meadowhawks in North America.

Alternatively, as she skims over the water, the female lays her eggs directly into it, either among vegetation or straight into deeper water. Again, some *Sympetrum* species dragonflies favor this method. The male may even help in some instances: For example, in the European ruddy darter dragonfly, *S. sanguineum*, the two sexes fly in tandem. The male leads and holds the female behind her head with the claspers at the end of his abdomen. She releases the eggs in batches onto the end of her abdomen, and he then swings her downward so that the eggs enter the water. There they are washed from the female's abdomen and fall among submerged water plants. In a slight variation the female of the European keeled skimmer dragonfly, *Orthetrum coerulescens*, dips toward the water and flips a droplet of the water, where the eggs have fallen, up onto the bank

⬆ *With the males standing above them to keep other males away, two azure damselfly females,* Coenagrion puella *from Europe, lay their eggs among pond vegetation.*

or onto the leaves of water plants so that the eggs stick to the plants. A more simple strategy is for the female to drop her eggs into the water as she flies over it without making contact with the water surface.

Some variations in these egg-laying methods occur. Females of the setwing dragonfly, *Dythemis cannacrioides* from Mexico, perch for a while before egg laying commences. During that time they produce a large mass of eggs, like a bunch of grapes, on the end of the abdomen. They then seek out a place where a cluster of plant roots hangs from the bank into a stream or river. They drop the mass of sticky eggs into the cluster of roots.

Runaway Eggs

A dragonfly species whose females seem to adopt different methods of laying is *Zygonyx natalensis* from Africa. They are found along streams and rivers with frequent waterfalls and rapids, and which contain mats of vegetation washed over by currents. When she is ready to oviposit, the female sits on one of the mats and releases her eggs into the water. They swell up and become sticky as they are washed away by the current, and they become glued to the first thing with which they come into contact. Sometimes, however, the female will sit by shallow water and lay her eggs directly onto the bottom of the stream or river. Alternatively, she will dip her abdomen into the water during flight and drop her eggs directly into it.

The ovipositing behavior of the dragonfly *Tetrathmis polleni* from southern Africa has been seen to involve males as well as females. The males set up a territory of their own on the single leaf of a waterside plant, and they defend it from other males that attempt to take it from them. Following successful mating, the male takes his mate back to his chosen leaf, where she lays a batch of eggs on the underside. As she does so, the male flutters excitedly around the leaf, landing on it every now and again close to the ovipositing female. Within a couple of days the eggs hatch out, and the tiny nymphs fall into the water below.

Egg to Adult

Eggs are of two types, depending on how they are laid. Those laid straight into the water are roughly spherical, while those laid into plant tissues are more elongate. Being inside the plant helps protect the eggs, but those laid in water are covered in a layer of sticky jelly. This not only means that they stick to objects, such as plants, in the water but also makes it difficult for predators to eat them. While in some species the eggs may hatch within a few weeks, in colder climes the eggs may overwinter, hatching the next spring.

When the young hatch from the eggs, they do so as a prolarva, which is covered in a membrane. If the egg has hatched under water, the membrane immediately splits, and the first instar nymph emerges. Quite a number of species of dragonfly lay their eggs out of water but fairly close to it. In this instance the prolarva is able to leap, by bending and straightening its body, to carry it to the main body of water in which it will spend its nymphal life. Once in the water, the membrane again splits to release the first instar nymph.

Varied Development

Development time is mainly dependent on the temperature of the water in which the nymphs live, as long as adequate food is available. In warmer regions nymphs develop more quickly than those in colder areas. There can even be differences in rate of development over quite a short distance. In Britain, for example, nymphs of the blue-tailed damselfly, *Ischnura elegans*,

take one year from egg to adult in the south but two years in the north. A few hundred miles farther south in France, and there may be two or even three generations per year.

Once the final instar nymph is fully grown, it leaves the water and climbs up onto a suitable piece of vegetation, either doing so directly from the water or by crawling out onto waterside plants. Emergence in Aeshnidae, which go by the common name darners in the United States, takes place during darkness so that they are ready to fly as soon as it gets light, a useful way of escaping predation by birds. Most of the other damselflies and dragonflies start emerging at dawn so that they are fully emerged and drying off as the sun rises.

Emergence itself is much as in other insects. The last instar nymph must sit head up, as near vertical as possible. The top of the head and thorax then splits, and the adult forces itself out, using gravity to help it fall back and pull itself free from the old skin. Once out of the skin, it sits head up, inflates its wings, dries off, and then makes its first flight. When newly emerged, the young adults are called tenerals, differing from the mature adult in having very shiny wings and drab colors, the full adult color taking up to a week to appear.

⊙ *A newly emerged 4-spotted skimmer dragonfly,* Libellula quadrimaculata, *hangs from the old nymphal skin as it dries off its freshly inflated wings.*

⊙ *A new adult* Aeshna juncea, *known as the sedge darner in North America, emerges from its old nymphal skin.*

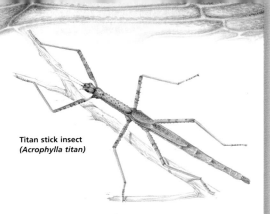

Titan stick insect
(*Acrophylla titan*)

Common name Walkingsticks (stick insects),
leaf insects, timemas

Order Phasmatodea (Phasmida)

Class Insecta

Subphylum Hexapoda

Number of species About 2,500 (32 U.S.)

Size From about 0.5 in (13 mm) to 13 in (33 cm)

Key features Body shape varies from short and broad in
leaf insects to very long and thin in
walkingsticks; antennae slim, very variable in
length; compound eyes fairly small; simple
eyes in flying species but often only present
in the male; wings (when present) usually
only full size in males, many species wingless
in both sexes; forewings leathery to protect
hind wings; nymphs resemble adults, but are
wingless

Habits Almost all species sit around on vegetation
and are active at night

Breeding Courtship mainly absent; many males guard
the female during egg laying; eggs dropped
anywhere or inserted into crevices

Diet All species feed on living vegetation of some
kind

Habitat Forests, grassy areas, scrub, semidesert, and
desert

Distribution Worldwide, but most common in the
tropics; absent from cool, temperate regions

⤒ *Acrophylla titan, aptly named the titan stick insect or the
great brown phasma, is the longest Australian species. The
females are generally much larger than the males and are
abundant egg layers. Two captive females were observed to
lay over 4,000 eggs between them during their lifetime. Body
length up to 10 inches (25 cm).*

Walkingsticks and Leaf Insects

Phasmatodea

*The order Phasmatodea contains not only some of the
weirdest-looking insects in the world but also the
longest. Females of the Malaysian walkingstick,*
Pharnacia *(or* Phobaeticus) kirbyi, *can grow to
13 inches (33 cm) long.*

THE TWO MAIN FAMILIES of the order are the
Phasmatidae (the walkingsticks or stick insects)
and the Phyllidae (the leaf insects). Most of the
walkingsticks encountered live up to their
common name, since they have a long, thin
body that closely resembles a stick.

Heavy Females

In the majority of species the females are
considerably longer and therefore heavier than
the males. In some species it is not unusual for
the female to be more than twice as long as her
mate, although in other species they may be
closer in size. The northern walkingstick,
Diapheromera femorata from North America, is
a good example. Males reach 3 inches (7.6 cm)
in length, while the females are a little longer,
at 3.8 inches (9.5 cm). In winged species the
skinny males and the fatter, larger unwinged
females could easily be mistaken for members
of two different species. While many
walkingsticks are smooth, others may be
covered in spines. Although long and thin is
more common, shorter and stouter shapes are
also found, with a number of species being
torpedo shaped.

  The leaf insects are extremely well named.
Their leaflike wings are held flat over their
broad, flat body and are green or brown so that
they resemble either living or dead leaves. Their
leaflike nature is further enhanced by having
flattened extensions from the legs. It has been
found that a number of species of walkingstick
are actually able to change their color. This has
nothing to do with camouflage but is to do

⊘ *The North American
slender-bodied
walkingstick,* Manomera
tenuescens, *is difficult to
find during the day. Its
presence only becomes
apparent at dusk.*

⊘ *A pair of 2-striped
walkingsticks,*
Anisomorpha
buprestoides *from the
southeastern United
States. The male is the
smaller of the two.*

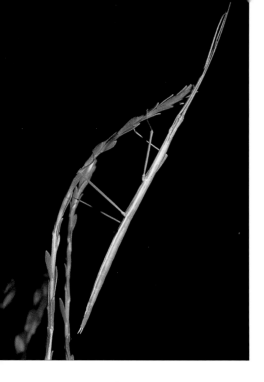

Podacanthus wilkinsoni, can strip the leaves from eucalyptus trees in Australia, and the coconut stick insect, *Graeffea crouani* from Polynesia, can be a pest in coconut plantations.

with the regulation of body temperature. On cool days they can make their body darker so that it absorbs more heat from the atmosphere.

In *Phasmida* the jaws point forward on the head and are used to chew and shred the leaves on which the insect feeds. While most of them pose no problem to humans, just a few can reach large enough numbers to become pests. For example, Lauri's ring-barker,

Lengthy Coupling

The Phasmatodea are not known to have any particular form of courtship. Males simply walk up to receptive females and mate with them. Males may ride around on the backs of the females for days at a time,

⊕ Quite a number of species of walkingsticks are thorny, presumably as a means of defense. This Circia species walkingstick comes from the rain forests of Madagascar.

sometimes coupled together, at other times not. The male does this to ensure that no other male gets to his mate.

There are, however, examples of species in which males will deliberately try to remove a male from a female and replace him. Males of the North American walkingstick, *Diapheromera veliei,* have hooked "fighting spines" situated on the femora of the middle pair of legs. If a mating male sees another male approaching, his first action is to push his mate's reproductive opening out of reach of his rival. Normally the intruder ignores this and moves in on the mating pair. The two males engage in combat, dragging the fighting spines across one another and sometimes drawing blood. While they fight, they are actually hanging head down, gripping onto the tip of the female's abdomen by means of a pair of modified cerci that act as strong claspers. The fight can last for several minutes, and in more than half of such fights the intruder wins.

In species in which the males engage in active disputes over females, the males tend to be closer in size to their mates than in species that do not fight. Males of *Oncotophasma martini* from Thailand are actually slightly larger than the females.

Females of some Phasmatodea do not have to bother with mating, since males are either extremely rare or unknown. In that case parthenogenesis is the normal method of reproduction. This is true of *Carausius morosus,* the common laboratory or Indian walkingstick.

Three-Tiered System

There are three basic egg-laying strategies in the Phasmatodea. Females of primitive species lay elongated eggs in the ground, in crevices beneath bark, or in hollow stems. The eggs of more advanced species tend to be spherical and are glued onto leaves or other surfaces. The most advanced species produce spherical eggs

⊖ *A* Phyllium *species leaf insect from New Guinea mimicking a green leaf. It is able to survive quite happily despite the loss of one of its front legs.*

⊕ *When alarmed by the approach of a predator, the female giant stick insect,* Acrophylla titan *from Australia, opens her wings to show a pattern of black-and-white warning colors.*

that are simply dropped onto the ground below the vegetation on which the female is feeding. A few females are more particular, giving the eggs a strong flick as they are laid so that they are hurled some distance away. It is believed that this helps the eggs avoid contamination from the large amount of droppings under the tree on which the insects are living. The smell of the feces may also attract egg parasites such as various species of wasp.

Ants are known to pick up walkingstick eggs and carry them back to their nests. The walkingsticks remain free from danger until they hatch, and they are able to

The Timemas

The Timemidae is a small family within the Phasmatodea found mainly in California and neighboring states. Its members resemble some of the broader-bodied walkingsticks in appearance, but they have only three segments to each tarsus rather than the five found in the rest of the order. They are not particularly large insects, the largest females reaching a length of around 1 inch (2.5 cm) and the males around two-thirds that length.

They have one feature in common with the earwigs: The abdomen in both sexes ends in a pair of well-developed cerci that are straight in the females but more like forceps in the males. Neither sex has wings. They feed on the foliage of various trees, blending in well with the color of the leaves. They are much more mobile than the slow-moving walkingsticks and rush off at speed if disturbed, producing an unpleasant smell at the same time. Of the 12 or so species so far discovered, two reproduce by parthenogenesis, and males have not yet been found for a further two species. As with the walkingsticks, it is common to find males (in those species in which males are present) riding around on the back of the females.

The eggs are simply dropped onto the ground, where they overwinter and then hatch the following spring. It takes a further 12 months for the nymphs to reach adulthood.

leave the nest without being harmed by the ants. From the ants' point of view that is not as generous as it seems. Attached to the egg is a structure called the capitulum. The ants cut it off and use it as a source of food before discarding the rest of the egg, which has a very hard shell that they cannot break into.

Tropical walkingsticks can be very abundant in trees, and the large numbers of their eggs falling at any one time can make it sound as if it is pouring with rain. The eggs are quite large in relation to the size of the female and are laid only a few at a time. Development can take anything from three to 18 months. The nymphs that emerge look like miniature adults. Male nymphs then go through five instars and female nymphs through six instars before molting into the adult form.

Walkingsticks and leaf insects are slow-moving, fairly soft-bodied creatures that are therefore vulnerable to attack by predators such as lizards, birds, and insectivorous mammals. As a result, they have a number of ways of defending themselves. The most obvious of them is their resemblance to sticks or leaves. They do not actually have to sit among sticks or leaves for the disguise to be successful, since fallen sticks and leaves can end up anywhere. The most important thing is for them to stay absolutely still. If they move, they will be spotted. When they do move in daylight, their walk is slow and deliberate, and they often sway slowly from side to side. The insect then seems to resemble a twig moving as if it is being blown by a light breeze.

Chemical Warfare

If a predator is more persistent and makes a closer approach to the phasmid, then alternative defenses can be brought into play. A number of winged walkingsticks have the ability to produce a startle display. If molested, they flick their wings wide open, revealing warning colors that will deter many smaller predators. Alternatively, there are quite a few stick insects that are able to use chemical warfare on their enemies. Such species have glands on the

thorax that manufacture very unpleasant chemical compounds. When the insect is molested, the chemicals are squirted straight into the face of the attacker. The effect is to blind it temporarily while the walkingstick makes good its escape.

One of these squirting species, the southern walkingstick, *Anisomorpha buprestoides* from North America, has been studied at some length to see how it reacts to various attacks. The glands that produce the spray are situated just behind the insect's head, and one or both can be used at a time and directed very accurately at an attacker. Ants are immediately repelled by the spray, as are carnivorous beetles. Small mammals, such as mice, sniff at the insects but usually back off as soon as they are sprayed. If they persist, however, the spray eventually runs out, and the mouse eats the walkingstick. In the laboratory possums just picked them up, waited until the spray ran out, and then ate them.

One amazing ability of these walkingsticks is that they seem to be able to recognize one of their main enemies, the blue jay, *Cyanocitta cristata*. The unfortunate birds are sprayed even before they have made contact with the insect. Like the southern walkingstick, *Agathemera* species walkingsticks from South America are also able to squirt their defensive chemicals very accurately. If the spray comes into contact with the human eye, it causes excruciating pain accompanied by temporary blindness, so these insects should be approached with some care. Rather than

Not all walkingsticks look like sticks. This very robust **Agathemera** *species comes from Argentina. It is able to squirt a corrosive liquid from its thoracic glands.*

spraying, the New Guinea stick insect, *Eurycantha horrida*, releases a foul-smelling brown liquid when it is molested.

Dangerous Pets

As an alternative to chemical defense, a number of walkingsticks are known to use physical attack. These larger species have spines on their legs and are able to rake them across attackers, often drawing blood in the process. This is a point worth remembering by those who keep exotic pets such as the jungle nymph stick insect, *Heteropteryx dilatata*. Females can reach 7 inches (18 cm) in length, and they have sharp spurs on the inside of their thighs. If handled carelessly, the spurs can be squeezed together over a human thumb or finger, drawing blood as they pierce the skin.

If all else fails, and an attacker gets close enough to grab a walkingstick's leg, it has one final line of defense: The leg breaks off along a predetermined line of weakness, and the walkingstick hurries away. For nymphs that is no great loss, since they may be able to regenerate the leg at the next molt.

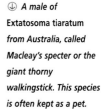

This unidentified walkingstick from the rain forests of Madagascar has chosen a suitable background against which to spend the hours of daylight.

A male of **Extatosoma tiaratum** *from Australia, called Macleay's specter or the giant thorny walkingstick. This species is often kept as a pet.*

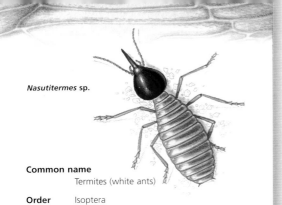

Nasutitermes sp.

Common name
Termites (white ants)

Order   Isoptera

Class   Insecta

Subphylum Hexapoda

Number of species About 2,300 (44 U.S.)

Size   From about 0.2 in (5 mm) to 1 in (2.5 cm)

Key features Social insects with kings, queens, soldiers, and workers; jaws typically used for biting and chewing; compound eyes (may be reduced or absent); antennae slim and about the same length as the thorax; membranous wings present in sexual forms, absent in workers and soldiers; soldiers often with large jaws or a snoutlike extension of the head; nymphs resemble wingless adults

Habits   Social insects with colonies of up to millions of individuals; live in the ground, often within mounds, or burrow into wood

Breeding   Winged sexual forms fly from colonies; females land and release pheromones to attract males; queens lay large numbers of eggs and are fed and looked after by workers

Diet   Fungi and decaying plant material

Habitat   Forests, savanna, semidesert, and desert

Distribution Worldwide, but mainly tropical; just a few species in warm, temperate zones

⊕ *A soldier-caste* Nasutitermes *species termite, known as a "nasute" soldier. The species is found in forest undergrowth in lowland areas of Central and South America. Length 0.2 inches (5 mm).*

Termites   Isoptera

As far as variety of forms and social structures are concerned, it is no exaggeration to say that the termites are among the most complex of all insects.

ABOUT SEVEN FAMILIES of termites are recognized by biologists. The so-called "higher" termites are collected in one family, the Termitidae, which contains many species. The remaining families form the "lower" termites and contain considerably fewer species. Whichever family they form, however, termite colonies are made up of a number of distinct types, or "castes." There are a king and a queen, both of which formerly had wings that were cast off once mating had taken place. The king and queen are called primary reproductives, and they may survive for 20 or more years.

Kings and Queens in Waiting

If either the king or queen were to die, reproduction would stop, which would result in the death of the colony. To prevent this possibility, there are a number of other undeveloped nymphs in the colony called supplementary reproductives, or neotenics.

⊕ *A colony of western subterranean termites inside a tree. Termites live in their colonies of millions of individuals either below ground (sometimes forming mounds) or by burrowing inside wood.*

⊕ *A male termite,*
Odontotermes obesus, *on*
the left, finds a female.
At this stage his wings
are still intact, but he will
break them off after
mating has taken place.

Depending on their sex, one or other can replace a lost king or queen by continuing its development to adulthood. All the other members of the colony are unable to reproduce (they are sterile) and consist of workers and soldiers. Unlike ant, bee, or wasp colonies, where all the sterile workers are female, termite workers and soldiers can be both sexes.

The workers are often very pale in color, which is how the common name of "white ants" has arisen for the Isoptera. Workers have what may be thought of as normal-sized jaws in relation to the size of the head. Soldiers, on the other hand, can have bigger heads than normal. Their jaws may also be much larger than usual for attacking enemies. Some termite species also have what are called "nasute" soldiers. They have a snoutlike projection on the front of the head through which they can squirt defensive secretions.

In some genera of lower termites there are no workers. The workers' tasks are carried out instead by the nymphs of soldiers and supplementary reproductives.

The Termite Colony

Termite colonies can exist for more than 100 years and contain millions of individuals, yet the balance between all of the different castes is somehow maintained at all times. It has been shown that in colonies kept in laboratories, removal of numbers of one particular caste—for example, the soldiers—will result in the production of extra soldiers to replace them.

In order to fully understand how that is achieved, it is necessary to follow the development of a colony from its very beginning. Regardless of family or termite species, the colony is founded by a queen and the male with which she has mated—the king. They set up a royal chamber either in wood or in the soil, where the queen first lays a few eggs. When the eggs hatch, they are fed by the queen on food from her own gut, which she regurgitates through her mouth. After a while the young begin to feed themselves and develop into workers that begin to take all work (other than producing fertilized eggs) away from the royal couple.

In the lower termites the queen does not get much bigger than when she first founds the nest, and she only produces small numbers of eggs. In the higher termites the queen becomes huge, her abdomen reaching an inch or so

The Termite Nest

The most obvious signs of termite activity are their nests. Clearly, those species that live inside wood or under the ground do not show their presence, but those with aboveground nests are instantly noticed. In South and Central America, for example, dark-colored oval masses attached to tree trunks or branches are likely to be the carton nests of *Nasutitermes* species termites. Carton is a mixture of chewed wood and feces that is used to make the nest in much the same way as chewed wood is used by social wasps. Running down the tree to the ground are covered galleries through which the termites pass as they go foraging.

The largest nests, however, are the termitaria, the mounds built by the higher termites, which can reach nearly 30 feet (9 m) in height and the same sort of distance across at the base. These termitaria are complex examples of animal architecture. Not only do they provide a home and protection for the colony, but they are also air-conditioning units. Tunnels and chimneys within the mound ensure that air circulates efficiently throughout the nest. Each nest contains millions of individuals, each of which requires oxygen and produces carbon dioxide that has to be disposed of. Apart from that, the large number of termites produces a great deal of heat that has to be vented to the outside; otherwise the whole nest would overheat, killing not only the termites but also their precious fungus "gardens."

The compass termite, *Amitermes meridionalis* from northern Australia, builds a mound that has two broad sides and two very narrow sides. The broad sides always face west and east, while the narrow sides face north and south. This means that as the sun rises in the east, it warms up the long east side; but as it swings to the south and gets hotter toward noon, it faces a narrow side, preventing the nest from getting too hot. As the sun goes around to the west and begins to lose its strength, it falls on the long west side, keeping the nest warm until sunset.

The termite Constrictotermes cyphergaster *from Brazil is one of the species that builds its nest off the ground in a tree. Interestingly, these termitaria are often dug into and nested in by birds such as parrots.*

(several centimeters) in length, and she may lay as many as 3,000 eggs each day.

In species that build nests, the workers collect food and construct the nest. As more and more food is collected, more workers are produced until eventually there are enough workers for the colony to begin soldier production. As the colony matures, winged males and females are produced, which will leave and found their own colonies.

The balance of castes in the colony is maintained by a combination of pheromones that in turn control the hormone balance inside each individual termite. When the colony is very young, there is no need for anything other than workers. The king and queen secrete pheromones that prevent any of the nymphs from becoming secondary reproductives or winged adults. When it is time for soldiers to be produced, pheromones from the king and queen stimulate some of the nymphs to become soldiers. As the number of soldiers increases, pheromones that the soldiers produce themselves inhibit the production of further soldiers. As the colony grows and the workers forage farther and farther away from the nest, more and more soldiers are needed to guard them. The pheromones that inhibit soldier

⊕ *Termite mounds on the African savanna can reach 30 feet (9 m) high. Towers and cellars provide ventilation and cooling. Below: The queen (1) needs to be much larger than the king (2) to produce her eggs. Large workers (3) forage; smaller ones (4) work inside the nest.*

production are reduced, and the king and queen are able to stimulate further soldier production to fill any gaps in the colony defenses. As the colony enlarges, the distances between the laying queen and the nymph-rearing areas increase. As a result, the amount of pheromones reaching the nymphs is reduced, and winged, sexual males and females begin to develop. They will eventually leave the colony and found new ones.

Feeding the Colony

All termites feed on plant material of one form or another. Many species feed on highly indigestible materials and require the assistance of other organisms to break down the food. Help in digesting the food in the lower termites comes in the form of single-celled animals, protozoa, that live in the gut. In return for their

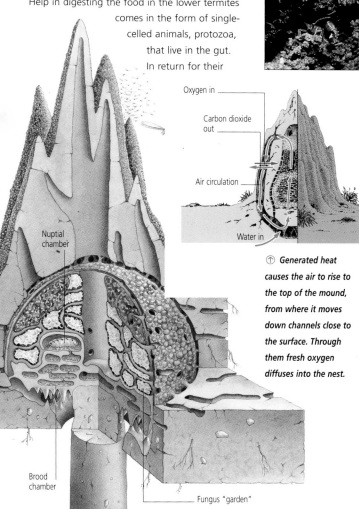

Oxygen in

Carbon dioxide out

Air circulation

Nuptial chamber

Water in

⬆ *Generated heat causes the air to rise to the top of the mound, from where it moves down channels close to the surface. Through them fresh oxygen diffuses into the nest.*

Brood chamber

Fungus "garden"

⬆ *These workers of the South American termite* **Nasutitermes ephratae** *have broken out of the old outer layer of their nest and are now enlarging it.*

help the protozoa live in a stable, protected environment. Each time the termite molts, it loses its protozoa and has to replace them by feeding from the anus of an already infected colony member.

Higher termites do not have protozoa. Instead, their place in the gut is taken by bacteria. The bacteria are not as efficient as the protozoa at breaking down the food, but that is not important, since the termites also use fungi in the nest to convert the collected vegetable material into a more digestible form.

The lower termites are mainly burrowers in damp or dry wood, where the galleries they dig as they feed form a sort of nest. Therefore they do not have to travel to collect food. Some species, however, make a nest in the ground and then tunnel to the nearest supply of wood, on which they then feed. Once they reach the open air, they build covered pathways using soil and droppings, through which they move back

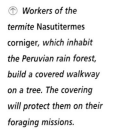

↑ *Workers of the termite* Nasutitermes corniger, *which inhabit the Peruvian rain forest, build a covered walkway on a tree. The covering will protect them on their foraging missions.*

and forth to feed on the wood. The covering prevents them from becoming dehydrated in the heat of the sun. The termites are a particular problem in tropical and subtropical regions, since they attack the wood of human habitations, often causing them to collapse as the structure of the wood breaks down.

Foraging for Food

The higher termites build complex nests in or above the ground, and the workers collect food from the surrounding area. Foraging for food is highly organized, and each species seems to have its own way of doing it. In the rain forests of Southeast Asia, *Macrotermes* species and *Longitermes* species walk along the ground, smoothing it down to make pathways as they collect fallen leaves. *Hospitalotermes* species, on the other hand, avoid walking across the ground if possible, preferring to travel on twigs, leaves, and other objects lying on the ground.

A study of *Hospitalotermes umbrinus sharpi* has revealed just how ordered these foraging expeditions can be. In this species expeditions to collect food only take place every few days. The outgoing columns are led by soldiers that, as the column gets longer, peel off to the side and stand guard over the passing workers. When the column reaches the tree on which they are to forage, the workers collect a bundle of food and then make their way back along the same pathway to the nest. Outgoing workers walk on the outside of the path, while loaded workers walk back along the center. If a worker in either lane becomes confused as to which direction it is supposed to be heading, it is soon put right: As it tries to go the wrong way, it meets hundreds of fellow workers coming from the other direction, and after receiving numerous head butts it turns around.

Even the act of foraging is ordered in these termites. Rows of workers cut away at lichens,

Defending the Colony

Termites live protected inside wood, under the ground, or in covered galleries on the surface—a fairly good means of defense. If the galleries or the mound are damaged by termite feeders such as anteaters breaking their way in, thousands of workers soon attend the site to repair the damage.

Many species forage openly at night, when, although they may be safe from daylight hunting birds and lizards, they are not safe from one of their greatest enemies—the ants. It is the role of the soldier termites to ward off the ant enemies to the best of their abilities. Many soldiers have huge jaws with which they lock onto and immobilize the ants. Others, called nasute soldiers, have snouts from which they squirt a foul-smelling, sticky liquid that gums up the ants' antennae and legs. When large numbers of nasutes are present, the overall effect of their secretions is able to deter even large termite feeders such as anteaters.

⊕ A group of Hospitalotermes *species termite workers foraging for lichens on the surface of a tree in a Malaysian forest.*

Two large-jawed Macrotermes *species soldier termites stand guard over a group of workers harvesting dead leaves in a forest in Malaysia. It is the role of the soldiers to ward off enemies—especially ants.*

⊕ A termite feeds on fungus in a nest. Many termite species grow their own fungus "gardens" inside their nests.

algae, bark fragments, and other suitable matter and hand the food back to another set of workers waiting behind them. They make the food into a ball-shaped mass and carry it back to the nest.

At any point in the process a new arrival may take over from a cutter. The cutter then becomes a ball maker, so it seems they are able to sense which job they need to perform at any particular moment.

Fungus "Gardens"

While many species of termite feed directly on the food they collect, others use it to form fungus "gardens" within the nest. The fungi in the gardens are only found in termite nests, and each species of termite has its own particular species of fungus.

The termites collect food and bring it back to the nest to make it into combs on which the fungus grows. After a while the fungus grows special structures, which are collected by the worker termites and used to feed the colony.

37

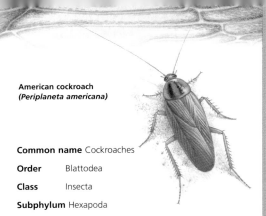

**American cockroach
(Periplaneta americana)**

Common name Cockroaches

Order Blattodea

Class Insecta

Subphylum Hexapoda

Number of species Around 4,000 (over 50 U.S.)

Size From about 0.15 in (4 mm) to 4.8 in (12 cm)

Key features Body tends to be rather flattened; head with well-developed compound eyes (except cave dwellers), long, thin antennae with many segments, and chewing mouthparts; pronotum usually forms a shield over the thorax and may extend forward to cover the top of the head; forewings toughened, covering the membranous hind wings; wings may be absent, especially in females; 1 pair of cerci on the end of the abdomen; nymphs resemble wingless adults

Habits Many species are nocturnal, while some come out in the day and feed from flowers

Breeding Mating may be preceded by courtship; stridulation (hissing) is known to occur in some species; eggs laid in a special purselike structure, the ootheca; parental care is known for a number of species

Diet Scavengers; many species will eat almost anything edible that they come across

Habitat Grassland, forests, deserts, sand dunes, caves, and human habitations

Distribution Worldwide, but most species found in the tropics

⊕ *The American cockroach,* Periplaneta americana, *is also known as the waterbug because of its preference for living in damp places such as water pipes and sewage systems. It is thought to have been introduced to the United States from Africa as early as 1625 and has spread across the world by crawling into grocery packages and being transported to new locations. Body length 1.5–2 inches (3.8–5 cm).*

Cockroaches Blattodea

Most people think of cockroaches as dirty creatures that spread diseases and cause food poisoning. That may be true for a few widespread species, but most cockroaches seldom come into contact with humans and are not a problem.

COCKROACHES ARE SOMETIMES confused with beetles, but careful examination makes them fairly easy to distinguish. Both cockroaches and beetles have leathery or toughened forewings, but those of beetles do not overlap along the centerline of the abdomen, while those of cockroaches do. Wingless species of cockroaches have a pair of cerci at the rear end of the abdomen. They are not present in beetles. Finally, the beetle's antenna has no more than 11 segments, while the cockroach's has many times more. The cockroach's flattened body is very useful, since it helps it hide in narrow gaps, for example, under peeling bark, beneath stones, or more unfortunately in the many nooks and crannies in human habitations.

Living with Humans

Of the 4,000 or so known species of cockroach only about 25 are a nuisance because of their habit of living alongside humans. Some species have lived with humans for so long that their origins are now unclear. The American cockroach, *Periplaneta americana*, for example,

⊕ *On the rain-forest floor in Trinidad a female cockroach,* **Homalopteryx laminata,** *makes a good job of mimicking a dead leaf.*

is found virtually everywhere in the world in association with humans. Despite the word *americana* in its scientific name, it is believed to have originated in Africa. These pest species owe their success to the fact that cockroaches can eat almost anything, and the waste food that humans leave around provides them with a veritable feast 24 hours a day.

Almost all the other cockroaches are also scavengers, eating anything suitable they come across. The exceptions are in the few members of the family Cryptocercidae, with five species from North America and two from Asia. *Cryptocercus punctulatus*, the wood roach found in the western United States and in the Appalachian Mountains in the east, is typical of the family. The wood roach lives in and feeds exclusively on dead and decaying wood. Such wood is normally highly indigestible, but the wood roach overcomes the problem with the aid of harmless protozoa that live in its hind gut. These single-celled animals are able to

⊕ Adults of the American cockroach, Periplaneta americana, feed on a discarded sandwich. The cockroaches live indoors, where they eat and contaminate foodstuffs with their droppings.

⊖ Most cockroaches, such as this Ectobius panzeri lesser cockroach in England, live well away from humans and cause them no problems.

39

In South Africa the cockroach Aptera fusca *stands hissing, its body raised ready to release a stream of unpleasant fluid at a perceived attacker.*

digest the cellulose in the wood, thereby providing the wood roach with a source of carbohydrates. The smallest known cockroach, *Attaphilla fungicola* from North America, lives in the nests of leaf-cutting ants, where it feeds on the fungus cultivated in their underground fungus "gardens."

Senses and Pheromones

Cockroaches are very much insects of the hours of darkness, and as a result, their courtship behavior tends to rely on touch, scent, and taste rather than on sight. In general, female cockroaches release pheromones to attract males and to bring about courtship, while male pheromones induce the female to mate.

Courtship behavior in *Latiblatella angustifrons* from Central America is typical of the behavior found in many other cockroaches. The female first attracts a male by sitting with the tail end of her abdomen drooping down (the so-called "calling" position). It is thought that this position helps release and spread her pheromones into the air. This type of calling has been observed in three of the five cockroach families. It can attract a male from as far as 33 feet (10m) away.

Once a pair has made contact, they touch one another's antennae. The male then starts his part of the courtship routine. He sways his body from side to side, turns his back on the female, droops his head and abdomen downward, and lifts both pairs of wings upward at an angle of about 60 degrees, uncovering a pheromone-producing gland near the tip of his abdomen. This is highly attractive to the female, and she walks forward to nuzzle and nibble at the gland and then moves along his abdomen until she contacts his raised wings. He senses her position, moves backward until their reproductive structures are in contact, and they mate. The female then steps off his back and turns around so that they are in the normal end-to-end mating position found in all cockroaches. The male then transfers his spermatophore to the female.

Battering Rams and Armor Plating

Courtship is not quite so straightforward in *Gromphadorhina portentosa,* the Madagascan hissing cockroach, since the male often has to compete with other males to win his chosen female. The males are bigger than the females and have a heavily armored pronotum. When they make contact, competing males first touch one another with their antennae. Using their pronotums as battering rams, they then engage in a pushing battle. The loser is the male that eventually gets pushed backward. As he turns to run, he may suffer further attacks from the victorious male. The contests can be very noisy, because as they fight, the males push air out of their breathing systems. This produces a hissing sound that—under different circumstances—is used to warn off attackers.

The male is much gentler in his dealings with the female, exchanging antennal caresses with her and hissing, but quietly. However, as they reach the point of mating, the male suddenly produces a series of hisses that stimulate the female to couple with him. The hisses are essential for mating to take place: If the male is prevented from hissing, the female will not mate. In *G. portentosa* the hissing replaces the nudging and nibbling of the male pheromone gland in other cockroaches.

A mating pair of a Pseudomops *species cockroaches from Brazil. They are in the normal end-to-end position adopted by cockroaches when mating.*

Males of *Xestoblatta hamata*, another Central American cockroach, actually provide their females with a special supply of food that is rich in nitrogen. The female obtains it from the male's reproductive opening. The gift of food is a form of investment by the male in his future offspring, because some of it ends up in the eggs that he will eventually fertilize.

Brood Chambers

Female cockroaches do not lay their eggs straight into any physical structures. Instead, the eggs are kept in a special purselike structure called the ootheca. Depending on the species, the ootheca may then be abandoned by the female in a suitable hiding place, or she may keep it attached to the end of her abdomen until the eggs hatch out. In some cases the ootheca is kept in a brood pouch, a chamber in the female's body where the eggs can develop without any outside interference.

Amazingly, the Pacific beetle cockroach, *Diploptera punctata,* produces live young. Females of the species make very small eggs that do not contain enough yolk to produce a full first instar nymph. The eggs are held in a very thin-walled ootheca that is inside the female's uterus (part of her reproductive structures). Inside her uterus the developing embryos are fed with a nutritious fluid, a sort of "milk." The first instar nymphs leave their mother's body when they are fully developed.

Cockroach nymphs are similar in appearance to wingless adults, and they grow through a series of instars before eventually molting to the adult form.

ⓣ *A female* Parcoblatta *species wood cockroach from the southeastern United States. She is carrying her ootheca, full of eggs, on the end of her abdomen.*

Family Units

Although most cockroaches live apart as adults, and the females leave their young to develop independently, a number of species have a degree of sociality in their life cycle. At its simplest it consists of nymphs from the same batch of eggs remaining together until they become adult. Studies on the widespread German cockroach, *Blatella germanica*, have revealed that this behavior occurs due to the production of a special pheromone. Each batch of youngsters seems to be able to recognize the pheromone produced by their own brothers and sisters, preferring to be with them rather than with an unrelated group.

Females of Australian giant burrowing cockroaches, *Macropanesthia rhinoceros*, dig burrows in eucalyptus woodland. They take leaves and other litter from the trees into their burrows and feed on them. The males go in search of female burrows to find a mate and tend to be aggressive toward any other males that they come across. The nymphs stay with their mother in her burrow for up to six months of the year, and sometimes an adult male may stay with the family group.

Mother's "Milk"

The wood roaches of the genus *Cryptocercus* also live together as a family. They dig galleries in the dead wood that forms their food, and nymphs live there with their mother or with both parents. The adult wood roaches wander around the galleries, usually feeding at some distance from the nymphs. At intervals the adults (more often the female) return to the nymphs, which cluster around them. From its rear end the adult produces a secretion that is eaten by the nymphs. They feed in this way for up to a year. Gradually the nymphs can feed themselves, having developed a set of protozoa in their gut with which to digest the wood.

ⓣ *The giant burrowing cockroach, or litter bug,* Macropanesthia rhinoceros, *from Australia, is the world's largest cockroach, reaching 5 inches (13 cm) in length. This is one of its front legs, which is adapted for digging, much like that of the mole crickets.*

⊖ *In the wild there is often safety in numbers. These warningly colored cockroach nymphs clump together on the trunk of a tree in southern Africa.*

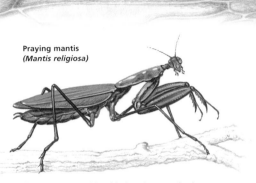

**Praying mantis
(Mantis religiosa)**

Common name Mantids (praying mantises)

Order Mantodea

Class Insecta

Subphylum Hexapoda

Number of species About 2,000 (20 U.S.)

Size From about 0.4 in (10 mm) to 6 in (15 cm)

Key features Males normally smaller than females; head roughly triangular when seen from front; eyes large and well separated; antennae thin; jaws for cutting and chewing prey; head held well away from the body on elongated first thoracic segment; front legs adapted for grasping prey; forewings leathery, covering membranous hind wings; 1 pair of cerci on the end of the abdomen; nymphs resemble adults or are ant mimics, at least in the early instars

Habits Most species sit on vegetation waiting for prey; some sit on bark, others live on the ground

Breeding Females attract males to them—courtship then follows; eggs laid in an ootheca; maternal care known in some species

Diet Predators, feeding on other insects and also spiders; occasionally take small vertebrates such as lizards

Habitat Grassland, scrub, forests, semideserts, and deserts

Distribution Mainly tropical in distribution, with a few species in warmer temperate areas

⊕ *The praying mantis,* Mantis religiosa, *is found waiting for smaller insect prey on flowers and foliage. It was accidentally introduced from southern Europe into the United States in 1899. Length including wings 2.5 inches (6 cm).*

Mantids Mantodea

Although mantid is the accepted common name for the group in scientific circles, the Mantodea are more often known as praying mantises. The way they stand as they wait for passing prey, with their front legs held forward side by side, looks like they are praying.

THE MANTIDS ARE PERFECTLY adapted for their role as one of the major groups of assassins in the insect world. On the normally triangular head is a pair of large compound eyes, which, together with the ability of the head to swivel in all directions, give the mantid a very broad field of vision when on the lookout for prey. Not only are the eyes large, but they often protrude some distance away from the head. The highly efficient jaws point down from the bottom of the head and allow the insect to demolish prey at quite an amazing speed. The antennae are slim and seldom particularly long.

Killing Machines

In order to fit in the long, grasping front pair of legs, the first segment of the thorax is very long, giving mantids the appearance of having a long neck. The coxa (the basal section) of the front leg is much longer than in other insects, nearly as long as the femur. That gives the mantid its long reach for grabbing its prey.

On the undersides of the femurs and tibiae are rows of sharp spines. As the tibia and femur come together during the grab, the spines dig into the prey, helping the mantid maintain a tight grasp on it before the first fatal bite is delivered. The other two pairs of legs vary in length according to the species: Some have short legs and a rather dumpy appearance; others are longer legged and look a bit like walkingsticks. The forewings are leathery and protect the more delicate membranous hind

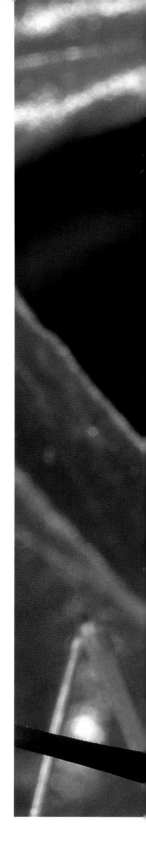

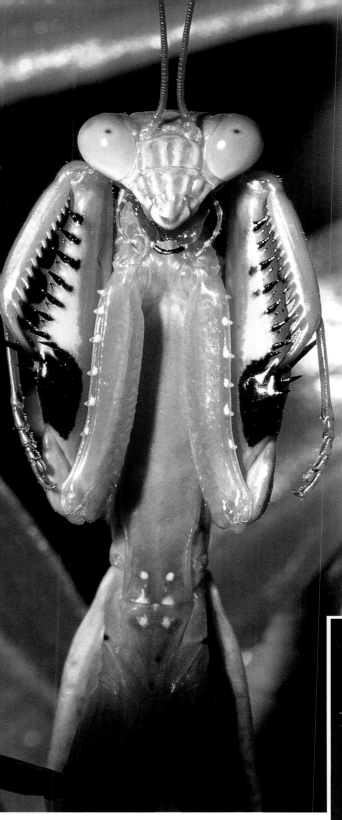

wings. In general, mantids are fairly good fliers. Many species, however, are wingless, especially those that live on the ground.

Second Helpings

Mantids will eat almost anything that comes their way, as long as they are able to handle it. While insects and spiders form the main prey, some of the larger species have been seen feeding on small birds, lizards, and frogs. Most mantids do not actively search for prey but are "sit-and-wait" predators, watching out for anything that comes along and grabbing it once it is close enough. While feeding, they are capable of grabbing another prey item in one front leg, while at the same time holding onto the original prey with the other leg. They then consume the second prey item after polishing off the first.

Nymphs of the African flower mantid, *Pseudocreobotra ocellata*, have been seen stretching up and grabbing flies out of midair. Another African mantid, *Tarachodes afzelii*, lives on the trunks and branches of trees, where it keeps company with multitudes of ants on the

⊙ *The face of death: What an insect would see, if it could, just before it was pounced on by this nymph of the mantis* Polyspilota aeruginosa *from Africa.*

⊙ *Gripping it tightly in her front legs, a* Parasphendale agrionina *mantis female munches away at an assassin bug, itself a predator of smaller insects.*

way from their nests on the ground to collect food in the forest canopy. Third instar larvae up to adult ants form its main prey. Instead of waiting for the ants to run past, however, the mantids chase and grab them.

Dawn Calls

Not a great deal is known about mantid courtship, since only a few species have been studied in detail, and most studies have been made under laboratory conditions that might not give a truly accurate picture of events in the wild. Studies made of the behavior of the leaf-mimicking mantid, *Acanthops falcata* from tropical America, may give a clue to the way in which the sexes come together.

In order for them to find a mate, males of *A. falcata* face two problems. First, the females are spread thinly around the forest in which they live, and they also resemble dead leaves, which are abundant in the forest. Second, the male must find a female that is actually willing to mate. He is helped to overcome these problems because females who are themselves seeking a male sit and "call." They do this by hanging from a twig, raising their wing cases, and curving their abdomen to uncover a pair of black glands from which they release a cloud of pheromone molecules. Females have been observed to attract more than one male at a time by "calling." The first male on the scene walks toward her, rocking from side to side so that he is recognized. He then climbs onto her back, and they mate.

The "calling" process was seen taking place for a short period of time just before dawn, presumably so that flying males and

Although to us these Stagmatoptera septrionalis *nymphs from Trinidad are clearly mantids, to a predator they look more like a group of ants. That gives them some protection, since ants are avoided by many predators.*

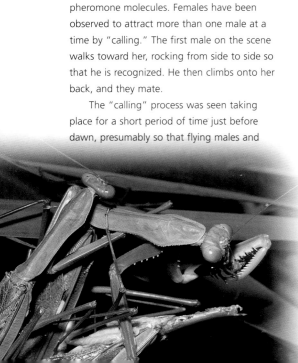

A female eats the head of the male with whom she is mating. The possible reason for this cannibalism, which is not common in the wild, is that they have been disturbed by a second male, seen on the left.

mating pairs would complete their activities before the birds and other vertebrates began their daily hunt for prey. Examples of males flying into the presence of females have also been observed in the wild for other species of mantid, and it can be assumed that the females of these species were also calling by emitting clouds of pheromones.

Female Cannibals

It has often been claimed that, having mated, the female mantid proceeds to eat the male; but is that really true? In the case of *A. falcata*, although many observations were made of mating pairs in the laboratory, the female was never seen to eat the male.

However, studies on the praying mantis, *Mantis religiosa* from Europe, indicate some cannibalism in the wild—about one in four males lost their heads, chewed off by the female during mating. It may be, therefore, that

*↑ This female
Polyspilota aeruginosa
mantis from Africa is
busy laying her eggs. The
white structure is the egg
case, made from a foam
secreted by the mantis,
which rapidly hardens on
contact with the air.*

in some species there is
occasional cannibalism.
Whether this is normal,
however, or whether other
factors, such as old, weak
males or disturbance are the
cause, is a matter still to be
investigated.

Discovery in the wild of
a pair of African *Polyspilota
aeruginosa* revealed that the
female was busy chewing
her way down her mate's body. There was,
however, another male attempting to mate
with her at the same time, and it may be that
as a result of this disruption she had become
confused and bitten off her mate's head.

A similar occurrence with an *Acontista*
species mantid in Trinidad revealed a contrary
result. A pair was observed mating when a
second male flew in, clambered across the front
of the female, and began a tussle with the
mating male. As he fought, the contender was
actually supporting himself on the female's
head, a seemingly dangerous position for him
to be in. She, however, completely ignored the
second male, which eventually gave up his
attempt and flew off.

A Rare Occurrence

It would appear, therefore, that sexual
cannibalism is rather rare in the wild, and much
of what has been observed may be a result of
the abnormal conditions that occur during
laboratory investigations. One such investigation
did, however, bring up an interesting point: An
introduced male was far more likely to be eaten
by a poorly fed female than by a well-fed
female. In the wild the female is unlikely to
begin calling for males until she has fed well
and her egg batch is complete, in which case
she will have no need to eat the male. It is

possible that the occasional poorly fed female attracts a male and then, to complete the growth of her eggs, eats him.

Egg Laying

Having mated, the next task for the female mantid is to lay her eggs. She makes a special egg case, or ootheca, that may be left attached to vegetation or under bark or stones, depending on the species. The ootheca is made from a foam released by special abdominal glands. The foam soon hardens to the consistency of expanded polystyrene foam.

While it is still soft, she forms a series of small chambers in it and lays a single egg in each one. Each chamber has a little valve at the top through which the newly hatched nymph can escape. The nymphs are miniatures of the adults, except that they lack wings. In a number of species, however, the earliest instars are quite successful mimics of ants. For most mantids, once the female has laid her eggs, her work is done, and she deserts the cocoon.

Sentry Duty

Females of the genera *Galepsus, Tarachodula,* and *Oxyopthalmellus*—most of which come from Africa—remain and guard their oothecae. These species produce a long, narrow ootheca (attached to a plant stem or twig) that fits neatly beneath their body as they lie along it. As is the case with many insects, this protection is mainly to keep parasitic wasp females away from the eggs. How long they remain on guard and whether they then protect their nymphs are not yet known. In species in which the female does not guard her ootheca, she will catch and eat any of her nymphs should she come across them at a later date.

A female *Oxyophthalmellus somalicus* in Kenya was observed apparently standing guard over her nymphs, which were clustered at the end of a twig above where she was sitting. Therefore ants or other predators would have to get past her to reach the nymphs. It is possible, at least in this species, that the female cares for her nymphs, even just for a short time.

⊙ *Many mantids gain protection from their enemies by being leaf mimics. This* Acanthops falcataria *male mimics dead leaves in its home in the Brazilian rain forest.*

⊙ *By appearing to be a pink flower, this* Pseudocreobotra ocellata *flower mantis nymph from Kenya not only fools its enemies but also attracts prey such as bees.*

A Predator at Risk

Mantids may be highly efficient assassins, but they are not immune from attack by bigger, stronger predators. Many wildlife films show mammals such as bush babies tucking into a mantid that they have stumbled on during their nocturnal foraging. Even the house sparrow may be seen on occasions with the long, green body of a praying mantis hanging from its beak as it takes it to feed its hungry nestlings.

To avoid such large predators, the majority of mantids are cryptically colored, including greens to match the leaves among which they live and mottled browns and grays for those that live on bark. There are also mantids that are very good mimics of leaves and flowers. One African mantid, *Pseudocreobotra wahlbergi,* which normally sits on flowers, is actually able to alter its colors to match its background, although it takes several days to achieve the transformation.

As long as it remains still, a mantid is usually safe. Yet if a would-be predator gets too close, then many of the camouflaged species have another trick: They use a startle display by suddenly revealing a brightly colored pattern or eyespots on their body. In Ghana, for example, 15 out of 25 mantid species that had camouflage colors or were mimics of twigs or grass were also able to perform a startle display. Although these displays are of little use against nocturnal predators, experiments have shown that they are quite good at frightening off monkeys—another mantid predator.

Gladiators

The word gladiator is associated with men fighting with one another and wild animals in the Roman amphitheaters, but it is also the common name for the first new order of insects discovered since 1915. These insects were first found in southern Africa in 2002, but a gladiator has also turned up in Tanzania. The taxonomic name for the order to which they have been assigned is the Mantophasmatodea, indicating that they appear to share characteristics with both the mantids and the walkingsticks. They are nocturnal insects and have been found in clumps of grass growing in the cracks in rocks, where they catch insects and spiders as prey.

At first glance they look a bit like a walkingstick—one of the timemas from North America is similar—but the gladiator body is more cylindrical. The antennae are slim, and the mouthparts, as expected in a predator, are designed for cutting and chewing. All of the specimens found so far lack wings. The life cycle includes nymphal instars that are small replicas of the adults. There is still much to be learned about the way of life of such a new and apparently rare group of insects.

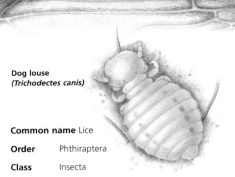

Dog louse
(Trichodectes canis)

Common name Lice

Order Phthiraptera

Class Insecta

Subphylum Hexapoda

Number of species About 5,500 (1,000 U.S.)

Size From about 0.02 in (0.5 mm) to 0.4 in (10 mm)

Key features Flattened, wingless insects; antennae short; eyes small or absent; mouthparts used for chewing in 2 suborders and for sucking in the 3rd suborder; legs with strong claws on the foot to grasp the hair or feathers of host mammals and birds; nymphs are like tiny pale adults

Habits Live on or near their host birds or mammals, including humans

Breeding Eggs are attached to the hair or feathers of host animals

Diet Feed either on bird feathers or mammal skin, or suck blood

Habitat Found wherever their hosts are, as well as terrestrial mammals and birds; hosts also include seals, penguins, and oceanic birds that only come to land to breed

Distribution Worldwide

⊕ *Trichodectes canis, the dog louse, is found all over the world. Large infestations of the parasite can cause considerable irritation to dogs (especially pups), which will try in vain to remove the pests by scratching vigorously. Body length 0.04 inches (1 mm).*

Lice

Phthiraptera

The very word lice makes most people feel itchy—few of us escape even a small infestation of the troublesome human head louse.

ALL MEMBERS OF THE ORDER Phthiraptera are totally dependent on the bird or mammal on which they live as parasites: If they become separated from their host, they soon die. In many instances the relationship between parasite and host is a very close one, with a particular species of louse being found on just a single host species. Often a particular genus of lice is associated with a particular family or genus of birds or mammals. Knowing which lice they carry has even helped scientists decide which family a bird belongs to. Since lice cannot fly, they have to pass from one host to another when the hosts are in contact with each other, such as in the nest or during mating or fighting.

The Phthiraptera is divided into two suborders of biting lice (the Amblycera and the Ischnocera) and one suborder of sucking lice (the Anoplura). The biting lice have a broad head and chewing mouthparts, and one or two tarsal segments, usually with two claws. The sucking lice, however, have sucking mouthparts and a single tarsal segment with just one claw.

The biting lice are mainly parasites of birds, with just a few species associated with mammals. They have sharp-edged mandibles that they use to cut off bits of feather and dead skin, their main food. They will, however, take blood from any available

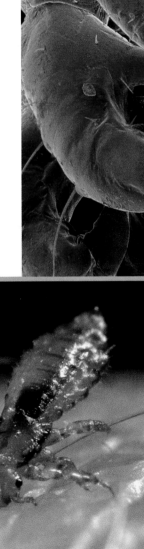

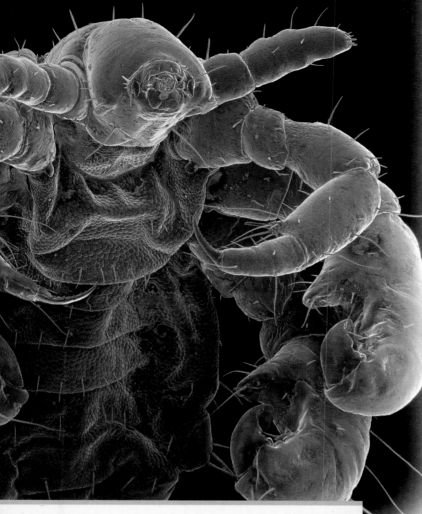

This scanning electron micrograph of the crab louse, Phthirus pubis, *clearly shows the claws used to hold itself in place while sucking the blood of its human host with its biting mouthparts.*

wound. Heavy infestations can result in feather loss. Birds are often seen dust-bathing to try to reduce the numbers of lice living on them. The best place to see some of these parasites is on domestic chickens, since they often carry biting lice.

Close Neighbors

Of the two suborders of biting lice the Amblycera wander around on the host, fitting themselves into nooks and crannies on the surface in order to avoid being removed during preening. However, the Ischnocera feed in one spot, hanging on tightly to feathers or fur to avoid being preened off. An animal can have two or more species of biting lice living on it at one time; but it appears that, simply by living on different parts of the host, they may not interfere with one another. For example, in North America *Geomydoecus* and *Thomomydoecus* species lice live together on *Thomomys* species pocket gophers. Studies have shown that *Geomydoecus* lice tend to live on the upper side of the gophers, with some moving down onto the sides, while the *Thomomydoecus* lice live on the underside, with a few living on the sides as well.

Of the sucking lice it is the superfamily Rhyncophthirina that has the biggest problem feeding, because they include the elephant lice. Elephants are, of course, very thick skinned; but to overcome the problem, the lice have a long, proboscislike structure that allows them to get at the elephant's blood through its thick skin.

Lice on Humans

Unfortunately, there are two species of lice that live on humans. The most common species in the western world is the head and body louse, *Pediculus humanus*. It was originally thought that head and body lice were two different species, then it was later decided that they were just two subspecies. Research on their genetic material, however, has indicated that they are in fact a single species. Their main claim to fame—apart from the irritation they cause—is that as they bite and suck blood, they transmit more different human diseases than any other single form of insect. The diseases they spread are caused by bacteria, the most important being relapsing fever, epidemic typhus, and trench fever, all of which can be fatal to humans.

The human head louse, Pediculus humanus capitis, *commonly infests schoolchildren because close physical contact allows the lice to move from host to host.*

Dog flea (Ctenocephalides canis)

Common name Fleas

Order Siphonaptera

Class Insecta

Subphylum Hexapoda

Number of species About 2,380 (325 U.S.)

Size From about 0.04 in (1 mm) to 0.5 in (13 mm)

Key features Adults very flattened from side to side; wingless; hind legs modified for jumping; head without compound eyes; simple eyes may be absent or well developed; mouthparts adapted for sucking blood

Habits Adults live on their hosts; hosts are mainly mammals, but also a few birds; larvae live in nests or close to where the hosts live

Breeding Breeding cycle of fleas often linked to that of the host; eggs normally laid in the host's nest or living area

Diet Blood for the adults, shed skin and other edible bits and pieces for the larvae

Habitat Wherever the hosts are found

Distribution Worldwide

⊕ *The dog flea,* Ctenocephalides canis, *and the cat flea,* Ctenocephalides felis, *are probably the most common domestic fleas, with a worldwide distribution. The flea life cycle takes about three weeks, but eggs can remain dormant for long periods in cool weather. Length 0.1 inches (3–4 mm).*

Fleas
Siphonaptera

Europe in the Middle Ages was ravaged by bubonic plague, a disease that killed an estimated 20 million people. The plague was transmitted from one person to another by rat fleas.

FLEAS ARE PERFECTLY ADAPTED for their life as parasites of mammals and birds: Their flattened bodies allow them to slip easily through fur and feathers to escape from grooming teeth, claws, and beaks. Lack of wings also makes it easy for them to move over the host; and if they need to get to another host, they simply jump.

Nest Invaders

The closest relations of the fleas are the flies, and like them, fleas have legless, wormlike larvae. Flea larvae, at least in the wild, live in or near the nests of their host animals. That helps explain the fact that large animals, such as horses and cattle and their relatives, do not have fleas, because they do not have nests. Yet domestic cats and dogs do not have nests as such, but they still have fleas. The fleas drop their eggs around our homes, where the larvae feed on the bits and pieces of skin and other edible scraps, such as crumbs, that are left lying around the house. When adults hatch out and find no cat or dog around, they are quite happy to jump onto the nearest person and take a quick meal. When their proper host comes in for a pat or a stroke, the fleas make their way from us to them.

In a wild mammal or bird nest the flea larvae feed on bits of skin, feathers, or other edible material, as well as the blood-rich droppings from adult fleas. The larvae pass through two molts before they pupate, which takes place inside a silken cocoon. After they leave the cocoon, adult fleas may have to wait a considerable time before they get the opportunity to find a new host. As a result, they

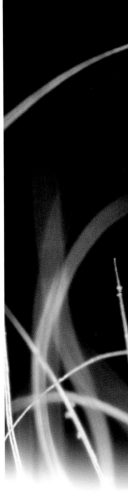

⊕ *Spilopsyllus cuniculi, the rabbit flea, feeds on the ear of its rabbit host. The flea is a major carrier of the rabbit disease myxomatosis, which is fatal in Old World and Australian rabbits. Its effects are fairly mild in North American rabbits.*

are able to go for long periods without feeding. Female fleas, however, must feed on blood before they are able to lay a batch of eggs.

Specific Hosts

Many creatures have just one single flea species normally associated with them. Humans, for example, have the human flea, *Pulex irritans*. The name *irritans* is appropriate, since the anticlotting substance the fleas inject into the wound is very itchy and is what causes us to scratch at a flea bite. Some creatures are not so lucky and have more than one species of flea to irritate them. The European house marten, *Mustela foina*, for example, is host to three different flea species. However, spare a thought for the poor old mountain beaver, *Aplodontia rufa*. This North American mammal, thought to be the most primitive of all rodents, is host to the largest known flea—*Hystrichopsylla schefferi*. Females can grow between 0.3 and 0.5 inches (8 to 13 mm) in length.

The life cycle of any kind of parasite has to tie in very closely to that of its host, otherwise the parasite

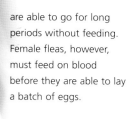

⊙ The flea's remarkable jumping ability comes from a special structure known as the pleural arch, a modified wing hinge made of an elastic protein called resilin.

Jumping

The flea's jumping ability is awesome. Some have been recorded as covering 150 times the length of their body in distance and 80 times the length of their body in height. In human terms this is equivalent to a 6-foot (1.8-m) human—discounting the length of the legs—jumping about 600 feet (182 m) in length, while rising 320 feet (98 m) in the air. While in the air, high-speed photography has revealed that fleas have little control of their movements, since they turn over and over with their legs sticking out in all directions. They are unable to control which part of their body hits the ground first, but they are extremely light and suffer no damage from such improvised landings. In fact, fleas are amazingly powerful little creatures that are even able to wriggle their way out when held between finger and thumb. They also have a very tough exoskeleton, which makes them difficult to squash.

might lose its host. The life cycle of the European rabbit flea, *Spilopsyllus cuniculi*, has been studied in detail, although whether the biology is typical of all fleas will take a long time to research.

Close Ties

The activity of rabbit fleas is closely tuned to the activity of the rabbit. When rabbits are mating, their temperature rises substantially. As they warm up, the fleas on the rabbits get agitated, and some of them move from one rabbit to the other. Not long after mating, the female rabbit begins to produce sex hormones in her blood. The fleas, when they feed, are affected by the hormones, and they gather near the ears of the female rabbit and settle down there without moving.

Around 10 days before the female rabbit is due to give birth to her kittens, her pituitary gland begins to release a different hormone. The feeding female fleas detect this hormone, which causes them to begin development of their eggs. They also begin taking in lots of blood from the female rabbit.

Hormone Changes

Birth of the kittens results in yet another hormonal change in the blood of the female rabbit, causing the fleas to make their way onto her face. As the mother rabbit licks her babies, the fleas jump across from her face onto them. They then begin to feed from the rabbit kittens' blood. That blood contains yet another hormone, in this case a growth hormone, which sets the fleas off mating again.

The result of heavy feeding on blood is that the fleas produce lots of blood-rich droppings, which fall into the nest. They provide food for the flea larvae, which hatch from the eggs laid by the female fleas. When they are around one week old, growth-hormone production in the baby rabbits begins to fall off, and the fleas

⊙ *An electron micrograph of a cat flea,* Ctenocephalides felis, *sucking blood. The specialized piercing stylet can be seen entering the skin.*

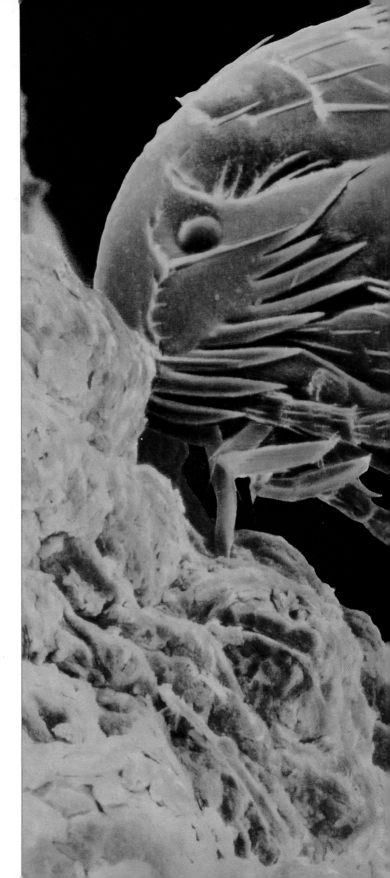

then leave the youngsters and return to the mother rabbit. The fleas now cease any form of reproductive activity until the female rabbit mates again, and the whole cycle is repeated once more.

In the meantime the flea larvae are feeding on the bloody droppings and eventually pupate. At around the time that the young rabbits are ready to leave the nest, the new generation of adult fleas has already emerged from the pupae and made their way onto them. So as the young rabbits enter the big wide world, they already have their own contingent of fleas to accompany them.

⊕ *A colored scanning electron micrograph of the rat flea,* Xenopsylla cheapis. *It is seen here clinging to the rat's fur. Extensive control measures against both fleas and rats have virtually eliminated the plague in the developed world.*

Fleas and Disease

Perhaps the most important and best-known disease transmitted by fleas is bubonic plague, caused by the bacterium *Yersinia* (formerly *Pasturella*) *pestis*. The disease organisms are passed on when the fleas feed on an infected person and then move onto the next person to feed. Plague killed millions of people in the past and still exists in many parts of the world, including the western states of North America. Here it exists in rodent fleas, such as those found on ground squirrels. The bacterium is just as deadly to the rodents as it is to humans. Although the rodents carry the disease, it is seldom passed on to humans, since people in the area know not to come into contact with them and to keep the immediate area around their homes rodent free, especially from rats. Luckily, plague is fairly easily controlled these days through the use of antibiotics.

Depending on one's point of view, the transmission of a disease by a flea can in fact be quite useful. The rabbit flea, for example, carries the myxoma virus, which causes the fatal disease myxomatosis of Old World and Australian rabbits. The disease was introduced into both Europe and Australia from its native North America, where its effects on the native rabbits are relatively mild. The introduction of the disease was an attempt to wipe out, or at least severely reduce, the huge crop-damaging rabbit populations of these areas. The fact that the disease was carried by fleas was a major factor in the rapidity with which the disease spread.

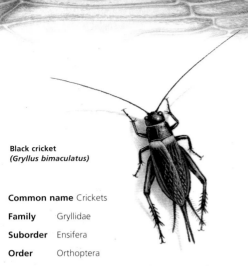

Black cricket
(Gryllus bimaculatus)

Common name Crickets

Family Gryllidae

Suborder Ensifera

Order Orthoptera

Number of species About 2,000 (about 100 U.S.)

Size From about 0.06 in (1.5 mm) to 2.3 in (6 cm)

Key features Separated from related insects, such as katydids, by the fact that crickets have only 3 segments in the tarsus of the middle leg, while katydids have 4; jumping hind legs short and fairly stout; antennae long and slim, sometimes more than twice the body length; female ovipositor straight and cylindrical; hearing organ on each front leg

Habits During the day generally found on the ground, sheltering under stones and logs or among vegetation; most are active at night, but some are day active; some males dig burrows

Breeding Males usually attract females by "singing"; mating takes place at night and therefore not often seen; females use ovipositor to insert eggs in the ground, into crevices, and sometimes into plants; females lay just 1 egg at a time

Diet Perhaps the most omnivorous of the Orthoptera, feeding on both plants and other insects; flowers—especially the pollen-rich anthers—a favorite of some species

Habitat Meadows, parks, gardens, forests, mountains, deserts, and caves; also ants' nests

Distribution Widespread around the world

⊕ *The black cricket,* Gryllus bimaculatus, *is native to southern Europe. It is bred commercially as lizard food. Being large and stocky it cannot fly, and the male sings a birdlike song day and night. Body length 1–1.2 inches (2.5–3.0 cm).*

Crickets   Gryllidae

Crickets are well-known for their "singing." In Asia they are kept in cages and take part in singing competitions. Their sound is also familiar across North America, as the males sing to attract a mate.

IN COMMON WITH THE KATYDIDS the crickets are a mainly nocturnal group that can be heard singing more often than they are seen. They are usually drab shades of brown or black, although one or two are more brightly marked.

As with the katydids, females have a long ovipositor. It looks even more like a sting than that of katydids, since it is more needlelike in shape. Food of both plant and animal origin, including animal droppings, figures in the diet of the crickets. As well as eating leaves, many crickets are particularly fond of flowers—especially the pollen, which is rich in protein—and will climb up plants to reach them. When they occur in large numbers, some crickets can be destructive pests of cultivated crops.

Sneaky Matings

As with most other orthopterans, male crickets "sing" to attract a mate. On summer nights in North America males of the field cricket, *Gryllus integer*, sing loudly in suburban gardens. Like many other species of cricket, males will fight one another over the best areas in which to dig their burrow, the place from which they sing. The largest and strongest males will also attack and upset the mating of already established couples, increasing the likelihood that they will mate with the female instead.

In *Gryllus integer*, however, having the loudest voice does not always ensure the greatest mating success. As the top cricket's loud voice attracts females, so weaker-voiced males are also attracted to him. They wait on the sidelines and sneakily mate with females on their way to the top cricket's burrow.

⊕ *A 4-spotted tree cricket,* Oecanthus quadripunctatus *from the United States, sings from a leaf. In the tree crickets (subfamily Oecanthinae) the body is longer and slimmer than in other crickets.*

While most male crickets sit on the ground or on vegetation to call, a number have developed ways of increasing the volume of sound produced and the distance it travels. Males of some *Oecanthus* species tree crickets cut a pear-shaped hole in a leaf a little larger than themselves. They then brace the edges of their wings against the side of the hole and begin to sing. It has been shown that by using the leaf in this way, the cricket produces up to three and a half times the volume of sound produced without using a leaf.

⊕ *Most crickets from around the world are brown or black (straw-colored in tree crickets) and nocturnal. The strikingly marked* **Rhicnogryllus lepidus** *is a day-active species from Kenya, and its colors are an indication that it might be poisonous.*

Wall of Sound

Just as enterprising are the black-and-white males of the Asian cricket *Gymnogryllus elegans*. In common with a number of other species of cricket the male digs a burrow, where he spends the daylight hours. He builds a wall of mud around the mouth of his burrow, leaving a gap at one end. As darkness approaches, the male emerges from his burrow and sits so that his tail end faces the gap. He then begins to sing. The sound he produces is amplified to such an extent by the wall that it is painful to the human ear if one is too close.

Having attracted a mate, courtship can vary from the simple to the quite complex. In the American species *Hygronemobius alleni* there is usually some antennal stroking of the female by the male until she mounts him. They then couple, and he attaches his small spermatophore to her. She then walks around for a while before eating the spermatophore, by which time the sperm it contained should have entered her reproductive canal. The process may be repeated twice more before the male begins to call to attract another female.

One disadvantage of producing small spermatophores one after the other is that the female might lose interest and leave the male before he has passed on enough of his sperm to her. An alternative is to produce a larger spermatophore, but that means the male must keep the female occupied in some way while the larger quantity of sperm passes into her. Otherwise she will eat the spermatophore before it is empty. In the black-horned tree cricket, *Oecanthus nigricornis* from North America, the attention of the female is secured by providing an alternative food source. Having accepted the male's spermatophore, she occupies herself in feeding from a special gland, the metanotal gland, on the male's thorax. Similar behavior is found in the European wood cricket, *Nemobius sylvestris*, the female feeding from the base of the male's forewings.

Females are even more voracious in *Pteronemobius* species crickets from the United States. Here, once she has mounted the male and he has passed his spermatophore to her, the female remains on his back and nibbles

away at spines on the inner surface of the tibia of each of his hind legs. She may remain there for up to 40 minutes before dismounting and eating the spermatophore, which by now should have emptied.

In another North American species, the restless bush cricket, *Hapithus agitator*, the female is kept busy feeding from special glands on the male's body and wings. Males of the species in the north of its range cannot sing. Instead, they must actively search out females to mate with.

Lengthy Courtship

In one *Nisitrus* species of day-active crickets from Southeast Asia both stridulation and visual displays play a part in courtship. Males of the species sit on large leaves and begin to sing, raising their tegmina vertically and producing a short "tsssp" once every three to four seconds. As the female comes within a few inches, the male stops singing and begins his visual display, vibrating and jerking his

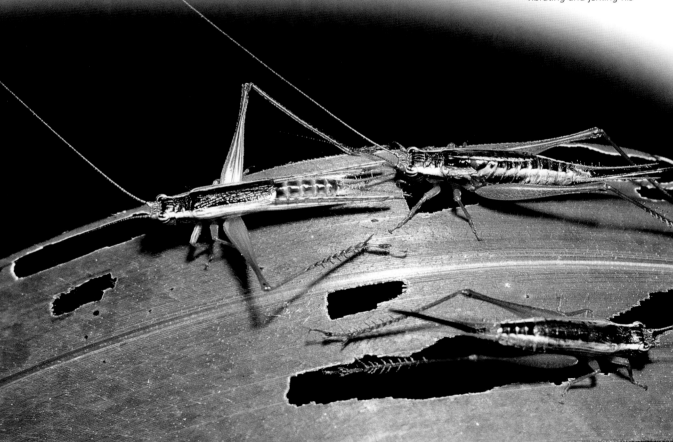

⊕ *In a rain forest in Uganda a female Euscyrtus bivittatus (right) creeps toward a male (left), which spreads its legs to the sides so that the female can mount its back.*

The attractive Nisitrus crickets from Indonesia are active during the day. This small nymph is tempted by a wild raspberry growing on Mount Kinabalu in Borneo.

Ant Guests

A number of small species of cricket have been found living in the nests of ants. This is rather an unusual lifestyle, since ants are formidable hunters and could clearly be a great danger to the crickets. The ant guests include the world's tiniest orthopterans, some reaching just 0.06 inches (1.5 mm) in length. Most of our knowledge of ant-guest crickets comes from the study of *Myrmecophila manni,* a 0.12 inch- (3 mm-) long species from western North America, which lives in the nests of the western thatching ant, *Formica obscuripes.* The cricket spends the whole of its life in the ant nest, but has to be very careful when dealing with its host, which remains generally hostile. The cricket uses its agility to jump away from any ants that appear too threatening.

Ants recognize each other by smell. It seems that the crickets pick up the ants' smell, allowing them to approach the ants closely without being attacked. The crickets are then able to feed by encouraging the ants to regurgitate food from their mouths. Ants normally use signals to determine which of them should regurgitate food. The crickets seem able to mimic the ants' signals so that the ants feed them without question. The crickets have also been seen combing the surface of the ants, their eggs, and their larvae to obtain oils that coat the surface of their hosts. If the ants move nests, the crickets have been seen to follow them.

antennae and rapidly vibrating his raised tegmina. He then raises and rotates his hind legs one after the other.

Suddenly his behavior changes. He faces the female, tegmina still raised, and walks rapidly and jerkily toward her, emitting a series of rapid chirps. He then turns away from the female, who walks onto him and begins to nibble at his metanotal glands. The male then quickly pushes back under his mate and attaches a spermatophore to her. He repeats the whole procedure up to five times during a single courtship and mating session.

Means of Defense

Most crickets are rather drab creatures, clothed in browns and blacks, that spend much of their life hidden from the view of would-be predators during the hours of daylight. At night their dark colors make them difficult to spot even by large-eyed hunters.

Some species, however, live a more exposed life on the bark of trees. They are both shaped and colored accordingly, with a more flattened body than the average cricket, so that when pressed against the bark, they have virtually no shadow. Instead of the usual brown or black coloration, they are speckled in greens, silvers, and grays. They blend nicely into the surrounding bark, which is often covered with similarly colored lichens. If they are spotted, and a predator tries to attack them, they can shoot rapidly across the bark before stopping and immediately disappearing from view again.

Just a few crickets are active in the daytime. They seemingly have no worries about being spotted by predators, since they will sit in full view in the sunshine. Such species are, however, warningly colored, and it may well be that they contain some form of unpleasant chemical, making them inedible to most attackers.

Some minuscule members of the cricket family even live in the company of ants in their nests.

A Brachytrupes orientalis male calls loudly from the mouth of his burrow in a rain forest in Thailand.

Oedipoda miniata

Common name Grasshoppers (short-horned grasshoppers), locusts

Family Acrididae

Suborder Caelifera

Order Orthoptera

Number of species About 7,000 (550 U.S.)

Size From about 0.4 in (10 mm) to about 6 in (15 cm)

Key features Antennae short, sometimes clubbed; wings fully developed in most species although often absent in mountain-dwelling species; hind legs long and powerful for jumping; sound usually produced by rubbing hind legs against the forewings; ears on sides of the abdomen

Habits May be found on the ground, on grasses, low plants, bushes, and trees; some species jump, others fly readily to escape danger; locusts migrate over long distances

Breeding Males attract females with a song; alternatively, they may look for them in a silent, active search followed by visual courtship; females of most species lay their eggs into the ground or at the base of plants

Diet Many different kinds of plants; only a small number feed on grass

Habitat Meadows, parks, gardens, savanna, forests of all kinds, mountains, deserts, marshes, and salt marshes

Distribution Widespread around the world in all but the very coldest regions

⊕ *At rest this European grasshopper, Oedipoda miniata, resembles mottled stone. When disturbed, however, it flies off on an erratic course and flashes its brightly colored wings to startle its attacker. Oedipoda miniata is found across southern Europe. Body length up to 0.8 inches (20 mm).*

Grasshoppers

Acrididae

Members of the family Acrididae vary enormously in size, shape, and color. However, almost all of them can immediately be recognized as grasshoppers by their well-developed hind legs, perfect for jumping, and their short antennae.

AS A RESULT OF THE LARGE VARIATIONS in appearance, there is some disagreement as to how the grasshoppers should be classified. Here the typical grasshoppers, toad grasshoppers, bladder grasshoppers, lubber grasshoppers, and gaudy grasshoppers are included as subfamilies within the family Acrididae. In other books they are often classified as separate families.

Array of Color

Members of the subfamily that contain what might be called the typical grasshoppers—the locust being a good example—are the insects most likely to be found in the temperate regions of North America and Europe. Typical grasshoppers show a great deal of variation in color. Many are shades of brown or green and well camouflaged against their surroundings, while others are brightly colored. The American *Dactylotum* species painted grasshoppers, for example, are dark blue to blackish with white, yellow, and orange or red markings.

Even within a single species there may be much variation in color. The European common field grasshopper, *Chorthippus brunneus,* for example, exists in all shades of brown from pale to almost black. It even displays stripes and mottling. There is also a green form with pale-brown tegmina, a brown form with the top of the pronotum green, and a flamboyant form that is almost completely bright pink.

As well as differences in color between the adults within a species, there may be marked differences between the sexes and also between the adults and the nymphs within a single species. The variation in color between males and females is called sexual dichromatism

⊖ *Most grasshoppers from temperate regions are drably colored. The mating pair of common field grasshoppers, Chorthippus brunneus seen here in England, also show that the male is smaller than his mate.*

and can be quite apparent. Often the male is brightly colored, while the female is a somber brown or green. A possible explanation for the color difference lies in the differing roles of the sexes. The males can actively seek out females, protected from vertebrate enemies by their bright warning colors.

Meanwhile, the females, with their precious egg batches, sit around camouflaged in the undergrowth. Some males and females have such marked differences that they have even been described as different species. The same has happened with species in which the nymph is marked in a strikingly different way than the adult.

⊕ *The* Dactylotum *painted grasshoppers come from from the arid regions of the American Southwest and Mexico. Here nymphs of the species are on a cactus.*

Locusts

Locusts have been an enemy of humans for thousands of years. According to the Bible, a plague of locusts was sent to punish the Egyptians. The two locusts known for their huge, devastating swarms are the desert locust, *Schistocerca gregaria*, and the migratory locust, *Locusta migratoria*. To be a locust, a grasshopper must have two distinct phases in its adult life—a solitary phase in which individuals are fairly well spaced out, and a gregarious phase in which masses of the insect are in constant contact with one another. The two phases are so different both in appearance and behavior that they were once thought to be different species.

During the normal dry weather in the areas where locusts live there is little food. As a result, few offspring are produced. The young are rather drab creatures that are well camouflaged against their dry surroundings. When it rains, perhaps for the first time in years, a dramatic change occurs in the locusts. The rain stimulates rapid growth in plants, especially grasses, and the locusts also feed, grow, and breed rapidly. As numbers of nymphs increase, they form bands of what are called hoppers. They are now brightly colored, and they march across the land, eating the lush supplies of grass until they eventually become adult. It is not long before the adults run out of food, causing millions of them to take flight in a vast swarm. They often follow the wind, which leads them to new sources of food. When the fresh supplies of food are people's crops, the effect is devastating, since they eat every piece of plant food available. A swarm of the desert locust can cover hundreds of square miles and may include 50 billion insects, weighing 80,000 tons (79,000 tonnes).

Scientists have only recently discovered what may cause the locusts to change from their harmless, solitary phase into a ravaging eating machine. Touch-sensitive hairs have been discovered on the insects' hind legs. When there are just a few locusts around, the hairs are rarely touched by other locusts. As numbers increase, however, and the locusts come into contact with each other more often, the hairs are stimulated, and swarming starts.

Other grasshoppers can be just as destructive as the desert and migratory locusts, even though they do not have solitary and gregarious phases. The Australian plague locust, *Chortoicetes terminifera,* can produce countless millions of offspring in a good

year, which take to the air, clearing millions of acres of pastureland along the route. Even in the United States grasshoppers can achieve locust numbers. One of the largest swarms ever recorded anywhere was between California and Oregon in 1949.

Left: Nymphs (known as hoppers) of the migratory locust and desert locust feed voraciously on virtually any green plants they encounter. Right: A swarm of locusts takes to the air against bright sunlight in the Nuba Mountains in Sudan.

Varied Diet

From their common name you might expect the main food of grasshoppers to be grass. Perhaps unfortunately, the name grasshopper originates from the British Isles, where the 11 described species do feed mainly on grass. Elsewhere, however, many grasshoppers feed on anything but grass. In North America the widespread two-striped grasshopper, *Melanoplus bivittatus*, feeds on a wide range of different plants, and its numbers can reach pest proportions on alfalfa crops. Equally unchoosy, and just as widespread, is the red-legged grasshopper, *Melanoplus femurrubrum*, which can also be a pest. In addition, it is an intermediate host for a parasite, the poultry tapeworm, *Choanotaenia infundibulum*. The grasshopper contains the developmental stage of the tapeworm in its body. When eaten by a chicken, the parasite continues its life cycle within the bird.

Many plant families contain species that are poisonous to animals and are therefore avoided by grasshoppers. Yet some grasshoppers are able to survive quite happily feeding on plants that would kill most other species. The creosote bush, *Larrea tridentata*, of the American deserts, for example, is most unpalatable, its leaves being covered in unpleasant-tasting resins. But it is the home and sole food plant of the creosote bush grasshoppers of the genus *Bootettix* and the desert clicker grasshopper, *Ligurotettix coquilletti*.

Finding a Mate

While katydids and crickets are generally songsters of the night, grasshoppers sing during the day, especially when the sun is shining. The song is produced by drawing a row of pegs on the hind femurs across prominent veins on the tightly flexed forewings (known as stridulation). Each species has its own song, and it is only recognized by the female of that particular species. Although the males do most of the singing, some females

⊕ *Most grasshoppers lay their eggs in soft ground. This female elegant grasshopper,* **Zonocerus elegans** *(subfamily* **Pyrgomorphinae***) from Africa, is accompanied by her mate.*

The gold-horned lubber grasshopper, *Taeniopoda auricornis, is a large species from Mexico. It "flashes" bright-crimson wings when alarmed.*

also stridulate. However, in the female the pegs on the hind femurs are much smaller than in the male, and the song produced is very quiet.

The male European large marsh grasshopper, *Stethophyma grossum*, produces his song in a different way. Instead of using his femurs, he flicks the end of the hind tibia against the flexed forewings, producing a series of sharp clicks. Males of the subfamily Oedopodinae, well represented in North America, show yet another method of attracting a mate. The males leap into the air and either emit loud cracking sounds from their wings or flash their brightly colored hind wings. Sometimes they use a combination of the two.

While songs are important for bringing together males and females of many grasshoppers, probably just as many are silent. In the quiet types males may first search out females on suitable plants, sometimes

drumming with their legs on leaves to announce their presence. Such methods are employed by many brightly colored tropical species living in dense vegetation, where songs do not carry far. Having come together, males and females usually perform a visual courtship before mating takes place. Male grasshoppers are normally smaller than the females on whose back they sit while mating. The average mating time for grasshoppers is about 45 minutes, during which the male passes his spermatophore directly to the female.

Eggs are laid in the ground or just above the ground in places such as grass tufts. As she lays them, the female covers them in foam, which hardens and forms a protective layer, mainly to prevent the eggs from drying out. Two North American grasshoppers—*Leptysma marginicollis*, the cattail toothpick grasshopper, and *Stenacris vitreipennis*, the glassy-winged toothpick grasshopper—are unusual in that the females lay their eggs directly into the waterside plants among which they live.

Grasshoppers hatch as a white, wormlike creature that wriggles its way out of the egg case and, if necessary, up through the soil. The white skin is then cast, and the larva takes on the appearance of a normal first instar nymph.

Lubber Grasshoppers—Romaleinae

The lubber grasshoppers include the largest of all grasshoppers, *Tropidacris cristatus*, from

⊝ The eastern lubber grasshopper, Romalea microptera *from the United States, wears a typical brightly colored "warning" uniform advertising its ability to produce an unpleasant defensive froth.*

⊕ The color and texture of the Lamarckiana *species toad grasshopper from South Africa are a perfect match for the rocks in the desert where it lives.*

Costa Rica. Females of the species can reach 6 inches (15 cm) in length, with a wingspan of 10 inches (25 cm). If disturbed, they explode into flight and may look more like a bird than an insect. Most of the 200 or so known species come from North and Central America, with just a few from the Old World. They are mainly warningly colored insects. They are known in Mexico and North America as lubber grasshoppers since they are relatively slow moving. Lubber grasshoppers are found from desert to tropical forest feeding on foliage in general but seldom grass.

Perhaps the best known of the North American species is the eastern lubber grasshopper, *Romalea microptera*. It can be fairly common along roadsides and field edges from North Carolina and Tennessee south to Florida and Louisiana. Warningly colored in red, yellow, and black, it has an interesting chemical defense mechanism. If attacked, it may first hiss and buzz its wings. If that deterrent fails, it produces a brown froth from the spiracles of the middle segment of the thorax. The froth contains a cocktail of complex chemicals with an evil smell. As the bubbles burst, they form a protective mist around the grasshopper, scaring off all but the most determined attacker.

Toad Grasshoppers—Pamphaginae

The amazing thing about the toad grasshoppers is that most of them, both adults and nymphs, are excellent mimics of stones, lumps of earth, sticks, or dead leaves. It is often not until they move that their presence becomes evident. They are called toad grasshoppers because—like toads—they have a heavy, thickset body, often rather warty in appearance. Like toads, they also tend to be slow moving. The pronotum tends to be thick and heavily built, and often has a raised crest along the center. In many species the males have wings, while the females lack them. However, since they are ground-dwelling insects, the males are not great fliers. The subfamily has a somewhat restricted distribution—they are found in the stony desert regions of Africa and southwest Asia, as well as similar areas in the Middle East, Spain, and Greece.

Not all of the subfamily stridulate. There are two species in which the males, not having full-size wings, are known to just tap their short wing cases against the second pair of legs when calling to attract a mate.

Bladder Grasshoppers—Pneumorinae

The bladder grasshoppers are a small subfamily of 20 or so species from southern Africa. The largest species reach 4 inches (10 cm) in length. Although most are green, a few are marked with colored bands or spots. The name bladder grasshopper comes from the fact that the males of some species have a transparent, balloonlike body. It is used to amplify the sound they make by scraping a comb on each hind leg against ridges on the sides of the abdomen. The sound produced is so loud that it would seem to be coming from a much larger animal. The males can fly, giving rise to another common name of flying

65

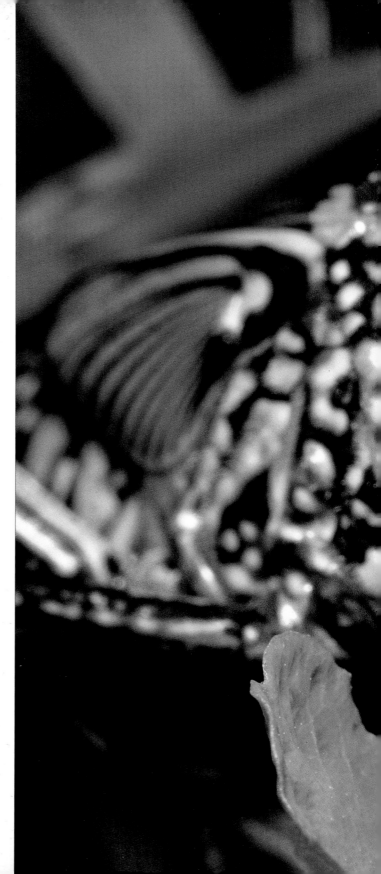

gooseberry. The females have no wings, however, and their body is not swollen.

Gaudy Grasshoppers—Pyrgomorphinae

The gaudy grasshoppers include species that are perhaps the most colorful of all insects. There are about 450 species so far described, the majority of which come from tropical Africa and Madagascar. In the New World Mexico has the largest number of described species. They are most easily recognized, at least in the majority of species, by their conical head and decidedly receding chin. Most gaudy grasshoppers live above the ground in tall herbs and bushes on which they feed, and many of them are well camouflaged in their surroundings. There are, however, several warningly colored species with bright reds, blues, oranges, yellows, and purples in their general coloration. The nymphs of some species, which often do not resemble the adult in their color patterns, may form large groups much like the locusts.

It is in Africa that some of the nastiest and gaudiest grasshoppers occur. They are rather leathery, slow-moving creatures that sit openly on their food plants, showing off their bright, "keep off" colors. The reason for their nastiness is that they feed on the leaves of plants containing poisonous chemicals. The toxins do not harm the grasshopper but accumulate in its body. If any animal tries to eat the grasshopper, the poisons induce vomiting, so it soon learns to leave such prey alone. The buildup of poison is so strong that in South Africa a child died after eating a single grasshopper of the species *Phymateus leprosus*. A close relative, *P. morbillosus*, spews out an unpleasant frothy liquid if it is attacked, as does *Dictyophorus spumans*. The foam produced has a terrible stench, which makes anybody nearby nauseous. It can be detected from up to 1 yard (1 m) away and so forms an effective protective chemical umbrella around the insect.

⊖ **Phymateus** *species gaudy grasshoppers are among the most brightly colored and poisonous grasshoppers found in Africa. This is a final instar nymph.*

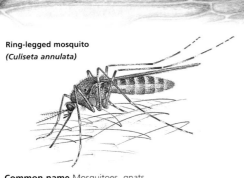

Ring-legged mosquito
(Culiseta annulata)

Common name Mosquitoes, gnats

Family   Culicidae

Suborder   Nematocera

Order   Diptera

Number of species About 3,000 (over 150 U.S.)

Size   From about 0.2 in (5 mm) to around 0.3 in
        (8 mm)

Key features Slender body, long legs, and rigid, piercing
        mouthparts (except in the gnats); ocelli not
        present; males of most species have
        featherlike antennae

Habits   May be diurnal or nocturnal; tend to rest
        in the shade; blood feeders attracted to
        host animals by the carbon dioxide they
        breathe out

Breeding Females whine to attract males; often form
        mating swarms; females lay their eggs on the
        surface of water

Diet   Male mosquitoes feed on nectar and fruit
        juices; females feed similarly, but a number
        are also blood feeders; larvae are aquatic
        filter feeders or nibble at underwater plant
        remains and algae; a few feed on other
        mosquito larvae

Habitat   Usually found near water in which they can
        breed; also forests with plenty of water-filled
        holes in trees; lake- and pond-side
        vegetation, marshes, estuaries, human
        habitations, outhouses, stables, and so on

Distribution Worldwide even into the Arctic

⊕ *The ring-legged mosquito,* Culiseta annulata, *can be
easily identified by the black-and-white bands on its legs. It
is one of the largest mosquitoes, whose bite can be painful,
although it probably does not carry any diseases. It is found
all over Europe. Body length 0.2 inches (5 mm).*

Mosquitoes and Gnats

Culicidae

*It is difficult to believe when looking at a mosquito
that such a tiny creature could cause so much misery.
However, a number of species carry some of the worst
of human diseases, especially malaria.*

MOSQUITOES AND GNATS, with their fragile, spindly
appearance, do not immediately look like flies.
The main difference between mosquitoes and
gnats is the structure of their mouthparts. The
mosquitoes have a long proboscis and can bite,
while gnats have short mouthparts and do not.

Whining Females

At the base of each of the antennae of an
insect is a structure called the Johnston's organ.
In the Culicidae it contains cells that are
sensitive to sound and is used by males to
detect the whining sound made by the wings of
the female. The females of one species produce
a whine to which only males of their own
species respond, ensuring that only members of
the same species come together to mate.

Having mated, the female mosquito or gnat
is now ready to lay her eggs, which in all but a
few species will be laid on water. There are two
main types of laying site: those that are
permanent, such as lakes, large ponds, and
estuaries, and those that are temporary and
soon dry out, such as puddles or rot holes in
trees. Culicid larvae are completely dependent
on water, and if it dries up, they die. For those
species that breed in temporary water, the
timing of egg laying is crucial, and the
development from egg to hatching of the pupa
has to be quick. Females that lay on permanent
water, such as estuaries, must choose the
correct degree of saltiness or the right degree of
light or shade for their eggs.

Each egg laid on water has a float. The
float is more elaborate in species such as
Anopheles and *Aedes* that lay eggs one at a

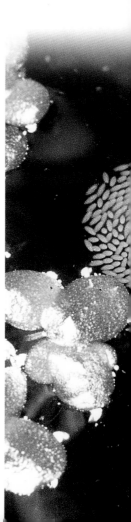

⊖ *The feathery antennae typical of male mosquitoes are fully expanded in the male ring-legged mosquito,* Culiseta annulata *from Europe, sitting beside a female.*

time. The mosquitoes either land on the water or drop the eggs onto the surface during an egg-laying "dance." *Culex* species and others lay their eggs stuck together in rafts and so do not need such elaborate floats.

Trichoprosopon digitatum females often lay their eggs inside empty fruit husks that have filled with rainwater, including those discarded on cocoa plantations. The females stand guard over their eggs until they hatch. It appears that by staying with them, the females can help prevent the eggs from being washed out of the husk if it overflows during heavy rain.

Delayed Development

Female culicids whose larvae live in temporary water are unable to predict exactly when water will be present. As a result, the female has to use a different egg-laying strategy. Instead of laying in water, she lays in soil among leaves. She may even lay on the open ground in an area where she is somehow able to detect that there will be water at a future time. The embryo larva forms normally inside the egg, but then development suddenly stops. If and when water covers the egg, after heavy rain, for example, the larva hatches and

⊖ *This female mosquito from Europe is using her back legs to maintain the circular shape of the raft of eggs she has laid on the surface of the water.*

⊕ *Culicid larvae hang beneath the surface film. They use tubes (siphons) extending from their abdomen to breathe directly from the air.*

continues its development. Such eggs are resistant to both drying out and frost, and are therefore found in areas that have dry seasons as well as in the colder regions of the world. In fact, the egg stage is the way in which many mosquitoes hibernate in the coldest areas of their range, while in less hostile environments they hibernate as adults, quite often in our homes.

Like the larva, the culicid pupa can only survive in water; but unlike the pupae of most insects, it is quite active. The pupa breathes air through trumpet-shaped extensions from the spiracles on the thorax. The pupa usually remains below the water surface but swims up now and again to breathe through the wide end of each trumpet. It finally comes to the surface to allow the adult to hatch out. The pupal casing acts as a platform on which the adult stands to open up its wings and take off.

Taste for Blood

Scientists believe that in the past the adult females of all members of the Culicidae were blood feeders, while the males fed on nectar alone. Many species behave in the same way

⊕ *Toxorhynchites moctezuma from Trinidad is unusual among mosquitoes because the adult does not feed on blood. Here, it is visiting flowers for nectar.*

⊕ *Wyeomyia species from the American tropics hover in front of ants to sip honeydew from their open jaws, as seen here in Trinidad.*

today, but in some the females have given up blood as food and, like the males, feed only on nectar. Each blood-feeding species tends to specialize on a particular group, so there are those that feed only on birds, some that feed on reptiles or amphibians, some on other insects, and of course, some on mammals.

The majority of culicid larvae are filter feeders of one kind or another, taking small edible particles out of the water in which they live. Some also have the ability to "nibble" at larger food sources, including algae.

However, larvae of *Toxorhynchites* species mosquitoes are carnivorous. They feed on the larvae of another species of filter-feeding mosquito that shares their home. Since female *Toxorhynchites* are no longer blood feeders, the larva has adopted the role of taking in enough protein to produce a fully mature, egg-filled female at the end of the life cycle.

Ant Hypnotists

Some mosquitoes in both the Old and New Worlds have been found to associate in an unusual way with ants: Many species of plant-feeding bugs such as aphids produce honeydew—a sugar-rich fluid that is a by-product from the sap that they drink. Ants in particular enjoy feeding on honeydew, and some actually "herd" the bugs in the same way as cows are herded by humans. The ants then return to their nest with a globule of the liquid produced by the bugs held in their mouth.

The mosquitoes hover in front of the ants until, for an unknown reason, the ants open their jaws. The mosquitoes then push their proboscis into the ants' mouths and drink the honeydew that they have collected. Quite how the mosquitoes are able to "hypnotize" the ants, which are aggressive and would ordinarily attack them, is not known.

Mosquitoes and Disease

To those of us who live in temperate climates mosquitoes are undoubtedly a nuisance, but to people living in the tropics they bring disease and death. The females require a blood feed to ensure that they develop a full batch of eggs. By feeding from different people in turn, they pass on diseases that they have picked up. In the case of virus diseases such as yellow fever, dengue fever, and encephalitis the mosquito picks up viruses from one person and passes them onto the next person it bites.

However, in the case of malaria, caused by a single-celled parasite, and filariasis, caused by nematode worms, the situation is somewhat different. Both the malarial parasite and the filarial worm actually spend part of their life cycle in the mosquito. Malaria is transmitted only by *Anopheles* species mosquitoes, the most important being *A. gambiae*. Of the 380 species of *Anopheles* mosquito so far described only 60 are capable of transmitting malaria. The other species seem to be resistant to the malarial organism in some way. When biting her human host, the female injects the parasites into the bloodstream, where they continue their life cycle. Later, another female mosquito will bite the infected person, picking up the stages of the parasite that infect mosquitoes.

Although a mosquito bite may not transmit malaria, it is almost always itchy and painful. That is because after a bite some of the mosquito's saliva remains in the wound. The alien proteins from the saliva send the body's immune system into battle. The bite area swells (the bump around the bite area is called a wheal) and itches while the immune cells do their job of breaking down the saliva proteins.

Malaria is found mostly in the tropical areas of the world—in Africa, Asia, and South and Central America. Although medical science has improved the treatments for and preventatives against malaria, and attempts have been made to wipe out the mosquito carriers, the disease seems once again to be on the increase. At the beginning of the 21st century about 300 million people around the world are affected by malaria, and there are 1.5 million deaths per year from the disease—most of them children.

Fortunately for the owner of the hand, the female ring-legged mosquito, Culiseta annulata *(a day-biting species seen here in England), will not transmit malaria or any other disease. In many countries—especially in the tropics, but also in England in former times—malaria and other serious diseases are transmitted exclusively by mosquitoes.*

Stratiomys sp.

Odontomyia sp.

Common name Soldier flies

Family Stratiomyidae

Suborder Brachycera

Order Diptera

Number of species About 1,500 (250 U.S.)

Size From about 0.3 in (8 mm) to 0.8 in (20 mm)

Key features Thorax may be armed with spines; abdomen rather flattened; often brightly colored or with striped abdomen; at rest wings folded one over the other to cover up the abdomen; males may have holoptic eyes (meeting at the top of the head)

Habits Adults usually found sitting on or under leaves or feeding at flowers

Breeding Not well known, but males of some species form hovering swarms and mate with passing females; may be true for most soldier flies

Diet At least some adults known to be flower feeders; larvae eat decaying plant material, rotting wood, and dung; some aquatic species eat algae

Habitat Forests and watersides; preferably in damper situations, both in the soil and in rotting wood, fresh water, brackish water, and salt marshes

Distribution Widespread fairly uniformly around the world

⊕ *The larvae of the larger soldier flies such as* **Stratiomys** *and* **Odontomyia** *species are carnivorous, feeding on worms, small crustacea, and insects in moist ground. Both species are found in the Northern Hemisphere. Body length of* **Stratiomys** *sp. 0.5–0.6 inches (13–15 mm);* **Odontomyia** *sp. 0.3–0.6 inches (7–15 mm).*

Soldier Flies

Stratiomyidae

The common name of soldier flies for the family would seem to be rather a misnomer—far from being tough predators, the flies feed harmlessly on flowers.

SOLDIER FLIES ARE USUALLY SEEN on warm, sunny days, most likely sitting around on leaves. Their wings are usually kept closed, so it is not always possible to view their often bright coloring. That is because the wings fully overlap one another when at rest so that the abdomen is covered by a double layer of wing membrane. It is their bright colors of shiny reds, blues, and greens, or black-and-yellow stripes—a bit like those of old-fashioned uniforms—that probably gave the soldier flies their common name.

The bright colors are only visible when the insect is in flight. Since swarming is the most common method for males to attract a mate, this may be the way in which the flies recognize members of their own species. The sudden disappearance of the colors as they land and fold their wings over the abdomen makes them less visible to passing predators.

Mating Territories

As well as gathering in swarms in order to attract passing females, some soldier fly males establish and defend distinct territories. *Hermetia comstocki*, found in the deserts of Arizona, establishes territories on agave plants. Clearly some plants are better than others, and those are taken by the biggest and strongest males. Females that are ready to mate seem to be most attracted to the agaves over which the males have fought the hardest. They approach, fly in a circle around the agave, and then mate with the first male to fly out and grab them.

While there is no particular form of courtship with those flies, in a few other soldier

⊕ *The unusually long, conspicuous antennae typical of soldier flies are easily seen in the banded general,* **Stratiomys potamida,** *a large wasplike species from Europe.*

Rough Skin

Soldier fly larvae have unusually rough skins owing to the presence of a deposit of calcium carbonate in the outer layer. The chalky deposit probably helps keep the larvae from drying out: Stratiomyid larvae are known to survive for a long time in conditions such as drought.

The soldier flies are also unusual in the way that they pupate. Like the more advanced flies such as bluebottles (Calliphoridae), the pupa forms in a puparium inside the last instar larval skin that has been shed.

⬆ *The common green colonel,* Odontomyia viridula, *is a European species. Its larvae live in small bodies of fresh water, such as drainage ditches.*

⬇ *The long-horned general,* Stratiomys longicornis, *is unusual among soldier flies in its mimicry of bees such as the honeybee,* Apis mellifera. *The fly is widespread in Europe.*

flies courtship takes place after the male has grabbed the female by ambushing her in midair. Males of *Himantigera nigrifemorata*, a Costa Rican species, perform a rather rough form of courtship: Having taken possession of the female, the male then sits on her back. He lifts one front leg at a time above his head and smacks her across the head with it, apparently aiming for her antennae. Alternatively, he sways his body from side to side in front of her and twitches his legs across her antennae. If he is acceptable, she will then allow him to mate with her.

"Blinder"deerfly (Chrysops caecutiens)

3-spot horsefly (Tabanus trimaculatus)

Common names Horseflies, deerflies (elephant flies, clegs)

Family Tabanidae

Suborder Brachycera

Order Diptera

Number of species Around 3,000 (350 U.S.)

Size From 0.2 in (5 mm) to 1 in (2.5 cm)

Key features Eyes large, usually with brightly colored patterns; body stout; wings often with darker patterning; biting proboscis; eyes of male nearly touching on top of head

Habits Tend to be active on sunny days; usually avoid shade when biting; stealthy flight when approaching hosts to feed

Breeding Males either form individual territories and mate with passing females or gather in swarms

Diet Males feed only at flowers; females take nectar and blood; larvae mainly predaceous, while others feed on decaying vegetable matter

Habitat Wherever the mammals they feed on are found; larvae in water or damp soil

Distribution Worldwide—tropics, temperate zones, and the Arctic

⊕ *The 3-spot horsefly,* Tabanus trimaculatus, *is found in the United States and feeds on deer, moose, and domestic livestock. It can also attack humans. Body length 0.5–0.6 inches (13–15 mm). The "blinder" deerfly,* Chrysops caecutiens, *is from Europe. It is called the "blinder" because it bites its host's eyelids, causing them to swell up and reduce the animal's ability to see. Body length 0.5–0.6 inches (13–15 mm).*

Horseflies and Deerflies

Tabanidae

The biting habits of horseflies and deerflies, coupled with the fact that some transmit disease, make the tabanids one of the least pleasant fly families. However, they have some of the most beautifully marked and colored eyes of all insects, although the hues soon fade after death.

APPROPRIATELY FOR A FAMILY in which sight plays an important part in finding prey and in courtship, the eyes of tabanids are large. In common with the March flies (Bibionidae), the eyes of the male almost meet on top of the head. Also like bibionids, in most species the upper part of the eye has fewer, larger facets than the rest of the eye. The colors and patterns on the eyes can be remarkable, with bands or patches of brilliant red, green, and gold. Horseflies can be distinguished from deerflies by the way they hold their wings at rest. While deerflies sit with their wings held horizontal, horseflies hold their wings at an angle above the body, like a tent.

Tabanids seem to be attracted to water. During hot weather both males and females will visit mud at the edges of puddles or small streams. Here they drink from the mud, perhaps taking in essential salts as well as water. Rather unusual, however, is the way that males have been seen behaving over open water. During the hottest part of the day they swoop down and touch the water's surface. It is assumed that they are drinking, but it is also possible that they are cooling down.

Grabbing a Partner

Like the familiar hover flies, tabanid males also hover when they are trying to grab a passing female. Hovering numbers may vary from single males up to large swarms depending on the species. Males of the large black-and-gold banded horsefly, *Tabanus barbanus* from Europe, will often be found hovering in the area

In England Rhagio scolopaceus (Rhagionidae) is commonly called the downlooker snipe fly because of its habit of sitting head downward on a tree or plant stem.

The iridescent eyes typical of most members of the family Tabanidae are very conspicuous in the Philopomyia species from Europe. The antennae are quite small.

Snipe Flies

The Rhagionidae is one of the smaller fly families, with just over 100 species in North America and only 15 in the British Isles. In appearance snipe flies resemble the tabanids, but with a more slender body. Like tabanids, they also have sucking mouthparts. It would seem that the mouthparts are mainly used to suck nectar, but snipe flies are secretive, so their habits are not well understood. It is known, however, that a number of species also resemble tabanids in their need for a blood meal. Humans may sometimes fall victim to their appetites. A number of *Symphoromyia* species snipe flies live in North America, especially in the western states. In the Rockies they are especially persistent in their attacks and give quite a painful bite. British *Symphoromyia*, on the other hand, are not known to bite.

Snipe fly larvae live mainly in damp soil, but a few are aquatic, and some are known to live in dead wood. It would seem that they are in general carnivorous, since they have well-developed mouthparts. In addition, the European species, *Chrysopilus cristatus*, appears to produce poisonous saliva, probably to paralyze its prey. Another European species, *Spania nigra*, is called the liverwort snipe fly and is unusual for the family as a whole. It is found in leaf mines in *Pellia* species liverworts. It is not known whether it feeds on the plant itself, producing the mine as it does so, or whether it feeds on the larvae of gall midges, which do make mines in the plant.

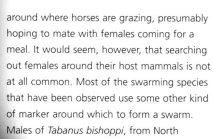

around where horses are grazing, presumably hoping to mate with females coming for a meal. It would seem, however, that searching out females around their host mammals is not at all common. Most of the swarming species that have been observed use some other kind of marker around which to form a swarm. Males of *Tabanus bishoppi*, from North

75

⊝ *The large mass of eggs attached to a plant stem beside a lake was laid by a female of the European dark giant horsefly,* Tabanus sudeticus.

America, for example, seem to swarm in what might be called an arena—a ring of trees with the canopies forming a complete circle. Each fly hovers by bobbing up and down and making darting back-and-forth movements. *Tabanus bishoppi* species make a loud hum while hovering. When in a large group, the sound can be heard by humans as far as 150 feet (46 m) away. With the appearance of females and following successful matings, the hovering of the males lessens but becomes more frenzied again as the numbers of females diminish.

Once the eggs have fully developed in their body, the females lay them in tight masses on vegetation in or near water. In species whose larvae live in the water of rot holes in trees, the eggs are laid on bark near the hole. One of the only examples of female parental care in the Diptera exists in the tabanids. Females of the American horsefly, *Goniops chrysocoma*, lay their egg mass beneath a leaf. They have long, hooklike claws on their feet. They dig their claws into the leaf to anchor themselves in place over the eggs to protect them. The females die soon after the larvae hatch out.

Vampire Females

Rather than the delicate mouthparts of the mosquitoes, the tabanids have a short, stout, daggerlike proboscis. Like the vampire bats of the night, tabanid flies use stealth to approach their victims, flying quietly and landing gently

⊕ *It is clear from the way the huge eyes meet on top of the head that this black horsefly,* Tabanus atratus *from North America, is a male.*

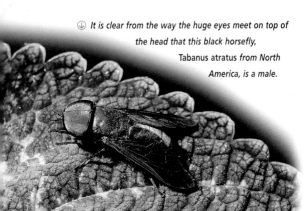

on them before feeding. With a mosquito the bite feels like a tiny prick; but when a tabanid bites—even a small specimen like a deerfly—it is very painful. As often as not, when the proboscis is withdrawn, a spot of blood will ooze from the wound.

Apart from feeding on human blood, tabanid females will feed on most domestic animals, as well as deer and similar wild creatures. Horseflies can be such a problem with domestic animals that in some countries the native herdsmen move their animals from place to place to avoid attacks. Like mosquitoes, it is the females that bite, since they need to take a blood meal after mating to ensure that the eggs develop fully. Although the larger species will often approach a human, they will usually fly away without biting. It is the smaller species that tend to use humans as a source of food.

Flower Feeders

While female tabanids need at least one blood meal for the development of their eggs, for the rest of the time they—like the males of the family—feed on nectar. In fact, one of the best places to have a good look at a horsefly or deerfly is when it is feeding from a flower.

One subfamily of the Tabanidae—the Pangoniinae—has become highly specialized for flower feeding, to the extent that their proboscis may be twice the length of the body. The appendage enables them to obtain nectar from flowers with long tubes. It is the sucking part of the proboscis that is so long; the parts that cut into animal skin to get at blood are of a more usual length. However, the female in the subfamily still needs her blood meal. In order to get it, she has to push the sucking tube to one side as she uses the

→ *Diachlorus ferrugatus is a small species from North America. As in many tabanids, this female has targeted a human finger to sink her proboscis into.*

shorter stylets to cut a hole through the skin. At the other extreme one small group of tabanids has almost lost its mouthparts and seems to just suck up a little liquid from dead and decaying animals.

Larval Habits

Tabanid larvae live in either water, mud, or damp soil. Some horsefly larvae are highly carnivorous; and as a consequence, they have strong, curved jaws that can even pierce human skin. Their prey consists of worms, small slugs and snails, and other fly larvae. Deerfly larvae generally live in water and are not carnivorous, feeding on dead and decaying plant material. Of the species that lay their eggs in rot holes in trees, some of their larvae eat vegetable matter. Other species are carnivores, consuming small animals living in the same habitat. Of the carnivorous forms, usually only a single larva is found surviving in a single rot hole, presumably having eaten any smaller competitors.

→ *The "blinder" deerfly, Chrysops caecutiens from Europe, is usually found near water, in which the aquatic larvae develop.* Chrysops *is also found in North America.*

Milesia crabroniformis

Drone fly (*Eristalis tenax*)

Common name Hover flies (flower flies)

Family Syrphidae

Suborder Brachycera

Order Diptera

Number of species About 6,000 (around 950 U.S.)

Size From about 0.2 in (5 mm) to 1 in (2.5 cm)

Key features Body often striped, mimicking bees or wasps; mouthparts adapted for sucking up nectar; eyes quite large

Habits Sun loving; visit flowers; often form large swarms; usually spend much of their time in hovering flight, sometimes for no obvious reason

Breeding Hovering males attract females, or males may seek out females on foliage and hover over them; eggs laid in various places depending on food requirements of larvae

Diet Adults are nectar feeders; some species also feed on pollen; larvae carnivorous or feed on vegetable matter

Habitat Almost anywhere with flowers from which they can feed

Distribution Worldwide, including the tropics, but at their greatest numbers in temperate zones

⊕ Hover flies are common visitors to garden flowers. Many people mistake some of the commonest species for bees. Milesia crabroniformis is found in southern Europe and the Mediterranean region. Body length 0.9–1 inches (23–27 mm). The drone fly, Eristalis tenax, is an important pollinator, with worldwide distribution. Body length 0.5–0.6 inches (12–15 mm).

Hover Flies

Syrphidae

Hover flies are great sun lovers. While many types of fly hover in order to attract a mate, it seems that both males and females of the family will sometimes hover just for pleasure. Hovering is often accompanied by a loud whining sound.

MOST ADULT HOVER FLIES feed either on nectar or on nectar and pollen. They are probably nearly as important as bees when it comes to pollinating flowers in places such as orchards. The hover fly proboscis tends to be quite short, with few species able to feed from long-tubed flowers. The end of the proboscis is rather like a sponge, which soaks up the nectar. From there it can be sucked up into the mouth.

Grooming for Pollen

How a fly with sucking mouthparts manages to feed on pollen as well is less straightforward. The process has been well studied in the drone fly, *Eristalis tenax*, which has an almost worldwide distribution outside the tropics. Rather than taking pollen directly from the anthers, the drone fly picks up pollen on its body as it wanders around feeding on nectar from flowers. At frequent intervals it uses its front legs to comb pollen off the head and middle legs. The front legs also brush pollen off each other. The back legs are used to comb the middle legs and any parts of the body that the front legs cannot reach.

Following general grooming of the body, the pollen is gathered together by combing the front legs against one another. A mass of pollen forms on the front tarsi and is sucked up through the proboscis. The back legs carry out a similar gathering process. The pollen obtained is then transferred to the front legs to be eaten while hovering.

While the drone fly and other similar feeders use flowers that are insect pollinated, some hover flies feed on wind-pollinated flowers, such as plantains and grasses. These

⊕ Rhingia campestris from Europe is unusual in having a conspicuous protruding "snout" that houses the very long proboscis, seen here scraping pollen from a flower anther.

flies have been seen to hover over the flower, grasp an anther in the front legs, and take pollen directly from it. The New Zealand hover fly species *Melanostoma fasciatum*, for example, pushes the whole of the end of its proboscis into an anther. It sucks it dry of all the pollen before moving onto the next one.

The Next Generation

Males and females of the same species of hover fly can often be found feeding together on the same flower. However, they seem not to take any notice of each other—despite the fact that

→ Baccha obscuripennis from Europe is a rather dark, slim-bodied species. This female is feeding on aphid honeydew that has splattered down onto a leaf below.

both of them may be ready to mate. The reason for their apparent indifference is that most hover flies do not mate on flowers. Instead, they choose places where females come to lay their eggs, such as a group of leaves, a twig, or a rot hole in a tree. Males will spend long periods hovering near such a landmark, chasing off any males of the same species that come anywhere near. Males without a landmark may hover at some other point in the hope of picking up a passing female, usually without much luck. The females seek out the landmarks, since they instinctively know that the males guarding them will be fit partners with which to mate. In turn, the males know that visiting females are there for the sole purpose of mating.

There are, however, some male hover flies that spend at least part of the day actively searching for suitable mates among the females feeding at flowers. Males of the bulb fly, *Merodon equestris*, use the tactic to find a mate. They hover above the female as she feeds, bouncing down toward her and back up again several times, the tip of the abdomen bent downward. The male will court in this way

Cow Pie Removers

Evidence suggests that the larvae of the earliest hover flies fed on dung or decomposing plant material, as a number of species still do today. In Europe larvae of the black-rimmed snout hover fly, *Rhingia campestris*, are important to cattle farmers because they help with the decomposition of cow pies on grassland. A few years ago cow pies were not disappearing at their usual rate and were beginning to accumulate in the fields. The numbers of adult *Rhingia* had also fallen dramatically. It was found that a chemical treatment given to the cows was passing into the dung and killing all the insect larvae that normally feed on it. A change in the treatment resulted in a normal rate of removal of the cow pies, and the *Rhingia* are back in their usual numbers. Such incidents illustrate how human activities can upset the delicate balance of nature.

Larvae of some closely related species have moved away from dung. Some now feed on decomposing plant material in rotting wood, rot holes in trees, and sap runs. Despite the attractive appearance of the adult of the species, the bulb fly has become a pest, since it has moved onto the damp, mushy food provided by onions and flower bulbs.

Living in Water

From a reliance in the past on mushy plant material hover fly larvae have now mostly either become aquatic or live on dry land. The ability to live in water has probably resulted from successive generations being able to cope with increasing degrees of bogginess. All hover fly larvae have spiracles (breathing apparatus) on the tail end. The spiracles of flies living in wet places gradually became extended. Eventually, the rat-tailed larva (maggot) of the *Eristalis* species hover flies evolved. *Eristalis tenax*, the drone fly, has a typical rat-tailed maggot. It can extend its tail siphon, which is longer than its body, to reach up to the water surface. With this "snorkel" it can wander around and feed from the bottom of quite deep water while still breathing air. It returns to dry land to pupate.

↑ With a whine from his rapidly vibrating wings, a male Eristalis nemorum *from Europe hovers in courtship over a female. She ignores him and continues to feed on a flower.*

for about 10 minutes or so, taking an occasional break for a quick circling flight, before the female eventually allows him to mate. Mating itself may take as long as 15 minutes to complete.

Once she has mated, the female will go about laying her eggs. Her choice of egg-laying site is dictated by the lifestyle of the larvae that will hatch from them. While the structure and lifestyle of adult hover flies do not vary a great deal, a much wider range of habits can be observed in their larvae.

Two other adaptations have been made by water-dwelling syrphid larvae. Instead of a siphon, some species have a tuft of gills (as in fish) around the rear end and take oxygen directly from the water in which they live. Others have a short, sharp rear end so that they can push the spiracles into the stems of aquatic grasses and take oxygen—produced in the plant by photosynthesis—directly from them.

The aquatic hover fly larvae are mainly scavengers, as are some of the terrestrial larvae. *Volucella* species larvae, for example, live in the nests of ants and bees, feeding on anything that comes their way. More important to humans are the many species of hover fly whose larvae feed on aphids, which are pests of crops and flowers. The female flies lay their eggs under leaves close to an aphid colony. The blind larva that hatches wanders around until it finds an aphid, which it seizes in its jaws and sucks dry of its internal fluids. The youngest larvae take just two or three aphids per day, but a fully grown one may eat as many as 60. The larvae have also been seen to feed on the larvae of other flies, as well as the caterpillars and pupae of some moth species. When aphid-feeding larvae first hatch, they are white; as they get older, they become green. It is not known why this color change occurs.

Wasp, Bee, or Fly?

Many species of hover flies are known for their mimicry of bees and wasps. Some are so convincing that they even confound the experts. However, close examination shows that they have the single pair of wings associated with flies, rather than the two pairs of wings found in the bees and wasps that they copy. As with mimics in other insect groups, their mimicry helps protect them from some predators—mainly birds—that have learned to avoid bees and wasps because of their sting. The mimicry does not have to be perfect, however, since what can fool humans can easily fool a small-brained bird.

The larvae of *Volucella* species hover flies scavenge for food in the nests of wasps and

↑ *Found on both sides of the Atlantic,* Volucella bombylans *is one of the best bumblebee mimics in the Syrphidae. Another form is all-black with an orange tail end.*

bees. The adults resemble bumblebees or wasps, depending on the species, which gives them some protection from predators. However, such mimicry does not protect them from their bee and wasp hosts. Since the female *Volucella* are able to enter their hosts' nests unharmed, it must be assumed that they are protected from attack in some other way.

Other hover flies have different strategies: *Merodon* species live in daffodil bulbs; *Criorhina* species inhabit rot holes, and *Eriozona* species

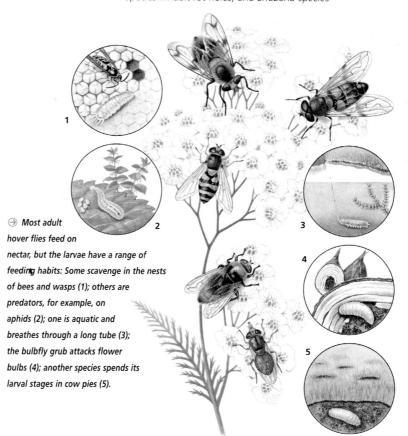

→ *Most adult hover flies feed on nectar, but the larvae have a range of feeding habits: Some scavenge in the nests of bees and wasps (1); others are predators, for example, on aphids (2); one is aquatic and breathes through a long tube (3); the bulbfly grub attacks flower bulbs (4); another species spends its larval stages in cow pies (5).*

feed on aphids. Nonetheless, they are all excellent mimics of bumblebees. They even have forms that resemble different species of bees. The flies are conspicuous visitors to flowers and may gain advantage against predators by being mistaken for bumblebees.

Masters of Disguise

The bumblebee plume-horn hover fly, *Volucella bombylans*, found in both North America and Europe, also mimics bumblebees. Like them, it is hairy. The fly occurs in two forms, one of which is a close mimic of the black-and-white bumblebees; the other mimics the red-tailed species. Another bumblebee mimic, the bulb fly *Merodon equestris*, shows even more variation in its color forms. A closely related European species, the hornet plume-horn hover fly, *Volucella zonaria*, is a large insect and a passable mimic of the common hornet.

Excellent wasp mimics are found among the *Chrysotoxum* species of hover flies, which include the yellow jacket fly, *C. integre,* from North America. Almost certainly the best of them is the giant prong-horn hover fly, *C. cautum,* from Europe. Not only does it look like a wasp, but it behaves like one, especially in the way in which it appears to be looking for prey in flight, just like a wasp. The best of the honeybee mimics is the drone fly, *Eristalis tenax*, which often forages for pollen on the same flowers as the bees.

While their mimicry may fool predators such as birds and lizards, it does not protect them from other arthropod predators. Both orb-weaver and flower spiders take large numbers of hover flies as prey. Hover flies captured by spiders may produce a characteristic whining sound until the attacker's poison eventually quietens them forever. Some of the smaller species of solitary wasps, which specialize in flies for their larvae to feed on, may also take large numbers of the smaller hover flies.

⊙ *Although vaguely wasplike,* Metasyrphus luniger *from Europe, along with many other similar species, is too small to be a convincing wasp mimic.*

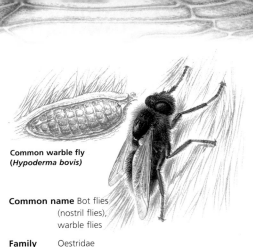

Common warble fly
(*Hypoderma bovis*)

Common name Bot flies
(nostril flies),
warble flies

Family Oestridae

Suborder Brachycera

Order Diptera

Number of species 65 (41 U.S.)

Size From 0.4 in (10 mm) to 1 in (2.5 cm)

Key features Adults heavily built, rather plump; may
resemble bees

Habits Adult flies are generally short-lived and stay
close to the host animal on which their larvae
will feed

Breeding Males of some species defend territories;
females lay eggs or deposit live larvae on
host; some species use other insects to carry
eggs to host

Diet Adults not known to feed; larvae are internal
parasites of vertebrates, including humans

Habitat Adults seldom seen; larvae of some species
may be seen under the skin of the host

Distribution Worldwide, with a number of species
having been spread by humans

⊕ *The common warble fly,* Hypoderma bovis, *is found in the
Northern Hemisphere between March and the end of May. It
lays its eggs on cattle, which recognize the sound of the fly
approaching and attempt evasive action, known as
"gadding." These disturbances in feeding can result in
decreased yield of milk or meat from the cattle. Body length
0.4–0.6 inches (10–14 mm).*

Bot and Warble Flies

Oestridae

*The Oestridae is perhaps one of the most unpleasant
of the fly families. Although the adults look quite
harmless and do not even feed, their larvae live inside
the body of warm-blooded animals, including humans.*

ADULT MEMBERS OF THE OESTRIDAE show differences
both between and within the four recognized
subfamilies—Hypodermatinae, Oestrinae,
Gastrophilinae, and Cuterebrinae. For example,
warble flies (Hypodermatinae) are big and hairy
with beelike patterns. Also, nose and
pharyngeal bots (Oestrinae) include both the
common sheep nostril fly, *Oestrus ovis* (which is
wrinkled, pale, and not very hairy), and the deer
bots, which are hairy and colorful.

Invasion Beneath the Skin

The main interest in the family Oestridae lies
not in the adults, which are seldom seen, but in
the larvae and how they find their way into
their hosts. Once mating has taken place, the
female fly has to get her eggs, or in some cases
her larvae, onto the host animal.

Hypoderma warble flies have a northern
distribution. They are associated mainly with
cattle, although the reindeer also has its own
species, *Oedemagena tarandi*. Eggs are usually
laid on the hairs of the host animal's lower legs.
The larvae emerge after about three days, climb
down the hair, pierce the skin, and enter the
animal's body. They make their way through the
body to the chest or abdomen. From there they
come to lie beneath the skin, where they make
a small breathing hole to the outside air. Here
they complete their growth, eventually forming
a swelling—the "warble." Finally, when fully
grown, the larvae break out through the
breathing hole, fall to the ground, and pupate.

The females of the stomach bots
(Gastrophilinae) target horses and other animals
on which to lay their eggs. The eggs are placed

⊕ *The beelike warble
fly,* Hypoderma lineatum,
*produces a humming
noise that may warn her
cattle hosts away and
prevent her from laying
eggs in their hair.*

do not feed directly on the horse's flesh but share the food digesting in the horse's stomach. The term for the stealing of another animal's food is "kleptoparasitism."

The nose and pharyngeal bots (Oestrinae) use sheep, deer, antelope, camels, and elephants as hosts. The female fly waits until the larvae in her eggs are ready to hatch before she seeks a host animal. Having found one, she then shoots her larvae directly into its nostrils. Some species of bot larvae—for example, those of sheep and deer—then spend their lives in the host's nose, hanging onto the membranes inside the nose and feeding until they are fully grown. The animal then sneezes them out, and they pupate on the ground. Larvae of other species live instead in the gullet or windpipe.

⬆ *On a rock by a stream in the mountains in Arizona a female* Cuterebra *species rodent bot fly sits waiting for a passing rodent on which to lay her eggs.*

on hairs that can be reached when the animal licks itself. Licking the eggs causes the larvae to emerge and burrow down into the horse's tongue. From here they make their way down the throat and into the animal's stomach. They attach themselves to the stomach wall by means of hooks on their head end. The larvae

Targeting Humans

Last of all is a wholly American subfamily, the rodent or skin bots (Cuterebrinae). They mainly use rabbits and rodents as hosts, with one notable exception—the so-called human bot, *Dermatobia hominis*, which can live in a range of different species, including humans. The presence of the larvae under the skin is unpleasant. To reach the host, the female first catches another fly of a species that is likely to make contact with the host, although occasionally hover flies are taken by mistake. She then lays a batch of eggs on the fly before she releases it. When the carrier fly containing ripe eggs lands on a warm-blooded host, the increase in temperature causes the larvae to hatch. They then burrow into the host's skin, where grow to maturity.

Common housefly (*Musca domestica*)

Common name Houseflies, face flies, stable flies, horn flies

Family Muscidae

Suborder Brachycera

Order Diptera

Number of species 4,000 (622 U.S.)

Size From 0.1 in (3 mm) to 0.5 in (13 mm)

Key features Mostly small; differ from other families in lack of certain bristles on thorax; common housefly is a typical muscid

Habits Typically sit around on vegetation or in houses, stables, and other buildings

Breeding Some species court in flight; female lays eggs on or near food

Diet Adults feed on blood, sweat, and plant and fruit juices; larvae feed on decaying plants, dung, and dead animals; can be predators

Habitat Outside in all types of habitat in all types of climate; human habitations, trash heaps, cowsheds, and stables

Distribution Worldwide—many common species have been spread by humans

⊕ *Musca domestica*, *the common housefly, breeds in manure, garbage, and rotting vegetable matter. It is found all over the world and can spread diseases and cause food poisoning due to its habit of feeding on both excrement and human food. Body length 0.2–0.3 inches (5–7 mm).*

Houseflies and Relatives

Muscidae

The activities of the Muscidae would probably go unnoticed if it were not for a few members that have an unpleasant relationship with humans.

WHILE MANY SPECIES OF MUSCID flies just suck up nutritious liquids such as plant and fruit juices with their spongy proboscis, others have become blood feeders. In the latter it is the blood that supplies the protein for the development of the female's eggs. In the plant-feeding species, however, it is the maggot stage that has to acquire enough protein to produce a female full of eggs.

Spongy Proboscis

The spongy proboscis is not capable of piercing the skin of host animals, although it can take blood that is already flowing, such as from the site of a wound or an area where some other insect has already bitten. To get through skin, some modifications have occurred. Some muscid flies have "teeth" or hardened areas on the end of the proboscis. The teeth scratch away at an animal's skin until it bleeds; the blood is then sucked up. The European species *Coenosia tigrina* is roughly the size of a housefly but is a tiger among muscids. It catches other flies and tears into them with its teeth, sucking their body fluids through the incision.

In other muscid flies the labium of the mouthparts is a sharp, stiff tube that can pierce the skin to make the blood flow. The same arrangement exists in another human pest, the stable fly, *Stomoxys calcitrans*. The little fly, which resembles the housefly, is sometimes called the biting housefly. As its name implies, it is usually found around domestic animals such as horses and cattle. It is widespread in northern temperate regions. Careful inspection will reveal the forward-pointing proboscis. It

⊕ *This noonday fly, Mesembrina meridiana from Europe, is feeding on a blackberry. It has the plump body typical of most members of the Muscidae.*

likes to come into houses; and since it tends to bite around the ankles, it has often bitten before it is noticed. It is not known to transmit human diseases.

The stable fly's African relative *Stomoxys ochrosoma* has a fascinating breeding stratagem. A female fly seeks out the foraging columns of driver ants, *Dorylus nigricans*, as the workers bring food back to their nest guarded by the larger soldiers. She hovers just above the column with a batch of about 20 eggs held on the end of her abdomen, seeking out a worker ant that is not carrying any food in its jaws. She drops her egg batch right in front of the chosen worker, cleverly avoiding the fierce, snapping jaws of the soldier ants. Instinctively, the worker ant picks up the egg batch and carries it back into the ants' nest. There the eggs hatch, and the larvae live and feed alongside the ants without apparently coming to any harm.

A Variety of Larvae

Like housefly larvae, the larvae of most of the species within the family Muscidae feed on dung or other decaying vegetable matter. The alternative is to eat fresh plant food. Of the muscid flies whose larvae feed on plants a number are significant crop pests. Notable among them are the onion fly, *Delia antiqua*,

⊖ *With its bright-red eyes,* Alloeostylus diaphanus *from Europe is a particularly attractive muscid. This female is about to lay eggs in a fungus.*

the cabbage-root fly, *Erioischia brassicae*, and the wheat-bulb fly, *Leptohylemyia coarctata*.

Plant food is not particularly nutritious, and evolution has led to a number of species whose larvae feed on a more protein-rich animal diet. One method of getting enough protein—practiced by a number of different genera—is for the larvae to begin on a vegetable diet but to move on to other, smaller larvae as they grow. The larvae of a North American *Fucellia* species fly go one better: They live on the shore and feed on the eggs of fish that lay in the sand. Another easy source of animal protein is baby birds. The larvae of *Passeromyia* species flies suck the blood of helpless nestlings.

The Horrendous Housefly

Despite the fact that it looks so harmless, there are few insects in the world that cause as much misery as the housefly, *Musca domestica*. The fly is found just about everywhere that humans live, from temperate zones into the tropics. In hot climates it is present at all times of year. In temperate areas, however, it disappears in the winter, sheltering in cowsheds and stables.

Adult houseflies will feed from almost anything liquid that they find attractive, including moist dung. They will also regurgitate onto solid foods, which then are digested to a liquid to be sucked up through the fly's proboscis. The larvae are also fairly easy to

⬆ *The adult housefly,* Musca domestica, *just after emerging from the pupa. The wings are crumpled from the recent confinement.*

Tsetse Flies

The family Glossinidae (tsetse flies) is a small but important group of flies with just 22 species, all in the genus *Glossina*. The flies carry the disease-causing organisms of sleeping sickness in humans and nagana in cattle and horses. Nagana is widespread among the native African hoofed mammals, but does them little harm. That is probably because the disease has infected native animals for hundreds of thousands of years, so they have become tolerant to it. Cattle and horses were, however, introduced to Africa in fairly recent times and have only been in contact with nagana for a few thousand years. As a result, it is a disease that causes many deaths among domestic stock. Both sleeping sickness and nagana are caused by parasitic single-celled animals called trypanosomes that live in the blood of the host animal. Tsetse flies feed from the blood of living animals and pass the trypanosomes on as they feed.

Feeding in tsetse flies is carried out only by the adult fly—the larva does not have to provide for itself at all. Almost all female tsetses mate as soon as they hatch. One egg is released at a time, but is not laid. Instead, it hatches inside the female, and the larva feeds on secretions inside her. As soon as it is fully developed, the fly searches out a suitable shady area and drops the larva to the ground, where it burrows and pupates.

The tsetse fly, Glossina mortisans, *feeds for blood from a human arm. The fly transmits the parasites* Trypanosoma gambiense *and* T. rhodesiense, *both of which are responsible for the sleeping sickness disease in tropical Africa.*

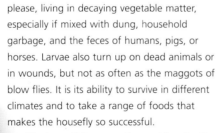

please, living in decaying vegetable matter, especially if mixed with dung, household garbage, and the feces of humans, pigs, or horses. Larvae also turn up on dead animals or in wounds, but not as often as the maggots of blow flies. It is its ability to survive in different climates and to take a range of foods that makes the housefly so successful.

The housefly's success is a problem for the human race. It has been shown to carry at least 100 different kinds of disease-causing organisms, including those of human diseases such as cholera, bacterial dysentery, typhoid, anthrax, and eye diseases. Houseflies also pass on the infective stages of parasitic worms. They

⊜ *The feeding habits of* Musca domestica, *the housefly, are varied. Here it enjoys the sweetness of a sugar-coated cake left uneaten by its owner.*

transmit infantile diarrhea, a fatal disease of children in many poorer countries. The relationship between infant deaths and the housefly was known as long as 50 years ago, when new insecticides were used to reduce housefly populations in poor villages. Removal of the flies cut infant deaths by around half. But the houseflies—great survivors that they are—became resistant to the insecticide, and infant deaths soon rose again.

The lesser housefly, *Fannia cannicularis*, is often mistaken for the larger common housefly. The flies are often seen circling around lamp fittings, chasing other members of the same species. The behavior is in fact just an adaptation of normal outdoor activity, when the flies circle around the end of a twig in what is part of their courtship behavior.

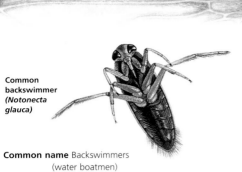

Common
backswimmer
(*Notonecta
glauca*)

Common name Backswimmers
(water boatmen)

Family Notonectidae

Suborder Heteroptera

Order Hemiptera

Number of species About 300 (35 U.S.)

Size From about 0.2 in (5 mm) to 0.6 in (15 mm)

Key features Body boat shaped, flat on the underside;
usually hang head down from water surface,
showing underside; eyes large; ears present in
both sexes; rostrum strong and sharp; front
legs used to grasp prey; hind legs long,
fringed with hairs and used as paddles; wings
well developed; underside of abdomen bears
water-repellent hairs

Habits All species are strong swimmers, coming to
the surface regularly to replenish air supply;
also strong fliers, moving from one area of
water to another

Breeding In some species males stridulate to attract
females; eggs attached to objects in the
water, such as stones or plants

Diet Aquatic animals including insect larvae,
tadpoles, and small fish as well as insects that
have fallen into the water

Habitat Lakes and ponds, water tanks, and animal
water troughs

Distribution Worldwide

⬆ *The common backswimmer,* Notonecta glauca, *is
widespread throughout Europe and lives in ponds, ditches,
and canals. It swims upside down, propelled by two long legs
that paddle like oars, making it look like a rowboat. Length
up to 0.8 inches (20 mm).*

Backswimmers Notonectidae

*Backswimmers are well named for their habit of
swimming upside down with their undersides
pointing toward the water surface. The large eyes,
located near the top of the head, are therefore able
to look down into the water as the bug searches
for suitable prey.*

Looking down into a pond, it can be quite
difficult to pick out backswimmers as they hang
upside down just beneath the water surface
because their general coloring matches that of
the pond. Their camouflage colors presumably
hide them quite well from any water birds on
the lookout for an easy meal. Their upper side,
on the other hand, is pale, which means that
they blend into the background of the sky
when viewed from beneath, probably making
them more difficult for a fish to spot.

They are efficient killers, easily immobilizing
prey smaller or even bigger than themselves by
stabbing it with their sharp, powerful rostrum.
Digestive juices are injected into the prey
through the rostrum, and the liquid contents of
its body are then sucked out. As with bugs in

⬇ *A North American species of backswimmer from
Arizona hangs motionless at the water surface while it
refreshes its air supply.*

⬇ *The common
backswimmer,* Notonecta
glauca *from Europe,
shows two important
lifestyle adaptations. The
paddle-shaped hind legs
used for swimming have
rows of hairs along them
to increase their surface
area. The large eyes are
of importance in spotting
prey in the murky water
in which it often lives.*

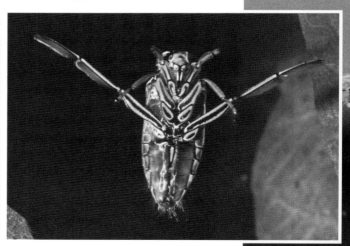

other families, backswimmers can deliver a painful jab to a human finger if they are picked up carelessly. In order to study their upper sides, it is best to restrict them in a small glass tube where they may be examined without the observer coming to any harm. Not all backswimmers hunt below the water—some specialize on insects that have fallen into the water and are struggling on the surface. The backswimmers have the ability to detect the difference between ripples in the water produced by prey and ripples produced by individuals of their own species. They are strong fliers, enabling them to move from pond to pond; they can also literally jump out of the water and immediately take flight.

Despite the fact that they live under the water, both sexes have ears, and the males of many species stridulate. They produce sounds attractive to females by rubbing rough areas of the front legs against the rostrum. In some backswimmers the bubble of air held under the wings acts as an amplifier for the sounds. For example, it appears that the sounds produced by a number of *Buenoa* species males can be heard from several yards away. They start with a series of clicks; but as they get closer to the female, it turns into a rapid hum.

The life cycle of *Notonecta* species, which are found all over the world, is quite typical of the family as a whole. Once mating has taken place, the female lays her eggs in or on various pondweeds. The female of *N. glauca* from Europe is able to use her ovipositor to cut into plant stems where she lays her elongate eggs. Like their parents, all nymphal stages are active predators, catching suitable-sized prey and in some cases eating one another. While land-dwelling insects take in air to expand their body after they have molted, aquatic bugs either swallow water or take it in through their body surface in order to expand into their new skin. Depending on the species and the water

⊕ *The common water boatman or common backswimmer,* Notonecta glauca *from Europe, hangs onto submerged vegetation while waiting to pounce on passing prey items.*

temperature in a particular year, there may be one or two generations produced annually. When looking down into water where backswimmers live, it is not uncommon to find both adults and nymphs of all stages present at the same time.

Bubbles of Life

It is interesting to note how backswimmers and other water bugs manage to obtain the oxygen they need. They do so by coming to the surface

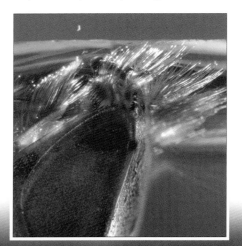

⊙ ⊙ *Right: This close-up of the end of the abdomen of a backswimmer shows some of the bristles that hold the bubble of air. Below: A common backswimmer,* Notonecta glauca, *hangs at the water surface with its underside in contact with the atmosphere. It is changing the bubble of air that it uses to breathe beneath the water, and that is trapped in rows of bristles beneath the abdomen.*

of the water at intervals to take on new air supplies. The air is trapped as a bubble under rows of water-repellent hairs on the underside of the abdomen in both nymphs and adults. Adults, being bigger, can hold onto an even larger quantity of air by trapping some between the wings and the top of the abdomen. The insect takes oxygen from the bubble as required through the spiracles. At the same rate as the oxygen is used, more enters the bubble from the surrounding water to replace it. Provided the bug is not too active, the slow removal of oxygen and the replacement from the water will keep it breathing quite happily. While its activity levels are low, it can remain beneath the water for as long as six hours without having to replace the bubble. If the bug is very active, however, or if the water is low in oxygen—for example, in warm weather—the insect has to make regular trips to the surface for fresh supplies of air. A second reason why the bubble may need changing regularly is that it contains nitrogen as well as oxygen. (Nitrogen makes up about four-fifths of the earth's atmosphere.)

Lesser Water Boatmen

Bugs in the family Corixidae are called lesser water boatmen because the members of the Notonectidae (backswimmers) are sometimes referred to as water boatmen. Clearly, both live in water, but it is not too difficult to distinguish them from one another. Instead of swimming on their backs, lesser water boatmen swim on their fronts so that the top of the body is always visible to the observer. The upper side of the body is flatter than in the backswimmers but still rounded, and all three pairs of legs are different from one another. The hind legs are the largest; they are flattened, with fringes of hairs, and are used for swimming. The middle legs are similar in length to the hind legs, but are slim and used for holding onto weeds and other objects in the water. The front legs are short and in the majority of the family are used for gathering food. The tarsus of each front leg has only one segment, along which is a fringe of tough bristles. The bristles are used to scoop up and filter out tiny algae, diatoms, and tiny animals on which the bugs feed. Males of some species also use the scoops on the front legs to hold onto the females during mating.

A few species in the family are predators. *Cymatia coleoptrata*, a European species, lives in pools where it rests among plants beneath the water. It will swim out and catch small water crustaceans, insect larvae, and even nymphs of other water boatmen, holding the prey in its front legs as it feeds. *Glaencorisa* species have similar habits but are large-eyed and nocturnal. They have long hairs on their front legs which they use as a type of net to catch small crustaceans and other small water creatures on which they feed.

Corixa punctata, *the lesser water boatman, is commonly found in weedy ponds and lakes where it feeds on algae and detritus on the bottom. As well as being powerful swimmers, these bugs can fly.*

The nitrogen in the bubble slowly dissolves into the water, and the bubble gradually shrinks in size. The smaller the bubble, the less oxygen it can take in from the water and the less use it is. As it shrinks, it eventually has to be replaced.

In *Notonecta* species, having taken on a bubble of air, the bugs swim down and hold onto water plants or other objects to prevent themselves from floating back to the surface. *Buenoa* species backswimmers from the warm temperate and tropical regions of the Old World and *Anisops* species from the temperate and tropical regions of the New World, however, are able to hang still in the water, unaided, at any depth they wish. They manage this by taking on a much smaller bubble of air and therefore becoming less buoyant than *Notonecta*, so they do not float upward. This means that they have a smaller supply of oxygen available to them. To overcome the problem, their body contains stocks of hemoglobin—the substance that carries oxygen in the blood. The bugs can store a certain amount of oxygen in the hemoglobin to use when submerged. They do not have to come to the surface as often as would be expected with such a small bubble of air. In addition, the presence of hemoglobin means that they are able to live in water that is low in oxygen.

93

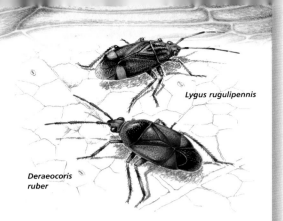

Lygus rugulipennis

**Deraeocoris
ruber**

Common name Plant bugs (leaf bugs, capsid bugs)

Family Miridae

Suborder Heteroptera

Order Hemiptera

Number of species About 10,000 (about 1,800 U.S.)

Size From about 0.12 in (3 mm) to 0.6 in (15 mm)

Key features Shape variable; some long and thin, others
short, broad, and rather soft bodied; usually
fully winged but may have short wings or
lack them altogether; often brightly colored,
but many species also have cryptic coloration,
usually rather shiny; separated from other
bug families by having a 4-segmented
rostrum, 4-segmented antennae, and by
absence of ocelli

Habits Most often found running around on the
plant species with which they are associated

Breeding Females insert eggs into the tissues of their
food plants or beneath bark

Diet Many species feed on plants and include
pests of crops; others are predaceous, feeding
on small insects; some species rob spiders'
webs

Habitat Found from the ground up to the tops of the
highest trees in almost any habitat where
suitable plants grow

Distribution Worldwide

⊕ *Lygus rugulipennis is a pest of greenhouse cucumber
crops. Length approximately 0.2 inches (5–6 mm). Deraeocoris
ruber feeds on the developing fruit and seeds of numerous
plants, as well as on aphids and other small insects. Length
0.2–0.3 inches (6–8 mm). Both species are widespread in the
Northern Hemisphere.*

Plant Bugs

Miridae

*The Miridae is the second largest family in the
Hemiptera, exceeded in numbers of species only by
the leafhoppers. A random sweep with a net through
any vegetation will almost certainly catch one or
more species of plant bugs.*

WITH SUCH A LARGE NUMBER of species in the family
there is some variation in structure among its
members. Typical members are fully winged
with oval to elongate bodies when viewed from
above. Some species, however, have wings that
are reduced in size or completely absent, while
others have individuals with full or partial
wings. Other species may have fully winged
males and wingless females. Coloring ranges
from camouflage browns and greens to bright
reds and yellows, often with black markings.

Walking on Leaves

The success of the family, with its thousands of
species, can be explained partly by the ability to
walk easily on any kind of leaf, even the shiniest
ones. That is because in adults the tarsi (the
"feet") have modifications—varying from one
subfamily to another—that help them stick to
the surface on which they are walking. Nymphs
have an even more interesting way of holding
on in an emergency: They push the rectum, the
end part of the intestine, out of the tip of the
abdomen. The rectum sticks hard to the surface
on which they are standing, preventing them
from falling or being pulled off. When the
emergency is over, they pull the rectum back in
again and continue about their business.

In the Miridae the second segment of the
legs, the trochanter, is rather unusual. It appears
to be made up of two sections, a feature not
found in any other bugs, but occurring in
spiders. The point where the segment is
apparently separated into two is in fact a line of
weakness. If a predator grabs a bug by the leg,
the trochanter breaks in two, and the bug
escapes on its remaining legs. The predator is

⊙ *Adults of the
common green capsid
bug,* Lygocoris pabulinus,
*feed on flowers of
charlock,* Sinapis arvensis,
*a member of the cabbage
family. This common and
widespread European
bug can be a pest at
times, especially on fruit
bushes and trees.*

left with just a leg, which is of no particular use since it contains little in the way of food.

Ant mimicry is not uncommon in the family. In some species the nymphs resemble the ant; in others it is the adults. Some bugs are shaped like ants, while others are colored in such a way that they look like ants at first glance and will easily fool a predator, if not an observant human. Among four aphid-feeding *Pilophorus* species, all of which mimic ants, the aphids that they feed on are tended by ants. By mimicking them, the bug escapes the attentions of predators, which keep away from the biting ants. The ants, however, are not fooled by the deception, so the bugs have to be both observant and agile to prevent themselves from being attacked.

In temperate regions there is usually just one generation each year, and overwintering occurs at the egg stage. In the tropics breeding may take place all year round. The female plant bug has a sawlike ovipositor that she uses to cut a slit into plant tissue where she lays her eggs—up to 200 during her lifetime.

Diverse Feeders

Although the common name for the whole family is plant bugs, they are by no means all plant feeders. For example, the members of the subfamily Deraeocorinae are all predators. They feed on small insects, their larvae, mites, and

⊕ *The European bug,* Miris striatus, *is one of the larger species in the family Miridae. It lives on a range of tree species and preys on aphids, scale insects, insect eggs, and small moth larvae.*

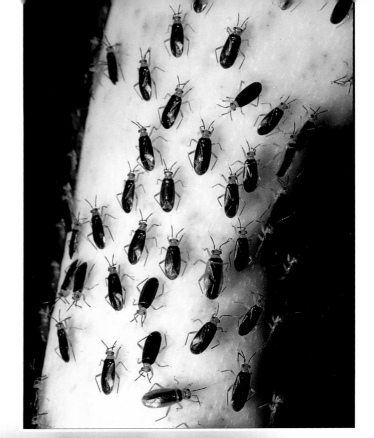

other small arthropods, although they will occasionally probe plant material. *Stethoconus* species in the family specialize in preying on lace bugs. *Stephanitis pyrioides*, the azalea lace bug, was accidentally introduced into North America, where it has become a pest on cultivated azaleas. Fortunately, its main predator, *Stethoconus japonicus*, has now been deliberately introduced. It is hoped that it will help control the pest lace bug.

Among the plant-feeding mirids there are those that use just one or a few species of plant, while others are generalists and can feed on almost anything. One subfamily, the Bryocorinae, specializes in ferns or orchids, although *Sahlbergella singularis* is a major pest on cocoa plants. The group is mainly tropical in distribution, but it is also represented in North America and Europe by a number of species that feed on ferns. The small, shiny brown bugs are in fact among the few creatures that actually feed on ferns, which tend to be rather distasteful. Yet another subfamily, the grass

A large group of tiny **Pachypoda guatemalensis** *on the flower of an* **Anthurium** *in rain forest in Costa Rica. Mirids are generally not common in tropical rain forests.*

All members of the subfamily Deraeocorinae are believed to be predaceous. An adult **Deraeocoris ruber** *feeds on a newly emerged seven-spot ladybug,* **Coccinella 7-punctata,** *by the side of an English meadow.*

bugs (Mirinae), is confined to feeding on the leaves, flowers, and seeds of grasses, sedges, and rushes at all stages of the life cycle. The adults are often very difficult to pick out since they are pale green to yellowish in color and often resemble grass seeds. They can occur in very large numbers in grassland. The European grass-feeding meadow plant bug, *Leptoterna dolobrata*, has been accidentally introduced into North America, where it is something of a pest.

Pest and Pest Controller

Plant bugs feed by pushing the rostrum into the plant tissue and injecting saliva into the wound, leaving damage marks on the plant. As a consequence, a number of plant bugs are considered pests of human crops. One such species is the tarnished plant bug, *Lygus lineolaris*, from North America. The problem is that it will feed on almost anything, making it a pest of both crops and forestry. For example, it feeds on young pine trees growing in nurseries, damaging the growing point and making the plants useless. It also likes strawberries: It eats the seeds on the fruit surface, damaging the surrounding flesh and making the fruit unfit for human consumption. In the warm south the bug can have up to five generations each year, so the problem can be very serious.

At the other end of the scale are plant bugs that benefit humans. One example is *Tytthus mundulus*, an Australian species that was introduced into Hawaii early in the 20th century to control the sugarcane leafhopper, *Perkinsiella saccharicida*—itself an introduction from Australia. The leafhopper is now found on sugarcane in Florida, but it seems to cause little damage to the crop there.

Living with Spiders

Strange as it may seem, *Ranzovius* species mirid bugs have become dependent on a number of different species of spiders and live alongside them in their webs. The bugs spend the whole of their life cycle in the presence of the spiders, relying on them for shelter and for a supply of food. These so-called spider bugs are only found in the New World, with three species in North America.

A good example of a bug successfully living with spiders is *Ranzovius contubernalis* from eastern North America. The bug has been found living with both *Anelosimus studiosus*, a comb-footed spider, and *Agelenopsis pennsylvanica*, a sheet-web weaving spider. During the day both bug adults and nymphs can be found on the spiders' webs or on vegetation close to them. They seem to be less active at night, possibly because that is when the spiders are most active. Webs of both spider species contain a platform consisting of a sheet of silk, and the bug is able to walk both above and beneath the sheet without getting stuck. As the bugs move around on the web, their antennae are in constant motion, but their movements appear not to be noticed by the resident spider. It seems that the small size of the bugs and the vibrations they make in the web are totally unlike those of an insect that has fallen in and is struggling to escape, so the spider ignores them.

The bugs mainly feed on insects trapped in the web that are too small for the spider to bother with. Adults have also been seen to feed on larger insects from which the spider hosts have already fed. It would seem that the dried corpses still contain enough food to interest the bugs. The bugs also feed on any suitable plant material that falls into the web. *Ranzovius contubernalis* occasionally betrays its host spider: It has been seen feeding on the newly molted baby spiderlings belonging to *Anelosimus studiosus*.

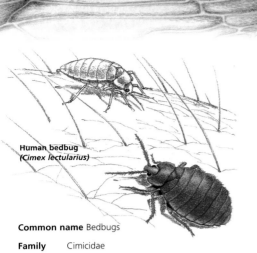

Human bedbug
(*Cimex lectularius*)

Common name Bedbugs

Family Cimicidae

Suborder Heteroptera

Order Hemiptera

Number of species About 80 (4 U.S.)

Size From about 0.1 in (3 mm) to 0.2 in (5 mm)

Key features Body oval and flattened (appearing more rounded after a blood feed); color yellowish to brown; wingless

Habits All species are parasites on surface of birds and mammals, including humans; active by night, when they come out to feed

Breeding Male bugs penetrate the body of the female and inject sperm into the body fluid; eggs are laid in crevices near the host animal

Diet Blood feeders

Habitat Birds' nests, cellars, and caves inhabited by bats; human habitations

Distribution Worldwide, but mostly in the tropics

⬆ *The human bedbug,* Cimex lectularius, *is a notorious worldwide pest. It feeds not only on humans but also on bats, chickens, and other domestic animals. When feeding, it moves slowly over the skin, biting every few steps. It can survive for over a year without a blood meal. Length 0.2–0.3 inches (4–7 mm).*

Bedbugs

Cimicidae

Imagine what it must be like to go to bed knowing that when the light goes off, a host of tiny blood-sucking bugs will emerge from nooks and crannies in the room. Unfortunately for their host, they are sure to indulge in a blood feast.

IN POORER COUNTRIES the bedbug is extremely common, but in the developed world the bedbug is rare today thanks to improved living standards. However, that was not the case even as recently as the middle of the last century. In London, England, just before World War II (1939–1945) as many as 4 million people had bedbugs in their dwellings.

When they do occur, they can be a problem. One family had to vacate their house after they experienced an infestation of bedbugs after bringing them back in their luggage from Europe.

Sending the Bugs to Sleep

One way to get rid of the bugs, however, is to use sleeping tablets—not on the bugs but on the humans. When the bugs feed on people who have taken the tablets, they also take in the drug and fall asleep, leaving themselves to be discovered and destroyed the next morning. The problem bugs are gone in just a few nights.

There are two species of bedbugs that feed on humans. *Cimex lectularius* is the bedbug found in the temperate regions of the world, while *C. rotundatus* (also called *C. hemipterus*) is the bedbug found in the tropics. Both species are similar in appearance: They have a flattened, rounded body that is dark brown and wingless. There are differences in the behavior

⊕ **Cimex lectularius,** *the bedbugs of temperate regions, crawls across a bedcover in search of human blood. Its flattened body allows it to squeeze into narrow cracks to hide during daylight hours.*

⊕ *A* **Cimex** *species bedbug showing the rostrum with which it sucks up its blood meals. From the swollen state of its body it is clear that it has just fed.*

of the two species, which mainly relate to the difference in temperatures where they live. The tropical bedbug is a much faster mover than the temperate species, which means that it is capable of traveling greater distances and spreading more quickly from one place to another.

Virus Spreaders?

Nymph and adult bugs of both species spend the hours of daylight in any suitable nook or cranny, coming out to feed at night. Although their bites are a minor irritation producing itching and swelling, they are not dangerous. Generally bedbugs have not been known to transmit any important human diseases. Recent studies, however, indicate that they may be involved in passing on the hepatitis B virus.

Females attach their eggs to a surface, usually in their resting place. The eggs take between 10 and 20 days to hatch. Female bugs may lay between 150 and 345 eggs during their average life span of nine to 18 months. On hatching, the nymphs must take a blood meal during each of their six instars; otherwise they cannot molt into the next instar.

Flower Bugs

The flower bugs, or minute pirate bugs (their other common name), in the family Anthocoridae are small bugs with a worldwide distribution. They are closely related to the bedbugs and are sometimes included within the family Cimicidae. The flower bugs are usually fully winged, rather flat insects with an oval or oblong shape when viewed from above. The front of the head juts forward like a sort of snout. While a few of them feed on blood, including that of humans, most of them eat other insects and mites.

They are very careful predators. In fact, biologists call them "timid predators" because they usually only feed on prey that is smaller than themselves and that moves relatively slowly. Their prey includes aphids, thrips, barklice, whiteflies, and mites as well as the eggs and smaller larvae of various insects. As a result, the little flower bugs are quite important in helping control the numbers of some important pests.

One interesting feature of some species is that either by accident, or perhaps by design, they will also attack humans. As its name implies, the European common flower bug, *Anthocoris nemorum*, is common on flowers during the summer months. It flies freely and often lands on bare human skin. At that point it will insert its proboscis into the victim, who will usually brush it away immediately. Whether the bugs attempt to suck blood is not recorded, but the site of the puncture wound usually swells up and can itch for a considerable time.

**Assassin bug
(Acanthaspis sp.)**

Common name
Assassin
bugs

Family Reduviidae

Suborder Heteroptera

Order Hemiptera

Number of species About 5,000 (106 U.S.)

Size From about 0.3 in (8 mm) to 1.6 in (4 cm)

Key features General shape oval to elongate, some actually resembling small stick insects; short, stout, curved, 3-segmented rostrum that fits in a groove beneath the thorax when not in use; noticeable groove across head behind the eyes; front legs adapted for clasping prey, so they usually walk on the hind 2 pairs; pronotum may have a crest or may bear spikes, which may also occur on top of the head

Habits Walk around on vegetation and on the ground in search of prey, often moving slowly and stealthily; blood-sucking species find their prey by flying in search of it; some species attract prey by using "tools" such as resin

Breeding Females of a number of species exhibit parental care, as do males in some species

Diet Other insects and their larvae; spiders; the blood of vertebrates; one species known to feed on liquid from fermenting dung

Habitat Many species live on vegetation, while others live on the ground or on tree bark; some species inhabit the nests of termites; found in all kinds of habitat—grassland, forests, marshes, and deserts

Distribution Worldwide, but with the greatest variety of species in the tropical regions

⬆ *An Acanthaspis species assassin bug feeds on a caterpillar. Acanthaspis species have been found in West Africa, where they prey on ants. They camouflage themselves by attaching the sucked-out bodies of ants to their back by means of fine hairs and silk threads. Length 1 inch (2.5 cm).*

Assassin Bugs

Reduviidae

The Reduviidae are a bit like "hit men": quiet assassins that kill without remorse. Not only that, they are such efficient killers that they can take on prey considerably larger than themselves.

THE LARGE, MAINLY TROPICAL family Reduviidae varies considerably in body form, from heavily built to delicate and gnatlike, and from short and broad to long and thin. However, they all have common features that separate them from other bug families. Their three-segmented rostrum is a fearsome piece of equipment: short, broad, and used for stabbing through a weak part of the prey's exoskeleton. At the same time, the victim is held in the powerful front pair of legs. Saliva is then injected, which rapidly paralyzes the prey and then digests its internal organs, leaving behind a "soup" for the bug to suck up. As with other predaceous

⬇ *A close-up of the head of* Canthesancus gulo *from Sumatra reveals the robust, curved mouthparts with which it stabs and then feeds from its victims.*

A warningly colored assassin bug, Eulyes amaena *from Malaysia. Its overall shape is representative of what might be termed "the typical assassin bug."*

bugs, larger members of the family should be approached with care, since if picked up they can bite very painfully. The rostrum also has a second use as a stridulatory organ. In nearly all male assassin bugs the tip can be rubbed against a sort of file on the underside of the thorax to produce sounds. In some species that can be heard as a distinct squeak and is probably a warning to "keep off." Otherwise the sounds are produced to attract females.

Clever Assassins

While many species of assassin bug sit quietly until a suitable victim comes within reach or steal slowly around until they find a victim, others have developed more cunning ways of

⊕ *It is hard to believe that an assassin bug nymph from Kenya is hidden here. It is camouflaged beneath bits of wood, soil, and the empty husks of its victims.*

ensuring that they find a meal. One way is to live among their victims, but making sure they are not recognized. In Central America both adults and nymphs of the bug *Salyavata variegata* are found in the nests of *Nasutitermes* species termites. The adult bugs have camouflage coloring, while the nymphs disguise themselves by scraping off pieces of the termite nest surface and gluing them to their bodies. The bugs sit by the termite nest openings,

101

grabbing suitable-sized victims as they emerge. The third, fourth, and fifth instar nymphs go one step farther, using the sucked-dry body of one of their victims as a "tool" to attract more termites to their doom.

A Sticky Death

"Tools" are used by other assassin bugs to lure and trap prey. In Southeast Asia two species, *Ectinoderus longimanus* and *Amulius malayus*, have been given the common name of resin bugs. They dip their hairy front legs into resin that exudes from various trees. The resin is also used by *Trigona* species stingless bees to build their nests. As a result, they approach the resin-coated bugs, expecting some nest-building material, only to receive an unpleasant and fatal surprise. *Manicoris rufipes* from Brazil also catches stingless bees, but uses a mixture of pollen, nectar, and resin to coat its front legs.

The bug reaches out toward any bee attracted to it. On contact with the sticky legs the bee becomes trapped and ends up as a meal. Also in Brazil *Apiomerus* species assassin bug nymphs have been discovered "fishing" for termites. They attach sticky resin to their front legs, find a hole in the tunnels through which tree-nesting termites run, and sit and wait. As a termite runs past, they touch it on the back, it sticks to their legs, is hauled out of the tunnel, and speared with the rostrum.

Living in the south of the United States is the assassin bug, *Stenolemus lanipes*, which specializes in a creature that is itself a predator—the common American house spider *Achaeranea tepidariorum*. Clearly in order to avoid being eaten by the spider, the bugs have to behave in a very clever way. As its name indicates, the spider constructs its web on houses or other buildings, and the young spiders remain in the web with their mother for some weeks before eventually going their own way. It is the youngsters that the bug targets. On the bug's legs are tiny spines that become covered with either spider silk or some other silklike material, which acts to camouflage it and allows it to walk on the spider's web without getting stuck. The bug first steals up to the web and taps on it with its antennae. It then walks onto the web, vibrating its body, which

Bloodsuckers

All species within one subfamily of assassin bugs, the Triatominae, suck the blood of vertebrate animals, including humans. Such attacks are always painful and unpleasant experiences; however, in Central and South America the situation can be dangerous, since the bugs carry the infective organisms of Chaga's disease. The disease itself is caused by a single-celled animal, or protozoan, related to the organisms that cause sleeping sickness in Africa. Although it occasionally kills children early on in the infection, the disease does not normally produce any symptoms until 10 to 20 years after being bitten by the bug. The main effect of the disease is to damage the heart. People who contract it, mainly poor country folk, can expect to live on average nine years fewer than an uninfected person. It is believed that between 16 and 18 million people have the disease at any one time. However, only around 50,000 die as a result each year, making it nothing like as dangerous as malaria, another killer disease transmitted by insects.

Infection can occur through bites, but may also result if the bug's droppings are rubbed into an open scratch or other wound, or into the eye. Infection can also occur if food contaminated with the bug's droppings is eaten. One of the bugs that carries the disease, *Triatoma sanguisuga*, the eastern blood-sucking cone-nose, is found from Ontario down to Florida and across as far as Texas. Although it carries Chaga's disease farther south into southern Mexico, it does not carry it any farther north. While the bug is quite capable of flying to find a host when it is hungry, after a blood feed it is so heavy that it is unable to leave the ground.

⊕ *The bloodsucking cone-nose,* Triatoma sanguisuga, *is also called the Mexican bedbug. Its bites are hardly felt by its hosts, but the results can be fatal.*

This unusual bug lives both as nymph and adult in crevices under stones close to nests of the ant *Anoplolepis longipes* and nowhere else. No ants, no bugs! At night bugs of all ages emerge from their daytime hiding places and, accompanied by the ants, make their way to where they feed on masses of fermenting cow dung. The bugs feed on the liquid oozing from it. The dung has to be at just the right stage of fermentation to be of use to the bugs, which may have to travel some distance to find such a food source. As a result, groups of bugs living around a number of different ant nests may all end up at the same feeding place, returning to their own particular nest during the day. The ants appear to feed on the bugs' droppings.

Caring Parents

Some Reduviidae species indulge in parental care, but it is not common. Females of *Rhinocoris carmelita* and *Pisilus tipuliformis*, both from Africa, stand guard on or near their eggs until they hatch. *Ghilianella* species from South America do a bit more—the female carries her small brood around with her, the infants maintaining contact by wrapping their long, slim legs around her body.

Paternal care is very rare among insects, but occurs in some *Rhinocoris* species assassin bugs from Africa. The reason for its rarity is that no male insect can be sure that it was his sperm

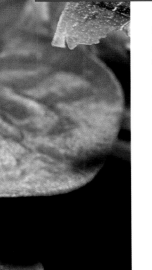

in turn vibrates the web in much the same way as a piece of leaf blown into the web by the wind might do. The movement of the web is ignored by the spider, and the bug is allowed to get within striking distance of a youngster while keeping well away from the adult spider.

Assassin bugs that are not killers are exceptional, but one such species is *Lophocephala guerini* from India and Sri Lanka.

⊖ *Some assassin bugs mimic social or parasitic wasps. The curved rostrum of* Hiranetis braconiformis *from Peru, however, reveals it to be a bug, not a wasp.*

that fertilized the eggs. Caring for eggs fertilized by another male would be a waste of time. *Rhinocoris albopilosus* has overcome the problem: Having found a receptive female, he mates with her several times and then stays with or very close to her while she lays her eggs. As soon as she has finished, he quickly moves in and sits over the egg batch, remaining there whatever the circumstances, foregoing any food unless some unwitting insect ventures too close.

While he is on guard, he is regularly visited by the female, with whom he again mates. She then adds more eggs to the batch he is guarding. The male gains a further advantage from his behavior: His presence at a batch of eggs is very attractive to other females that are looking for a male to protect their eggs. As long as they first allow him to mate with them (so that he is certain that he is the one that has fertilized their eggs), they are allowed to add to the batch that he is protecting. He stays with the eggs until all of the nymphs have emerged, when he abandons them. His natural predatory instincts are switched off in some way at this particular time, since he does not attempt to spear and feed on any of his offspring.

Why do the males protect their eggs? There are certainly insects around that feed on eggs, and the male will drive them off. However, the greatest enemies are tiny parasitic wasps that lay their eggs into the bug eggs in order for their larvae to feed on the developing nymph. *Rhinocoris* males have been observed darting at the female wasps, attempting to spear them on their rostrum. The presence of such attentive males certainly increases the survival rate of the offspring, but not all of the wasps are driven away; out of a number of the eggs a tiny wasp, rather than a bug, will eventually emerge.

The males of some *Zelus* species assassin bugs from Colombia are even more caring. They guard the egg batches until they hatch, but then they stay with the nymphs. They are attentive fathers, catching prey and holding it at the end of their stretched-out rostrum. The nymphs all cluster around and feed from the prey. The male's efforts are rewarded: Studies have shown that in unprotected egg batches 55 percent of eggs were found to be parasitized by wasps, compared with only 21 percent of eggs that were guarded.

Some larger assassin bugs, such as this Arilus *species from Peru, called a "wheel bug," are quite prepared to go into an attack posture if they feel threatened.*

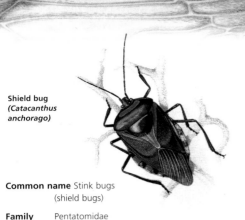

Shield bug
(Catacanthus
anchorago)

Common name Stink bugs
(shield bugs)

Family Pentatomidae

Suborder Heteroptera

Order Hemiptera

Number of species About 5,000 (222 U.S.)

Size From about 0.2 in (4 mm) to 1 in (2.5 cm)

Key features Broad-bodied, often oval-shaped bugs,
nearly as wide as they are long; often rather
flattened on top; scutellum is usually
triangular, extending over as much as half the
abdomen but not overlapping the
membranous area of the forewings by much;
front of the pronotum may have blunt or
pointed projections on either side of the
head; stink glands present

Habits Most often found on the plants on which
they feed; predaceous species found on any
suitable vegetation in search of prey

Breeding In a number of species the females care for
their eggs and young; in many species males
stridulate to attract females

Diet Many are sap feeders; others feed on insects,
especially soft-bodied ones such as larvae

Habitat Meadows, grassland, forests, sand dunes,
seashore, marshes, and deserts

Distribution Worldwide, but tropical zones are especially
rich in species

⊕ *The bright colors of the shield bug Catacanthus
anchorago from Asia give a clear indication to would-be
predators that the bug contains foul-tasting defensive
chemicals and gives off equally unpleasant smells. Length
about 0.5 inches (13 mm).*

Stink Bugs Pentatomidae

*With such a large family, it is difficult to travel
far in virtually any habitat without coming
across a member of the Pentatomidae. The
brightly colored species are easy to pick out,
but many are well camouflaged and are
not at all easy to discern against their
natural background.*

WHATEVER THEIR COLOR, stink bugs are fairly easy
to recognize. Their proportions are such that,
on average, they are about twice as long as
they are broad, and looked at from the side
they are usually rather flat on top. Members of
related families tend to have a more rounded
top to the abdomen. As their alternative
common name of shield bugs indicates, the
scutellum is quite large, normally reaching to at
least halfway down the abdomen.

Giant shield bugs are very similar, except
that their head is small in relation to the rest of
the body, while the head of stink bugs is a
perfect match for the size of their body. It is not
uncommon for the sides of the front part of the
pronotum to be extended outward in various
ways. Those of the North American spined
soldier bugs (*Podisus* species) and the European
two-spined stink bug, *Picromerus bidens*, for
example, form sharp points.

Adult shield bugs are always winged, but
members of the genus *Lojus*, from Central and
South America, are rather unusual. They have a
pair of forewings, but the membranous hind
wings are absent, and therefore these bugs are
unable to fly.

Why "Stink Bugs"?

The reason for the name stink bug is that the
insects produce unpleasant smells to ward off
their enemies. The smelly chemicals come from
glands in the thorax of adult stink bugs and
the abdomen of the nymphs. The chemicals
also make the bugs taste unpleasant, so that

⊕ *Feeding on sap
running through the
stem of a plant in the
Peruvian rain forest is an
adult Peromatus species
stink bug. Members of
the Pentatomidae tend to
have flatter backs than
other related families.*

⊖ *A pair of stink bugs,
Edessa rufomarginata,
mating as they sit on a
leaf in the rain forest of
Peru. Tail-to-tail mating is
normal, and the female
is the larger of the
two bugs.*

would-be predators avoid them once they have learned how disgusting they are. The unpleasant fluids are released through openings on the underside of the body, and the bugs may lift their abdomen up in the air to expose their underside when releasing them. The smell they produce can be very noticeable. The European green shield bug, *Palomena prasina*, for example, can be very common in gardens and often gets caught up in lawn mowers. The strong smell produced as a result can pervade the area for several feet around.

Adults of the stink bug *Cosmopepla bimaculata* have been examined in detail to find out more about how the bug emits its unpleasant fluids. It appears that the bugs have the ability to produce the fluid from the left or right glands, or both at the same time. They can also control how much fluid is produced, What is more, if it is not used, they can withdraw it back into the gland from which it was produced, avoiding any waste. The fluid is obviously very effective in deterring potential predators. Under experimental conditions a variety of different bird species, as well as anole lizards, rejected the bugs when they were offered them.

Like the caterpillars of many species of Lepidoptera, stink bugs have been found to obtain the defensive chemicals from the plants on which they feed. The North American harlequin bug, *Murgantia histrionica*, feeds on a range of plants from the cabbage family and is a pest of cultivated varieties. Although eaten by humans, cabbages tend to have a very strong smell, especially when they are going bad. That is because the plants contain substances called mustard oils, which deter some creatures from eating them. The harlequin bug is able to concentrate the mustard oils so that in its body they are 20 to 30 times as strong as they are in the plant. When the harlequin bugs were presented to several different species of birds, they were not prepared to eat them.

Helpful Bacteria

The majority of stink bugs feed on plant sap. In order for them to be able to make use of it, they enlist the help of special bacteria that live in small pockets in the side of the gut. The bacteria are absolutely essential, so female bugs smear their eggs with their own droppings, which contain the bacteria. When the young hatch out, they are able to take in the bacteria provided by their mother.

Members of the subfamily Amyoteinae take small animal prey, especially caterpillars or other slow-moving insects of a suitable size, and occasionally suck sap if they are hungry. Feeding mainly on animals means that they do not need bacteria to assist them. Predatory stink bugs appear to be very tolerant of some of the chemicals found in their prey: They are often found feeding on ladybugs or moth larvae, which contain substances that make insectivorous birds and mammals ill.

Timid Hunters

Sap feeders tend to have a narrow rostrum, but in the predatory species it is somewhat thicker. The latter are rather timid in their approach to prey. They wander around, reaching forward with their sensitive antennae for anything suitable. On contacting the prey, they gently push their stylets into it. If it reacts too violently, they pull them out and back off rapidly. However, if the prey is not too aggressive, the stylets spread out inside the prey's body so that it is unable to pull itself off. As the bug injects digestive juices, the prey becomes immobile, and it is then usually sucked dry.

Some species of predatory stink bug are quite important in helping control pests—for

⊖ *Some stink bugs are predaceous, but they tend to feed on soft-bodied prey. Oplomus dichrous from Mexico digs its proboscis into an unfortunate moth caterpillar.*

Plataspid Stink Bugs

The mainly tropical African and Asian family Plataspidae, related to the Pentatomidae, has no accepted common name. By virtue of the fact that they look very much like beetles, they could perhaps be called "beetle bugs," although that could be confusing. The reason for their beetlelike appearance is that they are flattened on the underside. Also, the scutellum is very large and curves over the abdomen, covering it completely. The easiest way to tell them apart is to look for the line down the center of the back, which separates the two wing cases in beetles. Since the scutellum is a single structure, the line is not present in plataspid stink bugs.

These bugs may be brightly colored and are often very shiny, as if they had been polished. Some species form groups of adults and nymphs, with the adults warningly colored while the nymphs are camouflaged. In some species the males have a pair of "horns" sticking out of the front of the head between the eyes; horns are not found in the females. All species are plant feeders, and one or two may reach pest proportions on certain pulse crops.

One species has been noted as having an interesting relationship with ants. *Caternaultiella rugosa*, from Cameroon in West Africa, lives in groups at the base of a particular species of tree. The ants build shelters—called pavilions—over the bugs and their eggs to hide the eggs from the attentions of female parasitic wasps. The pavilions are not always big enough, meaning that some bugs are left outside. The egg masses and the nymphs inside the pavilions are then deserted by the females and left in the care of the ants. Outside the pavilions, however, the female bugs continue to look after any eggs that were left out and the first instar nymphs. What is more, adults and final instar nymphs form protective groups around the first instar nymphs.

Left: Plataspid stink bugs resemble beetles, as seen in Ceratocoris cephalicus *from Uganda. The male has long "horns."*
Inset: Adults and nymphs are easy to distinguish in these Libyaspis coccinelloides *plataspid stink bugs from Madagascar. The adults are striped and warningly colored, while the nymphs are camouflaged.*

example, the eyed stink bug, *Perillus bioculatus*, which is widespread throughout North America. It is a major predator of larvae of the Colorado potato beetle, *Leptinotarsa decemlineata*. As a result of its success in controlling that pest, it has been introduced into Europe to see if it can carry out the same level of control there.

While the eyed stink bug is warningly colored, there are other useful North American predatory stink bugs that use camouflage. The *Brochymena* species live on trees, including those in orchards, where they feed on caterpillars and other soft-bodied insects. Their coloration is almost a perfect match for the bark of the trees on which they live.

Although the eyed stink bug should be encouraged, there are a number of stink bugs that are undesirable, since they feed on and

Giant stink bug nymphs are often an unusual shape. This is a group of Lyramorpha species nymphs from Australia, their bright-red color indicating that they are probably distasteful.

Oncomeris flavicornis from the dense tropical rain forests of New Guinea is one of the largest species of tessaratomids. It is a powerful flier and emits a loud buzz.

Giant Shield Bugs

The small family Tessaratomidae, with around 260 species, comes mainly from Southeast Asia and Australasia. A few species are known to live in the tropics of the New World. They are large insects, with adults of some species reaching 1.5 inches (4 cm) in length. They are similar in appearance to stink bugs, but they differ from them in the relationship between the size of the head and that of the body. In stink bugs the head looks the right size for the body, while in giant shield bugs the head looks too small for such a large body.

Another feature of the giant shield bugs is their nymphs, which can assume quite bizarre shapes when compared with the normally rather rounded stink bug nymphs. Those of the giant shield bugs may be rectangular, triangular, or even kite shaped and may have very pretty colors and markings.

One species in Australia is gaining notoriety. The bronze orange bug, *Musgraveia sulciventris*, has become something of a pest on citrus trees. (Its common name is derived from a combination of its main color—bronze—and its habitat—orange trees.) Both adults and nymphs feed from the young shoots of the citrus trees and can cause considerable damage in commercial orchards. The species has another unpleasant habit: If disturbed, it squirts out a foul-smelling brown liquid that can burn the skin and cause extreme discomfort if it gets into the eyes of predators or humans.

Burrower Bugs

The burrower bugs in the family Cydnidae are sometimes included with the stink bugs of the family Pentatomidae. However, they are perhaps best considered as a family in their own right, if only because of the unusual lifestyle of most species. They may grow up to 0.6 inches (15 mm) in length but are usually less than 0.4 inches (10 mm). They have the typical broad body of a stink bug or shield bug, but the most obvious features that distinguish them from related families are the heavily spined legs that they use for burrowing. They sometimes burrow as deep as 3 feet (9 m) in order for the females to lay their eggs in the soil. Nymphs of all but a few species then feed from plant roots.

A slightly less typical burrower bug, but one that is most likely to be seen, is *Sehirus* species. The reason it is not so typical is that the nymphs feed above the ground. *Sehirus bicolor* from Europe uses mainly the white deadnettle, *Lamium album*, as its food plant. The female still digs into the ground to form a chamber in which to lay her eggs, but the nymphs climb up onto the deadnettle to feed after hatching. *Sehirus cinctus* from North America feeds on *Stachys palustris*, but the female of the species has an extra trick up her sleeve. Like *S. bicolor*, she lays her eggs in the soil. But when the nymphs hatch, she carries seeds down from the plant for them to feed on. Only after they have molted into the second instar do they then emerge from the soil and climb onto the plant to feed.

The female of the Asian burrower bug, *Parastrachia japonensis*, goes even further. From the tree on which she lives she "picks" a fruit on the end of her rostrum. She then climbs down to the ground, digs a nest chamber, and lays her eggs. When the nymphs hatch, they feed from the fruit that she has so carefully provided for them. She eventually leads her second instar nymphs onto the leaf litter above the nest chamber, where they continue to feed on fruits that have fallen from the host tree.

One European burrower bug exhibits a kind of parental care that is very rare among bugs as a whole. Females of *Brachypelta aterrima* produce special secretions from the end of the gut, a sort of "baby food" on which the first instar nymphs feed. At the same time, the nymphs take in special bacteria that will help them digest their food throughout the rest of their life.

damage human crops. The harlequin cabbage bug or calico bug, *Murgantia histrionica*—another North American species—is a good example. It feeds on all sorts of plants of the cabbage family, leaving pale marks on the leaves and making the crop unsellable. The green vegetable bug, *Nezara viridula*, is even more of a problem: It is very common in the warmer parts of the world and attacks many crops, including tomatoes and various pulses.

Courtship Concerts

Some stink bugs stridulate, producing "songs" to attract members of the opposite sex. The songs are produced by scraping a row of pegs on the femur of the hind leg against a ridged area beneath the abdomen. Stridulation in a European species, the woundwort stink bug, *Eysarcoris fabricii*, can sometimes bring the sexes together in their hundreds. Humans are unable to hear the songs made by the bugs, but with the use of electronic equipment they can be picked up and recorded.

The green vegetable bug, *Nezara viridula,* demonstrates a complex use of song. A pheromone produced by the male is responsible for the initial gathering of the bugs. Once gathered together, the "singing" can commence. Scientists have found that the female bugs have three distinct songs, while the males can produce seven, although three of them are very similar. Rival males duet with each other, while males and females also sing to one another. Once a suitable pair get together, courtship begins. Courtship itself can

⬅ In England a male pied shield bug, Sehirus bicolor (left)—a burrower bug—head-butts the underside of a female in an attempt to make her accept him as a mate.

⬆ A group of woundwort stink bugs, Eysarcoris fabricii, in England. They have been brought together by the stridulation of the males, and the group includes both single bugs and mating pairs.

be quite complicated and may involve various actions. Males, for example, may tap or stroke the females with their antennae, and the females may respond by jerking their body up and down. Mating finally takes place with the sexes joined tail to tail and facing in opposite directions. In general, females are bigger than males, and it is not unusual to see a mating male being dragged unceremoniously backward as the female continues with her daily routine.

Pheromones are also used by many other species of stink bug to attract members of the opposite sex, an example being the males of *Thyanta pallidovirens*. Researchers have discovered, however, that this does not always result in a totally happy outcome—not only does the pheromone attract female bugs, but it also attracts female sphecid (solitary) wasps. The *Astata occidentalis* wasp provisions her nest with the stink bug for her larvae to feed on. It is likely that the female stink bug, attracted by the male's scent, will find that he has been taken by the time she arrives.

The Egg Burster

Stink bug eggs are normally laid in small groups and are often found stuck to the underside of a leaf. They are usually pale at first; but as the nymph develops inside, they darken. Once they are fully developed, the first instar nymphs use an "egg burster" to escape from the shell. The egg burster is a "t"-shaped tooth situated on the head. The first instar nymphs often stay together for a while before wandering off to feed. In certain tropical stink bugs the newly hatched nymphs cluster around the empty eggshells. In that state they resemble a hairy, stinging caterpillar. Another advantage is that, if molested by a predator, their combined chemical defenses are roughly equivalent to those of an adult bug.

⊙ *Newly hatched nymphs of a Peromatus species stink bug sit around the empty eggshells from which they have recently emerged. In this pose they are thought to resemble a stinging caterpillar and are therefore unlikely to be bothered by predators, especially birds.*

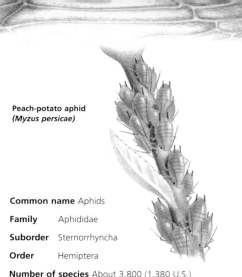

**Peach-potato aphid
(Myzus persicae)**

Common name Aphids

Family Aphididae

Suborder Sternorrhyncha

Order Hemiptera

Number of species About 3,800 (1,380 U.S.)

Size From about 0.04 in (1 mm) to 0.2 in (5 mm)

Key features Most commonly green or pink in color, but may be brown or black; females normally wingless; in males both pairs of wings transparent and folded tentlike over the body; body rather soft; abdomen with pair of cornicles on fifth or sixth abdominal segment

Habits Adults and nymphs usually found together in huge numbers on their host plants, on above-ground structures, or on plant roots

Breeding Life cycles can be very complex, including parthenogenesis and alternating of host plant species

Diet All suck the sap of plants, producing honeydew as a by-product; some species produce and live in galls

Habitat Forests, meadows, grassland, moorland, on waterside and floating plants, marshes, and seashore

Distribution Worldwide, but with the greater number of species in temperate regions

⊕ *Found all over the world, the very common peach-potato aphid, Myzus persicae, feeds on more than 200 plants, including peaches and potatoes, on which it is a pest. As a carrier of the fungal disease potato blight, this species helped cause the Irish potato famine in the 1840s, which was responsible for the deaths of almost 1 million people. Length 0.07 inches (2 mm).*

Aphids

Aphididae

With their complicated life cycles, various physical forms, and fascinating methods of defense the aphids include some of the most interesting and unusual of insect species.

THE 3,800 SPECIES INCLUDED within the Aphididae are composed of a number of subfamilies, which some scientists consider to be families in their own right. Therefore, classification of the group can be quite messy. It is not at all easy to define a typical aphid. Their appearance may depend on the species, which food plant they appear on, and the time of year.

Perhaps the most obvious feature of an aphid is the pair of cornicles, which produce wax and pheromones for defense purposes. The cornicles are a pair of tubes that stick up from the upper side of the fifth, or sometimes the sixth, abdominal segment. In a few species of aphid, however, the cornicles appear as rings on the surface of the abdomen or may be missing altogether.

Sugar Manufacturers

Aphids feed by inserting their rostrum into the phloem tubes of their host plants. The phloem is a tissue in the plant that is used for transportation of the products of photosynthesis. As a result, it is rich in nutrients, and the aphids grow quite rapidly. They take in more sugars and water than they need and as a consequence produce large quantities of honeydew. So much honeydew may be produced that, standing beneath a tree that is heavily infested with aphids, it can seem as if it is drizzling with rain. A few aphids are restricted to a single food plant or to one or two closely related species. Many change their food plants as the season goes alongs. The number of alternate plant species that they are capable of feeding on varies between species.

⊕ *Brachycaudus cardui from Europe lives on various thistle plants. In the group seen here the black individuals have been parasitized by a wasp and will die. The brown specimens are already dead, while the green ones are healthy.*

The most commonly seen aphids are those that rely on different species of plants at different times of the year. As a result, there are different generations of the aphid on different plants. However, things are not always so simple. A number of aphid species may alternate between three different hosts at different times of the season, and the number of plant hosts on which a single generation lives can also vary considerably.

An Aphid's Life

The bean aphid, *Aphis fabae*, which occurs in much of North America and Europe, is a good example of such host switching. At the end of the winter the bean aphid (along with many other species) exists only as eggs that have spent the harshest months of the year attached to a woody host plant. As temperatures rise in the spring, sap begins to rise in these plants, and the aphid eggs hatch. From them emerge only wingless females, which feed on the sap.

The females are able to produce offspring—all wingless females—without having mated, a phenomenon known as parthenogenesis. Further generations of wingless females may then appear, again by parthenogenesis, until the sap in the host plant becomes less nutritious. That is the signal for the wingless females to produce a generation of winged

↑ *Aphids mating.*
Reproduction without
mating—known as
parthenogenesis—is
common in aphids.

females, which then fly off to seek a secondary host. In the case of *A. fabae* a common host is field or broad beans, giving them their common name. On the new host plant the winged females produce a generation of wingless females. They in turn produce further generations of wingless females until the host plant begins to run out of supplies of food. Once again, this is the signal for more winged females to appear, which then fly on to more secondary host plants where the whole fascinating cycle continues.

As the end of summer approaches, the females on the secondary host plants start giving birth to winged females, which fly back to the woody primary host plants. In them the sap is now flowing well again and providing a good supply of food. A generation of wingless, egg-producing females is now born. In the meantime those females remaining on the secondary host plants are giving birth to winged males, which fly to the woody primary host plants, where they mate with the egg-producing females. Each of the females then lays four to six eggs on the bark of the primary host. The eggs then overwinter, and the whole cycle is repeated the following year.

Root Feeders and Gall Formers

Some aphids are seldom encountered, since they feed on the roots of their host plants, or they form plant galls. The colony remains mostly hidden inside the gall. The European cherry aphid, *Myzus cerasi*, for example, feeds from the underside of cherry leaves, causing the leaves to roll up and form a protective chamber around the insects. *Eriosoma* species, which are widespread on elms in the Northern Hemisphere, form galls by rolling the leaves of the host plants.

Eriosoma yangi, a Japanese species, however, goes about things in a more bizarre

⊖ *Adults and nymphs of the bean aphid,* Aphis fabae, *feed in large numbers on the flowering shoot of a string bean plant.*

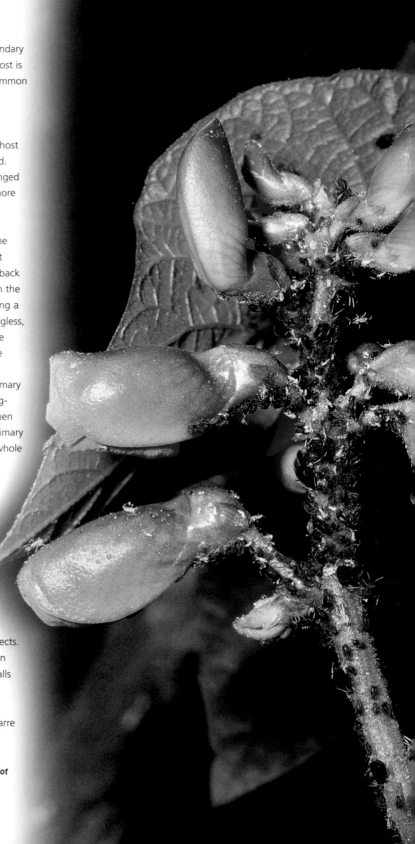

way. Individual females feed on young elm leaves until they molt into the third instar. The *E. yangi* nymph is apparently unable to induce galls by itself and so seeks out those created by other *Eriosoma* species aphids. The *E. yangi* nymph enters the gall, kills its real owner, and takes possession of the gall. Occasionally the original owner is not killed, and the two different species live together in the gall, feeding and producing live young, which remain clustered around their own mother.

"Superglue"

Being tiny and very soft-bodied, aphids have many enemies. At first glance they appear to have no defenses. This, however, is not the case. Birds do not normally feed on aphids unless they are very hungry, since aphids are not a particularly rich source of food for large animals. They do, however, provide an acceptable meal for other insects, including ladybugs and their larvae, lacewing larvae, and the larvae of a number of hover fly species. Another group of enemies is the parasitic wasps—tiny wasps that lay their egg onto an aphid, which then itself becomes the food for their larva to live on. Examination of any aphid colony will usually reveal the fruit of the parasitic wasps' labors: rather bloated, motionless aphids, normally an unusual color, which are slowly being devoured from the inside by the wasp larva.

The aphids defend themselves against such unwanted attentions by using the two cornicles on the abdomen. When the aphid is disturbed, perhaps by a tiny parasitic wasp landing on it,

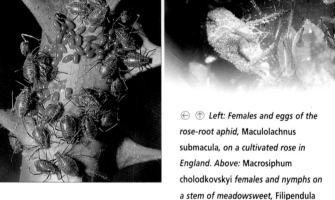

Left: Females and eggs of the rose-root aphid, *Maculolachnus submacula*, on a cultivated rose in England. Above: *Macrosiphum cholodkovskyi* females and nymphs on a stem of meadowsweet, *Filipendula ulmaria*, in an English hedgerow. The female at the top left is giving birth to a young one parthenogenetically.

the bug secretes a tiny drop of a waxy substance from each cornicle. It is a bit like superglue, since when the wax comes into contact with any part of the wasp, it immediately sets solid, gluing the attacker to its victim. As a result, both the aphid and its attacker will eventually die.

Such a strategy might seem like suicide for the aphid; but since nearly all the aphids in a group are sisters, one sacrificing her life is worthwhile for the group as a whole. A single parasitic wasp, hover fly larva, or ladybug could kill a much larger number of aphids if allowed to go free. Alarm pheromones are also secreted by the cornicles, which spread through the colony, warning other aphids that they are in danger of attack.

Soldier Aphids

Although the presence of soldier castes in ants and termites has been known for more than 200 years, it is only as recently as 1977 that some aphids were also found to have a soldier caste. Since then research has indicated that soldiers have appeared independently at least four times in different lines of aphid. The first report was of soldiers of the woolly aphid, *Colophina clematis*, from Japan. The soldiers, which are sterile first instar nymphs, attack predatory insects and their eggs by jabbing at them with their sharp stylets. They have also been observed to attack aphids of different species living on the same plant, perhaps in an attempt to reduce competition for space.

Other species of aphids produce soldiers complete with structural modifications for the job. An Asian bamboo-feeding species, *Pseudoregma alexanderi*, has first instar soldiers that resemble pseudoscorpions. Each soldier has enlarged grasping front legs and a pair of sharp horns on the front of the head. Predators, such as lacewing larvae, are attacked by groups of soldiers, which pierce them with their horns. The result is that the larva is either completely immobilized where it stands or falls to the ground with the soldiers still attached to it.

Investigations in Europe into the activities of the soldiers of *Pemphigus spyrothecae*, which make galls on the leaf stalks of the black poplar, *Populus nigra*, revealed that they were able to chase off ladybug larvae, young hover fly larvae, and the early instars of the flower bug, *Anthocoris nemoralis*. The aphids always lose a few soldiers in the attack. But considering that a flower bug nymph can kill off the whole aphid colony, the loss of a few soldiers is worth the sacrifice.

Sugar Cravings

Ants are known to "milk" aphids for their honeydew. There is some evidence to indicate

ⓔ *A ladybug beetle adult (Coccinellidae) feeds on an aphid in Transvaal, South Africa. Ladybugs and their larvae are important predators of aphids.*

Aphid Pests

Aphids include some of the worst pests of human crops in the temperate zones of the world. The list of pest aphids is long, and the list of plant species attacked almost endless. The bean aphid, *Aphis fabae*, for example, uses as secondary hosts not just members of the pea and bean family but also a variety of cultivated ornamental plants as well. A number of different species of aphid attack cereals such as wheat and barley wherever they are grown. Today the only way to control their numbers is by using insecticides.

In the United States rosy apple aphids, *Dysaphis plantaginea*, are a major pest of fruit orchards. They cause the apple tree leaves to curl up and the fruit to become misshapen and to ripen before it is fully developed. The green apple aphid, *Aphis pomi*, which was probably introduced into North America when settlers imported the first apple trees from Europe, is also a widespread orchard pest, damaging the soft young growth of apple trees and their ability to produce fruit.

Aphid pests continue to spread as people introduce new crops in new areas. Soybean has been an important crop in North America for some time, but it was only in 2000 that one of its major pests, the soybean aphid, *Aphis glycines*, a native of China, Japan, and Southeast Asia, was first discovered here. It was so widespread and present in such numbers on the soybean that it had obviously arrived some years previously and had become established without being noticed. How far it will spread in its new habitat and how damaging it will be in the long run is yet to be learned. Sadly, over recent years the aphid has also made its way into Australia, where soybean is now grown in some quantities.

that the ants are in fact attracted to the sugar in the honeydew. Investigation of three *Chaitophorus* aphid species from Europe revealed that two of the three species produced honeydew containing the sugar melezitose, much favored by ants. The two sugar producers are regularly visited by ants, but the nonproducer is not.

ⓣ *A cabbage aphid female,* Brevicoryne brassicae, *and the offspring that she has produced by parthenogenesis, pictured in California.*

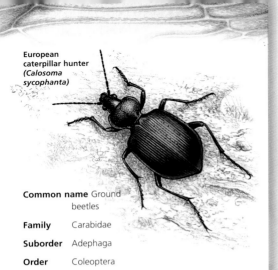

European caterpillar hunter (*Calosoma sycophanta*)

Common name Ground beetles

Family Carabidae

Suborder Adephaga

Order Coleoptera

Number of species About 25,000 (over 3,000 U.S.)

Size From about 0.1 in (3 mm) to 2.4 in (6 cm)

Key features Body mostly black, shiny, and metallic, often with a flush of purple or green iridescence over the ground color; so variable that no one characteristic is "typical"; a small number of brightly colored species; legs mostly long; jaws usually quite prominent; elytra usually with numerous furrows running lengthwise, often also pitted; antennae usually threadlike (sometimes beadlike); eyes usually large; often wingless

Habits Most are nocturnal; during the day usually found under stones, fallen logs, or among moss and fallen leaves, emerging at night to hunt for food

Breeding Mating not usually preceded by any kind of courtship; eggs mostly laid in the ground, sometimes in a special "nest"; adults often relatively long-lived, often 2–3 years, sometimes even 4 years

Diet Many species are predators of worms, snails, caterpillars, and other insects; a few species feed on seeds, fungi, pollen, and other vegetable matter; scavenging for dead insects probably common; larvae may be parasitic on other insect larvae

Habitat Common in gardens and woodlands, less so in more open habitats; many species on the seashore; several eyeless species in caves

Distribution Widespread around the world, except in the polar regions and the driest deserts

⊕ *The European caterpillar hunter,* Calosoma sycophanta, *lives in gardens and woods. It has been introduced to parts of North America. Length up to 2 inches (5 cm).*

Ground Beetles Carabidae

A shiny black ground beetle running across the backyard may well be the first beetle that most people encounter as children.

ALTHOUGH MANY GROUND beetles give a first impression of being just plain black, a closer look will reveal that in many species there is a beautiful flush of purple, green, bronze, red, or blue iridescence—sometimes even a mixture of several colors. Ground beetles are closely related to tiger beetles, which are often included in the family Carabidae.

Night Hunters

Most ground beetles are nocturnal hunters, although a few are mainly found by day. Some of the nocturnal species will also hunt by day if the conditions are right, such as in damp, warm, thundery weather when prey is likely to be active. Ground beetles are restless hunters, constantly on the run as they scout around for food. They search every likely place where prey could be hidden, poking their heads into nooks and crannies and using their sensitive palps to detect the presence of a possible meal.

The fiery searcher, *Calosoma scrutator* from North America, is often called the caterpillar hunter. Its common name sums up its main diet; and like other members of its genus, it may be useful in controlling pest caterpillars. That is partly because, unlike many other ground beetles, both adults and larvae will climb trees in search of prey. The European ground beetle or caterpillar hunter, *Calosoma sycophanta*, was bred and released in large numbers into the wild in North America. This was in an effort to control the catastrophically destructive caterpillars of the gypsy moth, *Lymantria dispar*, which had been accidentally introduced from Europe. In some ground beetles the front legs are broadened and used for digging through the ground in pursuit of subterranean prey.

them by making a lightning strike downward with its antennae. The antennae have a special "cage" of hairs that ensnare the springtails before they can jump to safety.

Liquid Lunch

Not all ground beetles use their large jaws to tear their prey to pieces before swallowing it. Instead, many adults and most larvae practice external digestion, during which digestive fluids flow down special grooves in their jaws and onto the prey. The victim is quickly dissolved into a semiliquid state and then pumped up into the stomach. In the snail-eating ground beetles (tribe Cychrini) the long, narrow head is inserted into the opening of the snail's shell. The inner surfaces of the beetle's mandibles are armed with many small teeth to hold onto the slippery prey. The snail is torn apart, dissolved, and eaten from its shell like soup from a can. By carrying a large supply of air beneath its elytra, the beetle avoids being smothered in the copious amounts of slime released by the snail. Many ground beetles are beneficial in gardens because they eat slugs despite their

Two species of ground beetles from Arizona have adopted a rather unusual and highly specialized diet. They follow the scent trails laid down by raiding columns of army ants. When a beetle meets one of the ants carrying an item of insect booty back to the nest, the ant drops it in alarm, and the beetle promptly picks it up and eats it. If the ant fails to deliver, the beetle will "mug" it, forcing it to give up its prize. The beetles also raid the nests of the ants and gorge on their larvae to such an extent that the beetles' abdomens become noticeably swollen. One European species, *Loricera pilicornis*, specializes in catching springtails (small wingless insects), trapping

⊕ *The fiery searcher,* Calosoma scrutator *from the United States, is a typical shiny, long-legged ground beetle. It is also called the caterpillar hunter.*

⊕ *Some species of ground beetle tear their prey apart.* Pterostichus madidus *from Europe is using its large jaws to rip open the nutritious thorax of a day-flying clearwing moth (Sesiidae). Other ground beetles practice external digestion.*

protective slime, which most other predators will avoid. In the British Isles ground beetles are one of the few predators willing to tackle the introduced New Zealand flatworm, which has become a pest, killing the native earthworms.

Some of the smaller ground beetles feed on seeds. The seedcorn beetle, *Stenolophus lecontei*, is a pest in the United States, where it feeds on germinating seeds. Seed eaters have short, broad, blunt jaws that break up the seeds and grind them into an easily swallowed mush.

Reproductive Habits

As in many beetles, most ground beetle males simply jump onto the back of a female without carrying out any courtship in advance. However, the *Cychrus* snail-eating beetles produce a sound—presumably sexual in purpose—through stridulation (rubbing the tip of the abdomen against the edge of the elytra.) Once

Chemical Weapons

The most famous of the ground beetles are the *Brachinus* bombardier beetles, which employ an unusual explosive means of driving off their enemies. By mixing various chemicals in a special chamber in the abdomen, the beetles can discharge from the tip of the body a sudden blast of extremely hot and unpleasant spray. It emerges with an audible "pop" and a puff of smoke. The beetle can fire off its spray up to 20 times in rapid succession before running out of "fuel." The beetle can direct its spray with great accuracy, aiming straight at the target. Ants are quickly disabled and take several minutes to recover. A praying mantis that is blasted in the face will instantly drop the beetle and start cleaning off the offensive chemicals.

Bombardier beetles deter would-be assailants by blasting them with a spray of boiling hot, noxious chemicals.

on the female's back, the male tries to persuade the female to mate, often by kicking the sides of her abdomen repeatedly with his back legs. Special adhesive hairs on the undersides of his feet help him stay in place. The males are often very insistent and will follow females for hours trying to mount them and generally making a nuisance of themselves. Because of such over-pushy behavior, some females have evolved an effective method for getting rid of their stalkers. The female of *Pterostichus leucoblandus* from the United States can hit the male right in his face with a squirt of a stop-dead spray from the tip of her abdomen. The spray knocks him into a stupefied state so that he cannot move for an hour or two, leaving the female plenty of time to make a getaway. Such measures would only be used if the female had already mated or was not yet ready to mate.

Eggs are generally laid right into the ground, although some species make rather more elaborate arrangements, constructing nests of mud, leaves, or twigs. *Percus navaricus* from Europe molds a bowl of soil with her jaws, lifts it onto the tip of her abdomen, and lays an egg in it. She then settles it on the ground and covers it with a lid of earth. The North American *Tecnophilus croceicollis* lays each egg in a ball of soil particles suspended from

↑ **Someticus bohemani** *from Africa's Namib Desert inhabits one of the most arid regions in which ground beetles are found. It hunts on rocky slopes in full sunlight.*

a twig by a silklike strand. In a small number of species the female stays with her eggs inside a special brood chamber, excavated beneath a log or stone or in soft, rotten wood. She stays there for about three weeks, not feeding and keeping her precious eggs free of molds that would spoil them. In *Carterus calydonius* from Europe the mother constructs a network of tunnels and brood cells below ground, laying an egg in each cell. There is just one entrance, where she stands guard, feeding both herself and her developing babies on a stockpile of seeds that she has assembled. In *Pseudomorpha*, which inhabit ants' nests in Arizona, the eggs hatch immediately after being laid. They have developed fully while still within the mother—a phenomenon known as ovoviviparity.

Where Ground Beetles Live

Many species live in gardens, but woodlands have the largest number of species. Some species live only in marshes, including coastal salt marshes, a rather hostile environment in which the Carabidae is the major beetle family. Species that live at the top of sandy beaches on the coast dig into the damp sand when the tide comes in and remain buried under the water until the tide recedes. Ground beetles are also among the highest living of any insects. Certain wingless kinds are found on the edge of glaciers at altitudes of up to 18,000 feet (5,500 m). At the opposite extreme ground beetles are also particularly well represented among the insects living deep inside caves, where many blind species are found.

← *The male of this six-spotted saber-toothed ground beetle,* Anthia hexasticta *from Kenya, is trying to persuade a female to mate by nibbling her thorax and kicking her sides with his back legs.*

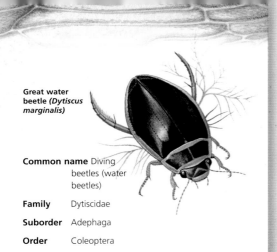

Great water beetle (*Dytiscus marginalis*)

Common name Diving beetles (water beetles)

Family Dytiscidae

Suborder Adephaga

Order Coleoptera

Number of species About 3,000 (about 475 U.S.)

Size Adults 0.06 in (1.5 mm) to 1.8 in (4.5 cm); larvae up to 2.7 in (7 cm)

Key features Adults mostly blackish or brownish with a streamlined elongate-oval shape, convex both at the top and on the underside; hind legs flattened as paddles and fringed with hairs; antennae quite long and threadlike; larvae long and narrow with conspicuous curved jaws

Habits Aquatic beetles that come to the surface to breathe air; both adults and larvae actively hunt prey in daytime; most adults can fly and will migrate in order to find new habitats

Breeding Mating takes place underwater; eggs are attached to underwater plants or laid inside them; larvae may pupate underwater or move to the shore to do so; in areas subject to drought both larvae and adults can survive dry periods by burrowing into mud

Diet Tadpoles, adult frogs, small fish, shrimp, worms, leeches, snails, and water mites; insects such as dragonfly and damselfly larvae; also cannibalistic

Habitat Streams, roadside ditches, ponds, lakes, and pools (including those that are stagnant or temporary); also in hot-water springs and salty pools on the coast

Distribution Worldwide except in the coldest or driest areas

↑ *The great water beetle,* Dytiscus marginalis, *is found in European ponds and still water with plenty of vegetation. It is a voracious predator, including frogs, newts, and small fish in its diet. Length up to 1.4 inches (3.5 cm).*

Diving Beetles

Dytiscidae

Aquatic diving beetles are ruthless predators and excellent swimmers. Yet when in flight, they are not easily able to distinguish water and sometimes dive onto the nearest shiny surface, having mistaken it for a pond or lake.

DIVING BEETLES ARE PROBABLY the most ferocious killers among the aquatic insects. They will not hesitate to tackle prey much larger than themselves, nor will they shy away from those equipped with formidable weaponry, such as dragonfly nymphs. Water beetle larvae will attack almost anything of a suitable size that moves, earning themselves the deserved name of water tigers.

Adults are particularly good swimmers, having shiny streamlined bodies that slip easily through the water, propelled by powerful thrusts of their broad, paddlelike hind legs. The legs have wide fringes of hairs, which improve their function as flippers. As in frogs, the legs kick in unison when swimming hard. The larvae are much longer and narrower than the adults and are slower swimmers, but can move in a series of rapid somersaults by instantly contracting the muscles of the abdomen.

Air Supply

Adults spend most of their time underwater, but return to the surface at intervals to breathe. Keeping the head downward, they stick the tip of the abdomen out of the water and take in a fresh supply of air. The air may be stored beneath the elytra or (in smaller species) held as a bubble at the tip of the body, anchored in place by specially shaped ridges.

The adults fly well and will leave the water to migrate to a fresh habitat, often leaving at night, when they may be attracted in great

↑ *With its prey of a goldfish speared on its long, sharp jaws a great water beetle,* Dytiscus marginalis, *shows the broad, shiny domelike back typical of the family.*

numbers to artificial lights. Their movements on land are awkward; and when migrating, they will often try to plunge straight into the nearest suitable body of water. They sometimes surprise people by bouncing noisily off the roofs of cars, having mistaken them (or sometimes shiny roads or greenhouses) for the surface of a pond.

Both adults and larvae are predators and take the same kind of food, which consists of anything from mosquito larvae to tadpoles or small fish. In the larvae the jaws are conspicuously long and curved. In some species they act as fangs, having hollow centers down which digestive fluids can be injected into the body of the prey. The resulting liquid can then be sucked out.

Mating takes place underwater. Broad adhesive pads on the male's front legs help him stay in place on the female's shiny, domed, and slippery back. The eggs are attached to aquatic plants. In some species the mature larvae construct a special pupation chamber in the mud at the bottom of the pond; others leave the water and pupate in moist earth nearby.

Adult diving beetles can live three years or more; some species remain active under the ice during the winter.

Chemical Defenses

Adult *Dytiscus* large diving beetles use chemical warfare to protect themselves from attack by fish and other predators. A milky secretion from glands on the thorax can quickly transform a large, fierce predator such as a pike into a helpless zombie. The adult beetles also smear their bodies with other glandular secretions. The fluids are known to prevent the growth of harmful microorganisms.

The larva of Dytiscus marginalis *has a long, slender body. Moving more slowly in the water than the adult beetle, it uses its "fangs" to feed on prey as it goes along.*

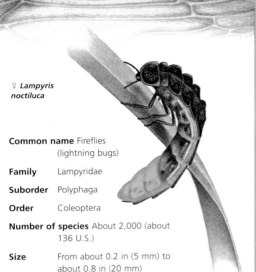

♀ *Lampyris*
noctiluca

Common name Fireflies
(lightning bugs)

Family Lampyridae

Suborder Polyphaga

Order Coleoptera

Number of species About 2,000 (about
136 U.S.)

Size From about 0.2 in (5 mm) to
about 0.8 in (20 mm)

Key features Body drab brown or blackish; when viewed
from above, head is more or less concealed
beneath the pronotum, which is also very
broad (almost as broad as the elytra); body
soft and flattened with sides generally
parallel; females often with short wings or
wingless and larvalike (larviform); antennae
threadlike or often sawtoothed; luminous
organ usually present on tip of abdomen

Habits All larvae and most adults are luminescent;
light production takes place only during the
night; by day the adults rest on foliage and
are inconspicuous

Breeding Males fly around flashing their lights at night;
the perched females reply with their own
lights, acting as a beacon to which the males
can easily fly for mating; some species are not
luminescent or only weakly so and are active
in daytime

Diet The adults of most species apparently do not
feed; females of some species attract and
feed on males of unrelated species; the larvae
are carnivorous, feeding on insect larvae,
mites, snails, and slugs

Habitat Mainly in forests; also in grasslands, gardens,
riversides, and swamps

Distribution Worldwide, avoiding very cold or dry areas;
most abundant in the tropics

⊕ *The wingless, larvalike female of the firefly Lampyris*
noctiluca has light-producing organs that are carried in her
last three abdominal segments. This European species of
grassland firefly reaches 0.6 inches (15 mm) in length.

Fireflies

Lampyridae

*In tropical regions the evening sky is
often alight with the luminous glow of
fireflies. The insects use their internal
flashlights to attract the opposite sex,
sometimes with fatal results.*

THE FLASHING GREENISH OR yellowish light of fireflies
shines with an intensity that belies the small size
of the insect producing it. Although tropical rain
forest is the richest habitat for fireflies, North
America is also comparatively rich in species.

Drawn to the Light

In most species of fireflies the bright light
produced from the luminous organ at the tip of
the abdomen is devoted solely to the business
of attracting a mate. The luminescence is
generated through a highly efficient
biochemical process, which succeeds in
producing an intense illumination, but avoids
creating any wasteful heat as a by-product.
Basically, a protein called luciferin reacts with an
enzyme, luciferase, causing the protein to
become luminous—simple yet effective.

Fireflies use their light in two ways. First,
females sit on the ground or on leaves and
shine a constant beacon of light toward which
the males fly. Females generally only have a
single light situated on the last two or three
segments of the abdomen. However, the
strange, wormlike *Phrixothrix tiemannii* from
South America has 11 pairs of greenish lights
set along the top of the abdomen, plus a
reddish glowing zone on the head. Its local
name is the railway worm.

Second, the males themselves flash their
lights while flying around. Each male fires off
his lights in a sequence that is different for
every species. When a blacked-out female
perched down below spots the correct
sequence for her own species, she switches on
her own lights in reply, also using a species-
specific code. In addition to using differently

→ *The common eastern
firefly,* Cotinus pyralis, *is
the most familiar firefly
over the eastern half of
the United States. Its
rather long, narrow build
is typical of most fireflies
throughout the world.*

coded light flashes,
the males also fly at
different heights above
the ground, keeping strictly to
their particular height level
according to species. In males that fly around
looking for females the eyes have a high
number of facets. They are extremely large,
almost meeting on top of the head so that they
give binocular vision. Sometimes it is the males
who sit with the signal lamp and attract flying
females. In the tropics of Southeast Asia the
males of certain fireflies gather in huge
numbers (often in millions) in riverside trees.
Here they flash their lights in unison, producing
an effect like a huge lamp being switched on
and off by some unseen hand.

Mated females lay their eggs (usually also
luminous) in the ground or among rotting
wood or debris. Most larvae are luminescent.

*➔ In some male
fireflies the antennae
are developed into
prominent featherlike
structures. This is a
Calyptocephalus
gratiosus male from
the tropical rain forests
of Peru.*

Fatal Attraction

Firefly larvae crawl around
on the ground, feeding on
insects and worms. They will
also follow slime trails in order
to track down slugs and snails to
feed on. They digest prey
externally, secreting fluids onto the
prey, which is then dissolved into a
soup. *Luciola* larvae from Asia live
underwater and are the only examples of
luminous aquatic insects. Most adult fireflies do
not feed at all, but in North America certain
kinds do and have evolved a highly original
method of securing a meal. Female *Photuris*
"pretend" to be females of other species by
giving the expected answer to the flashes from
Photinus males. When the male responds by
homing in, he flies straight into the female's
waiting grasp and is eaten.

Thanasimus formicarius

Common name Checkered beetles

Family　Cleridae

Suborder　Polyphaga

Order　Coleoptera

Number of species About 4,000 (about 260 U.S.)

Size　From about 0.1 in (3 mm) to about 0.6 in (15 mm)

Key features Mainly brightly colored beetles, often with checkered elytra; body usually fairly long and narrow, covered with bristly hairs; head prominent, usually as wide or wider than the pronotum, which is much narrower than the elytra; eyes bulging; antennae varied, usually clubbed; also threadlike or sawtoothed

Habits　Adults active in daytime, often sitting for long periods on flowers; usually seen singly; larvae mainly live in the galleries of bark beetles or in the nests of bees and wasps

Breeding　Mating probably mainly takes place soon after the female has emerged from her pupa; eggs are laid on flowers, in the ground, on trees inhabited by bark beetles, and in plant galls

Diet　Adults often feed on nectar and pollen, but also prey on insects such as caterpillars and adult bark beetles; larvae eat bark beetle larvae, the grubs of bees and wasps, or grasshopper egg pods; a handful of species eat stored food products

Habitat　Mainly in woodlands; also in meadows, deserts, mountains, gardens, and houses

Distribution Worldwide, but prefer warmer regions; most of the U.S. species occur in the Southwest

⊕ **The checkered beetle Thanasimus formicarius from Europe lives on tree trunks, the larvae feeding on bark beetles. Length up to 0.4 inches (10 mm).**

Checkered Beetles

Cleridae

Adult checkered beetles are among the most colorful of all beetles. However, they are never common, which adds to the pleasure of chancing on one lounging on a flower or clinging to the bark of a dead tree.

CHECKERED BEETLES ARE ABUNDANTLY hairy with a bright checkered pattern not found on any other beetles. However, some of the smaller, drabber species could easily be confused with members of other families, such as soldier beetles. A number of the scarlet-and-black species of *Trichodes* in Europe (known as bee-wolf beetles) are among the most boldly colored members of the family. It is possible that the beetles are attempting to mimic poisonous burnet moths (Zygaenidae) with whom they share similar markings. Most bee-wolves are themselves highly distasteful to a range of predators, and their colors serve a "warning" function.

Mating and Feasting

Mating habits are only known for a few species. The first action of a newly emerged female of the California checkered beetle, *Aulicus terrestris*, is to find and kill a caterpillar. As she gets busy with her meal, a male will arrive, and they quickly mate without causing the female a moment's pause in her feeding. Even if several more males show up and fight on her back about who is going to be her partner, she will not take a break from her meal (her abdomen swelling visibly all the time as she stuffs herself nonstop). Once she is alone again, she will lay her eggs one at a time in soil that contains the egg pods of grasshoppers; the egg pods will provide the food for her larvae.

Many other species lay their eggs on the bark of trees infected by bark-feeding or wood-boring beetles, whose larvae provide a nutritious source of food. As a result, checkered

⊕ **The European bee-wolf beetle, Trichodes apiarius, is most often seen feeding singly on flowers. Its larvae develop inside the nests of bees.**

beetles often act as an important control on the numbers of harmful bark beetles and other species that destroy living timber. In the *Cymatodera* slender checkered beetles, found throughout North America, the females lay their eggs next to gall-wasp eggs on the leaves of oaks and other trees. The beetle eggs delay their hatching until a gall (a swelling of plant tissue) has developed from the wasp eggs. The beetle larvae then hatch and break into the gall, where they live as parasites on the wasp larvae within, eventually killing them.

Hitching a Ride

A number of the larger species, such as the European bee-wolf beetle, *Trichodes apiarius*, and the rather similar red-blue checkered beetle, *Trichodes nutalli* from the United States, lay their eggs singly on flowers. Sooner or later a bee or wasp will happen along, and the beetle larva jumps on board. It hitches a ride back to the wasp's nest, where it will feed on the brood. Females of the tiny red-legged ham beetle, *Necrobia rufipes*, which is found worldwide, lay their eggs in stored foods derived from animals, such as ham or cheese. In Europe *Opilo domesticus* mainly lives in houses, where its larvae do a good job attacking highly destructive woodworm beetles (Anobiidae).

↑ Trichodes ornatus bonnevillensis *from the United States shows to perfection the bright warning colors and rather bristly body of most checkered beetles. Note the very wide head.*

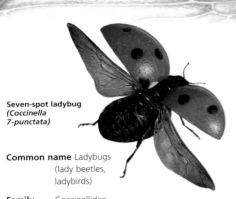

Seven-spot ladybug
(Coccinella 7-punctata)

Common name Ladybugs
(lady beetles,
ladybirds)

Family Coccinellidae

Suborder Polyphaga

Order Coleoptera

Number of species About 4,500 (about 400 U.S.)

Size From about 0.04 in (1 mm) to about 0.4 in
(10 mm)

Key features Mainly brightly colored red or yellow,
usually spotted or blotched with black;
distinctive oval or almost round body,
noticeably dome shaped on top and flattened
beneath; antennae short and weakly clubbed;
head hardly visible from above

Habits Mainly active during the day on plants, where
adults and larvae of many species are
beneficial in eating pests; some species
hibernate in huge swarms

Breeding Males usually mate without any courtship;
males guard females in some species; females
of predatory species lay batches of eggs near
aphids; larvae highly mobile and actively
move around in quest for prey; pupa (with no
appendages visible) attached by rear end to
some form of support

Diet Many species feed on aphids; others prefer
scale insects, mealybugs, mites, and other
soft-bodied invertebrates and their eggs;
some species are vegetarian and may damage
crops; others graze on molds growing on
leaves

Habitat Gardens, fields, orchards, hedgerows, forests,
and mountainsides; rarely in deserts

Distribution Worldwide except in the driest and coldest
regions; commonest in temperate countries

⊕ *A seven-spot ladybug, Coccinella 7-punctata, in flight
revealing its true wings under its hardened and colorful
elytra. Length up to 0.3 inches (8 mm).*

Ladybugs   Coccinellidae

*Ladybugs are among the few insects that are
almost universally recognizable. Indeed,
most people have positive feelings about
these colorful little insects and give
them special names.*

THE DEGREE OF POPULARITY enjoyed by ladybugs
must surely be connected with the helping
hand these voracious predators give us in
controlling aphid pests on vital crops. As long
ago as the Middle Ages in Europe, ladybugs
were credited with wiping out serious
infestations of pests on grapevines. In thanks
and blessing, the name ladybugs was coined for
them, dedicated to "Our Lady." Most languages
have a special name for ladybugs: "God's little
thief," "God's lamb," and "sun calf" being just
a few such distinctions.

In Britain the usual name for these little
insects is ladybirds, but in the United States they
are known as ladybugs. However, they are not
actually true bugs, which are members of the
order Hemiptera. Unfortunately, not all species
are beneficial, and in some parts of the world
vegetarian ladybugs are quite a nuisance, eating
valuable crops themselves rather than
protecting them from pests.

Variation in Patterns

Although the pattern in many ladybugs is quite
constant, in others it is so variable that it is
difficult to believe they are a single species. A
familiar species showing such variation is the
two-spotted ladybug, *Adalia 2-punctata*. It is
the most successful and widespread ladybug,
common in Europe, Asia, and North America,
and the species most likely to be found in
gardens. *Adalia 2-punctata* commonly occurs in
two forms; the most frequent has red elytra
with two black spots, but almost as common is
a form with black elytra and four red spots. The
two forms often mingle together and are
frequently seen mating. Other variations occur,

⊕ *One of the
most common color
combinations in ladybugs
is orange with black
spots. This is the nine-
spot ladybug, Coccinella
9-notata, from the
United States.*

⊕⊕ *A range of color
and pattern variations is
seen in ladybugs, even
within a single species.
All these ladybugs are
Adalia 10-punctata from
England, but the
background color and
number of spots varies
from individual to
individual.*

mainly involving a steadily increasing number of black spots in the red forms, but they tend to be rarer.

Color variation is even less straightforward in the European 10-spot ladybug, *Adalia 10-punctata*. In this hopelessly confusing, yet common, species more than 80 different color forms have been described. A common form has black elytra with two red shoulder blotches; an alternative form is black with five large yellow spots; a third is yellow, with anything from two to eight black spots, while a fourth is pinkish-orange, with as many as 12 black spots of variable size. Few variations actually have the 10 spots suggested by the common name; but fortunately for the naturalist trying to make a positive identification, 10-spotted forms tend to far outnumber the others in most situations.

Anything Goes

As with many beetles, male ladybugs are not too choosy in their selection of a partner and will try to couple with any shiny, domed object that seems to resemble a suitable female. Since a number of leaf beetles (Chrysomelidae) fit that profile perfectly, both males and females may be subject to amorous approaches by male ladybugs. Even weevils that are not remotely like a female ladybug beetle may be mounted. Staying in place on the female's shiny, domed carapace is not easy, but the male's broad feet stop him from slipping off.

Cradle Snatchers

Males of the Australian *Leptothea galbula* choose a sexual partner unusually early—while the female is still in the pupal stage. The male is able to identify the sex of a pupa by stroking it with the sensory organs on his antennae and palps. If the pupa is female, he climbs on top. If the pupa is a long way from hatching, it will resist being touched and will respond by flipping upward to throw off the intruder. Pupae that are closer to emergence will allow

⊕ *Wriggling their way free of their eggs, these two-spot ladybug (Adalia 2-punctata) larvae need not move far to start feeding on the aphids that surround them.*

Pest Controllers

Ladybugs were the first insects to be used as a form of biological control against a pest insect. The first (and highly successful) venture involved the introduction of the *Vedalia* beetle, *Rodalia cardinalis*, from Australia. It was pitted against the cottony cushion scale, *Icerya purchasi*. The cottony cushion scale had been accidentally imported to the United States from Australia years earlier and was ravaging California's citrus orchards, threatening the survival of the entire citrus industry. The first *Vedalia* beetles were released in 1888. More releases soon followed, and within two years they had brought the problem under control. Introductions of Australian ladybugs to control Australian mealybugs and black scale in California have also been successful. The principle of introducing an enemy from the original native home of an introduced pest has remained the cornerstone of biological control ever since. However, disasters have occurred through unwise introductions: It seems that lessons were not learned when the European seven-spot ladybug was introduced into North America to control aphids that were not being held in check by the native ladybugs. Unfortunately, the foreigners have been too successful and are now outnumbering the natives.

the male to retain his perch on top for anything up to four days. During his stay he will usually be involved in a series of fights with other males trying to steal his place. The duels become more frequent and intense the nearer the female is to emerging. The event seems to be sensed by most of the males in the vicinity, who crowd excitedly around the pupa and its male attendant. He will desperately try to climb onto the female's back the moment she emerges. At the same time, he attempts to fend off the barrage of headbutts, jostling, and biting that rain down on him from his rivals. He may finally manage to mate with his "bride" an hour or so later, once she has dried her wings and is ready to accept him.

Fertilized females of predatory species seek out colonies of aphids near which to lay their

Ladybugs, especially the larvae, have no problems simply mowing their way through their massed ranks, leaving behind a litter of drained corpses. Newly hatched ladybug larvae ride on the backs of the larger aphids while they drain them dry.

Eating Each Other

In some of the larger ladybugs each larva will kill around 25 aphids per day, and an adult can devour over 50. Not surprisingly, a whole aphid colony can be wiped out in just a few days. The famished ladybug larvae will then be forced to wander off in search of fresh colonies. If they fail to find any, they will probably turn on each other as substitute food, and in hard times the smallest are eaten by the largest. In a real shortage of prey pollen and nectar from flowers seem to tide them over for a while. If really desperate, they will even bite human skin in search of a meal. During periods of drought adult ladybugs will drink from dew, raindrops, or from the flowering stems of thistles chewed off by wasps. They will also visit soft, juicy fruits such as blackberries.

At least two species of North American ladybugs are specialized predators on leaf beetle larvae. *Neoharmonia venusta* attacks both larvae and pupae of the willow leaf beetle, *Plagiodera versicolora*. The ladybugs are probably the only predators that are undeterred by the larvae's ability to discharge a volley of unpleasant defensive chemicals when molested. If ladybugs are not present, the leaf beetles soon reduce their host plant to shreds. In Australia the strange, flattened larva of *Scymnodes bellus* fattens itself on the larvae of ants living beneath the bark of eucalyptus trees.

Certain "rogue" ladybugs feed on crops. By far the worst offender is the Mexican bean beetle, *Epilachna varivestis*. The feeding depredations of adults and larvae will quickly reduce the leaves of crops such

eggs. Clusters of five to 50 yellow, spindle-shaped eggs are carefully packed in bundles, usually on the underside of a leaf near a throng of aphids. Depending on species and food supply, females can lay as many as 1,500 eggs over a life span of two to three months. The larvae hatch in just three to four days. They resemble rather spiky, miniature alligators with broad heads. Their first act is to eat their eggshells, after which they begin feasting on the aphids nearby. Ladybugs have some of the fastest-developing larvae within the Coleoptera, and they are fully grown in only a few days. They stop feeding a day or so before they pupate. Adults emerge quickly, often after only nine to 10 days, and are very pale at first. They take some time to gain their full coloration (up to several months in the red species).

Aphids are the chief prey of most ladybugs, both as adults and larvae. Being basically a packed lunch perched on six spindly legs, aphids can do little to resist when attacked.

During periods of drought adult ladybugs will resort to gleaning moisture from a variety of sources. Here a seven-spot ladybug, Coccinella 7-punctata, is feasting on a juicy blackberry.

as pole and lima beans to skeletons. If numbers are so great that they then run out of food, they will turn their attention to the pods and stems, ruining the whole crop. In the warmer parts of the United States up to four generations are born each year, so the beetle can be a major pest. In Europe the 24-spot ladybug, which bears the impressively long scientific name *Subcoccinella vigintiquator-punctata*, is a minor problem. The European yellow ladybug, *Halyzia sedecimguttata*, is one of the largest ladybugs, yet thrives on a diet of mildews grazed off leaf surfaces, often where aphid honeydew has fallen on them.

Warning Colors

Adults, larvae, and pupae of most coccinellids are clothed in warning colors, often wearing one of the two commonest "uniforms" of this type—either black and red or black and yellow. The colors warn that defensive secretions are available to be deployed against an attacker.

When severely handled, most ladybug adults and larvae react by forcing blood out through their leg joints, an action known as reflex bleeding that is also seen in other families of beetles. Most larvae can also leak blood through the membranes connecting each segment of the abdomen. The blood has an offensive odor and very bitter taste, and a quick

⬆ *When roughly handled, most ladybug larvae can force out droplets of their distasteful blood, as seen in these larval kidney-spot ladybirds,* Chilocoris renipustlatus, *from Europe.*

peck is enough to make most birds back off in disgust. The very common seven-spot ladybug, *Coccinella 7-punctata,* can be toxic to the nestlings of certain small birds. Yet strangely enough, many birds regularly feed ladybugs to their young. Spiders, robber flies, and various kinds of bugs also take them, although sometimes with little enthusiasm.

In addition to reflex bleeding, many ladybug larvae, especially those that feed on mealybugs, cover their backs with a dense secretion of defensive wax. It provides a protective shelter over the pupa when it is formed, concealing it from prying eyes. The pupae of most species are far from defenseless. Many can secrete distasteful chemicals from glandular hairs. Others use a gin-trap device consisting of jawlike openings between the body segments. By flipping suddenly upward, the pupa can open its "jaws," which then snap shut as the pupa drops downward again, trapping an ant's leg or antenna.

Migration and Hibernation

A few ladybugs are great migrants, the most famous of which is the convergent ladybug, *Hippodamia convergens*. Although the ladybug is found throughout North America, it is in the West that the great migrations of the species take place.

Vast swarms head up from the hot lowlands into the mountain canyons to hibernate during the winter. Here they form dense masses containing millions of individuals, covering rocks and leaves in a crimson carpet. At higher elevations they will be covered in snow during the worst of the winter. With the warmth of spring they awake and fly back to the lowlands below. Most ladybugs cluster together for hibernation, sometimes in the open, sometimes beneath bark or leaves, but no other species do so in such large numbers.

→ *The convergent ladybug,* Hippodamia convergens, *forms spectacular overwintering swarms in certain regularly used areas of high mountainside in the western United States.*

♂ European stag beetles (*Lucanus cervus*)

Common name Stag beetles (pinching bugs)

Family Lucanidae

Suborder Polyphaga

Order Coleoptera

Number of species About 1,250 (about 30 U.S.)

Size From about 0.3 in (8 mm) to about 3.5 in (9 cm)

Key features Body mainly large and black, brown, or reddish-brown; sometimes yellow or green, usually shiny; antennae distinctive, elbowed, with a comblike terminal club whose plates cannot be held together (unlike in scarabs); male jaws often large and antlerlike; many species flightless

Habits Adults mainly nocturnal, often flying to lights, sometimes in large numbers

Breeding Males use antlerlike jaws in fights to gain access to females; eggs are laid in cracks in the bark of dead trees or stumps; larvae of larger species take at least 5 years to pupate; it is then a further year before the adults emerge

Diet Adults feed on aphid honeydew and sap leaking from trees; a few feed on flowers; some species probably do not feed as adults; larvae eat wood inside trees

Habitat Mainly woodland; also in gardens, city lots, and city streets that are lined with old trees; absent from areas with no sizable trees

Distribution Worldwide, except in very dry or cold areas

⊕ *A pair of male European stag beetles,* Lucanus cervus, *spar for the attention of a female; the stronger one usually wins this pushing and shoving match. Length up to 3 inches (7.5 cm).*

Stag Beetles

Lucanidae

The huge, branching jaws of the males, like the antlers of a stag, give the family its common name. Because the jaws are held downward, the male can only succeed in walking by having exceptionally long legs.

IN THE UNITED STATES STAG beetles are often called pinching bugs, although the pinch from the large mandibles of the male is usually fairly feeble. Not all males have these prominent adornments. In the females the jaws are smaller, yet they are capable of inflicting a painful pinch. In *Chiasognathus granti* from Chile's temperate southern beech forests the male's jaws are spectacularly long, far exceeding body length.

Collectible Insects

Most species are reddish-brown or black, but there are also yellow examples. Many members of the subfamily Lampriminae from Australasia are a spectacular iridescent green, blue, violet, or bronze, making them the most beautiful of all stag beetles. Even in small-jawed species there should be little problem in identifying the family, since their elbowed antennae are distinctive. The scarabs (Scarabaeidae) have rather similar antennae, but the plates at their tips can be held together. Stag beetles are much sought after by collectors. Some species have declined in recent years due to habitat loss and other causes, so that conservation measures may be needed. The European stag beetle, *Lucanus cervus*, is now protected by law in most European countries.

Stag beetles are basically nocturnal insects. They are often only noticed when they visit lights at night, sometimes in large numbers. It is the males that are most active, flying in search of females. During the day stag beetles are most often found sitting on dead trees or logs. The adults of some species apparently do not feed at all. Others feed on aphid honeydew glistening on leaves or visit damaged trees for the sap running down their bark. The beetles

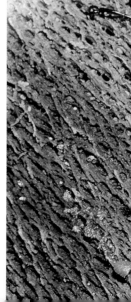

⊕ *With its well-developed antlerlike jaws held well to the fore, a male* Cyclommatus tarandus *poses on a fallen tree in the rain forest of Borneo. Note the elbowed antennae.*

are often attracted by the strong smell that usually permeates the air around sap runs as organisms of fermentation get to work on them. The amount of alcohol produced can have strange effects on the beetles, which gradually drink themselves into a state of such intoxication that they can no longer cling onto the trunk and fall off. Even on the ground they have difficulty in walking and cannot fully recover their faculties until they have "slept off" their overindulgence.

Clash of Jaws

Male stag beetles often seem to ignore each other if they meet. However, a fermenting sap run is worth fighting over, since it is likely to attract a female. Every male will try to monopolize the area so that he will be the only male present when a female arrives.

Jousting between males can be remarkably violent. With a clash of locked jaws the opponents try to wrestle each other off the trunk. The winning tactic is to use the mandibles to lift a rival off the tree so that his feet no longer grip and he falls to the ground.

Happy Families

Bessbugs (also called patent-leather beetles or betsy beetles) are closely related to stag beetles, but are grouped in the family Passalidae. They have one short, forward-projecting horn on the head. The mandibles are short but powerful and can bite through solid timber. The body is black and shiny, and the elytra are deeply scored with a distinctive series of parallel grooves.

Bessbugs demonstrate domestic arrangements that are more typical of "advanced" social insects such as honeybees and social (paper) wasps. The adults live in family groups alongside the larvae in rotting wood that is rich in microorganisms. The larvae do not thrive on wood that they have chewed themselves. Instead, they eat wood pulp prechewed for them by the adults. Some larvae eat the adults' droppings, which consist of partly predigested wood. Several generations may live together, helping one another. Newly emerged adults soon assist with chores in the nest, such as building the complex pupal cases for the next generation.

↑ *The shiny blackish elytra and almost parallel-sided body typical of passalids is obvious in this* Odontotaenius disjunctus *perched on a dead tree in a forest in the eastern United States.*

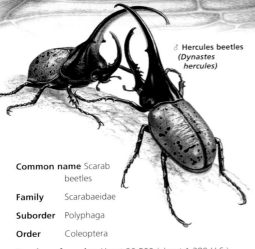

♂ Hercules beetles
(*Dynastes
hercules*)

Common name Scarab beetles

Family Scarabaeidae

Suborder Polyphaga

Order Coleoptera

Number of species About 20,500 (about 1,380 U.S.)

Size From about 0.2 in (4 mm) to about 7 in (18 cm)

Key features Body usually stout and heavy, oval or oval-elongate, often brightly colored, especially in the tropics; antennae unique, elbowed, and tipped with a series of flat, elongated leaflike plates (lamellae) that can be separated by opening them up like a fan or closed to form a club; a few species have divided eyes

Habits Enormously varied; some are associated with dung, some with flowers, and others with roots or leaves; many species only active at dusk or after dark, others only in warm sunshine

Breeding Many species have horned males that fight over access to females; some species form "balls" of males scuffling over a single female; male chafers tend to form aerial swarms to attract females; dung-rolling beetles collect dung, others make a "compost" from plant material; many species lay eggs in trees or roots

Diet Larvae feed on dung, leaves, fruit, roots, wood, fungi, carrion, fur, and bones; many adults only eat pollen and nectar

Habitat Almost anywhere; as common in deserts and pastures as in forests or gardens; some species inhabit the nests of mammals, birds, or termites

Distribution More or less throughout the world wherever insect life is possible on dry land

⊕ *Giant among beetles, male Hercules beetles,* **Dynastes hercules,** *from Central and South America fight using their horns as pry bars to topple each other over and off tree trunks. Length up to 7 inches (18 cm).*

Scarab Beetles
Scarabaeidae

Scarabs, with their characteristic antennae, form one of the most unmistakable families of beetles. They were worshiped by the ancient Egyptians, who associated scarabs with the deity Re.

APART FROM THEIR DISTINCTIVE antennae, scarabs can generally be identified by the deep body and rather short, powerful legs, in which the front pair is often modified for digging. In many species the elytra are chopped off short, leaving the tip of the (sometimes pointed) abdomen exposed. Many of the larger and more bizarre scarabs—often with spectacular horns in the males—are only active at night. In contrast, most of the more brilliantly colored species can be seen during the day. The diurnal species can be found feeding on flowers or the sap that oozes from wounded trees. They include some of the most beautiful of all beetles. Some species are clothed in a dense coat of scales, giving them a velvety, even shaggy, appearance.

Delicious Dung

Scarabs that feed on dung are found in the subfamilies Scarabaeinae, Aphodiinae, and Geotrupinae (often given their own family, Geotrupidae). The Scarabaeinae includes the sacred scarab of ancient Egypt, one of many members of the subfamily that rolls dung balls. Although they are not true bugs—which belong to the order Hemiptera—dung-rolling scarabs are called tumblebugs in the United States.

Dung is a valuable and nutritious material that is much sought after by a variety of insects. However, in many insects it only provides food for the immature stages. Dung beetles, on the other hand, feed on dung both as larvae and adults. Because it tends to be served up in large, relatively short-lived dollops at irregular

⊕ **Hexodon latissimum** *from Madagascar belongs to the same subfamily (Dynastinae) as the rhinoceros beetles, although its broadly rotund body shape is unusual within the scarab family.*

→ A scarab
beetle is depicted
on a cartouche at
the Temple of Karnak,
Egypt. The scarab was a
venerable symbol to the
ancient Egyptians, as sacred as
the cross to Christianity.

and unpredictable intervals, dung is rated a "bonanza" product for which there is often a great deal of intense competition. Dung beetles employ various methods for making sure that they secure their fair share of what is available.

Dung Rollers

On the open plains of Africa a heap of fresh buffalo dung will soon be a scene of bustling activity. The first dung beetles may arrive only minutes after the dropping was first produced. Their fanlike antennae are remarkably sensitive to the odor of fresh dung, enabling them to rapidly home in on the scent. The best way to

Sacred Scarab

The scarab beetle was the most sacred symbol for the ancient Egyptians. They associated it with the god Re. The way the beetle rolled its ball of dung across the earth reminded them of how the sun-god rolled the light across the sky each day.

Scarab beetles were represented in hieroglyphs on the walls of temples and were found stored in jars buried with the deceased. They were also found in graves during the First Dynasty (around 3,000 BC). Scarab carvings made from semiprecious stones were also used as protective amulets and as the seals of officials.

141

guarantee a private supply is to remove it from the scene, and that is what dung rollers do. Sometimes it is the female who makes the first ball. At other times it is the male. Some males first make a "nuptial" ball, which serves to attract a female. Males and females then work together to fashion balls, first for their own use as food and second as long-term provisions for their larvae. No matter who does what up to this point, it is always the male who rolls away the finished item. The female "rides shotgun" on top, ready to repel any attempts at hijacking. If a dispute occurs, the original owners generally come off best, since they have the advantage of the high ground: From their position on top of the ball they are usually able

Calling In the Cleaners

When European settlers introduced cattle to the range lands of Australia, the native dung beetles were unable to process the huge quantities of wet, often semiliquid dung that suddenly started to appear. The dung of the native kangaroos and wallabies is quite dry and arrives in relatively small packages that are easy to deal with. Millions of rocklike, sun-dried cowpats soon became a serious problem, stifling the growth of grasses and effectively sterilizing the pastures. There were simply no native insects available to get rid of them rapidly enough. The economic cost of the diminishing pastureland soon became enormous. To make matters worse, astronomical numbers of blood-sucking buffalo flies found cattle dung to their liking and soon became a huge additional headache.

The solution was to introduce several species of dung beetles from South Africa and southern Europe. The species were carefully selected after numerous trials and were all well adapted to dealing with large-scale quantities of runny dung in a hot, dry climate. One particular South African species was especially effective, being able to bury a whole cowpat in just two to three days, quickly putting it out of reach of the buffalo flies.

The episode highlights the enormous benefits that dung beetles of all kinds confer on mankind by cleaning up pastures that would soon become smothered in cowpats. Even in a wet climate like Great Britain's a cowpat on which there are no dung beetles takes many times longer to disappear than one with a healthy population of beetles and other insects.

to flip the intruder over onto its back. When rolling their ball away, the beetles walk backward, pushing the ball with their back legs, often moving at great speed. Some species enclose their ball in a covering of soil or clay.

Dung Burying

Eventually the dung ball will be buried, usually by the male while the female perches on top. The female then lays an egg in the still-moist dung. It is around now that the male normally leaves. Sometimes several brood balls are trundled into a large chamber prepared beneath the ground, as in the tumblebug *Canthon cyanellus* from Mexico. In this species it is the male who makes the first dung ball, joined by a female during his labors. He works swiftly and skillfully, raking in the dung with his

↑ In most dung-rolling scarabs the male and female work together to fashion the ball and roll it to a place where it can be safely buried. Above are Scarabaeus aeratus *from the savannas of Kenya.*

Not all dung rollers have to mold a ball from a mass of raw materials. Instead, many smaller species use single, ready formed pellets such as rabbit dung. A number of species—for example, *Phanaeus milon* from South America—fashion balls from carrion rather than dung, while some species of *Canthon* can use both. The North American *Deltochilum gibbosum* does not use dung at all, but makes its brood ball from a mass of feathers or hair covered with decaying leaves and soil.

Instead of rolling dung away, some species bury it directly underneath the main dung pat. Because all the dung is removed from the underside of the heap, often without disturbing its dry outer crust, the intense level of activity taking place beneath the undisturbed outer surface may not be obvious. Since the larvae of several species may occupy the limited space directly below the dung heap, conditions can become rather crowded. When developing larvae crash through into their neighbors' quarters, the ensuing fights can be fatal. Fortunately, the larvae can repair breaches in the walls by squirting liquid feces into the gap, which hardens to form a firm surface.

Parental Responsibilities

The amount of parental control over the developing larva's welfare varies in different species of dung beetle. Parents that leave their young to develop alone simply dig a series of brood chambers and stuff them with sausage-shaped masses of dung. Parents that intend to stay and care for their offspring need room to maneuver within the burrow, so they shape the dung into individual free-standing balls. A gap is left between them and the walls of the passage, giving the adults room to squeeze past and check on the welfare of the larvae inside.

Nest building is often shared between the male and female. In the European *Copris lunaris* both sexes excavate a chamber some 4 to 8 inches (10 to 20 cm) below the dung heap. The female does the digging work, shoving the soil up to the male. He stows the soil in the cavity created by the dung he sends down into the

strong, spadelike forelegs. He gradually forms it into a sphere, patting it to smooth it off. The completed ball is rolled away and buried in a substantial nest chamber excavated by the male and female together.

The male follows up the first ball with several more, all of which the female studiously forms into pear-shaped brood balls. If the male is slow in arriving with a new ball (he is often delayed by other males hell-bent on theft), the female will emerge from the nest to help him. Unlike in African dung rollers, the male stays on until the larvae are well developed. He drives out intruders and secretes protective chemicals onto the brood balls to make them unattractive to dung-breeding flies. Despite his best efforts, he cannot rear a brood successfully on his own, and the larvae will die if the female is absent.

Some scarabs lay their eggs in fallen timber on the rain-forest floor. Here, Macraspis lucida *from Costa Rica excavates a hole in the soft wood where she can place her eggs.*

burrow. Meanwhile, the outer skin of the dung heap is left undisturbed as a "roof." The male also collects fresh dung supplies for the waiting female, which she kneads into a single "dung loaf." If she starts to run low, she lets her mate know that she needs a further delivery by drumming on his body with her legs.

Once the dung loaf is complete, the female usually evicts the male from the brood chamber.

After a brief pause of about a week (possibly the time the dung takes to mature) she starts carving up the single hoard of dung into several ovoid brood balls. After laying an egg in every ball, she prepares a special breathing pore in each one so that the larva inside does not suffocate. Over the next few weeks she regularly licks the surface of the brood balls, probably helping prevent the growth of harmful fungi. Only when her offspring have safely begun to emerge does the female finally leave them, completing a period of devoted care lasting about four months. During that time she has taken no food for herself at all.

In many of the beetles that nest below dung heaps the males have horns. They probably use them mainly in disputes over the

Some animal dung is in such demand that it is soon covered in flies and beetles. This buffalo dung in South Africa is crawling with Gymnopleurus aenescens, *a small species of dung roller.*

right to nest alongside a female and father her offspring. The triple-horned males of the European minotaur beetle, *Typhoeus typhoeus*, ignore one another when on the surface collecting dung supplies.

However, below ground in the nest it is a different story. If an unattached male enters the nest, he will attempt to drive out the resident male and claim the female. When faced with a gate-crashing intruder, the resident male will endeavor to block the entrance tunnel with his armored and slippery rear end. As in all dung beetles, the males vary greatly in size, so large invaders with superior weaponry can use their horns to lever the defender aside and evict him from the burrow. Head-to-head combat also occurs, the outcome of which will determine which of the two will become a father. The defeated minotaur will be forced to return to the surface to look for a new mate. Meanwhile, the female continues making preparations for rearing her family, content to accept whichever of the two rivals wins the contest.

Because family care is so highly developed, dung beetles have no need to lay the vast numbers of eggs deemed essential for species with lower chances of survival for their larvae, such as blister beetles. In fact, the dung beetles that exhibit parental care lay the smallest number of eggs of any beetles. As a result, the female has only a single ovary, which contains a reduced number of egg-producing ovarioles.

Not Just Any Dung

While some dung beetles will use several kinds of dung, others are more specialized. In Africa the large *Scarabaeus platynotus* mainly gathers elephant dung. The material is ignored by most other dung beetles because it is so fibrous (elephants eat large quantities of bark and other high-fiber foods, which are passed through the animal relatively unchanged, resulting in stringy droppings). The rain forests of Central and South America are home to several kinds of dung beetles that harvest monkey droppings in the forest canopy. In Australia the only native grazing and browsing

A Liking for Leftovers

Hide beetles (subfamily Troginae) are drab, black insects that are often given their own family—the Trogidae. They are attracted to animal carcasses, but only when they have been lying around for a long time, and all the easily available flesh has been more or less cleaned off by fly maggots and other carrion feeders. When there is nothing much left but indigestible skin, fur, feathers, scales, or bones, the hide beetles arrive. They are members of a small band of insects that are able to make use of what others are obliged to leave.

By this late stage in decomposition the powerful odor emitted by a more recent carcass has started to decline. It is after a downpour of rain has wetted the tattered remains and increased the whiff of decay that the hide beetles are likely to show up. The larvae live in vertical burrows below the carcass, while the adults stay up above. Some species live in the nests of birds or in mammal burrows, especially those in which housekeeping is poor or nonexistent, and feathers or fur are allowed to build up. The adult beetles tend to become well coated with the mess, making them difficult to recognize. Some hide beetles have the rather curious habit of feeding on the indigestible exoskeletons of insects abandoned by spiders in their webs. The spiders have no further use for them, but the enterprising hide beetles can wring the last traces of nourishment from such unpromising raw materials.

mammals are kangaroos and wallabies. They produce droppings that are not only small but also very dry even when fresh. Some Australian dung beetles use special prehensile claws to attach themselves to the rear ends of wallabies, ensuring that only the freshest dung is used.

As in any kind of economy in which there is a hard-working majority, there are always a few freeloaders who take advantage of the system. In the world of dung beetles the scroungers consist of various kinds of *Aphodius*, whose larvae develop in the dung so laboriously hoarded by their larger cousins.

Making Compost

Dung is simply grass and leaves that have passed through an animal such as a cow, monkey, or rabbit. In the process the material becomes modified into a form that can be used by dung beetles and their larvae. Some scarabs have eliminated the need to wait for a large animal to eat the plants first and convert them into a usable material. Instead, the beetles themselves gather the plant materials and compost the results to create a kind of artificial dung. In Europe *Lethrus apterus* stocks its brood chambers with leaves. In the fresh state they are inedible for the larvae, but after a period of fermentation they become both palatable and nutritious.

Cephalodesmius armiger from Australia goes one step further and constructs a series of vegetable brood balls. The male gathers the raw materials, consisting of fallen leaves and fruit. The female crushes everything the male brings and adds it to a central supply. Fungi that grow from spores in the beetles' droppings then "digest" the tough materials. Once the fungi have transformed the tough, inedible material into a spongy, easily worked mass, the female begins to manufacture brood balls, laying an egg in each one. Unlike in most dung beetles, the brood balls do not contain enough food for the entire development of each larva. When the larva begins to run out of food, it rubs its mouthparts against its tail, producing a rasping sound that sends its mother scurrying to fetch fresh supplies.

At least one beetle takes advantage of abandoned compost. In the warmer parts of the Americas the vast underground nests of leaf-cutting ants are often a common feature. When deserted by the ants, the nests still contain large amounts of the fungus-infected compost that they have manufactured from leaves. It is in this ready-to-use material that the beetle *Choeridium granigerum* lays its eggs.

Chafers

Chafers belong to the subfamilies Melolonthinae (chafers) and Rutelinae (leaf chafers). Most chafers are rather dull in color. They are often brown, but some are iridescent, while others are hairy or scaly. Leaf chafers, on the other hand, are usually brightly colored and metallic, sometimes to the extent of seeming to be created from pure metal, as in the gold

beetles (*Plusiotis*) from the forests of Central America. In both subfamilies the elytra are often slightly foreshortened, exposing the tip of the abdomen. It is in the chafers that the fanlike nature of the antennae is most obvious, particularly in the males. In the European pine chafer, *Polyphylla fullo*—a large, handsome black-and-white spotted species whose fat, white larvae are often eaten by local people—the male has large, prominent flaplike tips to the antennae. The tips are composed of plates, which bear a large number of sensory cells on their surfaces. The plates can be spread wide like the fingers of a hand, for example, when the male is alert for the scent of some far-off female. In the United States the male of the 10-lined June beetle, *Polyphylla decemlineata*, has similar antennae. Like many chafers, they can chirp when handled roughly.

Mating Swarms

Like most scarabs, chafers are strong fliers. The males of many species form noisily buzzing mating swarms around trees or some other landmark, often toward dusk. European cockchafers, *Melolontha melolontha*, take their bearings from prominent landmarks such as the silhouette of a clump of trees on an isolated hill. They are also able to use the earth's magnetic field when commuting between feeding, mating, and egg-laying localities.

⊕ *The pine chafer,* Polyphylla fullo, *is the largest chafer in Europe. Females, like the one shown here, lack the large, prominent antennae typical of the males.*

The appearance of mating swarms seems to be triggered by certain weather conditions, such as thunder showers. Having emerged from their pupae, large numbers of adults remain underground until a torrent of rain softens the ground and signals their release. They scramble upward into the dusk in their millions, and suddenly the ground and air are alive with whirring beetles. The simultaneous mass emergence ensures that males and females are guaranteed to find each other. It also means

that several males will find each female, leading to an ultracompetitive spirit among the males. They will quickly form a dense, struggling mob around any female that lands.

In the Japanese beetle, *Popillia japonica*, the long-term presence of an entourage of fiercely competitive males seems to be actively encouraged by the female. As she emerges from her pupa in the ground, she emits a pheromone that ensures she will soon be surrounded by up to 200 males, clamped

⊕ *With the flaplike tips of his antennae spread like fingers, a male European cockchafer, Melolontha melolontha, sits alert for the scent of a distant female.*

around her in a frenzied, brawling scrum. Since she does not need to mate until just before she lays her eggs (which will not be for several days), it seems that she deliberately sets up a trial of stamina among as many males as possible. As in most beetles, it is the female which has ultimate control over whether or not a male can copulate, regardless of his efforts.

Crop Pests

Most chafers feed on plants and can be pests of field crops. The fat, "c"-shaped larvae generally live in the ground, where their constant nibbling on roots can affect the growth of the plant above ground. Trees and shrubs can even be killed if many larvae are present. It can take three years for the larvae of many species to develop. In the United States several members of the large genus *Phyllophaga* cause severe damage to crops. The mainly dark-brown adults, known as May beetles or June beetles, often emerge in such numbers that they swamp the trees, stripping them of their foliage with their voracious feeding. The larvae can be even more damaging, feeding on the roots of valuable range land grasses, as well as soybean and other field crops. The females lay batches of 50 to 100 white eggs, placing them inside a carefully constructed earthen cell.

In the United States the Japanese beetle is the most serious pest among the shining leaf chafers. It has made itself very much at home after being accidentally imported from Japan,

⊕ Members of the Cetoniinae are usually called flower chafers or flower beetles from their habit of feeding on flowers. Left is Oxythyrea funesta *from southern Europe.*

where it is not a major problem. Since 1916 it has gradually crept across most of the northeastern United States where its larvae injure the roots of many kinds of plants. The adults eat leaves, often bending down twigs under the weight of their numbers and causing severe damage. Among native members of the subfamily Rutelinae in the United States the most beautiful is the lustrous green *Plusiotis gloriosa*. It lives in the Southwest, where it feeds on the leaves of junipers. Like many chafers, it is most easily seen when attracted to sources of light at night. In Australia adults of *Anoplognathus*, known as Christmas beetles, can strip eucalyptus trees of their leaves.

Privileged Diners

The tough exterior of most scarabs comes in useful for a number of purposes, although none more unusual than in the ant acacia beetle, *Pelidnota punctulata*. Ranging from southern Mexico to northern Colombia, this grayish-green beetle needs to be built like a battle tank, since its sole food is the leaves of two species of acacias that enjoy a special relationship with ants. The acacia bushes supply the ants with food and shelter. In return the ants make sure that nothing eats the leaves.

⊖ With his front legs spread protectively, a male Polyphemus *beetle,* Chelorrhina polyphemus, *guards a female (on the left) while she feeds on fermenting sap in a Kenyan forest.*

Although small, they have a vicious sting. However, the ant acacia beetle is able to get past the ants, apparently immune to their frantic, yet futile onslaughts. Protected by its impenetrable armored hide, the ant beetle spends the day peacefully asleep on the ant acacias, clamped in place by its jaws. At dusk it wakes up and begins its nightly meal of fresh, tender leaves—the only animal free to dine on these heavily defended morsels of greenery.

Flower and Goliath Beetles

The flower beetles (subfamily Cetoniinae) contain some of the most flamboyantly colored of all beetles. Many species are metallic, while others are hairy and may resemble bumblebees, especially in flight. When in the air, a beelike buzzing is generated, as in the North American bumble flower beetle, *Euphoria inda*. The European bee beetle, *Trichius fasciatus*, is an even better mimic of a bumblebee. The newly hatched adult beetles are very furry, although they become rather balder as they age. Some flower beetles are confusingly variable in color. The gemlike Neptune beetle, *Neptunides polychromus* from tropical Africa, occurs in reddish-bronze, burnished gold, or brilliant green varieties.

Although generally powerful fliers, flower beetles and their allies are unusual in not holding their elytra upward to free the hind wings for flight. Instead, the hind wings are threaded through a slit in the edge of the elytra. Even the largest of the African Goliath beetles, which can reach a length of 4.3 inches (11 cm), can fly well

⊕ A chafer beetle (Dermolepida albohirtum) *sits on a stalk of sugarcane in Queensland, Australia. The species is a major pest of the sugarcane crop.*

despite being real heavyweights. A loud, penetrating, droning hum can be heard as they fly. If attacked in flight, the beetle instantly tucks its wings away and drops like a stone to the forest floor. Even if it lands on a log and bounces off, its tough armor will protect it. Male Goliath beetles have horns, although they are never as well developed as in rhinoceros beetles; but like them, male Goliaths enter into battles horn-to-horn like stags. Goliath beetles include some of the rarest of all beetles. They are highly sought after by insect collectors.

As their name suggests, many flower beetles feed on flowers as adults, although some prefer fruit such as peaches or tender young foliage. Several tropical species feed on fermenting sap on tree trunks. Many larvae, including those of most of the larger, more colorful tropical species, develop in rotting tree trunks. The larva of the North American green June beetle, *Cotinus nitida*, is one of many that live in the ground and eat the roots of plants. It can be a pest when it attacks agricultural crops

Ant Attacks

The 32 species of *Cremastocheilus* in the United States inhabit ants' nests, which are always rather hazardous places for any uninvited guests. The larvae repel attacks from their host ants by striking at them with their mandibles while simultaneously expelling a dark, foul-smelling fluid from their mouthparts. A few equally pungent pellets of wet droppings ejected rapidly from the larva's rear end are usually enough to convince the ant to stop bothering it. Repeated strikes with the mandibles on the body of the ant are often fatal. The adult beetles also penetrate deep into the ants' nest, where their shiny, convex armor usually offers them adequate protection. If the ants manage to tip an adult beetle over onto its back, it releases a droplet of smelly fluid from its anus, which quickly sends its attackers packing. In Australia the tiny *Microvalgus* species are thought to live inside termite nests. They are less than 0.2 inches (4 mm) long.

⊖ The bee beetle, Trichius fasciatus *from Europe, is the best example of a number of furry flower chafers that resemble bumblebees, especially when in buzzing, beelike flight.*

in some numbers. In common with other species, the larva has the strange habit of crawling on its back even on the surface of the soil, using a dense brush of bristles on the folds between the segments in its skin.

The Heavy Mob

Rhinoceros, Hercules, and elephant beetles are the heavyweights among the scarabs. They are not only some of the heaviest of all beetles, but are also among the largest of all insects—larger and heavier than many birds. Males of the Hercules beetle, *Dynastes hercules* from the rain forests of Central and South America, can weigh 2 ounces (57 g). That is 23 times as heavy as the world's smallest bird, the bee hummingbird, *Mellisuga helenae*, from Cuba. A male Hercules beetle can be up to 7 inches (18 cm) in length. Four inches (10 cm) is taken up by an enormous horn projecting forward from the pronotum. A second, slightly shorter horn curves upward from the top of the head, almost meeting the larger horn. In *Chalcosoma atlas* from Indonesia a long, sharp, curving horn juts forward from either side of the pronotum. A short horn from the center of the pronotum is joined by a fourth arching upward from the head. Such horns are typical of many of the giant males in the subfamily Dynastinae and are used in battle with other males for a prime position next to a sap run on a tree.

← *Many tropical flower beetles are brilliantly colored. The Neptune beetle,* Neptunides polychromus *from Africa, can be bright green, bronze (as in the male shown here), or gold.*

⊕ *The Goliath beetles from tropical Africa include some of the world's heaviest insects—larger and heavier than many birds. Here,* Goliathus druryi *rests on a log in a Kenyan rain forest.*

Male Hercules beetles use their horns like pincers; they can move them up and down, and that allows them to grab one another in much the same way as a pair of calipers. While fighting, the males will strive to scoop up their opponent's body between their horns in order to toss it violently off the tree.

In *Golofa porteri* from South America the horns are used to lever an opponent off the tree and away from any prospective sexual contact with females. They are helped by vicious raking actions of the long, well-armed front legs. As they toil away like sumo wrestlers, they set up a constant, belligerent chirping, rubbing a rough filelike area on the tip of the abdomen against a scraper on the underside of the elytra. The winner celebrates his triumph with a special "victory chirp." Although many species are horned, actual combat between males has only rarely been seen. Even then, it usually seems to take place on sap runs or rotting fruit, where females can be expected to arrive. However, it is not the presence of a female that appears to be the cause of a contest between males. There is also no need to "impress" her with their prominent

masculine headgear. In many species the tips of the horns are quite blunt and make little physical impact on an opponent's hard, shiny armor. Yet in some species, such as *Heterogomphus schoenherri* from tropical South America, the horns are more harpoonlike and capable of inflicting fatal damage.

Most of these giants breed in dead fallen trees. Because of their size the larvae of really mammoth species such as the tropical American elephant beetle, *Megasoma elephas*, need large, mature trees that will take several years to rot. In smaller trees the larvae would be deprived of their home by fungi and other organisms of decay before their four to five years of development are up. These huge beetles are therefore susceptible to forest destruction or even selective logging in which the larger trees are felled, leaving only smaller, unsuitable specimens.

Modest Sizes

In temperate northern areas sizes tend to be more modest. The horns of the male eastern Hercules beetle, *Dynastes tityus* from the United States, are relatively short, giving the species a maximum length of about 2.4 inches (6 cm).

Larvae of some of the smaller species eat roots rather than decaying timber. In North America the immature stages of the carrot beetle, *Bothynus gibbosus* (adults are drab black and hornless), damage the roots of parsnips, carrots, potatoes, and other root crops. The adults eat foliage, which is not a habit found in the tropical giants. The South American *Scatophilus dasypleurus* is one of a number of species that lay their eggs in dung. The female makes one enormous sausage-shaped mass of dung in a subterranean chamber and then seeds it with eggs every half an inch (2 cm) or so. In Australia *Cryptodus* lives in association with ants and termites.

⊖ *At about 5 inches (13 cm) long the elephant beetle,* **Megasoma elephas** *from South America, is one of the world's largest beetles. The prominent horns of the individual shown here clearly identify him as a male.*

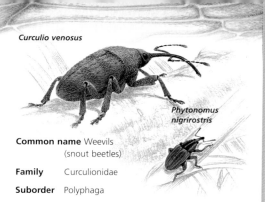

Curculio venosus

Phytonomus nigrirostris

Common name Weevils (snout beetles)

Family Curculionidae

Suborder Polyphaga

Order Coleoptera

Number of species About 50,000 (about 2,500 U.S.)

Size From about 0.04 in (1 mm) to about 3 in (7.5 cm)

Key features Color very variable: brown, black, yellow, orange, red, blue, purple, green, gold, or silver; body often covered with iridescent scales; some species very hairy; downcurved snout usually well developed, sometimes broad and flat, more often longer (sometimes very long) and slimmer; antennae usually elbowed, tipped by a 3-segmented club; elytra often fused

Habits Adults are usually seen on vegetation; mostly active in daytime; larvae usually live concealed inside roots, stems, or galls

Breeding Male simply mounts female; in some species males conduct ritualistic "fights"; mating is often lengthy, and males often remain with females as "escorts" until egg laying starts; females drill hole in plant with rostrum before laying an egg in the hole; many species restricted to a single host plant; leaf-rolling weevils construct living "leaf cradles"

Diet Adults mainly eat pollen or leaves; larvae usually eat plant tissues within stems, roots, galls, fruits, or seeds; some feed externally on leaves, often in groups; 1 species eats dung, at least 1 other feeds on insect eggs

Habitat Most common in forests, but some prefer open habitats such as grasslands or deserts; larvae of some species live in aquatic plants, others inhabit rodent burrows or ants' nests

Distribution Worldwide except in the coldest and driest areas

⊕ *The acorn weevil,* Curculio venosus, *is found in southern England and Europe. Length 0.2–0.4 inches (5–9 mm). *Phytonomus nigrirostris *is from Europe and the U.S., where it is known as the cloverleaf weevil. Length 0.1–0.2 inches (3–4 mm).*

Weevils

Curculionidae

Weevils are known for the damage they can cause to crops and even to the timber in houses. However, their use in controlling pests, such as some introduced plants, is increasingly recognized.

THE CURCULIONIDAE IS PROBABLY the largest family in the animal kingdom. Moreover, with 50,000 species there are more weevils than mammals, birds, reptiles, and amphibians put together. A weevil can usually be distinguished from other beetles by its snout, or rostrum. It is generally curved downward and has a pair of (often) elbowed antennae set along its length. When walking, weevils have a somewhat waddling gait, otherwise only seen in the similar fungus weevils (Anthribidae). Many species are covered with iridescent scales, giving them a certain brilliance. The most spectacular examples occur in the tropics, such as the glittering *Eulophus* turquoise weevils from New Guinea or the large, shimmering green *Entimus* emerald weevils from the rain forests of South America.

Tough as Nails

The weevil's body is among the toughest of any insect. It can often be too hard to drive a pin through for mounting in a display. The impenetrable exterior is particularly pronounced in species such as the North American agave billbug, *Scyphophorus acupunctatus*. The billbug's tough outer skeleton protects it against its harsh desert environment and stops it from drying out. For the same reason many desert species have fused elytra and often spend their entire lives under bushes. Most weevils are robustly built and deep bodied, but some are long and narrow. A few are antlike, while some have enlarged hind legs and can jump. The adults of aquatic species have a dense pile of hairs on the underside, forming a plastron (film of air) that allows them to breathe underwater.

The correct way to classify the various weevil families and subfamilies is a matter of

⊕ *The long, downcurved snout or rostrum and elbowed antennae typical of the Curculionidae can be clearly seen in the male big-foot weevil,* Rhinastus latesternus, *from Peru.*

some dispute. Certain subfamilies have sometimes been given full family rank, most especially the leaf-rolling weevils (Attelabinae), the billbugs or grain weevils (Rhynchophorinae), and pear-shaped weevils (Apioninae).

Male Escort

As in many beetles, the males (which are noticeably smaller than the females) simply mount a prospective partner and try to persuade her to mate by making vigorous side-to-side movements of the body. Females usually react by using their back legs to try to push the male off. In many species mating is preceded by a long period of "escort" behavior, as seen in many long-horn beetles (Cerambycidae). The male weevil shuffles along behind the female with his front legs resting on her rear end, waiting for her to start drilling an egg-laying hole. When she has finished, he mates with her shortly before she lays an egg. In many species males outnumber available females, leading to severe competition: It is quite common to see as many as four males stacked up on top of a single top-heavy female. In a few species males challenge one another for the right to mate with a female

⊕ Not all weevils have a prominent snout. In many it is relatively short and blunt, as in the rough-backed emerald weevil, Entimus granulatus, *from the rain forests of Peru.*

⊕ In weevils the high degree of competition for females often leads to pushing-and-shoving matches between males, as in these eight-humped weevils, Brachyomus octotuberculatus, in Trinidad.

before actually meeting one, rather than while mounted on her back. In the peculiar giraffe-necked weevil, *Trachelophorus giraffa*, a leaf-rolling weevil from Madagascar, the males usually have spectacularly long necks, although the length can vary somewhat. They engage in ritualistic face-to-face displays in which they bob their long necks up and down. Apparently the one with the most impressive neck length is the winner, and he gets to remain on a leaf where a female is about to lay eggs. Actual fighting seems to be particularly prevalent in some other leaf-rolling weevils. Males of several European species struggle to expel one another from a leaf by employing their powerfully

enlarged rear legs as rams. *Byctiscus populi* uses its front legs and rostrum, rearing up on its hind legs to wrestle an opponent off the leaf.

Weevils on Stilts

In *Macromerus bicinctus* from Costa Rica the front legs of the males are very long and have distinctly clubbed tips. They swing them at one another in slugging matches over who will mate with the egg-laying female. A fallen tree in the rain forest is the arena for such battles. The sexual contests in the weird stilt-legged weevils (subfamily Zygopinae) are staged in a similar setting. A recently fallen tree will often play host to dozens of these weevils, running

⊕ *The common name of the giraffe-necked weevil,* Trachelophorus giraffa, *comes from the immensely long neck, as shown in this male sitting on a leaf in the rain forest of Madagascar.*

around with a peculiar jerky motion like clockwork toys. In many species the males are huge compared with the females and have enormous, lanky legs and a long, curving rostrum. The rostrum may be used as a weapon and thrust under the body of an opponent to throw him off the tree. The gangly legs form a mobile cordon around the females, fencing out rival males. As the females scuttle around on the bark searching for suitable egg-laying sites, the males keep them caged under the legs and long, overarching rostrum. In the bottlebrush weevil, *Rhinostomus barbirostris* from Central and South America, the long front legs and rostrum of the males are used in violent struggles that may drag on for some time.

In some species of *Otiorhynchus* females do not mate at all but lay unfertilized eggs (parthenogenesis) that give rise to generation after generation of exclusively female offspring.

⊕ *In the bizarre zygopine weevils the males are generally much larger than the females. Here a* Mecopus torquis *male guards a tiny female on a log in a Ugandan rain forest.*

Egg-Laying Sites

The long snout in weevils is mainly used as a tool for drilling holes into plants. The task usually takes only a few minutes even in timber, after which the female lays an egg in the hole. In many species the egg is followed by a creamy white liquid that soon hardens and plugs the hole, protecting the eggs from enemies such as ants. A number of species, such as the black oak acorn weevil, *Curculio rectus* from the United States, use a fecal pellet as a plug for the hole. In some cases females lay their eggs in the plant galls induced by other types of insects, like sawflies (Hymenoptera). The weevil larvae live alongside the rightful occupants, taking such a large share of the food that the sawfly larvae starve to death in their home without ever being attacked directly by the interlopers.

In some weevils the female has to modify the plant before it is suitable for her larvae. At its simplest this involves "girdling" a living twig, as in many long-horn beetles. The most advanced behavior is seen in a number of leaf-rolling weevils. In *Rhynchites cupreus* the female inserts her egg into an immature fruit. She then bites through the stalk until the fruit drops to the ground, where the larva completes its development. If the fruit were to remain on the tree, it would ripen, depriving the larva of the food it requires. A ripe fruit might also be eaten by birds, with the larva inside.

The most advanced leaf-rolling weevils devote many hours to the construction of a special crèche composed of a folded leaf. Methods vary from species to species, but in most cases the female's first act is to bite a series of holes or slits in selected areas of the leaf. They form zones of weakness that allow the leaf to be folded to a prearranged pattern.

Again, depending on the species, some leaves are rolled up from bottom to top, others from one side to the other. In many cases the female "sews up" the folded leaf by biting little holes in it with her rostrum. At some point during the process she lays one or more eggs in what will eventually become the center of the folded nest. In all cases the female spends several hours working with amazing precision and method. Sometimes her task is made more difficult by having a male perched on her back as she toils. The finished nest usually stays on the plant, gradually becoming brown as the leaf withers. It stands out clearly against the green, undisturbed leaves. In some species the female cuts the finished nest loose, and the larvae complete their development on the ground.

Legless Larvae

Weevil larvae are generally legless, maggotlike creatures that lead concealed lives within plants. Sometimes they inhabit the inside of a single leaf, where they create a mine. In *Rhynchaenus* the fully fed larva glues together the upper and lower "skins" of the leaf with a special secretion, then gnaws away a circle of tissue around itself, creating a disklike section that falls to the ground and forms the pupal chamber. A few species feed openly on leaves. They are often glistening, sluglike creatures that are just too unpleasant to eat. *Cionus* figwort weevil larvae from Europe are one example. Before pupation they migrate to the top of their food plant and construct spherical cocoons that resemble the host plant's seedpods.

⬅ *In most weevils the larvae feed concealed inside their food plant, but in* Phelypera distigma *from Costa Rica they form conspicuous groups and feed externally.*

Destructive Habits

The impact of weevils on mankind is often negative, and numerous species are classed as pests. However, there are exceptional cases, as with the *Rhynchophorus* palm weevils from South America. Their plump white larvae, which can often be pests in palms, are roasted on spits or fried in hot fat to make a tasty and popular dish. Many weevils are pests of fruit and field crops, ornamental plants, and timber.

The black vine weevil, *Otiorhynchus sulcatus*, is a pest both in Europe and the United States. It mainly attacks vegetables or pot plants grown as ornamentals, but can also live outdoors in the soil. Its larvae destroy the roots, causing the plant to collapse and die. Like many pest insects, it has become resistant to most insecticides, and in recent years its numbers have exploded in some areas. Being wingless, colonization of new areas happens when cultivated plants are shifted from one place to another by farmers or nurserymen.

The white pine weevil, *Lixus strobi*, causes economic losses not by killing its host plant but by deforming it, thereby making it useless. The female lays her eggs in the topmost shoots of eastern white pine (and occasionally other pines). By boring downward into the young shoot, the larva kills it, forcing a side shoot to take its place. The shoot eventually produces a tree with a noticeable kink in its trunk, destroying its value for lumber. Several species of long-snouted *Curculio* nut weevils can also be a problem. The pecan weevil, *C. caryae*, can wipe out some two-thirds of a pecan crop,

① *A female hazel leaf-rolling weevil,* Apoderus coryli *from Europe, carefully rolls up the leaf that will form a cradle for her offspring.*

⬇ *In the oak leaf-rolling weevil,* Attelabus nitens *from Europe, the leaf is rolled up from the tip inward, rather than from top to bottom.*

Counting the Cost

One of the most notorious pests in history, the boll weevil, *Anthonomus grandis*, is the most costly insect pest in North America. Accidentally introduced from Mexico in the mid-1800s, it rapidly became such a pest of cotton that even today the cultivation of that crop is uneconomic in some areas. The female lays her eggs in the unopened flower bud, which is eventually destroyed by the larvae, preventing flowering and the production of any cotton. With several generations produced in a single year, the boll weevil can cause serious losses even when costly and environmentally damaging insecticides are used.

Since their accidental introduction boll weevils have caused around $14 billion of damage to cotton crops.

while several species that breed in acorns reduce the crop so much that natural forest regeneration is held in check.

Helpful Weevils

The story is not all negative, and weevils are increasingly used to help control other pests. When Australian lakes and reservoirs were being swamped by a stifling carpet of *Salvinia* water fern, introduced from South America, modern science was helpless to find a sensible high-tech solution.

The answer came in the form of a tiny weevil, *Cyrtobagous salviniae*, imported from the problem plant's native home. Because the little weevil eats nothing but *Salvinia*, it could be relied on not to switch its attention to any native Australian plants or to valuable crops. In a number of less carefully researched introductions of insects for biological control the newcomer has itself become a pest. The success of the weevil was rapid and spectacular, soon solving the problem.

Playing Dead

The usual reaction of most weevils when alarmed is to tuck in the legs and play dead, often dropping off a leaf onto the ground. When on the ground, the weevil is virtually impossible to find among the jumble of twigs and other detritus. Some species can even roll themselves into a ball. Many of the weevils that spend time on the bark of trees resemble knobby protrusions, while some are sticklike or even copy a broken-off twig. A number of species mimic bird droppings, pebbles, or dead leaves. The coloration and bristly outgrowths of *Lithinus hildebrandi* from Madagascar make it look like a lichen-covered twig.

Many large *Gymnopholus* weevils from the rain-soaked highlands of New Guinea carry miniature gardens on their back as camouflage. Their elytra are covered with special pits and hairs that help plants such as mosses, liverworts, lichens, algae, and fungi get a foothold. The weevils are exceptionally long-lived, surviving up to five years. Their longevity allows plenty of time for a thriving mass of greenery to become established. Amazingly enough, these mobile "gardens" are home to minute creatures such as mites that are found nowhere else on earth.

⊙ *Like most weevils, when under threat the 12-spined weevil, Rhigus horridus from Brazil, simply falls off its leaf onto the forest floor where it is hard to spot.*

⊙ *Playing dead is a common ploy when weevils are disturbed, as seen here in the clay-colored weevil, Otiorhynchus singularis from Europe.*

Queen Alexandra's birdwing (Ornithoptera alexandrae)

Common name
Swallowtail butterflies
(apollos, swordtails, birdwings)

Family Papilionidae

Order Lepidoptera

Number of species About 550 (27 U.S.)

Wingspan From about 1.2 in (3 cm) to about 11 in
(28 cm)

Key features Mainly large butterflies (including the
world's largest), often with hind-wing tails;
colors varied, often consisting of just 2 colors,
such as black and yellow or black and green,
sometimes with red or blue spots; some
species (apollos) have semitransparent wings;
antennae knobbed but never with hooked
tips; all 6 adult legs of equal size; caterpillars
often with "Y"-shaped defensive osmeterium

Habits Adults feed on flowers or on salty ground,
where they may form large aggregations;
caterpillars mainly feed singly

Breeding Male and female of most species look very
similar; many males use pheromones from
androconial scales during courtship; eggs
spherical, usually laid singly; caterpillars with
smooth skins, often with knobby projections;
pupa suspended upright from silken girdle

Diet Adults feed on flowers, damp ground, or
dung; caterpillars eat leaves belonging to
plants of many families, including poisonous
Aristolochia vines

Habitat Commonest in tropical rain forest, but found
in many temperate habitats such as swamps,
parks, and gardens; some species found only
on high mountains or open tundra in the far
north

Distribution Worldwide, occurring as far north as
northernmost Alaska

⬆ *Queen Alexandra's birdwing,* Ornithoptera alexandrae, *is
found to the east of the Owen Stanley Ranges in southeast
New Guinea. It is one of seven protected butterfly species on
the island. Wingspan 6.6–11 inches (17–28 cm).*

Swallowtail Butterflies
Papilionidae

*Papilionid butterflies are mainly large, and
include the biggest butterfly in the world—
the Queen Alexandra's birdwing,*
Ornithoptera alexandrae, *from New
Guinea. Females can have a wingspan
of over 11 inches (28 cm).*

THE MALES OF SOME of the birdwing butterflies
from tropical islands such as New Guinea and
parts of Indonesia are among the most
spectacular of all butterflies. They are highly
prized by collectors, and special butterfly farms
now exist to breed the choicest species to
satisfy the market for perfect unmarked
specimens. That helps take the collecting
pressure off the remaining wild populations.

In common with other true swallowtails,
the birdwings constantly flutter their wings
while feeding on flowers, a characteristic
unique to the Papilionidae. The reason for the
behavior is unknown. The suggestion that it
supports the heavy butterfly's weight on a
flimsy flower seems unlikely, since some species
also vibrate their wings while sitting on the
ground puddling. During active flight the wings
in many species are only flapped a few times a
second, although some tropical swallowtails are
among the fastest and most acrobatic fliers of
all butterflies. Not all swallowtails have tails on
the hind wings. Many species are tailless; in
others tails are present in males but not in
females of the same species, while in the
subfamily Parnasiinae tails are largely absent.

The Three Subfamilies
The family Papilionidae is divided into three
subfamilies, all with very different habits and
appearance. The smallest subfamily is the
"primitive" Baroniinae, containing just a single
species, *Baronia brevicornis* from southern
Mexico. The forked hairs on the head and body

⬆ *The artemisia
swallowtail,* Papilio
machaon, *seen here in
France, is unusual in
being found on both
sides of the Atlantic. It
has the fairly short tails
typical of* Papilio *species
swallowtails.*

➡ *Puddling on a
riverbank in a rain forest
in Thailand, this fivebar
swordtail,* Graphium
antiphates, *displays the
long tails typical of the
genus* Graphium.

of the larva are unusual, while the arrangement of veins on the adult's wings is unique.

The biggest subfamily with the widest distribution is the Papilioninae (although the vast majority of species are tropical). It contains the most familiar and "typical" of swallowtails, represented in North America and Europe by *Papilio*, the largest "true" swallowtails. The 27 North American species are mainly found in the south, although one species—the artemisia swallowtail, *Papilio machaon*—ranges north into Alaska. It is also unusual in being the only swallowtail (and one of the few butterflies) found both in North America and Europe. Some species share communal roosts, which in the African citrus swallowtail, *P. demodocus*, contain from three to 12 (or more) individuals. Most return to the same spot night after night.

In *Eurytides* and *Graphium*, often called kite swallowtails, the hind-wing tails (where present) are much longer and more pointed than in *Papilio*. *Graphium* are known as swordtails in Africa and Asia. *Eurytides* is found in the tropics of Central and South America, with just a single species resident in the southeastern corner of the United States. The butterflies are seldom found feeding on flowers and often congregate in large numbers on damp, salty riverbanks and springs. They pass so much liquid through their systems that a jet of water is squirted from their rear ends every minute or so. In the poison eaters, such as *Parides* and *Troides*, the caterpillars can feed unharmed on poisonous *Aristolochia* pipevines. The most familiar species in North America is the pipevine swallowtail, *Battus philenor*, one of the few species found outside the tropics. The birdwings of the genus *Ornithoptera* also belong in the Papilioninae.

The subfamily Parnasiinae, with about 50 species, is unusual in being mainly found in the coolest parts of the northern temperate zones. Most species are restricted to mountainsides up to the snow line, while two of the three species found in North America are also found far to the north on the tundras of Alaska. A small selection of much more colorful species called festoons are found in warmer areas, such as around the Mediterranean Sea. Most of the high-mountain and tundra species are white, with two or more red eyespots, and are called apollos. In some species the scales on large

areas of the wings are soon shed, leaving them semitransparent. Both larvae and adults are poisonous to vertebrates such as birds and are generally left alone. The tough, densely hairy body of the adults is well able to withstand the kind of brief attacks mounted by inexperienced enemies before they learn better.

Eggs, Larvae, and Pupae

In most species the eggs are more or less globular and are usually pale green and lacking any surface sculpture. In some species the egg is coated with a waxy substance that is eaten along with the eggshell by the newly hatched caterpillar. Such eggs are usually laid away from the host plant or on tiny seedlings unable to support the caterpillar's appetite. Therefore the caterpillar probably needs the additional eggshell meal in order to fuel its search for a suitable source of food. In most species the eggs are laid singly on the food plant. The pipevine swallowtail is one of a number of species that lays eggs in clusters, and the young caterpillars feed shoulder to shoulder in ostentatious squads along the edge of a single leaf. The red-spotted swallowtail, *Papilio anchisiades*, found from Texas to Brazil, lays its yellow eggs in clusters of up to 40. The caterpillars always stay close together and feed and molt in unison. During the day they form densely packed

⊕ *Crawling around on the desert floor in Arizona in search of a fresh food plant, pipevine swallowtail caterpillars,* Battus philenor, *are protected by their distinctive "warning" uniform.*

⊖ *Caterpillars of the orchard swallowtail,* Papilio aegeus *from Australia, start out as bird-dropping mimics but change to this form as they grow. Here the red osmeterium is just being extruded.*

⊕ **Eurytides agesilaus** *is often seen in large numbers drinking on damp sand beside rivers running through rain forest, as here in Peru.*

throngs on the trunks of their host trees. Food plants vary, but some species can be pests on cultivated plants. The caterpillar of the giant swallowtail, *Papilio cresphontes*, is known popularly as the "orange dog" and can be a pest in citrus orchards in the United States. In some species the caterpillars feed openly; in others they make a shelter by curling a leaf over and fastening it with silk.

The papilionid pupa is attached in an upright position by the cremaster at the rear end and usually supported by a silken girdle around the middle. The pupa may take on different colors such as green or brown to correspond with its background. In some species the pupa is attached to a tree trunk where in shape, texture, and color it bears an extraordinary resemblance to the stump of a small snapped-off twig or branch, even to the extent of being decorated with splashes of green, resembling lichens.

Mimicry in Swallowtails

Mimicry occurs both between different members of the Papilionidae and between papilionids and members of various other

The Osmeterium and Other Deterrents

Swallowtail caterpillars are generally smooth bodied. In most species a "Y"-shaped defensive organ called an osmeterium can be suddenly protruded from just behind the head—like the forked tongue of a snake—when the caterpillar is prodded or otherwise molested. The osmeterium is red or orange in most species, and its protrusion is accompanied by an unpleasant smell (emanating from isobutyric acids) that presumably deters predators. If so, it is strange that birds generally seem to be resolutely undeterred. Parasitic (ichneumon) wasps may also walk around on the caterpillar while the osmeterium is in use. It could be that its main function is to scare away ants by emitting a copy of their alarm pheromones. The visual effect alone can be quite startling, for example, when a dense knot of *Papilio anchisiades* caterpillars sitting on a tree trunk simultaneously extend their brilliant scarlet osmeteria, producing a sudden and quite unexpected eruption of color.

The habit of feeding on toxic *Aristolochia* plants renders poison eaters such as the pipevine swallowtail poisonous to vertebrate predators such as birds. Pipevine swallowtail caterpillars wear a conspicuous warningly colored uniform of bright reddish-brown. They are often found crawling around on the ground in a life-or-death quest for fresh food plants, having exhausted their supply of some of the smaller *Aristolochia* species.

In a number of species, such as the North American spicebush swallowtail, *Papilio troilus*, the caterpillar bears a pair of prominent eyelike spots above the head, giving it the appearance of a small snake. The deception is reinforced when the tonguelike osmeterium is suddenly flicked out. A quite different ploy used by the caterpillars of a large number of species is to mimic bird droppings. The caterpillars make no attempt to conceal themselves but sit motionless all day in full view on a leaf of their food plant, killing time until night falls, when they can resume feeding in safety. In some examples the resemblance to a bird dropping is only found in the smaller larvae, being lost in the later and much larger instars, which may be green or some other color. In the American tropics the commonest species of bird-dropping caterpillar is the king swallowtail, *P. thoas*. The species is one that maintains its deception throughout its larval life.

⊜ *The female mocker swallowtail of the family Papilionidae (top) bears a remarkable resemblance to the common tiger butterfly, Danaus chrysippus (family Danaidae), its mimicry model.*

families of butterflies, and even a few moths. In some cases only the females are mimics, the males retaining a normal appearance. In North America the somber hues of the pipevine swallowtail, whose adults are rejected on sight by most birds, are mimicked by both sexes of the spicebush swallowtail and by the females only of the tiger swallowtail, *Papilio glaucus*. Male tiger swallowtails are always mainly yellow with black markings, and some females have the same colors. Nonmimetic females are generally found in areas such as Florida, where the nasty-tasting pipevine swallowtail is rare or absent. Females that resemble the mainly yellow males seem more attractive to them and mate more often. That means that dark-colored mimetic females only thrive in areas where their mimicry of the pipevine swallowtail gives a clear boost to their survival rates, outweighing any reduced sexual success. The pipevine swallowtail is also mimicked by the red-spotted purple, *Limenitis arthemis* (a member of the Nymphalidae). However, the mimicry only occurs over parts of North America within the exact geographic range of the pipevine swallowtail. To the north the red-spotted purple is differently colored and nonmimetic.

Harmless Copycats

In Central and South America the numerous species of *Parides* cattle-hearts feed on poisonous host plants as caterpillars, giving rise to adults that provide the central models for many mimics. As with *Battus*, the adult's body is very tough and can withstand attacks from inexperienced birds that have not learned to avoid butterflies of a certain color and pattern. Most female *Parides* look very similar, being

black with red spots. The males are more distinctive, usually having green spots as well as red. Both sexes may lack hind-wing tails. The females, being unpalatable themselves, are Müllerian mimics of each other. They form core role models for a wide range of Batesian mimics—harmless species that copy their warning coloration. They include species of true swallowtails (*Papilio*) and kite swallowtails (*Eurytides*).

The most complex and downright bewildering examples of mimicry occur in the African mocker swallowtail, *Papilio dardanus*. The males are pale yellow with black

⊕ *Perched in the open on a citrus leaf in Madagascar, a Papilio caterpillar extrudes its orange osmeterium as a response to being gently prodded.*

high ground. Instead, they devote their time to flying around looking for host plants on which to lay their eggs. Choosing the best mate from the selection assembled on the hill is made easy for the females by the males themselves, who compete for the highest point on the hill. It ends up being monopolized by the dominant male, making him easy to find by any female wanting the pick of the bunch to father her offspring. She just heads straight for the highest point and is sure to find a winner in residence. The males compete for "top spot" by engaging in "spiral contests" up into the sky for a considerable distance, during which the loser will suddenly peel away and leave possession of the area to the victor. In many tropical papilionids the males establish territories on a perch high up in the canopy of some rain-forest tree. The opposite strategy, seen in many common species, is for the males to patrol over a wide area, searching for females on flowers and other likely places.

After losing her virginity, there is usually no barrier to the female if she wants to take another mate in the future. But in *Parides* and some members of the Parnassiinae the females are prevented from mating again for some time by the presence of a genital plug called a sphragis. It consists of a hard, brown, horny material that is applied in liquid form by the male at the time of mating. It closes off the female's genital pore, preventing her from engaging in any further acts of copulation until she has laid her eggs. Eventually the sphragis falls apart, leaving the female free to mate again. In *Cressida cressida* from Australia the sphragis can be half as long as the female's abdomen, projecting well out from her rear end. It is so big that it persuades males that it is not worth trying to make contact with her, and saves her from wasting valuable time and effort staving off unwelcome mating attempts.

The act of copulation in swallowtails is quite lengthy; and if the pair is disturbed, they will usually (except in Parnassiinae) fly strongly, the female doing all the work and carrying the male drooping from her rear end.

⊕ *The female tiger swallowtail,* Papilio glaucus, *is a perfectly palatable mimic of the pipevine swallowtail. The males, being nonmimetic, look quite different.*

markings, have conventional hind-wing tails, and are not mimetic. In Madagascar, where no suitable unpalatable models exist, the females resemble the males. Over much of Africa, where unpalatable models are legion, the females lack tails and mimic various species of disgustingly inedible butterflies, including *Amauris* (Danaidae) and *Bematistes* (Acraeidae). Several other species of African *Papilio*, as well as some *Graphium* species, also mimic various members of these two families of very unpalatable butterflies.

Hilltopping and Chastity Belts

In common with insects as varied as flies and wasps, various swallowtails resort to "hilltopping" behavior in which the males wait on some prominent feature until females arrive. This form of sexual rendezvous is particularly common in species inhabiting flattish deserts, where a hill protruding from the landscape will be very noticeable and provide a distinctive landmark visible for miles around. Hilltopping is very important in many species of North American *Papilio*. Once the virgin females have visited their hilltop, selected a suitable partner from the assembled males, and mated, they no longer show any particular interest in areas of

⊕ *Shivering its dark wings continuously in the manner typical of many swallowtails, the pipevine swallowtail,* Battus philenor, *feeds on flowers in the United States. The distinctively colored and highly unpalatable species is the model for several mimics.*

Orange sulfur
(Colias eurytheme)

Common name Whites (sulfurs, brimstones, orange-tips, Jezebels)

Family Pieridae

Order Lepidoptera

Number of species About 1,500 (58 U.S.)

Wingspan From about 0.9 in (23 mm) to about 4 in (10 cm)

Key features Wings mainly with broadly rounded tips; wing color often white or yellow, sometimes with orange or red tips or even (in tropical species) with a brilliant colorful pattern; all 6 legs functional; caterpillar cylindrical, usually smooth and slender, often green; chrysalis supported by both cremaster and silken girdle

Habits Adults spend much time in flight, usually in open, sunny places; males of certain species congregate in large numbers to drink on riverside sand; a few species migratory

Breeding Sexes often look different—males normally brighter; some species with quite complex courtship involving both scent and sight; in most species males patrol in search of females, which often adopt specialized deterring posture

Diet Adults feed on nectar or on urine-soaked ground; caterpillars eat plants of a wide variety of families; some species are widespread pests of cultivated plants

Habitat Mainly open places such as grasslands, deserts, roadsides, gardens, and woodland clearings; many species are specialists on high mountains; numerous brightly colored species in tropical rain forests

Distribution Worldwide except Antarctica

⊕ *The orange sulfur,* Colias eurytheme, *is a common North American species. Its favored host plant of alfalfa gives it the alternative common name of the alfalfa butterfly. Wingspan 1.5–2.4 inches (4–6 cm).*

Whites
Pieridae

Although popularly called "whites," most butterflies in the Pieridae are in fact yellow—the typical color of the sulfurs and brimstones in the subfamily Coliadinae.

EVEN AMONG THE SUBFAMILY Pierinae, which includes the typical "whites," there are many color variations. They include the numerous species in which the wing tips of the males are orange, scarlet, or mauve, or the gorgeously multicolored and rich tapestrylike patterns of many Jezebels *(Delias)* from the tropics of Asia and Australasia.

The most exceptional members of the Pieridae are the mimic-sulfurs in the subfamily Dismorphiinae. With their long, narrow wings and brown-and-yellow pattern they mimic the tigers and longwings of the families Ithomiidae and Heliconiidae.

Living in Extremes

Pierids occur in a wide range of mostly open habitats. They are among the few butterflies able to survive the rigors of life on some of the world's highest mountain ranges, being found at the upper limit of where insect life is still able to maintain a foothold. In the Himalayas *Baltia shawi* flies at over 16,500 feet (5,000 m)—the same altitude reached by species of *Piercolis* and *Hypsochila* in the Andes Mountains of South America. Pierids also push farther north than most butterflies, with *Colias nastes* and *C. hecla* being found within the Arctic Circle. At the other extreme, most of the Jezebels are among the few pierids that thrive in the interior of the tropical rain forest. They flit around near ground level in the gloomy understory. They are particularly common to New Guinea, where more than half of the 130 or so species occur.

Pierid eggs are spindle shaped, usually yellow or white, with an attractive surface pattern. They are laid singly or in neat clusters.

⊕ *A male brimstone butterfly,* Gonepteryx rhamni, *feeds on a burdock flower in England. The long proboscis is sucking up the nectar.*

The larvae are slim and cylindrical, and lack protrusions. They are usually smooth or only a little hairy, but never have spines. Many species are hard to see because they blend in well with their food plants. Others, such as the caterpillar of the large white, *Pieris brassicae*, are warningly colored and often gregarious. Some, such as *Eucheira* from Mexico, live in strong communal nests made of silk.

⊖ *A common Jezebel,* Delias nigrina, *is perched on a leaf in the rain-forest understory in Queensland, Australia. The brightly colored undersides are typical of Jezebels.*

Cabbage Crunchers

A number of mostly white members of the Pieridae are often found in suburban gardens or among fields of crops and are some of the most notorious of all butterfly pests. The cabbage white, *Pieris rapae,* was accidentally introduced into North America from Europe in about 1860. By 1881 it had spread to the entire eastern United States and now occupies the whole of North America south of the subarctic and arctic zones, as well as pushing southward down into Mexico. This buoyant level of success has been repeated elsewhere, with accidental introductions into Australia, New Zealand, Bermuda, and Hawaii. The females lay their eggs mainly on plants of the cabbage family (Brassicaceae). It is on commercial varieties that the caterpillars can be such a pest. In Europe and North Africa the large white, *P. brassicae,* can be even more of a headache on cabbages, since its caterpillars are not only much bigger but also gang up in voracious squads to reduce the leaves of their host plants to ragged skeletons. The food plants all have one thing in common: They contain mustard oils, which are absorbed by the caterpillars in their food, making them unpalatable to most birds. The ability to ward off most enemies using chemical defenses is highlighted by the "warning" pattern seen in caterpillars of the large white. The use of naturally occurring bacteria and viruses to control numbers in the caterpillar stage has had some effect, but cases of resistance are now beginning to occur.

As in swallowtails, the pierid pupa is attached to the substrate by a silken girdle around the middle, as well as by the cremaster at the rear end. Pierid pupae are generally well camouflaged, resembling leaves, buds, flowers, or—in a few cases—bird droppings. Most species pupate alone, but a few species form crowded aggregations.

In most pierids there is some small difference in wing pattern between the males and females, usually involving slightly more black on the wings of either one of the sexes. In most of the orange tips (*Anthocharis* and *Colotis*) the prominent orange, red, or purple patches on the tips of the forewings are most characteristic of the males and are usually not as marked or even absent in the females.

⊖ *The pupae of Jezebels are unusual in being "warningly" colored and placed in full view on the tops of leaves rather than on the undersides. This* Delias *species Jezebel is from Australia.*

members of their own species. Females of the orange sulfur, *Colias eurytheme* from North America, are not bothered about the yellow or orange color of the males. Instead, the female is interested only in males that reflect ultraviolet light strongly from their upper sides. She will ignore males of the common sulfur, *C. philodice,* because they do not reflect ultraviolet. To further ensure cross-mating does not occur, females will only mate with males that emit the correct pheromone.

Pattern Displays

The male's ultraviolet reflectance markings may be displayed in specific ways during his courtship endeavors. In the North American barred sulfur, *Eurema daira*, the males seek out females feeding on flowers and drop in beside them. The male then executes a snappy "salute" to the female by flipping over the forewing nearest to her so that she can see its black-and-yellow upper side (which also includes a large patch of ultraviolet-reflecting scales). Next he converts the forewing into a flag, waving it up and down in front of the female's face so that the ultraviolet-reflecting area flashes back and forth. At the same time, a pheromone is brushed onto the female's antennae. If her interest is aroused, she begins flicking her wings and eventually protrudes her abdomen upward. During mating all pierids can fly if disturbed—the female will carry the male beneath her.

Basking and Migrating

Because most species feed on flowers, often at low level, they are among the most frequently seen of butterflies. In the tropics a wide variety of pierids are among the butterflies most often seen gathering in numbers to drink on riverbanks and puddles, especially where

⬆ What a mess! This is the kind of gardener's nightmare that can result from a massed attack on cabbages and related plants by caterpillars of the large white butterfly, Pieris brassicae.

⬅ The caterpillar of the cloudless sulfur, Phoebis sennae, *seen here in Costa Rica, is well camouflaged when on its* Cassia *food plants, which are covered with pale-yellow flowers.*

Hidden Markings

In many of the sulfurs and brimstones the males are a darker yellow than the females, which may often be almost white. Sometimes the differences are so slight that male and female appear almost identical.

However, the apparent similarity can be misleading: What is not evident to our eyes are the differences in pattern between males and females of certain species (*Pheobis* and *Eurema*, for instance) caused by ultraviolet reflectance that is visible to the butterflies but not to humans. When the butterfly is viewed through ultraviolet-sensitive cameras, the males of some species are seen to flash brilliantly in the ultraviolet. Such patterns play a vital role in enabling males and females to identify

animals have urinated or there is some natural mineral enrichment of the water. Such gatherings may contain hundreds of individuals of the same species, usually males, but occasionally also a few females.

The adults of some of the common white species found in temperate areas spend a lot of time basking using a special posture. Instead of holding their wings flat, as in most butterflies, the basking whites slope the wings upward to form a "v." This position enables the white wing surfaces to reflect much of the heat onto the black wing bases, which absorb heat very efficiently and warm up the flight muscles. In pierids from cooler northern climates or from high mountains the amount of black on the wing bases is more extensive, allowing greater and more rapid absorption of heat (black absorbs heat better than any other color).

Mass Migration

Some pierids are notable migrants. The brown-veined white, *Belenois aurota*, follows the rains in some of the arid regions of Africa, often arriving in millions within a few days of heavy rainfall in areas such as the Kalahari Desert. In India millions of *Catopsilia pyranthe* follow the northeast monsoon as the rains rejuvenate the arid land. By timing their arrival in such a way, the adults ensure that a fresh harvest of plant growth is available to sustain their larvae.

In the Americas spectacular clouds of sulfurs (*Pheobis*) have been reported crossing over mountain passes during massed migration, while other species have been seen migrating in numbers across the open sea. The cloudless sulfur, *Phoebis sennae*, is a committed migrant, setting off every spring across a broad track as far north as Maine and Montana from its permanent breeding grounds in the southeastern United States and Mexico. In fall there is a return migration southward.

↳ *Pierids in several different genera often form large flocks on riverbanks, where they drink from salt-contaminated sand. These* Pheobis *sulfurs are on a rain-forest riverside in Argentina.*

Red admiral
(Vanessa atalanta)

Common name Brush-footed butterflies

Family Nymphalidae

Order Lepidoptera

Number of species About 3,000 (125 U.S.)

Wingspan From about 1 in (2.5 cm) to about 3.5 in (9 cm)

Key features Colors bright and varied, often very flamboyant and beautiful; wing shape diverse, sometimes with frilly edges; some species with tailed hind wings; front legs in both sexes reduced to form tiny brushlike appendages, leaving only 4 walking legs; none of the veins at base of wings greatly swollen; caterpillars smooth, hairy, or spiky

Habits Adults usually found on flowers or feeding on damp ground; most species are fast fliers; some species strongly migratory; in temperate regions overwintering may occur in adult stage; caterpillars solitary or gregarious

Diet Adults feed on flower nectar, fruit, fermenting tree sap, animal dung, urine-soaked ground, putrid animal corpses, and human sweat; caterpillars eat green leaves

Breeding Male and female usually look alike, but sometimes look very different; adults often engage in "spiraling" courtship; females may release pheromones to attract males; eggs laid singly or in masses; caterpillars often very spiny, but smooth and green in many tropical species; pupa suspended upside down from its tail, often with silver or gold spots

Habitat In all habitats, but most common in tropical rain forest; many species among the commonest butterflies in gardens, others restricted to high mountain slopes

Distribution Worldwide, living northward as far as Greenland

⊕ *The red admiral,* **Vanessa atalanta,** *is a wide-ranging migratory butterfly that can be found almost anywhere with flowers and ripe fruit. Adults are particularly fond of overripe and fermenting fruit. Wingspan 1.2 inches (3 cm).*

Brush-Footed Butterflies

Nymphalidae

The large family Nymphalidae contains some of the most familiar butterflies found in gardens in both North America and Europe. It also boasts a high proportion of the world's most dazzling insects.

THE NYMPHALIDAE IS A highly successful group. One of the most familiar of urban species, the painted lady, *Vanessa cardui*, is the most widespread butterfly in the world. It is found on all the continents, probably owing to its strong migratory instinct.

This globetrotting species is unquestionably a nymphalid, but the situation is not always so clear-cut, since the classification of the Nymphalidae is in dispute. Nine families—the Satyridae, Brassolidae, Morphidae, Amathusiidae, Libytheidae, Heliconiidae, Acraeidae, Ithomiidae, and Danaidae—are often included within the Nymphalidae as subfamilies. Their inclusion is based mainly on the fact that in all nine families the front legs of the adult are reduced in size and resemble a tiny brush, as with the Nymphalidae. However, there are also certain differences between these families and the Nymphalidae, so here they are classed in families of their own.

Subfamily Charaxinae

The adults in the subfamily Charaxinae typically have short, stout, and rather hairy bodies, and are among the strongest and fastest fliers of all butterflies. They generally perch and feed with the wings closed, but may open them to bask. Many species spend most of their time high in the forest canopy, so are difficult to study. In South and Central America the subfamily contains the leafwings (*Anaea*), in which the underside of the adults resembles a dead leaf.

Agrias contains some of the world's most sumptuously colored butterflies, highly prized by

⊕ *The painted lady,* **Vanessa cardui,** *is found worldwide. It is seen here clearly sitting on just four usable legs. The compound eye and the long, slender proboscis probing into a flower are also in evidence.*

⊖ *The green-lined charaxes,* **Charaxes candiope,** *feeding on fermenting sap on a fallen tree in Kenya, has the attractively patterned "tailed" wings typical of the genus.*

→ *Like most members of the genus,* Anaea fabius *from the American tropics resembles a dead leaf when its wings are closed, even having a "tail" that resembles the leaf stalk.*

collectors. In Africa and Asia the "rajahs" (*Charaxes*) are renowned for the intricately ornamental patterns on their undersides. Most species have sharp teethlike projections on the hind wings, which the males may use as lances in aerial "dogfights."

Adult rajahs are often members of the eager throngs of butterflies pushing and jostling on the fresh dung of certain mammals. Dung is a typical diet in this subfamily, along with putrid carrion, rotting fruit, fermenting sap, and urine-soaked ground. Flowers seldom, if ever, figure

175

on the adults' menu; they prefer something stronger. After a long session of "boozing" on alcoholic drinks such as fermenting sap or fruit, the adults can often be picked up quite easily, having become too intoxicated to put up much of a struggle.

Charaxine eggs are generally rounded, with flattened tops and bottoms and some ribbing along the sides. The caterpillars are very distinctive. The body is generally smooth or slightly granular, and in many species there is a crown of between two and six horns projecting upward on top of the head. The crowns are especially well developed on the broad, flat-faced heads of the rajahs. Some species also have horns arising from the tail. Many leafwing and shoemaker (*Prepona*) caterpillars spend the day sitting head downward along a string of frass (debris or excrement produced by the caterpillar) hanging from a leaf. While hanging motionless on its support, the caterpillar—which has a rather crumpled brown skin speckled with green and silver and a somewhat humped shape—closely resembles the tip of a leaf that has shriveled and died, a common sight in the rain forests where it lives. Larger caterpillars simply sit on top of a leaf, where they resemble a dead crinkled leaf that has fallen from above. If touched, certain species can hunch their thorax upward, suddenly exposing two bulging

⬆ *Many tropical nymphalids never feed on flowers but prefer dung. These* Charaxes subornatus *in Uganda are feeding on the droppings of a civet, a catlike animal.*

⬇ *When hanging on its frass-string (made from its droppings), the caterpillar of* Prepona antimache *from the American tropics looks amazingly like the tip of a leaf that has died and shriveled.*

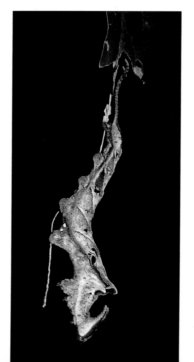

blue "eyes" and somewhat resembling babies of some of the deadly snakes of the area. In contrast, some species make a leaf roll in which to hide from their enemies.

Charaxine males tend to be very territorial, often spending days on end sitting on a tree trunk. They will dash out to inspect other butterfly intruders, but also birds and, in *Euxanthe* from Africa, any humans who dare to trespass too close.

Subfamily Apaturinae

The subfamily Apaturinae contains the hackberry butterfly, *Asterocampa celtis*—a very widespread North American species. It also boasts the splendidly colored emperors, such as the beautiful silver emperor, *Doxocopa laure*—a tropical species that regularly migrates northward to Texas. The species is one of a number observed feeding on flowers, but apaturine adults generally share with the Charaxinae a strong preference for dung or rotting fruit. The male of another North American species, the desert hackberry butterfly, *Asterocampa leila*, is very aggressive in excluding intruding males from a wide area around his own personal bush of the food plant, the desert hackberry (*Celtis pallida*). Apaturine caterpillars are generally smooth, with two tails and with long, often antlerlike horns projecting forward in front of the head.

Subfamily Nymphalinae

With about 1,000 species worldwide, the Nymphalinae is by far the largest subfamily and contains many of the most familiar garden butterflies found in North America and Europe. Gardens are a magnet for the butterflies because, unlike in the previous two families, the adults of many species prefer to feed on nectar. A fine show of flowering zinnias, buddleias, and other popular flowers makes a powerful lure. The Nymphalinae is split into several tribes. The Nymphalini contains the admirals, peacocks, buckeyes, crackers, anglewings, tortoiseshells, and painted ladies.

Members of the tribe Melitaeni are mainly found in the cooler parts of the Northern Hemisphere, extending almost to the Arctic, and include the checkerspots and crescents. The Argynnini consists largely of the fritillaries, chiefly found in North America and Europe, mainly brownish-orange butterflies with darker wing veins, often with beautiful silver spots on the undersides. Violets (*Viola*) are important food plants for their caterpillars, and the females are unusual in normally laying their

↪ This buckeye, Junonia coenia, *is from Mexico. The species is a strong migrant, moving northward throughout the United States in summer.*

↓ *Not all tropical nymphalids feed on dung or rotting fruit. The superb silver emperor,* Doxocopa laure *from Mexico, is feeding on flowers of the parsley family.*

⊕ *The extraordinary* Euthalia *caterpillar from Malaysia is protected by a canopylike stockade of spines that, on close inspection, have a "warning" pattern.*

eggs on tree bark, stones, or other objects near the host plants, rather than on them.

Eggs, Larvae, and Pupae

Nymphaline eggs are generally round and green; they are usually laid singly, but sometimes in large batches. Some species of crackers (*Hamadryas*) lay their eggs end to end in long chains suspended from the food plant. Nymphaline caterpillars are generally covered in a dense coat of hard branching spines, often accompanied by forked horns on the head. A few species mimic bird droppings, as in some swallowtail caterpillars (Papilionidae); others resemble twigs and dead leaves. In *Temenis* from the American tropics the color of the body changes with each molt. Nymphaline caterpillars tend to be very sociable, often lounging around in conspicuous spiky huddles on their food plant, which they often reduce to tattered shreds. In many checkerspots and fritillaries the eggs are laid in clusters. The young larvae rest together in a silken nest, hibernating when only half-grown. They then go solo in order to feed up before they mature in the following spring. Painted lady caterpillars live alone within a silken nest on their food plants, which encompass a huge range of plant species from many families.

Some nymphaline caterpillars create a homemade shelter by biting through the veins

➔ *A few (almost fully grown) caterpillars of the small tortoiseshell,* Aglais urticae *from Europe, mix with smaller caterpillars from a later batch of eggs.*

⊙ *The caterpillar of the red dagger wing,* Marpesia petreus *from the American tropics, sits in full view on top of its host plant. Its unusual pattern helps break the outline of the body.*

of a leaf so that it droops down like a tent; the occupant then feeds on the leaf tips, leaving the rest of its home intact.

Nymphaline pupae are as varied as the adults and caterpillars, assuming an enormous variety of shapes and colors. They are sometimes smooth and sometimes have prominent spines, horns, and other protuberances. The pupae are mostly camouflaged and in the zebra butterfly, *Colobura dirce* from the American tropics, resemble a snapped-off piece of wood.

Females usually take great care to place their eggs on or near the correct food plant. That done, the female leaves her eggs to develop as best they can. However, females of *Hypolimnas anomala* and *H. antilope* from islands in the Pacific generally remain on watch beside their eggs. In *H. anomala* about half the females stay and guard their egg batch, which usually contains about 500 eggs.

The female will try to drive ants away by fluttering her wings at them, although the larger species just ignore her and steal the eggs anyway. When the caterpillars hatch, they remain densely packed near their eggs. About half of females remain with their offspring, finally quitting when the family has made a safe migration to a new leaf.

Scent and Sound

Where males and females are different colors, it may seem that color must be a key issue in sexual relationships. Yet females seem surprisingly ready to accept partners whose bright colors have been artificially concealed. In actual fact, scent may be far more important reproductively, especially since males are very generous with the amounts of pheromone-rich "love dust" particles with which they will bombard a female as they flutter around her. The males of some species also have hair pencils that can be protruded from the abdomen and used to dust the female with pheromones. In the crackers from the American tropics the males make loud whiplike cracking sounds as they interact during brief flights from communal perching sites on tree trunks. Nobody knows the reason for the piercing sound, and it is uncertain how it is generated, although it probably originates from the wings.

A common male strategy is to wait for females on a piece of flat ground or perched on twigs. Alternatively, the male may set up a territory near the food plant and try to keep it until females show up ready to lay their eggs. This is an uncertain gamble; so if a female finally arrives nearby, the waiting male immediately begins courtship tactics, chasing

179

the female and buffeting her with his wings. If his endeavors fail to tempt her, she raises her abdomen upward almost vertically and holds her wings open. This creates both a "get lost" signal and a physical barrier that prevents him from reaching her abdomen and coupling up.

Patience Pays Off

For the male of *Aglais urticae,* the European small tortoiseshell, any chance of sexual conquest means establishing a temporary territory near a bed of stinging nettles (*Urtica dioica*)—the food plant. He chases off other males; but as soon as a female appears, he shadows her closely until she lands and perches with wings spread. He must now sit and wait close behind the stationary female. He reminds her of his presence occasionally by bringing his twin antennae sharply down and rapping them against her outstretched wings. The sexual stalemate can last for hours, but eventually, toward dusk, the female will move down among the nettle stems to roost. At that point she will finally consent to mate with her attendant. In *Aglais urticae*, and in many other species, disputes between males over territory are settled through spiraling helter-skelter flights high up into the air. The male who achieves topmost position gains the territory.

In another European species, the silver-washed fritillary, *Argynnis paphia*, it is common to see a female performing a slow and rather fluttering straight-and-level flight just above the ground. Close behind follows the male, busily performing a kind of aerial ballet that involves weaving a pattern of loops down and around the female as she flies. If she accepts his advances and settles on a leaf, he takes her antennae in his wings and claps them repeatedly, coating the receptors on her antennae with his male pheromone. The female of *Argynnis paphia* can actively promote sexual encounters by "calling" for partners, luring them toward her by releasing a pheromone from pouches at the tip of her abdomen.

Defense and Mimicry

In some crackers the upper sides of the wings bear a mottled pattern that camouflages the butterfly as it perches on a tree trunk. In most other nymphalids the upper sides are brightly colored, and the undersides are camouflaged. In some species such as the African blue pansy, *Junonia orithya*, or the European peacock, *Nymphalis io,* the butterfly normally rests with its wings closed; but when disturbed, it flicks them open to reveal two large, staring eyespots designed to scare off an enemy. In *Polygonia,* the anglewings from North America and Europe, the edges of the wings are ragged, so that with wings closed, the butterfly resembles a dead oak leaf.

Many nymphalids are mimics. In North America the viceroy, *Limenitis archippu*s, is a Müllerian mimic of the monarch, *Danaus plexippus*. In South America various species of *Phyciodes* are mimics of tigers in the family Ithomiidae; butterflies and moths from several other families are also involved and mimic tigers as well. In Africa *Pseudacraea* mimic various species of unpalatable butterflies.

⬅ *In Trinidad a mating pair of coolie butterflies,* **Anartia amathea,** *are disturbed by a male hovering above the female, buffeting his wings against her.*

➡ *In many mating butterflies, as in this pair of Arachne checkerspots,* **Poladryas minuta** *in Arizona, the male dangles from the tip of the female's abdomen.*

American monarch
(*Danaus plexippus*)

Common name Milkweed butterflies

Family Danaidae

Order Lepidoptera

Number of species About 250 (5 U.S.)

Wingspan From about 2 in (5 cm) to about 6 in (15 cm)

Key features Color range restricted, often brownish-orange spotted with black and white; some pale blue or lemon marked with black; a few lacelike, black and white, others very dark brown, sometimes with blue patches; wings generally broad; antennae without scales; 4 walking legs; larvae have fleshy outgrowths

Habits Adults are powerful fliers and include the most migratory of butterflies; 1 species (the monarch) overwinters in huge aggregations; all species often seen on flowers

Breeding Males generally have large hair pencils that release pheromones during courtship; males procure sexual pheromones by feeding on certain withered plants; eggs are flattened domes with prominent ribs; pupae sometimes covered with gold or silver spots, or may even be mirrorlike

Diet Adults feed on nectar from flowers; caterpillars eat toxic plants, mainly milkweeds and frangipani plants

Habitat In all habitats from deserts to mountains and from gardens to city lots

Distribution Mainly tropical, only reaching northern temperate areas by migrating northward in summer

⊕ *Danaus plexippus, the American monarch, is the only butterfly that migrates annually both northward and southward. It forms spectacular overwintering roosts, the largest being in the mountain forests in the state of Michoacán in Central Mexico. Wingspan 3.5–4 inches (9–10 cm).*

Milkweed Butterflies

Danaidae

The Danaidae contains the most famous of all migrant butterflies, the American monarch. Its dramatic overwintering roosts are one of the great spectacles of the natural world.

DANAIDS ARE MOST LIKELY to be seen flapping in their typically lazy fashion along the edge of some rain forest in the Asian tropics, where the largest range of species is located. All species are warningly colored and have tough, leathery bodies that are not easily damaged by birds or other predators.

The range of colors is limited, being mainly brownish-orange in the Americas and Africa, but more varied in Asia. Here, the largest of the danaids, the black-and-white *Idea* lacewings, can be found feeding on flowers on the rain-forest edge. The somber blackish *Euploea* "crows" are common in gardens throughout the region. Both species are mimicked by other more palatable butterflies. Asian *Danaus* are also more varied than in other regions, with several powder-blue or lemon-yellow species, streaked with black. Like all danaids, the adults can often be seen on flowers in sunny places such as roadsides and gardens. Unlike most other closely related tropical butterflies, danaids are not attracted to dung or rotting fruit, but they may sometimes sip water.

Neutralizing Plant Defenses
The eggs form a rather flattened dome and bear prominent ribs along the sides. They are always placed singly on the food plant. The caterpillars, which are solitary, are smooth-skinned and usually marked with a prominent combination of "warning" colors. There are usually between one and four pairs of rather fleshy, flexible, threadlike tubercles at the front end. The tubercles probably help reinforce the

⊖ *Danaid caterpillars are smooth-skinned and have fleshy outgrowths on their head, more well-developed in some species than others. All species are warningly colored, as seen in this caterpillar from Trinidad.*

⊖ The novice, Amauris ochlea, *is one of several species of black-and-white danaids found in Africa. This is a common "warning" uniform, advertising that the butterfly is very unpalatable.*

"keep-off" message by making the caterpillars appear especially memorable to their enemies.

Danaid caterpillars feed mainly on milkweed plants in the family Asclepiadaceae, and to a lesser extent on plants such as the frangipani (Apocynaceae) and the fig (Moraceae). All the chosen food plants usually contain toxic compounds that are stored by the caterpillars as they feed. However, there are limits to the caterpillar's ability to deal with an excess of toxic chemicals. Milkweed plants contain large amounts of milky latex that bleeds profusely from damaged leaves or stems. The latex could gum up the caterpillar's mouthparts as it feeds. To reduce the flow of toxins, the caterpillar will usually chew a broad trough in the stem leading to the leaf or flower head on which it intends to feed. The supply of latex is then cut off, and the affected area sags downward. When feeding on milkweed leaves, small caterpillars of the American queen, *Danaus gilippus*, create a "moat" by first chewing out a circular furrow in the leaf surface. The moat isolates the area within its boundaries from the main supply of latex. After waiting for about an hour for the moat to fill up and drain the "islet" that it surrounds, the caterpillar can safely begin feeding. Another tactic is to sever entire leaf veins to cut off the latex supply to a larger area.

The danaid pupa is suspended head downward from a small silk pad. It is generally a squat, rounded shape with few noticeable projections. It is often green, but many species are decorated with brilliant gold or silver spots.

It may even be entirely metallic gold or silver, with a mirrorlike sheen.

The toxic chemicals absorbed by the caterpillar as it feeds consist largely of poisons that act on the heart, called cardiac glycosides, normally passed on through the pupa to the adults. The adults have distinctive "warning" uniforms that are copied by a wide variety of other Lepidoptera, both palatable and unpalatable. In Africa the brownish-orange plain tiger or African monarch, *Danaus chrysippus*, is the model for many butterfly mimics from other families, as well as a few moths. Even within a particular species of danaid some individuals may actually be mimicking others. This is known as "automimicry." The caterpillars of certain individuals may have eaten plants that are not toxic or only slightly so, producing adults that are not chemically protected—despite their "warning" livery. Such individuals, looking exactly like genuinely unpleasant butterflies whose caterpillars have fed on toxic food plants, benefit from the deception.

Secondhand Chemicals

In all male danaids there is a pair of brushlike hair pencils that can be extruded from the tip of the abdomen. During courtship the male inserts the hair pencils into pheromone-producing glands on his wings. He then bombards the female with pheromone-rich particles from the hair pencils. The particles contain a "glue" that sticks them to the female's antennae, where their sexual message is transferred. The pheromones are derived from pyrrolizidine alkaloids that the males collect by feeding on dead or withered plants of certain families, especially heliotropes.

The method of applying the pheromones from the hair pencils varies from species to species. In the American queen the male brushes the female's head with his hair pencils after overtaking her in flight. The action transmits a chemical signal for the female to land immediately. The male then hovers over her, drenching her with more pheromones. Eventually the female folds her wings, allowing the male to move in beside her and mate.

The Monarch

The American monarch, *Danaus plexippus*, is found in the Americas, the West Indies, on some islands of Southeast Asia such as the Philippines, and in New Guinea and Australia. It is occasionally driven by storms to Europe, where it is unlikely to establish a breeding population because of the cool climate and scarcity of suitable food plants. In North America the monarch is mimicked by the viceroy, *Limenitis archippus* (Nymphalidae).

Monarch caterpillars feed on a variety of different milkweeds, some more toxic than others. The adult butterflies therefore range from perfectly palatable to highly unpleasant and distinctly poisonous. If a bird eats one of the nastier specimens, it will quickly become unwell and vomit up the entire contents of its crop. The bird soon recovers and has learned a valuable lesson—not to eat any butterfly resembling a monarch.

Courtship in monarchs differs from all other known danaids in that the male

⊙ *These males of the plain tiger (or African monarch),* Danaus chrysippus, *are stocking up on alkaloids by feeding on withered heliotrope plants trampled by elephants in Africa.*

does not deploy his hair pencils, which are very small. Instead, he sets off in pursuit of any passing female, dives onto her back, and locks his legs beneath her wings. Such tactics prevent her from any further attempts at flapping, and they glide to the ground on the male's outspread wings. Once landed, the male taps the female with his antennae, they mate (often with a protesting struggle by the female), and then the male flies off with the female dangling from the tip of his abdomen.

Mass Migration

The most well-known behavior of the monarch is its annual migration to and from its wintering grounds. The same places are used year after year by successive generations of butterflies. They will never have seen the hibernation sites, but they somehow know exactly where to go. Small sites occur in Arizona and Florida, and much larger ones on the California coast, from San Francisco down south into Baja. By far the largest and most spectacular roosts, containing millions of butterflies, occur in mountain forests in the state of Michoacán in central Mexico. Here the trees are draped throughout the winter months with a colorful coat of living butterflies. However, they are thinned out during the winter as thousands of monarchs are taken by various birds, some of which eat little else and seem immune to their poison. Unseasonable frosts may also wipe out millions.

In springtime the survivors fly northward from their wintering grounds, laying eggs as they go. Butterflies from the California coast head up to the Pacific Northwest and Great Basin; those from Mexico migrate into the Great Plains, the eastern United States, and southeastern Canada. In late summer the offspring of the northbound migrants head south to the wintering ground, feeding as they go and building up reserves of fat that will see them though the winter. Monarchs fly up to 2,600 miles (4,200 km) during these migrations.

Thousands of overwintering American monarchs, Danaus plexippus, *festoon the trees like garlands of bright flowers at Natural Bridge State Beach in California.*

Prominents

Notodontidae

From making faces to squirting chemicals, the defense mechanisms of prominent moth caterpillars are bizarre in the extreme. Even the adults are intriguing, with their near-perfect ability to disguise themselves as sticks.

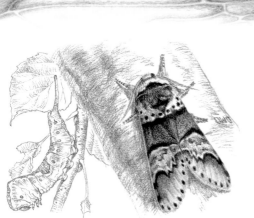

Common name Prominents

Poplar kitten moth
(Furcula bifida)

Family Notodontidae

Order Lepidoptera

Number of species About 2,600 (136 U.S.)

Wingspan From about 1 in (2.5 cm) to about 3 in (8 cm)

Key features Adult color usually drab, grays and browns predominating, often spotted or streaked with black; toothlike tufts of scales usually protruding from middle of inner edge of forewing; at rest adult holds wings rooflike or rolled tightly around body in a sticklike pose; body stout; proboscis usually well developed; antennae usually pectinate in males and in females of some species; hearing organs present on thorax; larvae variable, hairy or smooth, often weirdly shaped

Habits Adults generally nocturnal; seldom found when inactive in daytime, often coming to lights at night; occasionally found at rest on tree trunks or fence posts; caterpillars found singly or in family groups

Breeding Males generally smaller than females; females release pheromones to attract mates; eggs normally laid in large clusters on leaves of food plant; pupa attached to tree trunks, concealed beneath leaves, or formed in cell below ground

Diet Many adults probably do not feed, others visit flowers or leaking tree sap; caterpillars feed on wide range of plants, especially trees, on which they may be serious forestry pests

Habitat Mainly in forest but found widely in many habitats; some species breed in gardens

Distribution Worldwide in habitable areas

⊕ *The poplar kitten moth,* Furcula bifida, *is found in Europe and Asia, generally flying from April to July. Wingspan 1.4–1.8 inches (3.5–4.5 cm).*

ADULT PROMINENTS ARE MAINLY sturdily built moths that are exclusively nocturnal and rarely seen during the day. In the majority of species a tuft of scales projecting from the middle of the inner edge of the forewings is raised prominently above the level of the closed wings when the moth is at rest. It forms a pointed, curly tuft on top of the body, hence the common name of prominents. In males the antennae are usually comblike, unlike in many Noctuidae (owlet moths), with which the prominents could otherwise easily be confused. In owlet moths the antennae are threadlike.

Leaf and Twig Mimicry

The adults of many species from various parts of the world bear an amazing likeness to a rather short, stumpy, broken-off stick. In *Pavia undulata* from New Guinea the adult moth spends the day sitting at an angle to a branch, where it resembles a twig that has snapped— the moth's head having a rather tattered appearance corresponding to the broken end of the "twig." In the buff-tip moth, *Phalera*

↱ *The photographer who took this picture walked past this mating pair of European coxcomb prominents,* Ptilodon capucina, *several times, mistaking them for a piece of fallen bark.*

↓ *This* Rosema *species moth is proving itself to be a good mimic of a fresh leaf in a Peruvian rain forest.*

bucephala from Europe,
the adult's profile is rather long
and narrow due to the wings being held
closely rolled around the body. When at rest,
sitting openly on a leaf, the buff-tip's portrayal
of a short stub of fallen twig is very convincing,
with the yellow head duplicating the freshly
broken inner section.

Phalera sundana from Southeast Asia,
however, takes one more step toward total
disguise. The "splintered" yellowish tip of its
body protrudes upward between the wings;
combined with the uneven finish of its yellow
head, the effect is a "newly fractured"
configuration at both ends of the body. It too
sits in the open on leaves, not on broken twigs.

The tattered appearance of some
notodontid species comes from the typical
"prominent" tufts of scales along the top of
the body. They resemble scraps of fallen bark
that have peeled away from the tree trunk. A
pair of coxcomb prominents, Ptilodon capucina
from Europe, will spend all day mating in full
view. Yet they remain undetected by adopting a
peculiar pose, lying flat on their
sides so that their irregular,
zigzag, barklike body profiles are
emphasized. In Rosema from the
American tropics the green
adults spend the day sitting on
vegetation. All the legs are
tucked out of sight beneath the
wings, except for one front leg,
which is stuck out, thereby
becoming the "stem" of the
fallen green "leaf." The intriguing copycats can
be quite common in rain-forest habitats and are
some of the few adult notodontids likely to be
found regularly and fairly easily in daytime.

Female prominents generally lay their eggs
in ones or twos, or in neat batches on leaves of
the food plant, sometimes accompanied by a
protective secretion produced when laying.

The caterpillars of many notodontids are
exceedingly bizarre. Many have a very jagged

⊕ Phalera sundana,
seen here in rain forest
on the Indonesian island
of Sumatra, bears an
extraordinary
resemblance to a broken
twig that has fallen onto
a leaf below.

profile due to the presence of several raised peaklike tubercles. The sawtooth outline is even reflected in the specific name of one European species, the pebble prominent, *Eligmodonta ziczac*. When startled, the caterpillars of most species freeze and raise the front and rear parts of the body upward, retaining their hold with just the four pairs of middle prolegs. In the European lobster moth, *Stauropus fagi*, the caterpillar curves the flexibly hinged rear section of its body almost back on itself, while simultaneously raising its head and brandishing its long reddish legs in a threatening manner. The grotesque posture makes it looks more like some dangerous crustacean than a caterpillar, thereby giving it its common name.

In many notodontid larvae the rearmost prolegs are reduced or absent, but in certain genera, such as *Cerura* and *Dicranura*, they are modified into a pair of hollow tubercles. Each tubercle contains a single red filament, slender and whiplike in appearance. When aroused, the caterpillar can extrude the filament and flick it back and forth, secreting a pungent odor. In some species, such as the European puss moth, *Cerura vinula*, a gland behind the head can project a spray of corrosive liquid containing formic acid over a distance of up to 8 inches (20 cm). However, in an effort to minimize the need for last-ditch chemical defenses, the puss moth caterpillar first attempts to panic its enemies into retreat. It draws in its head, creating a rather intimidating, bright-pinkish false "face," complete with two black "eyes."

The glands present on the thorax of the North American variable oakleaf moth, *Heterocampa manteo*, secrete a dose of formic acid so strong that it can burn human skin. It seems to make the caterpillars immune to attack by birds, enabling their numbers to remain unchecked as they ravage huge areas of deciduous forest. Such destruction occurred in Missouri in 1971, when almost 2 million acres (800,000 ha) of oak trees were stripped bare.

Making Faces at the Enemy

The false "face" of the puss moth caterpillar is designed to intimidate its enemies by appearing rather snakelike. A similar illusion is created in a very different way by *Crinodes* from the American tropics. The caterpillar always sits beneath twigs or leaves rather than on top of them. Its instant reaction to danger is to flop its front end downward to reveal a pair of eyelike spots on either side of the front legs. The snakelike impression is reinforced by the rather fanglike legs between the "eyes."

In other caterpillars the defense strategy is to draw an enemy's attention away from the vulnerable real head by directing it toward a false head at the rear end, as seen in the adults of some butterflies. In *Lirimiris* from Central America the caterpillar reacts to a sudden threat

⬇ *The first line of defense in the caterpillar of the European puss moth,* Cerura vinula, *is to pull its head back into the first abdominal segments, creating a weird and colorful "face."*

← ⬆ *These two caterpillars were found within a few yards of one another in a forest in Costa Rica; both employ rear-end "false-head" mimicry. A* Lirimiris *(left) inflates its brown rear end and starts to turn its head around to make it less conspicuous. A* Naprepa *(above) starts to tuck its head out of sight beneath its body.*

Processionary Moths

During the day the caterpillars of many species of processionary moths gather in dense, hairy masses on their host tree trunks, as seen here in South Africa.

by inflating its false head at the rear end, making it a more conspicuous target. Simultaneously, it curves its real head backward and tries to conceal it alongside its body. Such behavior is by no means unique, and many other caterpillars from a variety of moth families take advantage of "false-head mimicry" in various ways.

Most of the more bizarre examples of notodontid caterpillar feed singly, but in some of the more conventional species they feed in family groups. The buff-tip moth larvae are warningly colored in black and yellow. The bright coloration, together with a hairy coat and the habit of forming dense groups as they strip their food plants bare, seems quite enough to make them immune to most enemies.

The moths in the subfamily Thaumetopoeinae (often given their own family) are well known for the gregarious habits of their larvae. The larvae always possess a full set of prolegs. They also have a warty exterior protected by a battery of short hairs that pack a powerful sting, sufficient to cause considerable pain in humans. The caterpillars of the pine processionary moth, *Thaumetopoea pityocampa* from Europe, live communally in large silk nests slung on the branch tips of pine trees. As they move out to feed at night, they follow one another nose to tail in single file along the branches and twigs of the pines, forming processions up to 12 yards (11 m) long.

In another European species, the oak processionary moth, *T. processionea*, the nests are large silken bags. They are slung on the trunks of oaks rather than on the twigs, and the larvae march out to feed in broader columns. Pupation takes place communally within the nest. In the pine processionary moth, however, the larvae disperse down to the ground to pupate just beneath the soil. Both species can cause serious damage to woodlands. Caterpillars with similar habits can also be pests in Africa.

Common name Tiger moths

Family Arctiidae

Great tiger moth
(Arctia caja)

Order Lepidoptera

Number of species About 10,000 (264 U.S.)

Wingspan From 0.5 in (13 mm) to about 3.2 in (8 cm)

Key features Adults often among the most brightly colored of all moths; may also be white, or drab brown or gray; wing shape very varied, sometimes long and narrow, otherwise relatively broad; proboscis often reduced in size; antennae in male pectinate or simple, always simple in female; hearing organs present on thorax; some species mimic other insects; caterpillars generally very hairy, some known as woolly bears

Habits Adults either nocturnal or day-active (diurnal); diurnal species often very active, feeding and mating by day; may be very prominent in localized colonies

Breeding Courtship very complex; several species form large groups (leks) for mating by day or night; males may inflate large sacs called coremata; some derive pheromones by feeding on certain plants; eggs laid in masses or scattered randomly over vegetation; caterpillars pupate in loose cocoon formed from silk mixed with their own hairs

Diet Adults of many species do not feed; others feed by day or night on flowers; caterpillars feed on lichens or a wide variety of plants

Habitat Found in all habitats from coastal sandhills and saltmarshes to deserts, grasslands, forests, and mountainsides; some species most common in gardens

Distribution Worldwide, but most abundant in the tropics

⊕ *The great tiger moth (also known as the garden tiger moth), Arctia caja, is found throughout the Northern Hemisphere. Its appearance is so variable that it is rare to find two individuals with the same markings. Wingspan 1.8–2.6 inches (4.5–6.5 cm).*

Tiger Moths   Arctiidae

The Arctiidae contains some of the most brilliantly flamboyant of moths. Many species mimic other insects and do not even look as though they belong to the Lepidoptera.

THE TYPICAL "TIGERS" BELONG in the subfamily Arctiinae, which has some of the most colorful moths to occur in temperate regions. An example is the great tiger moth, *Arctia caja*. It is relatively rare in North America, but in Europe it is often the most familiar of the tigers, even in urban settings—earning it the common name of garden tiger in Britain. As in several other tigers, its gaudy decoration is seldom displayed, since the adult moth hides away during the day. It only flies at night, when the ostentatious colors cannot be seen. Other similarly flashy species fly by day, which is a more logical behavior, because their colors can fulfill the "warning" function for which they are intended. Sometimes there is extra safety in numbers: On the Mediterranean island of Rhodes thousands of adult *Euplagia quadripunctaria* migrate every year to the same small area of woodland to hibernate—where they have even become a tourist attraction.

Cocktail of Chemicals
The caterpillars of all the more brightly colored species either absorb and store unpalatable and toxic compounds (histamines or alkaloids) from their food plants or manufacture them within their own bodies. Some of the adults—for example, *Rhodogastria* and *Utetheisa*—have a very active form of defense. They secrete poisonous blobs of a foamy liquid from glands on the thorax. The liquid smells and tastes unpleasant, and a predator never comes back for more. The moths, however, seem immune to their own poisons. By curving the proboscis upward over their head, they may suck the evil liquid back up again to avoid wasting it. The adults, along with other arctiids, will also visit

⊕ A Rhodogastria *species sitting on a fern in the*
rain forest of Borneo oozes a frothy blob of
distasteful liquid from its thorax in response to
being touched.

⊖ *A mating pair of* Gnophaela vermiculata *on a*
flower in the American West. The black-and-white
colors are a common "warning" pattern, although
quite rare in arctiids.

withered plants of the borage family to
stock up on their supplies of defensive
pyrrolizidine alkaloids, which the plants
produce. The moth dissolves the chemicals in
the plant by squirting liquid from its proboscis
onto it. The chemical secretions of some
arctiids have an instant and painful effect on
human skin, similar to a wasp sting.

The members of the subfamily Lithosiinae
are long, narrow-bodied moths. Their larvae
feed almost exclusively on lichens, giving them
the name of lichen moths in North America.
They fly mostly at night, but some species feed
on flowers in daytime, especially mimetic
examples such as the North American
Lycomorpha pholus. It mimics a net-winged
beetle in the family Lycidae.

Several other subfamilies are often given
family status. The most distinctive is the
Ctenuchinae (often listed as Ctenuchidae). It is

With its long,
narrow wings stuck out to the sides, Eurota
sericaria *from Brazil is a typical member of the subfamily*
Ctenuchinae. *Its body is warningly colored.*

a mainly tropical subfamily consisting of some 3,000 species of small or medium-sized moths with relatively narrow wings. The warningly colored adults are active in daytime and move only sluggishly, relying heavily on the defensive chemicals that make them unpalatable to most predators. Many species are mimics of other chemically defended insects, especially wasps. Some mimic the distasteful net-winged beetles of the family Lycidae.

Mimicry—where one insect copies the physical attributes of another more poisonous or better defended one—is also widely found in the subfamily Hypsinae. The moths tend to be larger than Ctenuchinae, with a well-developed proboscis and relatively large eyes. Most of the mimetic species are found in the tropics of Central and South America. Some, such as *Dysschema irene*, are members of the "tiger-striped" mimicry ring, involving similar-looking members of many different butterfly families as well as moths of the family Castniidae. Other genera of Hypsinae belong to mimicry rings involving transparent-winged members of the Ithomiidae and Danaidae.

Eggs and Caterpillars

Arctiid eggs are usually laid in large batches on the food plant, although in species that are unfussy about their food the eggs are scattered randomly, and the caterpillars feed on whatever comes to hand. In most species the caterpillars are solitary, but in some they form vast hordes that feed voraciously, as in the fall webworm moth, *Hyphantria cunea*. Originally native to North America (where its caterpillars attack and devastate more than 100 species of trees), the harmful forestry pest was accidentally introduced to Europe. It is now wreaking equal havoc in forests there. Some arctiids, however, are more helpful. The black-and-orange-banded caterpillars of the European cinnabar moth, *Tyria jacobaeae*, strip their ragweed (*Senecio jacobaea*) food plant down to the bare stems. Since the ragweed is poisonous to livestock—especially horses—the caterpillars provide a useful service. Ragweed is a serious pest in New Zealand, where it was introduced by mistake. The cinnabar moth was released there in an attempt to control the plant. Unfortunately, its numbers dwindled, owing to the tendency of the native birds to eat the caterpillars. The birds are not put off by a bold "warning" uniform and substantial chemical defenses—mainly poisonous pyrrolizidine alkaloids derived from their food plant. Yet cinnabar moth caterpillars are normally left alone by birds in Europe.

Arctiid caterpillars are generally hairy, sometimes extremely so, earning them the familiar name of woolly bears. The hairs are an irritant, and children tempted to handle such an attractively furry creature soon regret it. In many

⊕ *A warningly colored cinnabar moth caterpillar,* Tyria jacobaeae, *on a plant of common ragweed,* Senecio jacobaea, *a noxious weed that is poisonous to livestock.*

⊕ *The larva of the great tiger moth,* Arctia caja, *curls up defensively on a leaf in an English garden.*

temperate arctiids the caterpillar goes into hibernation for the winter when only half fed. It resumes feeding and pupates the following spring. Arctiid pupae are generally contained within cocoons that incorporate a copious supply of stinging hairs from the caterpillar.

Mating Flights

Some of the most complex sexual routines seen in moths occur in the arctiids; several species are known to gather to form mating "leks." The females may attract males by "calling" (releasing pheromones). In the North American ornate moth, *Utetheisa ornatrix*, the female does not pump out her scent in a constant plume. Instead, she releases it in pulses by a throbbing action of the tip of the abdomen. Along the East Coast salt marshes of North America, the onset of twilight is the signal for males of the saltmarsh moth, *Estigmene acraea*,

Sound Production

As in several other moth families, arctiids have "ears" (tympana) that can pick up the radarlike sounds produced by a hunting bat. The moth can then take evasive action by adopting a "ducking and diving" style of flight or by dropping to safety on the ground. Some of the distasteful, warningly colored arctiids use another form of defense: They respond by generating their own ultrasonic "replies" to the bat's radar. Experienced bats learn to associate the sounds with the unsavory taste of the moths and veer away as soon as they hear them. The perfectly palatable North American Isabella tiger, *Pyrrharctia isabella*, deceives incoming bats by copying the ultrasound responses of the genuinely nasty arctiids, thereby becoming a so-called "acoustic mimic." Arctiids also use ultrasound during courtship sequences, producing a sound by the buckling action of numerous tiny microtymbals on the thorax.

to come together in small groups for a night of sexual activity. Perched high up on the tips of plants such as grasses, each male inflates his coremata—long, curved, sausagelike hairy tubes—from the tip of his abdomen. Coremata occur in many species of arctiids and are thought to release a male pheromone. In the saltmarsh moth the pheromones attract females from far and wide to select partners from the assembled males. Any females that have failed to find a partner by the early hours of the morning will start to "call" as a fallback device. In the ruby tiger, *Phragmatobia fuliginosa*, found on both sides of the Atlantic, the male inflates his coremata at the last moment as he closes in on a "calling" female. The female confirms that she has detected the appropriate pheromone by fluttering her wings and generating ultrasonic clicks.

The day-flying scarlet tiger, *Callimorpha dominula* from Europe, forms spectacular leks in the late afternoon. Hundreds of individuals may assemble in an area the size of a tennis court. The females perch low in the grass and are courted by bevies of highly strung males all adopting a stylized, fluttering form of flight.

Black arches
**(*Lymantria*
monacha)**

Common name Tussock moths

Family Lymantriidae

Order Lepidoptera

Number of species About 2,500 (32 U.S.)

Wingspan From about 0.8 in (20 mm) to about 2.8 in (7 cm)

Key features Adults stout and hairy; wings mostly brownish or grayish; usually drab, but some tropical species brightly colored; some females have only stublike wings; wings generally held tentlike over the back; proboscis reduced in size or absent; antennae conspicuous and doubly pectinate in both male and female, but more so in male; females larger than males; females of some species wingless (sometimes without legs as well) or with poorly developed wings and unable to fly; caterpillars often brightly colored and generally hairy, causing a severe itching rash in humans

Habits Adults short-lived; nocturnal, hiding away during the day and seldom seen; caterpillars mostly found singly on leaves of food plant

Breeding Eggs usually deposited in dense masses, often covered with tufts of hair from the female's abdomen; pupa formed within loose cocoon of silk, often incorporating larval hairs

Diet Adults nonfeeding; caterpillars mostly eat foliage of trees and can be major pests

Habitat Mainly in woodland and forest; some species common in gardens

Distribution Worldwide; commonest in tropical regions of the Old World

⊕ *Lymantria monacha, the black arches, is common across most of northern and central Europe and is found in parts of Asia and Japan. Wingspan 1.4–2.2 inches (3.5–5.5 cm).*

Tussock Moths   Lymantriidae

The seldom-seen adults of the Lymantriidae are rather drab. By contrast, the caterpillars of many species provide a stunning visual impact—they are extremely colorful and often spectacularly hairy.

ADULT TUSSOCK MOTHS, WHICH are very short-lived and retiring, are seldom noticed. There are a few brilliantly colored exceptions, mainly in the tropics. They sometimes resemble butterflies more than moths. Wide color variation is rare, but is found in *Euproctis,* a genus that is widespread in the Old World.

Adults of the browntail moth, *Euproctis chrysorrhoea,* and the yellowtail moth, *E. similis* from Europe, are basically shining white in color. In the former a tuft of brown hairs forms the tail, while in the latter the tuft is yellowish-orange. The moth sits with its wings folded tentlike over its back, resembling a fluffy white feather. If disturbed, the moth parts its wings slightly, and the tail—whose warningly colored tuft has an irritant effect—is protruded upward through the gap. In *E. conizona* from tropical Africa the white of the wings is blotched with gray and black. There is also an untidy fringe of hairs that extends outward from the legs, blurring the moth's outline. The overall impression is very like a bird dropping, although the reddish brown-tipped tail can be displayed as a "warning" if an enemy gets too close. In the unusually flamboyant *E. edwardsi* from Australia the tail is bright red, as are large areas of the hind wings, contrasting with the black forewings tipped with yellow. Such markings make it the most striking member of the genus and one of the most showy of all lymantriids.

Exposed Eggs

The eggs are generally laid in substantial masses on the leaves of the food plant. In species whose females are wingless, or nearly so, the female does not even move away from the cocoon from which she has recently hatched.

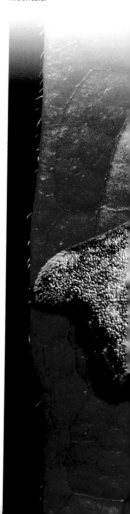

⊕ *A* Cobanilla *species tussock moth makes an excellent impression of a dead, fallen leaf in a rain forest in Sumatra, Indonesia.*

An example is the rusty tussock moth, *Orgyia antiqua*, found in Europe and North America. Instead, she advertises for a mate by sending out an "invitation" of pheromones. Once attracted, the fully winged male homes in on the squat, saclike female. She then smothers her empty cocoon with a great swath of eggs (400 to 500 is quite normal) and sits on top. She never sees her offspring, since she dies before the caterpillars hatch.

Overwintering on Mother's Cocoon

Hatching does not take place until the following spring. The eggs spend the entire winter on the cocoon, perched on the fork of a twig or in a cranny in the bark of the host tree, completely exposed to the weather. In most other temperate species the eggs hatch within a week or two. The caterpillars feed up until fall and then go into winter hibernation. In the European dark tussock moth, *Dasychira fascelina,* winter retirement happens when the caterpillar is still only small. It prepares to sit out the cold weather in reasonable comfort by spinning a small silken envelope—like a miniature cocoon—in the fork of a twig. In the browntail moth the caterpillars also enter hibernation while still very small, crowded closely together in a communal silk nest.

As in many lymantriids, the caterpillars of the rusty tussock moth are very striking, especially when fully grown. Four brushlike tufts of yellow hairs arranged along the back combine with jutting pencils of black hairs beside the head. The blend of blue-gray, red, and black creates a very distinctive appearance. As in most tussock moth

⊕ A pair of **Noroma nigrolunata** *in Uganda, resembling a feather that has fallen onto a leaf. They are mating on the female's pupa, where the male found her shortly after she emerged.*

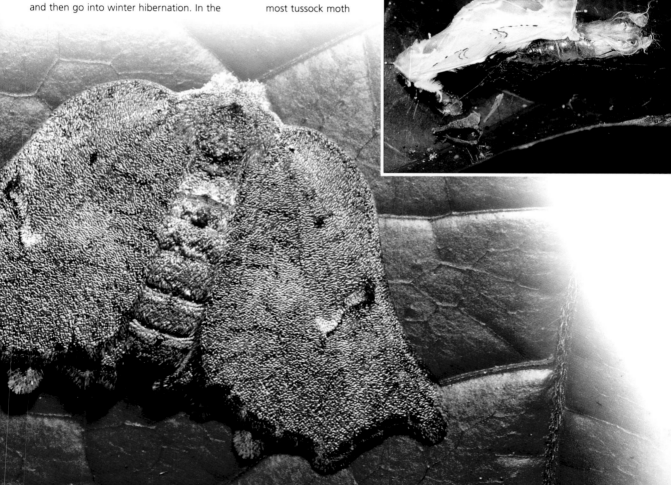

caterpillars, the hairs are urticating (causing itching) and can produce a painful rash on human skin. Such a deterrent makes them immune to attack from most large predators other than those adapted for dealing with very hairy prey, such as cuckoos. Some species also possess a gland that can release defensive chemical compounds when the need arises.

In *Orgyia* the eggs undoubtedly gain a degree of protection from being laid on the cocoon, which incorporates a mass of defensive, urticating hairs donated by the caterpillar. In other lymantriids the female protects her eggs by covering them with a clump of hairs detached from the large tuft on the tip of her abdomen. The females no longer require any protection for themselves, since they die soon after egg laying.

Group Feeding

Lymantriid larvae often feed in a group, and their numbers can rapidly build up to damaging pest proportions. In Europe caterpillars of the black arches moth, *Lymantria monacha*, can have devastating effects on spruce plantations. In North America several species of *Orgyia* may be the cause of local outbreaks of defoliation in a wide variety of trees. Most of the continental United States is blessed with long, warm summers that enable caterpillars to feed rapidly. The warmth also greatly reduces the time needed for the pupa to change to an adult. Two or more generations of moths can often be squeezed in during a single season, enabling numbers to rapidly reach plague proportions. When it was first introduced accidentally into the eastern United States, the browntail moth caused the same kind of defoliation that it commonly causes in the forests of Europe.

⊙ *A western tussock moth caterpillar,* Orgyia vetusta *from the United States, showing the tufts of hairs like shaving brushes down the center of the back typical of many lymantriid larvae.*

⊖ *The two black spots on this lymantriid caterpillar's face in South Africa may resemble eyes, but they are not.*

The Gypsy Moth

The most serious pest species in the Lymantriidae, and in fact one of the most destructive of all pest insects, is the gypsy moth, *Lymantria dispar*. For a long time it was a major pest in the forests of its European home. The gypsy moth launched a new and highly successful career as "destroyer-in-chief" of the far more extensive forests that still cover large areas of North America. As happens so often with major pest outbreaks, the gypsy moth was introduced into the New World by accident. In 1869 a French resident in the United States was importing consignments of gypsy moth caterpillars from Europe. He was hoping to cross the species with the silkworm moth, *Bombyx mori* (Bombycidae). His aim was to create a caterpillar that would produce an economically viable quantity of good-quality silk on a diet of the abundant local supply of oak leaves.

During unloading in Massachusetts one of the crates containing gypsy moth caterpillars was broken open. From that single event the species has spread like a modern-day plague through the forests of the northeastern United States and eastern Canada. Its success is partly due to the broad diet enjoyed by the caterpillars, which feed on a wide variety of trees, both wild and cultivated. It is also partly because in North America none of the natural controls (for example, parasitic wasps) present in Europe are on hand to temper its numbers. As a result, annual losses caused by this pest in North America run into hundreds of millions of dollars. Even in Europe the gypsy moth is subject to unpredictable population explosions, when caterpillar numbers rise to such high levels that thousands of acres of forest may be stripped of leaves. When that happens, the sound of hundreds of millions of tiny jaws chewing away at the leaves can clearly be heard by anyone standing nearby.

In North America the gypsy moth is still relentlessly extending its range, possibly aided by the ability of its caterpillars, while still tiny, to balloon upward on silken lines like spiders and be wafted along on a strong breeze to new areas. The rate at which they spread into new regions can be measured by baiting traps with synthetic versions of the female pheromone. The strongly winged males are attracted to the traps from far and wide; despite their broad wings, the females are poor fliers and can do little better than flutter weakly along the ground. Given the level of havoc caused in both Europe and North America, it is ironic that in the British Isles, where the species is native, it became extinct around 1907. It has remained so, despite several attempts to establish it once again in its old haunts!

Gypsy moth females normally come together to lay their eggs on the trunks of trees. The eggs are covered with a protective felt from the female's abdomen.

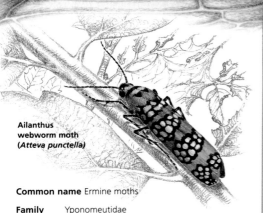

Ailanthus
webworm moth
(Atteva punctella)

Ermine Moths Yponomeutidae

Although ermine moths are seldom conspicuous, their caterpillars often make their presence very obvious, enveloping large areas of vegetation in swaths of silk.

Common name Ermine moths

Family Yponomeutidae

Order Lepidoptera

Number of species About 800 (32 U.S.)

Wingspan From about 0.5 in (13 mm) to about 1.2 in (3 cm)

Key features Wing pattern sometimes colorful, but often white peppered with black dots; body and wings quite long and narrow; wings wrapped closely around body at rest, giving torpedolike outline; wing tips blunt; antennae directed straight out in front of head, like horns; head covered with scales

Habits Adults generally rest on food plants by day; larvae often live in extensive silken webbing slung across their food plant or sometimes live as miners within leaves (larvae of different generations may attack different parts of the host plant); larvae generally gregarious, sometimes solitary; pupae often hung in large clusters within webbing

Breeding Male and female both release sexual pheromones; some species produce 3 generations per year; larva constructs cocoon in which to pupate

Diet Adults do not feed; larvae eat wide variety of plants

Habitat In all habitats; some species are major pests of agriculture

Distribution Almost worldwide; most common in the tropics

⊕ *The ailanthus webworm moth,* Atteva punctella *from Central and South America and the United States, seen in a typical pose with its wings tightly wrapped around its body. Wingspan 0.7–1.2 inches (18–30 mm.)*

WITH THEIR LONG NARROW bodies and fairly narrow, blunt-tipped wings ermine moths are quite distinctive. In some species, such as *Ypsolopha dentella* from Europe, the tips of the forewings are hooked backward. It is one of a large number of species in which the adults adopt a characteristic pose when at rest—the head pointing downward and the tip of the body tilted upward at a slight angle, supported just by the front two pairs of legs. When at rest, the forewings are rolled over the hind wings, giving many yponomeutid adults a rather twiglike appearance. Wing color varies greatly, from the gaudy appearance of the North American ailanthus webworm moth, *Atteva punctella* (one of the most beautiful members of the family), through browns and metallic grays, to what is probably the most common marking of all—silvery-white patterned with black dots.

Silk Sheets

Yponomeutid caterpillars are sometimes solitary, boring into fruit or eating out the tissue between the upper and lower surfaces of a leaf, causing distinctive mines. In most species the caterpillars construct extensive sheets of silk webbing across their food plants. Whole thickets of blackthorn, *Prunus spinosa*, may be enveloped in a grayish, smokelike carpet of webbing by the European *Yponomeuta padella*. While still tiny, the caterpillars mine within the leaves of the host plant, but then start to spin the silken tents in which they spend the rest of their lives. The pupae are eventually suspended inside the tents in large clusters.

Numerous species are pests. *Prays oleae* was originally native to the Mediterranean region, but is now widespread. By producing

⊕ *Yponomeuta padella from Europe often feeds in large numbers from flowers in daytime. The rather long, narrow wings and body are characteristic of yponomeutids.*

⊕ *Nematopogon swanmerdamella is a fairy moth (Incurvariidae) from Europe. The very long, hairlike antennae are typical of the males, but shorter in females.*

olive oil is pressed. Several species, including the European diamond-back moth, *Plutella xylostella*, are pests on cabbages, cauliflowers, and other crops.

As in most moths, female yponomeutids attract males by releasing pheromones. In some closely related species the pheromones can be so similar that males are attracted to females of the wrong species. Even so, accidental interbreeding is unlikely because the females can accurately identify the correct pheromones emitted by the males from the scent brushes on the abdomen. If the female detects the "wrong" scent, she refuses to make herself available.

three generations in a single year, it is able to build up massive populations on olive trees. The first-generation caterpillars form mines within the leaves; the second generation then switches its attention to the flowers; while the third generation causes the greatest amount of damage by ruining the fruits from which the

Fairy Moths and Yucca Moths

Although not closely related to ermine moths, the fairy and yucca moths in the family Incurvariidae also have rather long, narrow wings and could easily be mistaken for yponomeutids. In fairy moths the mistake is less likely, since they have very long antennae—especially the males of *Adela* and *Nemophora*, whose antennae may be four times as long as their body. The females' antennae, however, are much shorter. The males form large swarms and perform aerial "dances" around the tips of twigs. Incurvariid caterpillars are mostly leaf miners. In some species, such as the North American maple leafcutter moth, *Paraclemensia acerifoliella*, the caterpillar later constructs and carries around a case made of leaf segments.

Females of the North American yucca moth, *Tegeticula yuccasella*, have a close interdependent relationship with yuccas. By pollinating the yucca flower, the female enables it to set seeds in which some of her caterpillars will later develop. The untouched seeds will benefit the plant, which is unable to reproduce without the valuable services of the yucca moth.

Fire ant (*Solenopsis geminata*)

Common name Ants

Family Formicidae

Suborder Apocrita

Order Hymenoptera

Number of species About 15,000 (about 600 U.S.)

Size From about 0.04 in (1 mm) to about 1.4 in (3.5 cm)

Key features Body usually black, brown, reddish, or yellowish; eyes small; antennae elbowed; waist (known as a pedicel) with one or two beadlike or scalelike segments; stinger may be present; wings absent in workers—usually present in sexual forms, but discarded later

Habits All ants are fully social, often constructing very large nests containing thousands of individuals; some species live in the nests of others or take other species as slaves

Breeding Most species release large numbers of winged males and females, which form nuptial swarms; after mating, queens break off their wings and establish new nest, usually without help of male, who normally dies (unlike in termites, where male becomes "king" alongside his "queen"); queen ant stores all sperm needed for fertilizing many eggs over a long period

Diet Adults feed mainly on nectar and honeydew or on fungus; larvae eat food of animal (mainly insect) or plant (mainly seed) origin; sole diet for some species is a fungus that they cultivate in special "gardens"

Habitat Found in all terrestrial habitats, where they are often dominant; no aquatic species

Distribution Worldwide; commonest in the tropics, absent from very dry or cold areas

⬆ *Solenopsis geminata, the North American fire ant, is a serious crop pest. The common name derives from the burning sensation caused by the ants' venomous bites. Body length 0.03–0.2 inches (1–6 mm).*

Ants

Formicidae

Ants live in fascinatingly complex societies of often many millions of individuals that each know their place in the hierarchy. It has helped them become the dominant insect in many areas where they are found.

THE ANTS ARE THE MOST completely social members of the Hymenoptera. Unlike in bees and wasps, in which some species are solitary, some social, and some a mixture of both, all ants live in highly organized societies within a communal nest. Not all ant societies are equally well organized, and some rely on the press-ganged labor of other species for services such as the harvesting of food and rearing of young.

Dominant Insects

Wherever ants are found, whether in sun-baked desert or rain-shrouded cloud forest, they are almost always the dominant form of insect life. In terms of numbers and impact on their environment ants are rivaled only by the exclusively vegetarian termites. Most ants are considered beneficial to humans on account of their preying on insect pests. However, some ants are pests themselves. *Atta* leaf-cutting ants can damage orchards and plantations of trees; *Camponotus* carpenter ants may destroy wooden structures. *Solenopsis* fire ants damage plants and sting readily, while the Pharaoh ant, *Monomorium pharaonis*, is now a widespread pest in hospital and restaurant buildings.

All the hard labor in ant societies is carried out by the worker caste. They are sterile, wingless females that are not able to reproduce,

➔ *These* Oecophylla longinoda *weaver ants from Africa are about to carry their entire brood to a new nest. Note how the pupae are naked, not enclosed in a cocoon.*

⬇ *The various castes of* Messor *species harvester ants, showing all members of the colony.*

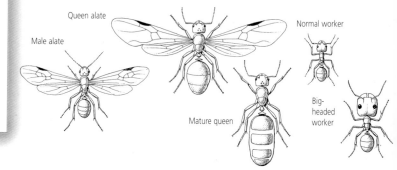

Male alate

Queen alate

Mature queen

Normal worker

Big-headed worker

⊕ *Note the antennae with their right-angled elbows and the typical narrow waist of the giant Paraponera clavata bullet ant from the rain forests of the American tropics.*

but devote their lives to the service of their mother, the queen. The queen's sole duty is to churn out an endless succession of eggs. In termite societies the workers consist of both males and females. Ant workers carry out all the daily tasks of housekeeping within the nest.

They keep the nest interior tidy, help extend its tunnels, and may rush to build earth ramparts around the entrance if heavy rain is on the way. One of their main duties is the gathering of food and care of the young, which is undertaken with close attention to detail. If the weather is too hot, the workers will carry the developing brood down to lower, cooler regions of the nest. If it is too cold, they will set out the larvae and pupae near the surface to warm in the sun. There is scrupulous attention to hygiene, and the young are kept constantly groomed. If threatened by flood waters, the workers will make an emergency evacuation of the brood to a safer spot on higher ground or in the branches of a tree.

Caring for the Queen

It is also the job of the workers to groom and feed their queen, who never leaves the nest. In some species the workers produce sterile so-called trophic eggs, which act as an additional source of food for the larvae and the queen.

Trophic eggs are much smaller and softer than the eggs produced by the queen.

In most species the workers can adapt to carry out any given task both inside and outside the nest, but in some species the bodies of some workers are specially adapted into a tool for performing certain tasks. In *Pheidole* some workers have outsize heads on which extralarge jaws capable of crushing seeds can be comfortably mounted. In other ants large heads and jaws are fitted to so-called soldiers whose job is to defend the nest and its workers, although they may also help in other tasks as needed. In *Paracryptocerus* and *Zacryptocerus* turtle ants disk-headed workers hurry to the nest entrance (in a hollow twig or branch) whenever the alarm is raised and use their smooth, armored heads as plugs to deny access to intruders.

Chemical Defense

Many species also use chemicals to defend themselves and their nests against attack. Some can sting; others spray an irritant chemical (usually formic acid) at an aggressor. The sting of some of the

→ Workers of **Camponotus detritus** *forage for food in the Namib Desert situated on the coast of southwest Africa. Gathering food is one of the main tasks for worker ants.*

⤵ In a forest in Thailand a weaver ant worker Oecophylla smaragdina *drinks a droplet of liquid from the jaws of a nestmate, a process known as trophallaxis.*

Language of Touch

Ant workers use the language of touch to communicate with each other. When one ant worker meets another, one of them will often beg for food by using its antennae to stroke its nest mate's face and antennae. The donor will usually respond by serving up a droplet of liquid and holding it on its jaws so that the recipient can feed on it. Such mutual feeding is known as trophallaxis.

The touch code that leads up to it, along with the "nest-scent" code, has been "broken" by a number of beetles and other so-called ant guests that spend their lives as spongers in ants' nests. The liquid donated during trophallaxis is often honeydew, a sugary secretion that the ants harvest from aphids, treehoppers, and other bugs in the order Hemiptera. Ants also glean nectar from plants, partly from flowers and partly from so-called extrafloral nectaries situated on the stems or leaves.

enormous bullet ants from South America is very painful and may be fatal even to humans. In smaller species the sheer number of stings from a massed attack can have a serious effect, and an onslaught by hordes of southern fire ants, *Solenopsis xyloni* from the United States, is believed to have been responsible for the death of a baby.

Defense of the nest is usually carried out with total disregard for individual safety and survival. That strategy is taken to its extreme conclusion in certain *Camponotus* workers from the United States. The workers are able to self-destruct in the face of an enemy, exploding with a force that disables an adversary beneath a shower of chemical debris.

Mexico raids are made against large parties of foraging *Nasutitermes* worker termites, which are guarded by a much smaller squad of soldiers. If the group of termites is not too large, the ants will try to encircle it and then rush in and attempt to overwhelm the soldiers by force of numbers before picking off the workers one at a time. In South America *Termitopone* scout ants wander randomly around on the rain-forest floor until one of them chances on a foraging party of *Syntermes* termites. The scout rushes back to the nest by the most direct route, laying down a "trail pheromone" along which it returns accompanied by a band of helpers. The group then launches a mass attack on the termites and returns to the nest in a column, each holding a termite in its jaws.

Some ants prey exclusively on other ants. An Australian species of *Cerapachys* that preys on *Pheidole* is so heavily armored that it can attack the adult workers without needing to bother about retaliation from its victim's powerful sting. Adult *Pheidole* are stung and killed, but larvae are only lightly anesthetized and remain in a torpid state for up to eight weeks, providing a long-lasting supply of fresh food for the conquering *Cerapachys*.

Predatory ants seize their prey in their jaws, which in some species are highly adapted for the purpose. In *Odontomachus* and other so-called "trap-jawed" ants the large, pincerlike jaws project prominently outward at either side of the ant's face. Between the open jaws there is usually one or two pairs of long, forward-pointing sensory hairs. When touched, these hairs trigger an instant snapping shut of the jaws, which in the larger species is accompanied by an audible click.

Swarms of Ants

Worker ants are both wingless and sexually inactive. One of their jobs is to rear more sisters like themselves to act as workers and maintain the life of the nest. At a specific time of the year, usually in late summer in cooler climates or at the start of the rains in the seasonally dry

⊕ *With a soldier termite held in its jaws, a Pachycondyla commutata worker hurries back to its nest. This South American ant preys exclusively on termites.*

Termite-Slaying Ants

Many ants are among the most omnivorous of all insects and will eat just about anything, whether of plant or animal origin. Yet some species are not only exclusively predaceous but will only attack a specific kind of prey. A number of them will only feed on termites. Termites are highly social insects with well-organized defensive capabilities involving specialized soldier castes. A successful raid against such formidable opposition needs to be mounted with care. In *Pheidole titanis* from the southwestern United States and

Queen ants are fully winged, enabling them to leave the nest on a brief nuptial flight that ends in mating. This is the large queen of Atta cephalotes, a leaf-cutter ant from Costa Rica.

Some ants' nests are only small. This is the fully formed nest of a Dolichoderus species ant from Trinidad, affixed to the leaf of a bush in the rain forest.

for her future reproductive career, usually by digging a small initial nest either in the ground or in wood, depending on the species. Before starting work, she sheds her wings, since their only function, to carry her on her nuptial flight, is now complete.

Varied Nests

Most ants' nests are in the ground, where many of the smaller species nest beneath stones or logs. Other species nest in dead wood or inside branches and twigs. *Camponotus* carpenter ants excavate extensive nesting galleries in dead wood, such as old tree stumps or dead standing trees. Unfortunately, they also use the old wood in houses, where they can become a pest, weakening the structure. They are not as destructive as termites, but may have to be

tropics, the workers start to rear larvae that are destined to be future queens, as well as the first male larvae. They are larger than the workers, especially the queens, with a fully functioning sexual apparatus. They also have a complete set of wings. These sexually functioning ants are known as alates.

Maiden Flights

At the appropriate time the workers herd these future colonists together near the nest entrance. When conditions are right, usually when the weather is warm and calm or shortly before a rainstorm that will soften the ground, every nest over a huge area will suddenly begin shepherding its alates to the entrance and spurring them into the air. Millions may emerge simultaneously so that the air and ground are suddenly swarming with winged ants. A nest does not usually commit its entire stock of alates on the first release. Some are usually held in reserve for departure on subsequent days.

With such huge numbers involved, males and females have no problems finding one another and mate on the ground or in the air. The males then die off, their sole reason for life having been fulfilled.

For the female the prospect of becoming a future queen by founding her own nest is bleak—only a tiny proportion will be successful. Stored within her body is a supply of sperm derived from her single mating that is sufficient to fertilize all the eggs she is ever likely to produce. Her task now is to lay the groundwork

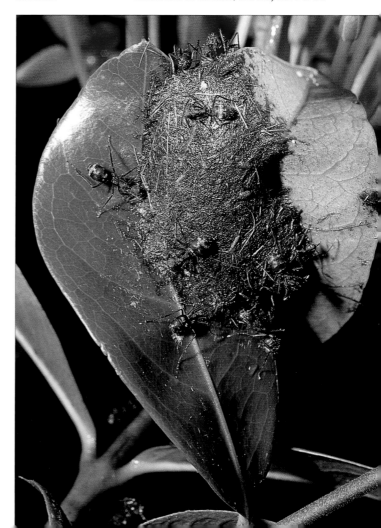

The large carton nests of Azteca ants are a conspicuous sight in many South American forests. This nest, about 2 feet (60 cm) long, is attached to a tree trunk.

controlled with chemicals. In the tropics many ants build packagelike carton nests attached to trees, using chewed-up wood mixed with bodily secretions. In Central and South America the carton nests of *Azteca* are a frequent sight on tree trunks and can reach a width of around 40 inches (100 cm) and a depth of more than 6 feet (2 m). Some tropical ants build nests of carton, earth, or detritus beneath leaves, which keep the rain off. Weaver ants build their nests from living leaves.

Founding a New Nest

Having established herself in a small breeding cell, the female lays her first eggs. She is usually alone, but in some species several queens club together to found a nest jointly. During that first stage the queen does not take any food. She feeds her brood on products derived from

Scent Trails

When away from the nest, ants navigate in a number of ways. Lone scouts, especially in desert-dwelling species, use the sun, which in more arid habitats is visible on most days. A scout that locates a good source of food navigates back to the nest by sight, where it recruits a single nest mate to accompany it back to the food source, a process known as "tandem running." When they return, they recruit two more, doubling up each time they return so that eventually quite large numbers may be trotting back and forth with food. In more sophisticated species the route between nest and food source will be precisely marked out with a trail pheromone. The pheromone can easily be followed by any number of workers, although in some species the actual numbers required can be defined by the strength of the pheromone laid down. The use of scent trails explains how hordes of ants crossing a road all follow the same narrow path even when they belong to species whose workers are blind. If a car crosses and disturbs the scent trail, the ants all mill around in confusion for a while until they relocate it.

Pheromones are also used by ants for communicating danger. These "alarm pheromones" are given off by the first ant to be disturbed, which causes its near neighbors to react likewise. That triggers a snowballing effect that very rapidly spreads the message to every ant in the vicinity. The pheromones differ not only from species to species but also within species, so that every ant belonging to a particular nest is "coded" with a scent specific to that nest. The ants' sensory apparatus is so finely tuned that they use the so-called nest scent to distinguish between members of their own nest and strangers from another one, which may even be attacked and killed simply because they do not belong. In ants there is no concept of acting for the good of the species—only for the good of the nest.

⊜ *Scurrying back to their nest, carrying their booty from a recent raid, worker* Dorylus nigricans *driver ants follow a trail pheromone that guides them across a track in Uganda.*

One Good Turn

Special relationships have arisen between ants and plants whereby a certain type of plant provides the ants with food and a home. In return the ants constitute a private army always at the ready to defend their host from leaf-eating animals with total disregard for self-preservation.

In Central America it is the hollow, grossly swollen bases of the thorns of various acacias that provide the *Pseudomyrmex* foot soldiers with secure living quarters. The ants only need to forage a short way from home to find all the food they need, which is laid on specially for them by their leafy host. Energy to fuel the ant colony is provided in the form of nectar secreted from the leaves.

Protein for rearing the ant brood is provided in the form of special egg-shaped modifications to the leaf tips called Beltian bodies. The worker ants harvest them, chop them up, and feed them to the larvae. In return for such hospitality the ants descend in furious cohorts on any animals—humans included—that dare so much as brush lightly against their acacia home. Despite the small size of the individual ants, a combined assault by a large squad is so painful that most intruders instantly retreat. As a result of employing their private armies, swollen-thorn acacias usually manage to keep all their leaves intact, while other acacias around them are stripped bare.

In Africa the whistling-thorn acacia, *Acacia drepanolobium*, provides even more spacious accommodation in its enormous bulbous thorn bases. Protein is provided from small outgrowths on the anthers inside the flowers. Back in Central America, the tree *Ocotea pedalifolia* provides a home for its ant guardians but no food. However, it does make feeding sites for two species of *Dysmicoccus* mealy bugs (Pseudococcidae) that supply the ants with honeydew. There are dozens of such relationships between ants and plants. Some plants "bribe" ants into dispersing their seeds, whose coats are equipped with special edible appendages (elaiosomes). The ants carry off the seeds, strip away the elaiosome for food, and dump the seeds on their garbage heaps, where germination is likely to occur far away from the parent plant.

The grossly swollen thorns of various acacia trees provide secure waterproof lodgings for their ant guardians. The entry holes are clearly visible. These Pseudomyrmex ferruginea *ants are from Costa Rica.*

breaking down her now functionless and quite substantial flight muscles, along with other energy reserves stored within her body. Her first brood of larvae are small and puny compared with what will come later, but their efforts will pave the way for future prosperity. In most ants the fully grown larvae spin a cocoon of silk in which to pupate; but in some, such as weaver ants, the pupa is naked.

The newly emerged pioneers of the first brood break free of the cell and begin foraging, bringing back enough food to rear a second brood of larger workers. They begin supplying the queen with her first food since her mating flight. She can now dedicate the rest of her life to being a committed egg-laying machine, permanently released from her initial brood-care duties. From now on the rapidly increasing force of workers will carry out all necessary tasks in the growing nest.

Once the nest has reached a certain size, the queen starts producing two types of eggs. Diploid (fertilized) eggs will eventually develop into queens after being afforded special treatment, including a richer diet. Haploid (unfertilized) eggs will become males.

Going Back Home

Sometimes a queen will return to her old nest rather than make a new one by herself. Her parent nest may eventually end up containing several queens, all of which are fertile and turn out eggs. When conditions get too crowded, some of these resident queens may leave home, accompanied by a retinue of workers, to found a new nest. This therefore presents an alternative and perhaps more reliable way of getting a new nest started without the hazards of life as a "single mother" during the early stages. In some ants in the primitive subfamily Ponerinae there is no queen at all. In *Pachycondyla sublaevis* from Australia egg laying is undertaken by the most highly ranked of the workers within the nests, which are usually small, sometimes with fewer than 10 members. If the top-ranked egg layer dies or is removed, another worker can quickly be

⊕ *The swarms of fully winged jet-black ants,* Lasius fuliginousus, *gathering at the entrance to their nest in a rotten stump, are queens ready for their maiden flight.*

"promoted" to take her place, since most of the workers within the colony are capable of laying productive eggs. In *Ophthalmophone berthoudi* from Africa up to 100 workers in each nest are inseminated and produce fertile eggs, although on a very slow and infrequent basis. They do not compete with one another or emerge above ground to forage.

Ant colonies are usually much longer lived than colonies of bees or wasps, especially in temperate regions where the latter die off during winter and have to start over again the following spring. Ant colonies survive the winter intact by going into hibernation, usually migrating deeper into the ground, after which the workers cluster closely around the brood throughout the coldest period.

Parasites and Slave Takers

As in most forms of life, the ants have their fair share of freeloaders who take things easy and profit from the industry of others. In the complex world of ants various versions of such a lifestyle exist, some more work shy than others. In one version there is a queen who does not attempt to establish her own nest but instead takes over the nest of a different species by killing the queen and taking her place. The queen's assassination is not necessarily accomplished in open combat or through the invader's superior fighting ability—in fact, the opposite may be true.

Off with Her Head!

Queens of *Bothriomyrmex decapitans* from North Africa gain entry to the nest of *Tapinoma nigerrimum* by allowing themselves to be treated like food and carried into the nest by the workers. Once safely within the nest, the invading queen sneaks up onto the back of the host queen and sets about the rather lengthy task of gnawing her head off. By the time this is done, the upstart queen has acquired enough of the vital nest odor to ensure her future acceptance, enabling her to foist her eggs on her adopted workforce. They dutifully rear the "cuckoo" eggs, producing large numbers of replacement workers belonging to the invading species. Eventually the new workers are left in sole charge of the nest, once the original workers have all died off.

In *Labauchena*, a tiny species from South America, several queens invade the nest of the *Solenopsis* host. The queens form an

Hooked on Honeydew

One of the most sought-after foods for many ants is a sugary liquid called honeydew. It is a waste product excreted mainly by various bugs, especially aphids and some kinds of hoppers such as treehoppers in the family Membracidae. Colonies of these bugs are tended by ants that "milk" them for their honeydew. In return, the ants will drive away many predators that threaten their precious food source. Some bugs become remarkably reliant on having a "police force" of ants on hand to deter undesirable intruders. Females of many treehoppers have a long-term commitment to their eggs and young. Yet *Entylia bactriana* stays for only a short time before handing over the job of guarding her family to the ants that have been hanging around from the start. The ants are so efficient at enforcing a "keep clear" zone around the mother and her family that she will desert her eggs if no ants are available.

In some species, such as the Texas shed-building ant, *Crematogaster lineolata*, the ants reduce the risk of losing their honeydew suppliers to enemies by constructing bowers around them made of chewed vegetable matter. They can then be milked under cover in relative safety. Some ants will pick up aphids and move them to plants nearer the nest, so that the honeydew supplies can be harvested more easily. *Dolichoderus cuspidatus* from Malaysia lives in temporary bivouacs that contain not only the adult ants, along with their eggs, larvae, and pupae, but also herds of their mealy bug "cattle," *Malaicoccus formicarii*. The ants cart the bugs off and pasture them on fresh sappy growth near the nest. When fresh growth near the bivouac has been exhausted, the ants break camp and move to a better area, carrying their domestic "cattle" along with them.

⬆ *Many ants have close relationships with lycaenid butterfly caterpillars. These green tree ants,* Oecophylla smaragdina *from Australia, are defending a* Narathura *species larva.*

➡ *In temperate regions aphids are often closely attended by swarms of ants. These red ants,* Formica rufa *in Europe, are "milking" aphids for their honeydew.*

assassination squad and work together to bite the head off the vastly larger host queen, a process that can take several weeks.

In some species the eggs laid by the replacement queen and reared by the host workers all turn into winged males and females. They leave the nest to invade other nests, leading to the eventual decline and extinction of the host colony once all the original workers have perished. The premature collapse of the colony is sometimes avoided when the invading queen spares the life of the host queen, enabling two production lines of offspring to be run side by side. The continued output of workers by the original queen is sufficient to keep the nest running smoothly.

Slave Labor

In slave-making ants the queens found new nests as normal, producing workers that at first perform their regular domestic duties around the nest. Once the colony has reached a certain size, the workers change from placid home helps into warlike raiders that set off to plunder the nest of a different species of ant, robbing the colony of its pupae. They are carried back to the raiders' nest to hatch into a lifetime of slavery.

From now on the slaves carry out all the daily tasks of the nest, leaving the workers free to go out in search of fresh conquests. In some species the original workers simply become degenerate parasites with no useful role in the nest. In other species, such as *Anergates atratulus* from Europe, there is no worker caste—only slaves—and the queen produces only males or queens. She cannot even feed herself without the help of her slave workers and becomes hugely swollen with eggs, turning out as many offspring as possible before her slaves die off, and the colony becomes extinct.

In most slave-making ants the mandibles are slender and sickle shaped, adapted for raiding, not for the day-to-day chores within a nest. In *Strongylognathus huberi* the muscles for the formidable-looking jaws are too weak to be of much use, so most of the fighting on

209

slave-making forays is done by existing slaves, which accompany their "owners" on raids.

Leaf-cutting Ants

Trails of leaf-cutting ants winding their way across the rain-forest floor are a familiar sight in the tropical regions of the Americas, although a single species, the Texas leaf-cutter, *Atta texana*, reaches as far north as Texas and Louisiana. Leaf-cutting ants have become farmers, cultivating a fungus that is their sole source of food. It is only found inside their nests. In order to thrive, the fungus needs a suitable compost. The ants manufacture it by harvesting large quantities of plant material, often stripping huge forest trees of their leaves in the process.

By using its jaws to cut in a semicircle, each worker quite rapidly snips away a small section of leaf, although sometimes fruits or flower petals are used instead. The ant then hoists the leaf section up in its jaws and carries it back to the nest. Hundreds of thousands of ants may be simultaneously hurrying back to the nest

with their little green "parasols," often forming processions over 12 inches (30 cm) wide and more than 100 yards (100 m) long. Both normal-sized workers and large-headed, pincer-jawed soldiers engage in cutting and carrying the leaves, some of which bear an additional cargo of tiny "minim" workers. Their task is to ride shotgun on the leaf fragments and deny their use to parasitic flies (Phoridae), which will try to use the leaf as a foothold in order to lay their eggs on the carrying ant's head capsule.

As the plant supplies pour into the nest in a continuous stream, the process of turning them into compost begins. Processing work is carried out by more minims that never leave the nest. First, they carefully cleanse and scrape the surface of each leaf, probably to remove the spores of undesirable fungi and bacteria. Each segment is then chewed up and anointed with saliva and feces to form a sticky pulp. It can now be added to the "garden" and "planted" with a few tufts of fungal material (mycelium). The warm, humid hothouse interior of the nest is ideal for fungal growth. Development is so rapid that swellings are soon produced that the

⊕ Holding their sections of leaf above their heads like parasols, a column of Atta cephalotes leaf-cutting ants heads back to the nest in a South American rain forest.

ants cut off and feed to the larvae. It is vital that the fungus beds are not contaminated with other fungi or bacteria that could act as weeds and spoil the garden. Leaf-cutters are remarkably adept at maintaining their fungus cultures in a pure state, possibly because they constantly apply salivary secretions that may be active against bacteria and foreign fungi.

⊙ Working around in a semicircle, a quartet of Atta *species leaf-cutting ants quickly and efficiently snip away sections of a leaf in a rain forest in Trinidad.*

Cultivating a Garden

A queen leaving the nest on her nuptial flight will always carry with her, stored in a special pouch within her body, a fragment of the fungus mycelium to act as "seed corn" in her new nest. Having mated several times high in the air on her single nuptial flight, the queen lands and breaks off her wings. She pushes them back one at a time at right angles so that they snap at predetermined zones of weakness. She then starts to dig a new nest, scooping out the soil with her mandibles and bulldozing it up to the surface with her head. She next ejects the pellet of fungal material from her mouth and manures it with her own eggs and droplets of fecal material. Once the garden is starting to

⊙ Once she has shed her wings, the first task for this newly mated queen 2-lobed leaf-cutter ant, Atta bisphearica *in Brazil, is to start digging a new nest in the ground.*

prosper, she will lay fertilized eggs and raise her first brood of workers. For the next four to five weeks she tends her miniature garden, neither feeding nor drinking, waiting for her first batch of workers to mature. If the garden fails now, she will die, since she cannot secure new supplies of fungus to make a fresh start.

Once the first workers emerge, they take on all the routine chores within the nest, cleaning their mother and tending to the garden. Once there are enough workers, some of them will start to forage for fresh leaves to develop the garden. After four to five years the colony will be as large as the mature one that the queen originally left. After a further three to four years it will probably decline and fade away after the death of its queen. However, some colonies have been known to last for at least 20 years. *Atta* nests in tropical rain forests can be extremely large, up to 50 yards (46 m) across and with dozens of entry tunnels. They

↑ *In the warm spring sun of the Arizona desert western harvester ants,* Pogonomyrmex occidentalis, *plod along carrying seeds back to their nest in the desert floor.*

are easy to spot because the surface is usually an open, bare, well-worn expanse of earth. Few plants are present, since the ants diligently remove most of them. The fungus gardens are deep undergound. The whole nest may contain as many as 5 million ants.

Harvester and Honeypot Ants

Pogonomyrmex harvester ants are found widely in the United States and Mexico, especially in the arid lands of the Southwest. They harvest seeds and grains (and sometimes other insects) and are active during the heat of the day even in the hottest desert regions. Their mating swarms are unique among ants, since they use the same meeting place year after year. The rendezvous point can be a hilltop, the crowns of tall trees, or even a piece of flat desert with no obviously distinctive features. Despite that, each generation of males and females knows just where to head after leaving their nests.

The males normally arrive first, and every female that appears is quickly deluged with suitors, all competing to be first to mate with her. The male has large, clamplike mandibles designed to grasp the female firmly around her thorax. Even so, males sometimes get hauled off their mounts by pressure of numbers and may accidentally snip off the female's abdomen.

Honeypot ants are found in arid regions of Australia and North America. *Myrmecocystus* is the main genus, although ants of several other genera have "honeypot" habits. During times of plenty they collect large quantities of nectar from plants or honeydew from aphids and other bugs. They then store it in a special worker caste called repletes, which use their bodies as living casks. Each replete accepts food regurgitated by incoming workers until its abdomen becomes so swollen that even small movements are virtually impossible. The repletes must devote their entire lives (which may last several months or even years) to being store pots, hanging head-upward from the ceiling by their claws. When food runs low outside the nest, the workers begin tapping the supply stored in the repletes, which regurgitate droplets of food on request.

Weaver Ants

There are two species of weaver ants, *Oecophylla longinoda* from Africa and *O. smaragdina* from Asia and Australia. In Asia *O. smaragdina* is reddish-brown and is known locally as the red tree ant, while in Australasia the same species is green. Both species use the living leaves of trees and shrubs to form a pouchlike nest. Sometimes a single large leaf is folded over on itself to form a pouch; in other cases several leaves may be fastened together. Large nests made up of over 20 leaves can measure over 12 inches (30 cm).

During nest construction rows of workers position themselves neatly along the edge of one leaf and use their jaws like a row of staples to hold the edge of the opposing leaf in the correct position. Squads of workers hurry to their required places like well-trained artisans. Yet scientists have no idea how they know where to go or which leaves to hold, where to hold them, or even how they know that nest

→ *Forming a highly disciplined team, these* Oecophylla smaragdina *weaver ants in Thailand are holding together the edges of two leaves until they can be set in place with silk.*

building is about to start. Once in position, they will stick tight, often for many hours or even days, until the two edges of the leaves have been securely fastened together with silk. That is mainly accomplished from within the nest. Since adult ants cannot produce silk, larvae are used instead. In the last instar larva of weaver ants the silk glands are disproportionately well developed for the task of nest construction. Unlike in most ants, there is no silken cocoon for the pupae, which lie naked within the nest.

Sewing Kit

Holding a larva in her jaws like a tube of glue against the edges of the two leaves to be joined, the worker ant uses her antennae to drum on the larva's body. That is an instruction for the larva to start squirting out silk into the required spot. By weaving its head from side to side as the silk is emitted, the worker ensures that gaps of varying widths can be fully sealed.

Being fashioned from living leaves, the finished nest is very durable and will last for many months, although eventually the leaves begin to wither and die. Scout ants then establish a site for a new nest. Once it is completed, the entire contents of their old home—consisting of eggs, larvae, and pupae, plus the queen—are assembled on the outside of the old nest in preparation for a mass exodus to the new living quarters.

Weaver ants cannot sting, but will bite fiercely and hang on with their jaws when molested. Much of the weaver ants' food consists of dead insects scavenged from the forest floor. Living insects are also killed. They are gradually torn apart by a ring of ants pulling in opposite directions.

Army Ants

Ants with army-style habits are mostly found in the tropics. One of the main characteristics they all share in common is their nomadic lifestyle. Nests, if they are made at all, are only temporary. Many species merely establish short-lived bivouacs that are soon abandoned as the army breaks camp and moves on. Army ant colonies are also usually extremely large, containing many thousands or even millions of individuals, all generated by just a single queen. All species are predaceous.

By far the largest raids are mounted by the tropical American species *Eciton burchelli*, during which entire areas of forest may be picked clean of every speck of animal life, large or small, that cannot either escape or buy immunity to attack through using chemical defenses. Certain insects are so distasteful that they can be surrounded by thousands of ants and remain completely untouched. Yet being armed with a formidable sting, usually a reliable way of avoiding trouble, is of scant help against such massed onslaughts. Paper wasps that are avoided by most other creatures in the forest can only hover helplessly nearby and watch their nests being stripped bare of their entire stock of larvae and pupae. Like an audience at a disaster movie, the wasps are powerless to intervene and protect their property.

Stashing the Booty

The victorious ants carry much of their booty back to their living quarters in one piece, often employing several ants like pallbearers to carry larger items. Especially bulky prey is usually cut to pieces and transported in parts. It will join a continuous column of workers and soldiers moving back and forth between the nest site and the assault front, returning one way laden with plunder and hurrying back empty-handed in the other direction to rejoin the fray. In such a

⬅ *Working under cover of darkness, an Oecophylla smaragdina weaver ant in India seals up a gap in the nest using silk secreted from a larva held in her jaws.*

"bombardment" style of warfare speed to and from the battlefield is essential. To make travel as smooth as possible, any tiny gaps in the roadway are crossed using the bodies of living workers to form bridges. When the amount of loot coming onstream is too great to handle, it will go into temporary storage in protected caches along the trail until labor is available to shift it. When a new source of food is discovered, a fresh gang of attackers can be recruited from the marching columns in about one minute, the fastest-known recruitment time in any social insect.

The most notorious of these massed raiders are the *Dorylus* driver or legionary ants from Africa and the *Eciton* army ants from Central and South America. Both are credited with attacking large animals such as snakes, chickens, pigs, and monkeys when they are confined in cages and cannot escape. Although unable to sting, army ant soldiers have large heads and long, curved jaws, which can inflict a painful bite. Once their jaws have sunk into yielding flesh, the ants will often die rather than let go. They rush to the attack as soon as they sense a threat to the column of hurrying workers. They use vibrations as their cue rather than sight, since they, like the workers, are blind. The whole complex battle scenario is arranged using scent trails to mark out the routes, which are initially laid down by scouts.

For several weeks at a time the ants roam through the forest, spending each night in a different temporary bivouac. They then settle

⊕ Hurrying back to their temporary bivouac, a column of Eciton burchelli *army ants in Trinidad crosses a living bridge made of interlocked workers clinging to one another.*

Bullet Ants

The largest ants in the world all belong to the subfamily Ponerinae. Some of the largest Central and South American species are called bullet ants. A single sting from some species is said to be fatal in humans. The sting is extremely painful and accompanied by considerable swelling. The shiny coal-black *Paraponera clavata* is one of the biggest ants in the American tropics. The heavily built workers reach up to 0.8 in (20 mm) long. They are a common sight over a wide area from Nicaragua to the Amazon Basin roaming around in the rain-forest understory. They may sometimes kill their own insect prey, but most food is probably picked up already dead.

Bullet ants are loners, and each ant forages singly. If a rich source of food is discovered, there is no rush to communicate the fact to other workers, and the finder exploits its discovery alone. Nectar is also an important source of food, and the ants are often seen trekking back to the nest with nothing more than a shiny droplet of nectar held in the mandibles. If two workers from the same nest meet, they temporarily abandon their solitary habits and may engage in an exchange of food through trophallaxis. If two workers from different nests bump into one another, they will fight to the death.

Foaming and Stinging

In the rain forests of Malaysia two slightly smaller species of ponerines, *Pachycondyla tridentata* and *P. insularis*, employ an unusual method of self-defense. They can spray out foamy threads from the venom gland to a distance of up to 4 inches (10 cm). It is particularly effective against swarms of smaller ants, which are instantly swamped by the foam and take some time to exctricate themselves. As well as foaming, the ants can also defend themselves by inflicting a painful sting.

⊖ Bullet ants are solitary and tend to forage alone, as in this Paraponera clavata *from the American tropics, seeking nectar on a* Heliconia *flower.*

⊕ With its large, curved sicklelike jaws bared in readiness for attack, an Eciton burchelli *soldier in Trinidad prepares to defend its nest mates. Like the workers, it is blind.*

down for about three weeks in a more permanent bivouac in which the queen can begin replacing the colony's losses. For the first week her body swells at an enormous rate as it fills with tens of thousands of eggs. Then over a period of a few days she suddenly slims down by disgorging her cargo of 300,000 or more eggs. They have developed into larvae by the time the colony breaks camp and resumes its nomadic lifestyle. The workers carry and feed the developing larvae and cluster around them each night in the temporary bivouac.

In the *Dorylus* driver ants from Africa the bivouacs are more stable than in *Eciton* and are established deep within the soil. In some areas chimpanzees "fish" for the ants by dipping a stick into the nest entrance. As soon as a few ants have leaped to the defense of their nest by running up the stick, the chimp lifts it out and uses its lips in a rapid swiping action to sweep the ants off into its mouth.

In the North American legionary ant, *Labidus coecus*, temporary nest sites are established under stones or in logs or tree stumps. Every two to three weeks the workers fashion tunnels made from leaf fragments leading from the nest to a new locality nearby. Using such a covered walkway, the colony is free to move either by day or night, taking their larvae with them.

Mutilla europaea

Common name Velvet ants

Family Mutillidae

Suborder Apocrita

Order Hymenoptera

Number of species About 5,000 (about 450 U.S.)

Size From about 0.2 in (5 mm) to about 1 in (2.5 cm)

Key features Body more sturdily built than in real ants (Formicidae), with less of a "waist"; densely covered in hair, usually brightly colored, often black and white or black and orange; females wingless, males fully winged; unlike ants, antennae are not elbowed; female has powerful sting

Habits Females usually seen running on open ground, less often across vegetation or up tree trunks; males usually found feeding on flowers

Breeding Males are often much larger than the wingless females and carry them off in a mating flight; females search for nests of bees and wasps in which to lay their eggs

Diet Adults normally feed on nectar, but females may attack other bees and wasps for food; larvae feed on larvae and pupae of bees, wasps, and flies

Habitat Most often found running on the ground in open, dry places such as deserts; in the U.S. most species restricted to the arid zones of the Southwest; also found in rain forests, meadows, and on mountains

Distribution Worldwide, but uncommon in cooler temperate zones

⤒ *The European velvet ant,* Mutilla europaea, *is a parasite whose larvae develop inside bumblebee nests. The females can be found running around on the ground, in leaf litter, or on tree trunks with an agitated, antlike gait. Body length 0.5 inches (13 mm).*

Velvet Ants

Mutillidae

Despite their common name, velvet ants are not closely related to true ants (Formicidae) and have different habits. Some may even be killers.

MOST VELVET ANTS ARE DENSELY clothed in a pelt of brightly colored hairs. Black and white and black and orange are two of the commoner color combinations, constituting a typical "warning uniform." The design advertises the agonizing sting that some of the velvet ants can administer if interfered with.

Fearsome Reputation

In some species the stinger is nearly as long as the abdomen, which can be bent around to ram the stinger home if the insect·is carelessly handled. In humans the venom causes huge swellings, and in one species it is reputed to be fatal. The fearsome reputation of some of the larger American species of *Dasymutilla* has earned them the name "cow killers." Although the sting is supposedly powerful enough to kill a cow, livestock are not normally at risk. As in all hymenopterans, only the females can sting.

Male velvet ants are most likely to be seen sipping nectar on flowers. Females are usually noticed first because of their habit of running restlessly around on open bare ground in an

⊕ *Clearly showing the absence of wings characteristic of female mutillids, a cow-killer velvet ant,* Dasymutilla occidentalis *from the United States, carries warning colors that advertise an agonizing ability to sting.*

Copycats of Velvet Ants

In the tropics the most common color pattern in velvet ants is black with white spots. On the savannas of Africa the wingless females of several species with such coloration run on the bare ground among the grasses. They are accompanied by other insects with similar patterns and habits, including the ground beetle *Eccoptera cupricollis* (Carabidae) and an *Ectomocoris* species assassin bug (Reduviidae). Both are also wingless. Like most members of its family, the ground beetle probably secretes a noxious defensive fluid, while the assassin bug jabs its sharp rostrum into skin with painful results. Both insects are known as mimics of velvet ants, since they copy them as a means of self-defense.

antlike way. Most desert species are active only at night or during cooler periods following heavy rain, although they also seem able to cope with surprisingly high temperatures in daytime. The dense velvety covering and armored body help them resist the high temperatures and reduce water loss through evaporation. Their solid build also enables them to walk straight into the nest of a bee or wasp through the front door, regardless of whether or not the owner is at home. Their impenetrable bodies cannot be accessed by the stinger of any of their adversaries, buying them time for finding the nest cells.

Scrounging Off Bees

Once inside the nest of its bumblebee host, the European *Mutilla europaea* female bites open each cell to check on the state of the larva inside. If it is only small, she reseals the cell and departs. If the occupant of the cell is fully grown and about to pupate, she inserts the tip of her abdomen into the cell and lays an egg on the larva. Unlike in some other species, the larva is not stung and paralyzed, but will be eaten alive by the ant's larva as it develops.

The larva eventually pupates in a thick cocoon within the host cell. Some species attack pupae rather than larvae, but the host is almost always a bee or wasp, usually of a particular species. For example, in the United States the western velvet ant, *Dasymutilla sackenii*, lays its eggs only in the nest of *Bembix occidentalis*, a sand wasp (Sphecidae).

In Africa two species of velvet ants invade the puparia of tsetse flies (Glossinidae). The flies are carriers of sleeping sickness, a serious disease of cattle and humans. Velvet ants may one day be used in the biological control of these harmful pests.

In sexual encounters the male velvet ant (normally much larger than the wingless female) sweeps his mate off her feet and carries her away clasped in his jaws and braced against his head. The males have specific modifications of the jaws and head for performing the task. Males stridulate as they drop in on the female, who replies with her own series of chirps.

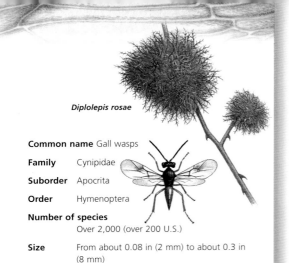

Diplolepis rosae

Common name Gall wasps

Family Cynipidae

Suborder Apocrita

Order Hymenoptera

Number of species
    Over 2,000 (over 200 U.S.)

Size From about 0.08 in (2 mm) to about 0.3 in (8 mm)

Key features Body black or dark brown, glossy, with humpbacked profile; abdomen of female flattened from side to side; wings with only a small number of veins; some species wingless; antennae long with 13 or 14 segments in females, 14 or 15 in males

Habits Adults small, secretive, and seldom seen; larvae form galls, which can be highly conspicuous on plants

Breeding Females lay eggs in plant tissues, usually restricting their attacks to just a single species of host plant; the plant responds by forming a gall in which the larvae feed

Diet Adults feed on nectar or honeydew or not at all; larvae mostly feed on plants, a few on other insects

Habitat Common in all terrestrial habitats, including deserts, from ground level to the tops of trees

Distribution Worldwide, but avoiding the driest and coldest zones

⊕ Diplolepis rosae, *the European gall wasp, makes a "robin pincushion" gall on the wild rose. Body length 0.2 inches (5 mm).*

Gall Wasps Cynipidae

The presence of gall wasps is more likely to be noticed from the often colorful and distinctive swellings they cause on plants than by seeing the tiny creatures themselves.

GALL WASPS, ALONG WITH fig wasps, are unusual among members of the suborder Apocrita in having a lifestyle that is mainly vegetarian. The female gall wasp lays her eggs in a host plant that is usually one particular species, but may be a closely related species in the same genus. In temperate regions the most popular hosts are oaks (*Quercus*) and other members of the family Fagaceae. The female oviposits in the specific part of the plant where the gall is intended to develop. All parts of a plant can be used, including the roots. Galls may contain one or more larvae, depending on species.

Inducing Galls

The gall only develops after the larvae have hatched: It is the plant's reaction to their salivary excretions. That is unlike the situation in sawflies such as *Pontania*, in which a gall develops as a result of chemicals injected by the female along with the egg.

By developing a gall, the plant limits the range of its attacker's operations. At the same time, the gall wasp larvae are provided with covered accommodation that doubles as a source of food. The shape of a gall varies among species: Its appearance, along with its position on the host plant (and the species of host plant), makes the occupants quite easy to identify.

Not all gall wasps induce galls—some act as "cuckoos" within the galls of others. The invader larvae do not always slaughter the

⊕ *The shape of these tiny galls on the underside of an oak leaf in England easily identifies them as the common spangle galls, the asexual generation of the wasp* Neuroterus quercus-baccarum *(Cynipidae).*

ground, with their occupants still developing inside. In April females emerge and lay their eggs in the young, developing flower catkins of the oaks, giving rise to bunches of "currant galls" that resemble red currants. By June they are mature and produce males and females. After mating, the females move to the undersides of the leaves, lay their eggs, and produce spangle galls, starting the cycle again.

⊕ *A tiny* Neuroterus numismalis *gall wasp lays her eggs on an oak leaf in England. The resulting silk-button spangle galls are similar to those depicted below left.*

rightful occupants, but they usually die anyway from starvation, their greedier lodgers having won the competition for food.

Alternation of Generations

Many gall wasps alternate between generations containing males and females and nonsexual generations restricted to parthenogenetic females which lay unfertilized eggs. Unlike in other wasps, the unfertilized eggs can give rise to female offspring as well as males, producing the next batch of males and females for the succeeding sexual generation. After mating, they lay eggs that give rise to nothing but females, which start the ball rolling all over again with their unfertilized asexual eggs.

Each of the two generations switches between a different part of the host plant or even between different species of host. In the live-oak gall wasp, *Callirhytis quercuspomiformis* from the United States, the asexual generation galls the stems of one species of oak, while the sexual generation generates leaf galls on a different oak. In *Neuroterus quercus-baccarum* from Europe the asexual generation develops in tiny disklike "spangle galls" that often cover the undersides of oak leaves. In the fall these spangles become detached and drop to the

Fig Wasps and Figs—a Perfect Match

Fig wasps in the family Agaonidae are also exclusively vegetarian. Their mutually beneficial relationship with certain fig plants is one of the most interdependent known between animal and plant. The partnership has reached the point where without fig wasps there would be no figs, and without figs there would be no fig wasps.

Newly emerged females wait inside their fig flower homes until males cut their way into them from the outside. Having mated, a female scoops up a quantity of pollen and stores it in special pockets on her front legs and thorax, then exits via the male's entry hole. Flying to a fresh fig flower, she enters, scraping her wings off as she forces her way in. She then lays her eggs in the flowers. Some of the flowers have short styles, enabling her ovipositor to reach their ovaries. Her larvae will feed on the developing seeds inside the ovaries. Other flowers have longer styles, preventing her from reaching the ovaries, so the seeds will develop normally. To ensure they do so, she carefully dusts the stigmas with the pollen from the supply she has brought with her from the other flower.

Yellow jacket (*Vespula germanica*)

Common name Social wasps (paper wasps, potter wasps)

Family Vespidae

Suborder Apocrita

Order Hymenoptera

Number of species About 4,000 (about 415 U.S.)

Size From about 0.2 in (5 mm) to about 1.4 in (3.5 cm)

Key features Body usually banded, often black and yellow or black and white; sometimes all black or brown, occasionally green; eyes with a distinct notch at the front; both sexes fully winged; pronotum reaches back to the wing bases; wings pleated when held at rest over back; females armed with stinger

Habits Mostly active during the day, a few species nocturnal; adults hunt for larval food on leaves or flowers; paper wasp nests often conspicuous on buildings; potter wasps may be conspicuous collecting mud around puddles

Breeding Potter wasps are solitary and build mud nests, which they fill with spiders; paper wasps are highly social; nests often large, usually made of "paper," in which overlapping generations of workers care for the young and eventually rear males and future queens; nests may be founded and dominated by one or more queens

Diet Adults mainly eat nectar from flowers, honeydew, juices oozing from ripe fruits, and leaking sap on tree trunks; larvae are mainly carnivorous

Habitat Common in all kinds of terrestrial habitats that are not too dry or cold

Distribution Worldwide, commonest in the tropics

⬆ *The yellow jacket,* Vespula germanica *(also known as the German wasp), builds its nest in suitable buildings or underground and is common in Europe. Body length (of worker) 0.9 inches (22 mm).*

Social Wasps
Vespidae

Although they are known collectively as "social" wasps, the Vespidae contains wasps that display a wide range of lifestyles. Some are solitary, laboring alone to construct their nests; others are highly social and work as a team to build their communal homes.

NEST BUILDING IN SOME MEMBERS of the Vespidae is a solitary business. Potter wasps in the subfamily Eumeninae (formerly placed in a separate family, the Eumenidae) work alone to build their beautifully crafted mud nests. The pollen-gathering wasps in the subfamily Masarinae (once in a separate family, the Masaridae) also engage in solitary labor. They build their nests in the ground or construct cells of mud or sand attached to rocks or twigs. The nests are filled not with the flesh of insects and other animals, as in most wasps, but with pollen and nectar, a habit more often associated with the bees.

Social Lifestyles
The paper wasps in the subfamily Polistinae have highly social lifestyles and work as a team to build their communal nests, usually of paper. The thread-waisted paper wasps in the subfamily Stenogastrinae, found from India to New Guinea, encompass almost the whole range of social development. Some are completely solitary, while in others communally living females give each other a helping hand. A number exhibit semisocial behavior bordering on the highly social habits of the Polistinae. The hornets and yellow jackets in the subfamily Vespinae build relatively huge paper nests inhabited by thousands of workers. As in ants, the workers are usually the daughters of a single queen (although some nests have several queens) and spend their lives raising her offspring while producing none of their own.

In wasps' nests all workers can carry out any required task, but in some species certain workers tend to become specialized for fixed roles, such as nest building. In many species a

⬇ **Polistes instabilis** *from Mexico is one of many paper wasps that store nectar from flowers. The worker shown is grooming her mouthparts with her front legs, having just fed.*

worker goes through a series of job changes as it grows older. It starts as a nurse caring for the larvae, then begins to make excursions from the nest to collect paper pulp or liquids. Building on its increasing experience, the next switch is to the more skillful and demanding task of prey capture, followed by a last move in approaching old age to a nest-bound job as guard. In some of the more primitively social species, such as *Belonogaster* from Africa, there is no worker caste, and all the females in the nest have equal status and can lay eggs. As in most insects, there are a few "cuckoo" species that benefit from the hard work of others while taking things easy themselves.

Sting in the Tail

For most people the mere idea of a "wasp" is summed up by the *Vespula* yellow jackets, some of which are also known as hornets in the United States. (The original hornets of Europe

and Asia are in the genus *Vespa*, so are more naturally segregated as a group.) The giant hornet, *Vespa crabro*, was introduced into the United States from Europe and is now established in some of the eastern states, where it is the only "true" hornet.

Yellow jackets are widely feared and detested because of their willingness to sting when molested. Unlike in honeybees, the stinger of most social wasps (except polybiines) can be

⊕ The giant hornet,
Vespa crabro, is the
largest European social
wasp. It was introduced
accidentally into the
United States, where it is
now established.

withdrawn in one piece and used over and over again. In all the social species the sting is used purely for defensive purposes and is not brought into play during the capture of prey. Prey is dealt with using the powerful jaws, which are highly efficient as hatchets. Adult wasps are unable to swallow solid materials, so they can only take their food in the form of liquids, such as nectar from flowers, juice oozing from overripe fruits, honeydew from aphids, and sap runs on trees. In times of drought yellow jackets will drink from streams and puddles. Where water is not available, they will show considerable enterprise by biting the flower heads off thistles and other flowers in order to drink the sap that flows out.

Potter Wasps and Mason Wasps

The potter and mason wasps (subfamily Eumeninae) are commonest in warm climates, with a world total of around 3,000 species. The females work alone in constructing and stocking their nests and in most cases never see their offspring. The main tool in capturing prey is the female's stinger. Prey items are taken to the nest in a paralyzed state and stored in one piece, rather than being dismembered as in other social wasps. In both respects the potter wasps have more in common with the solitary wasps in the family Sphecidae than with the other highly social members of the Vespidae in the subfamilies Vespinae and Polistinae.

The typical material used by potter and mason wasps for nest building is mud, but the ways in which it is used vary greatly. In mason wasps, such as *Ancistrocerus*, mud serves merely to fashion individual cells within a preexisting cavity, such as a beetle boring, hollow plant stem, rock crevice, or even inside a plant gall. Some species plaster their cells against a damaged area of wall and then cover the finished structure with a layer of mud. For the tiny *Euodynerus* a hole in a pebble gives enough space for squeezing in a nest cell. In *Odynerus* the nests are made in the ground, and the entrance has a long, curving chimneylike cylinder of clay above it. When the

⊕ *Some potter wasps, such as* Eumenes fenestralis *from South Africa, visit ponds and puddles to collect balls of mud that are ready-made for construction work.*

nest is complete, the wasp demolishes the chimney and recycles the material to seal the entrance. Mason wasps generally stock their nests with several small caterpillars of moths or butterflies or with the larvae of weevils (Curculionidae) or leaf beetles (Chrysomelidae).

Potter wasps belonging to genera such as *Eumenes* and *Delta* build self-standing, dome-shaped nests, rather than fitting their nests inside an existing cavity. In many species the little pots are erected in rows on twigs or leaves. In others they are placed on flat stones, rock faces, caves, walls, or inside buildings on chairs, china ornaments, or even on clothing. Because the wasp carries out its construction work in full view, it is easy to study its highly skilled mud-handling techniques.

Before she can start to build, the female potter wasp must first collect her supply of mud from a damp spot, such as the edge of a puddle. She gathers the mud between her jaws and front legs until it forms a ball. The finished ball looks wetter than the original source material, probably because it contains saliva for

⊖ *Many potter wasp females build a series of mud cells side by side, completing and stocking the first with paralyzed caterpillars before starting the second cell.*

strength and waterproofing qualities. In some desert species, where naturally occurring mud may be scarce or absent, the female fills her crop from a distant water source and transports it back to her work site. She then manufactures her own mud by mixing water from her crop with dry, dusty earth in the immediate vicinity. She can mix several pellets in this way until her internal reservoir needs to be replenished.

Master Builder

To form the foundation for her nest, the female potter wasp first lays down a circle of pellets. She then adds another circle on top, gradually

Nests Begun by Swarming

In many tropical members of the Polybiinae new nests are founded by swarming. One or more queens leave an existing nest, accompanied by a swarm of workers who make short work of establishing a new nest. The remarkable speed of construction is helped by the fact that in many species each worker sticks to a particular role in the construction process, providing increased levels of skill gained through experience. Some act purely as water gatherers, filling their crop from a nearby supply and ferrying it back to the nest. At the nest site the water is shared out among various specialist builders who mix it with the wood pulp that arrives from dedicated pulp gatherers. Unlike in most other wasps, workers are not multiroled. They do not gather wood pulp and add it to the nest themselves.

Right from the start the queens, freed of the need to take any part in the manual labor of getting the nest up and running, can devote their entire energies to laying eggs and never leave the nest. They are unusual in normally being smaller than the workers and in the number often present in the colony—up to 15 queens being possible. As in the vespines, the queens control their workers via pheromones, probably from a gland located in the head. They are assisted by high-ranking workers who constantly intimidate and harass the younger females to the degree that their ovaries fail to develop.

SOCIAL WASPS

tapering inward to form a dome. The outer surface of the nest reflects its multisegmented origin, being rough and unfinished like a crudely built mud wall. By contrast, the interior receives constant attention from the female's jaws, which are used to scrape it smooth like the inside of a pot. As she works, she constantly bends her antennae down into the interior, gauging its diameter and the standard of the finish. Finally she adds a little lip around the entrance, using her jaws and front legs with delicate precision to form the most neatly crafted part of the whole structure.

Once the nest is complete, the female potter wasp thrusts her rear end inside and suspends an egg from the roof on a short silk thread. She then stocks the nest with several stung and paralyzed caterpillars, feeding them through the smoothly lipped entrance with her jaws and front legs. Up to a dozen small caterpillars may be needed or just three to four larger ones. She then bites away the lip around the entrance to leave an uninterrupted dome-shaped profile and plasters over the whole structure with a smooth layer of mud. The covering is so resistant to abrasion that it is impossible to scrape off even a few grains of sand with a fingernail. Even a heavy downpour will not succeed in washing the walls away.

Inside its almost impregnable home the tiny newly hatched larva uses its tail to cling to its eggshell while it stretches down and takes its first meal from the nearest caterpillars. The insects are only lightly anesthetized and may wriggle around somewhat. Since their movement could damage the tiny larva, it remains temporarily out of harm's way by hanging from the ceiling on its egg thread. When it is larger and tougher, it will drop down among the caterpillars and feed directly.

Mass Provisioning

Most potter wasps stock their nests with large numbers of small insects, a process known as mass provisioning. It is the common method used by solitary or hunting wasps (Sphecidae). The insects are normally supplied intact, unlike

in the social members of the Vespidae in which the prey is chewed to a pulp before being fed to the larvae. A few potter wasps practice "progressive provisioning," in which the female supplies food to each larva only when it needs it. As a result, the female has to keep a constant check on her offspring's needs. Progressive provisioning is also seen in some sphecids; but as in mass provisioning, food is normally supplied whole. One potter wasp, *Synagris cornuta* from Africa, is highly unusual in supplying insects in the form of a chewed-up paste, much as in the social wasps.

Paper Nests

Most of the wasps in the subfamilies Vespinae and Polistinae use a kind of paper as their prime nest-building material. It is manufactured in approximately the same way in all species. Walking backward, the wasp uses its jaws to scrape a small pellet of fibers from a dead branch, wooden

Most social wasps make their nests from paper. Here several Polybia occidentalis workers in Trinidad are adding fresh building material supplied to them by foragers.

226

This fully enclosed mud nest of Eustenogaster calyptodoma *from Thailand is far more fragile than the solid structures made by potter wasps.*

⊙ *Paper wasps in the drier parts of the Americas often build their nests on some of the larger kinds of cacti. Shown above is* Mischocyttarus immarginatus *from Mexico.*

Producing a clearly audible scratching sound, a queen Dolichovespula media *yellow jacket uses her jaws to scrape a wad of wood pulp off a log in England.*

post, or other source of plant fibers. The material is mixed with saliva to form a pulp that can be molded into a variety of complex shapes. It dries out into a paperlike texture, which is remarkably tough and durable. The shape and internal architecture of the nest show enormous variation and are usually fixed for a given species. In most members of the Polistinae the nest consists of a series of hexagonal cells placed side by side. In *Polistes* nests, however, the outermost cells have rounded outer edges, rather than straight. The

nest is usually glued by a slender stalk to the underside of a firm surface such as a branch, large leaf, or rock overhang. The ceilings, windows, and overhanging eaves of buildings have become a popular location for *Polistes* nests, which may occur there in far larger numbers than in more natural situations. In desert areas cacti and other spiny plants are favored nest sites, probably because they afford extra protection against enemies. The stalk of the nest is usually smeared with a black, lacquerlike substance emanating from glands in the wasp's abdomen. Its main constituent, methyl palmitate, is highly repellent to ants. They are discouraged from entering the nest and destroying its contents (although it is ineffective against swarm-raiding ants such as *Eciton burchelli* army ants). In *Polistes* nests there is no outer covering, leaving the cells and their contents open, but in many other polistines there is an outer envelope of carton.

Storage in Vespinae Nests

In nests of the Vespinae, such as yellow jackets, the cells are built in tiers hung on a central comb and shielded by an envelope of tough

227

carton. The outer covering makes it impossible to see what is going on inside, but provides protection from bad weather. The carton also serves as a storage reservoir for surplus paper pulp when excess supplies are coming in. When supplies dwindle—as happens in bad weather—the workers chew off a portion of carton, mix it with saliva, and use it to build fresh cells.

During cell construction the worker adds a narrow strip of fresh material with her jaws. She uses her antennae as measuring calipers to maintain the precise hexagonal shape, as well as the position relative to neighboring cells. In most wasps each cell will be used for rearing a succession of larvae, being cleaned out between each occupant. Previously used cells are obvious from their frayed edges. The fraying is caused by the emerging adult wasp biting its way to freedom through the silken cocoon formed during pupation. In some species, such as *Polistes instabilis* from Central America, some of the outer cells are used to store nectar and fruit juices until the cell is needed for reproduction. The storing of vegetable products within nests is fairly widespread. In *Brachygastra mellifica*, also from Central America, large amounts of honey are stored within the nest, which, unlike in *Polistes*, has an outer envelope.

Cellophane Nests

In a few species of social wasps, such as *Pseudochartergus chartergoides* and *P. fuscatus* from South America and *Ropalidia opifex* from Asia, the nest is made of a transparent polyethylenelike material derived from secretions within the builders' bodies. The secretion is produced from the mandibles and takes more than 24 hours to set completely.

Construction work is carried out only by certain dedicated workers, which, if accidentally killed, take several days to replace. The finished nests resemble cellophane and are extremely efficient at shedding the heavy rainfall common in the wasps' rain-forest home. A number of social species also build with mud, creating nests of an elegant and delicate porcelainlike structure that is easily fractured. They are quite unlike the solid, almost indestructible structures crafted from mud by the solitary Eumeninae.

In temperate regions such as North America and Europe vespine nests last just a single summer. In the fall all the workers die, leaving the queens to overwinter and start fresh colonies the following spring. In the tropics polistine and polybiine nests may be much longer lived, lasting for several seasons. In areas with a prolonged dry season the workers may cluster together on the outside of the nest, hardly moving at all. Here they conserve their energies until the return of the wet season, when the abundance of prey triggers a resumption of activity. In very mild areas colonies of yellow jackets, such as *Vespula vulgaris* and *V. germanica*, may survive the winter into the following season. Some of the queens who left as unmated virgins the previous fall now rejoin their original nests, having subsequently mated. They become queens in their own right, producing nests with several queens that may eventually contain hundreds of thousands of workers.

Founding Nests

Nest-founding methods vary. In yellow jackets, hornets, and other members of the Vespinae the colony is inaugurated by a single queen, usually one that has emerged in springtime after a winter spent in hibernation. As in queen ants, the foundress does all the work herself to raise her first brood of workers. She chooses a nest site—a hollow tree, under the eaves of a house or shed, or among rubbish dumped near buildings. Alternatively, she may suspend the nest from a bush or place it beneath the ground, in a wall crevice, or abandoned rodent burrow. Unlike in nest-bound ant queens, the queen wasp does not rely on stored resources within her body to nourish her first brood. Instead, she feeds her developing larvae with pulped insects that she catches on regular forays. Once her first limited batch of workers is on hand, the queen usually retires from active nest duties. She now concentrates on being sole egg layer for the growing colony, although

⬆ *Fanning like mad with rapidly vibrating wings, two* Polistes fastidiosus *paper wasps direct a blast of cool air across their nest on the hot savannas of Africa.*

Cooling the Nest

Delivering food to the larvae is usually a job for the female workers, but in some species males also help out. They are even more likely to join in with a task that sometimes requires urgent remedial action—cooling an overheating nest. In unusually hot conditions or at certain times of the day when the sun strikes the nest directly, the cell-bound larvae, which cannot change their position for a cooler one, could overheat and die.

The first task to bring down the temperature is to stand on the cells most affected and fan vigorously with the wings. On larger nests several males and workers may stand by for long periods, energetically fanning away, but on smaller nests just one or two will take on the role. In the nests of species such as *Vespa* that are built inside natural chambers (for example, hollow trees) several colony members will stand at the single entrance and ventilate the interior by fanning cool air down inside.

If fanning alone fails to reduce the temperature, more drastic measures are taken. Most of the colony will give up whatever they were doing to ferry supplies of water back to the nest. The water is spread over the carton and cools it down by natural evaporation. Meanwhile, the bulk of the colony not involved in water gathering continues to fan the nest. The sudden switch to a collective effort shows just how dangerous excessive temperatures must be to the survival of larvae and pupae.

in *Vespula tropica pulchra* the queen carries out domestic chores right up to her death.

Chemical Control in Vespine Queens
Once the nest is well established, the queen needs to exert her authority over her workers and ensure that they do not start laying eggs on their own account. She uses a form of chemical control through pheromones to ensure their continued servitude. In "true" hornets (*Vespa*) the pheromone is secreted on the outside of the queen's body, from where it is eagerly lapped up by the workers, who find it irresistible. Controlling the colony by pheromones is probably the only viable option for the vespine queen. Nests may contain as many as 6,000 workers tending up to 14,000 cells, so control by individual bullying, as seen in many polistines, would not be practical. Vespine workers are smaller than their queen, being a true menial caste, and cannot be promoted to the top post if the original queen dies. The queen is also differently marked, and the proportions of her body parts are different.

→ *A female nectar-gathering wasp,* Ceramius tuberculifer *(subfamily Masarinae), adds an earthen chimney to her nest in the ground on a French hillside.*

Bullying in *Polistes* Queens

In *Polistes*—and other paper wasps in the Polistinae—nests are also usually founded by a single female working alone. But she may often quickly be joined by a number of other females, usually her sisters. They help her expand the nest and rear the first brood of workers. They are the offspring of just one of the females, who has won the right to act as queen by bullying her cofoundresses into accepting a submissive status that prevents them from laying eggs of their own.

The shakedown process may take several days during which the original group of foundresses chew one another up, battle with their stingers, and engage in vicious fights to decide who will be queen. The eventual winner will maintain her tyrannical attitude toward her companions thoughout the life of the nest and also toward her own offspring. The harsh treatment ensures that they accept their place as menial workers. Constantly persecuted by the queen, their ovaries fail to develop, so they can never reproduce.

The *Polistes* queen's dictatorship over her nest mates takes several forms. She eats any eggs that are laid (other than her own) and uses harassing behaviors such as biting her nest mates on the back of the head or wings and forcing them to feed her mouth to mouth (trophallaxis). She never allows them to relax or feel off guard. Such purely physical methods of control work in polistine nests, since they are usually much smaller than in vespines, with only a few dozen workers to keep in check.

The tyrannical habits continue right down the line through the other females in a "chewing order" from top to bottom. Each member of the hierarchy knows her correct place in the system at any one moment. If the queen is deposed, she drops straight to the bottom of the rankings. Because of the way the whole system is organized and developed, in polistine nests the queen is identical to her workers both in size and appearance. She can only be identified by her behavior. Unlike in vespines, *Polistes* queens still carry out some of the daily chores in the nest. They build cells, forage for food supplies and wood pulp, and feed the larvae, although they spend less time performing such tasks than the workers.

Daily Chores in *Polistes* Nests

The daily rhythm of activity in *Polistes* nests is easy to see, since the cells are exposed to view. The main duty for nest-bound "nurse" workers is to provide the larvae with a regular supply of food. The food is delivered in small packages by foragers. Back at the nest the foragers share out their bounty with one or more nurses, depending on the size of the parcel. Each worker holds the food in her jaws for a while and chews it in a special way called malaxation. The action serves to strain out much of the food's liquid content, which is swallowed by the worker herself, since she is unable to take solid food. The worker then takes the food to a larval cell and announces her arrival by drumming her antennae or abdomen tip against the nest. The larva sticks its head out, offers the adult a droplet of liquid food, and then takes a bite at the solid food proffered in the adult's jaws.

Drumming on the nest by adults who do not have any food to offer is also common, encouraging the larva to serve up a droplet of liquid food for the worker. The provision of liquid morsels by the larvae to the adults seems to be important in most social wasps. The solid food proffered by the adults is rich in protein, which the larvae require for growth. In return the liquid food is probably rich in the sugars that the adults need for fueling their day-to-day activities. Queens cannot survive without the dietary supplement, which seems necessary for egg production. In vespine nests the larvae themselves "beg" for meals by scraping their mandibles noisily against the paper walls of their cells. The commotion usually brings one or more workers running with a sample of food.

⊙ The heads of several larvae can be seen peeping out of their cells in this nest of Polistes instabilis *in Mexico. The topmost row of cells contains unhatched eggs.*

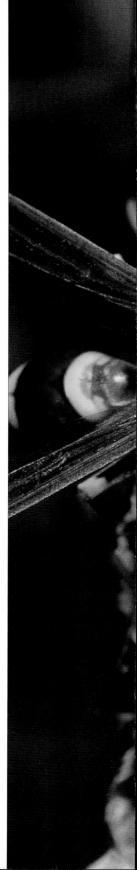

Another chore performed by workers of a number of species from Africa and Asia is to dispose of the accumulated waste products (meconium) vented by the larva just before it pupates. In *Belonogaster* and *Ropalidia* the worker cuts off the bottom of the cell just before the larva pupates and stands ready to receive the meconial sac, tugging it free as it begins to protrude from the larva's body. If the larva is denied the disposal service, it dies, being unable to vent the meconium fully on its own.

Despite the colony's best efforts, some pupae will always die within their sealed cells. The workers go around checking on each pupa's state of health, which can apparently be detected through the opaque cell cap. If the pupa is dead or diseased, the worker chews away the cap and extracts the remains. As long as it is not too rotten or diseased, it will be recycled back to the healthy larvae as food.

Thieving Habits

Yellow jackets often save time by stealing prey from spiders' webs and will take the spider as well if given the chance. The little stenogastrine *Parischnogaster nigricans* from Southeast Asia is a specialist in robbing spiders' webs and gets its food by no other means. It would seem to be a high-risk strategy for such a small wasp, but the females are adept at pilfering the web of its contents without being detected. Most wasps also collect nectar and honeydew, some of which may be stored inside the nest.

Like ants, wasps may visit homopteran bugs such as treehoppers (Membracidae) to collect their honeydew. At least 10 species of polistine wasps are known to tend homopteran bugs in this way. They "milk" them of their honeydew, herd them like cattle, and defend them against enemies. In Costa Rica *Parachartergus fraternus* is so possessive about its treehopper herds that it prevents access to them by any other hymenopterans, including

⊙ *When their colony is under threat, most members of a paper wasp nest respond quickly. These* Stelopolybia pallipes *workers in Trinidad are ready for battle.*

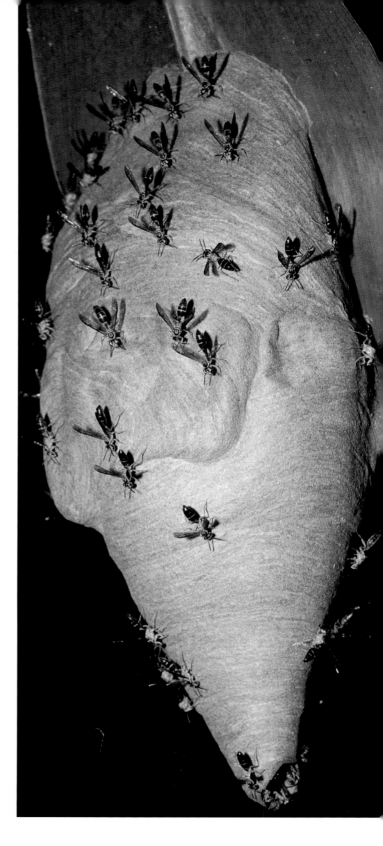

ants. Vespine wasps glean honeydew from leaves, which are covered in droplets falling from colonies of bugs higher up.

Continuing the Line

At some point during the colony's development, usually late summer in annual species living in temperate countries, the production of males and prospective new queens begins. In yellow-jacket nests the queen starts to lay haploid eggs, which will develop into males, as well as the usual diploid eggs. Although identical to the eggs that have been developing into workers all summer long, the eggs will be given special treatment that will ensure that they develop into queens. The queen communicates the need for "regal" nursery conditions by releasing a pheromone that triggers queen-rearing behavior in her workers. Future queens are spoiled with a super-rich diet and reared in extralarge cells, as befits their royal status.

Once the males and young queens have emerged, they may help with some of the nest chores, but their main role is sexual. The males do not mate with their sisters at home, but leave in search of unrelated females from other nests. In many species from temperate regions the males head for potential hibernation sites, such as rock crevices, holes in trees, or the eaves of houses. Such sites are likely to attract females from a variety of nests, making inbreeding less likely. In some species the males patrol near flowers that could be attractive to females. In a number of desert species, such as *Polistes commanchus* from the arid Southwest

⊕ *Dealing instant death with its powerful jaws, a common wasp,* Vespula vulgaris, *soon dispatches its unfortunate hover fly prey.*

Precision Butchery

Unlike the potter and mason wasps, which stock their nests with whole insects, the social species of vespids tend to be more wide ranging in their choice of food, which is fed to their larvae as a mashed-up pulp. Some kinds show a degree of conservatism in their choice of prey. *Belonogaster*, for example, mainly takes caterpillars, while some *Stelopolybia* specialize in collecting carrion from vertebrate corpses, such as dead mammals and birds. The tropical hornet, *Vespa tropica*, preys almost entirely on the brood of *Polistes* paper wasps, although adult wasps seldom seem to prey on other adults. The European hornet, *Vespa crabro*, takes a wide variety of prey, but can be a pest near honeybee hives, killing the workers as they come in and out. Yellow jackets have catholic tastes and will prey on most things. They will often sit by a patch of flowers and jump on insects such as hover flies, knocking them to the ground. The fly is then killed by having its head bitten off. The complete fly would be clumsy to transport back to the nest, and only the highly nutritious thorax and abdomen are required as food. The wasp prepares the corpse for delivery by first biting off both wings at their roots, followed by all six legs at their bases. The abdomen is then neatly folded forward against the thorax, leaving a compact parcel with only the most nourishing and digestible parts. The package is now no trouble to carry tucked beneath the wasp's body.

Such precision butchering is typical of wasps. With certain prey, such as bugs, they will use their jaws to carve the best strips of meat off the abdomen, leaving the rest of the carcass behind. They exhibit similar behavior with small animal corpses, such as mice, whose flesh will be steadily carved off the bones, leaving just the bare rib cage. With softer prey, such as caterpillars, most of the tissues are chewed up on site, enabling the wasp to fashion a compact bundle suitable for transport. Once a forager has found a prime food source, it has no way of quickly recruiting and guiding large numbers of its nest mates back to the site, as

In a Brazilian rain forest a Polistes cinerascens *worker methodically strips the flesh from the underside of an assassin bug.*

happens in ants. Nor can it notify the location of the food using a "dance," as in honeybees. In some hornets a few nest mates will follow the finder back to the food source, while in *Vespula* a returning forager seems able to communicate that it has found a good food source. Its nest mates find it, using scent as clues.

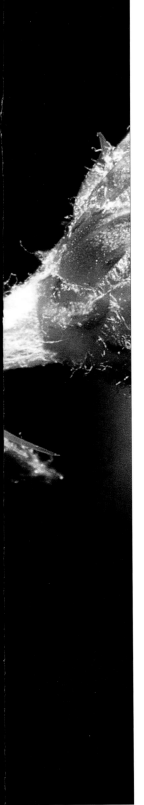

of the United States, the males assemble on hilltops to which females from many nests will come to seek a mate. "Hilltopping" is a much-used tactic that ensures a reliable rendezvous point for the two sexes.

Before mating there is little or no advance courtship. However, in most wasps—after the male has mounted onto the female's back—he will lasso her antennae in his own and stroke the tip of his abdomen up and down against the sides of her body. In temperate areas the virgin queen goes into hibernation once she has mated, emerging next spring to found her own colony. The sperm from her nuptial mating will be stored inside her body and will be enough for the fertilization of any eggs that need it (the ones destined to become workers or queens).

In some of the solitary vespids, such as certain *Ancistrocerus* mason wasps, the nuptial arrangements are different. The males hatch first from the outermost cells when the nest is placed inside hollow stems or crevices. The first action taken by the brothers is to fight for the privilege of staying beside the nest until their sisters emerge. The victor will mate with several of them, but cannot possibly manage to claim them all. Some females will escape and mate with males from other nests while visiting flowers. The victor himself will also spend some time searching on flowers, giving him a chance to mate with females other than his sisters.

Cuckoos in the Nest

Both *Vespula* and *Polistes* nests may suffer the attentions of "cuckoo" queens. In Europe there are three species of *Sulcopolistes* whose queens attack and take over the nests of the local species of *Polistes*. The *Polistes* workers are not killed during the takeover battles, but are retained to rear the usurping queen's offspring. In North America the nests of *Vespula arcadica* are invaded and requisitioned by queens of *Vespula austriaca*. After executing the resident

⊖ *After severing the stem with its jaws, a worker German wasp,* Vespula germanica, *sips the oozing sap during an unusually prolonged drought in England.*

queen, the *V. austriaca* queen exerts her domination over the colony's workers by submitting them to frequent bouts of abusive treatment. She mauls and bullies them relentlessly until they accept her status as queen and carry out her bidding, rearing her offspring as if they rightly belonged to the nest.

Call to Action

Defense of the nest is performed by all the workers, and in the most highly social species, such as swarm-founding polistines and all vespines, the call to action is made by means of an alarm pheromone. It consists of venom pumped into the air from the stingers. The odor rapidly spreads around the nest and, in species with outer envelopes, sends dozens of workers pouring onto the exterior. With wings spread wide and abdomens raised into the air in a threat posture, the workers fly out to inflict painful retribution on any aggressor.

In the tropics there is often a defensive arrangement between the nests of different wasp species or between wasps and ants. In Costa Rica *Mischocyttarus immarginatus* often places its small nests close to the much larger colonies of another polistine, *Polybia occidentalis*. Its chosen neighbor aggressively defends its nest and the surrounding area against larger predators such as monkeys. In Central and South America *Polybia rejecta*, *Synoeca chalybea*, and several species of *Mischocyttarus* place their nests on ant plants, which are inhabited and vigorously defended by symbiotic ants such as *Azteca* and *Pseudomyrmex ferruginea*. The ants seem to tolerate the presence of the wasps, probably because they help defend the ant plants against herbivorous predators.

⊖ *Sitting astride his slightly larger mate, a male* Ropalidia grandidieri *social wasp in Madagascar courts the female by stroking her antennae with his own and rubbing her with his abdomen.*

Apis mellifera

Common name Honeybees, stingless bees, bumblebees, orchid bees

Family Apidae

Suborder Apocrita

Order Hymenoptera

Number of species About 1,000 (60 U.S.)

Size From about 0.08 in (2 mm) to about 1.1 in (2.7 cm)

Key features Small, hairless, mainly brown or black body (stingless bees); medium-sized, slim-waisted, brown body (honeybees); stout and densely hairy rusty brown or black body, often with red or yellow bands (bumblebees); brilliant metallic-blue or green body, sometimes hairy like bumblebees (orchid bees); tongue long; pollen baskets generally present on hind legs

Habits Most species common on flowers and are important pollinators of many crops; honeybee often domesticated in hives

Breeding Most species often highly social, living in large nests containing thousands of workers (nonbreeding females); social species eventually rear males and females who leave nest for mating purposes; mated queens then establish new nest, usually in following spring after winter hibernation; some species are cuckoos in nests of others

Diet Adults feed mainly on nectar; in tropics orchid bees and stingless bees often feed on dung or urine-soaked ground; larvae eat pollen and nectar; larvae of some stingless bees eat carrion

Habitat In all terrestrial habitats from sea level to the limits of vegetation on high mountains; many species common in urban gardens

Distribution Worldwide in areas that are not too arid or permanently cold; honeybee introduced into the Americas, Australia, and New Zealand

⊕ *The honeybee Apis mellifera is found worldwide thanks to commercial beekeeping. It plays an important role in plant reproduction, transferring pollen from plant to plant. Body length (of worker) 0.5 inches (13 mm).*

Honeybees and Relatives

Apidae

The diverse members of the Apidae are united by a single outstanding feature—the presence of "pollen baskets" on the hind legs. They are used to transport food and building materials to the nest.

IT IS DIFFICULT TO BELIEVE that the tiny, naked-bodied stingless bees or brilliant metallic *Euglossa* orchid bees belong to the same family as the massive, stout-bodied, densely furry bumblebees. Even the familiar honeybee, *Apis mellifera*, seems to have little in common with any of them. The only shared feature—the "pollen baskets," or corbicula, on the back legs—consist of the smooth, slightly convex outer surface of the tibia fringed by a stockade of long, stiff hairs. The pollen basket is used to transport pollen, resin, or other materials to the nest. It has been lost in cuckoo species.

Most members of the Apidae are social, although the orchid bees are generally solitary. A few species of orchid bees and bumblebees are cuckoos in the nests of other bees. Unlike in other bees, female Apidae do not construct nest burrows but always nest inside existing cavities or build external nests.

Orchid Bees

The orchid bees are some of the most brilliantly colored of all bees. Many species of *Euglossa* are jewel-like green or blue, gleaming with a metallic splendor as they dart around in the tops of rain-forest trees. By contrast, *Eulaema* are more like bumblebees, with attractively banded furry bodies. Most species of orchid bees have long tongues, and all are restricted to tropical Central and South America.

Orchid bee females construct their nests underground or as free-standing structures in the open. They use mud or resin as building materials, sometimes blended with animal

⊕ *A male orchid bee (subfamily Euglossinae) collecting essential fragrances from an orchid flower in the rain forests of the Amazon Basin in Peru.*

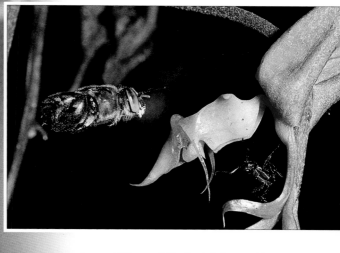

Euglossa orchid bees are brilliant metallic insects with a fast, darting kind of flight. This male in Costa Rica is about to land on an orchid flower.

Eulaema males are not associated with orchids but collect aromatic substances from rotting logs. Despite many experiments and observations, scientists are still uncertain what the role of the perfumes could be. Males sit and "display" on trees around light gaps in the forest, and it is possible that the perfumes are used to mark the display sites.

Bumblebees

Bumblebees are among the most familiar and well loved of insects. Although they are armed with a stinger—which, unlike honeybees, they can use over and over again—they seldom resort to stinging. They are only likely to sting if provoked, for instance, when roughly handled.

Bumblebees belong to the single genus *Bombus*. They are spread throughout the world except in Australia and Africa south of the Sahara Desert. In New Zealand they have been introduced by humans. Bumblebees are more common in cool, temperate areas than in the warm tropics, where they mainly occur on mountains. However, they are also present in permanently warm, humid areas such as the Amazon Basin in Brazil.

dung or chips of wood. A number of species, especially in *Eulaema*, are communal or even bordering on the social, with several females building and stocking a single nest.

Male *Euglossa* have a relationship with certain species of orchids for which they may be the sole pollinators. The orchids do not offer either nectar or pollen as a reward, but instead provide the male bees with special perfumes contained in oily droplets on the flowers. The males brush the drops off with special pads on their front feet and pass them back to storage organs on the rear legs while in hovering flight.

Bees and Flowers

Bees and flowers have a close relationship that is normally beneficial to both parties. The bees are rewarded with the pollen and nectar, without which they could not survive and reproduce; the flowers are rewarded by a pollination service that is both reliable and adaptable. Worldwide the value of crops pollinated by bees runs to more than $1.5 billion annually. Honeybees are the main providers of this vital activity, although with their short tongues they are unsuited to pollinating certain valuable crops such as red clover, *Trifolium pratense*. For this the longer tongues of bumblebees are needed.

We are familiar with the bright colors flowers use to attract insects such as bees. Unlike humans, bees can see into the ultraviolet end of the spectrum and can see colors and patterns on flowers that are invisible to the human eye. Yet bees cannot see red, which appears black to them. While visiting flowers, the dense clothing of branched or feathery hairs on the bodies of most pollen-collecting bees becomes dusted with pollen grains. The bee uses its front and middle pairs of legs to comb the pollen off its body and onto the pollen-storing apparatus, usually situated on the hind legs. Bumblebees often hang by their jaws while combing pollen, leaving all their legs free.

Many flowers are specialized for visits by bees. The powerful hinge on antirrhinum flowers can only be depressed by large, powerful insects such as bumblebees. They are therefore the only insects that can reach the pollen and nectar inside. However, the bees do not always play fair in their relationship with flowers. Short-tongued bumblebees often rob certain kinds of tubular flowers of their nectar by biting a hole at the base of the flower tube. Since the bee no longer enters by the legitimate route, it does not come into contact with the pollen-bearing anthers or the stigma. So while the bee gets the nectar, the flowers remain unpollinated.

Founding the Nest

In cool temperate regions a bumblebee nest gets underway in early spring. It is founded by a queen who mated the previous fall and spent the winter in hibernation under moss, in a crevice, beneath bark, or in some other protected site. With the first warm days of springtime the queen begins to spend most of the daylight hours on flowers. She sips nectar for energy and eats pollen to build up the bodily reserves she needs to produce her first batch of eggs. She also devotes a lot of time to searching for a suitable nest site. In the many

↙ *The pollen baskets on the back legs of this buff-tailed bumblebee,* Bombus terrestris *from Europe, are well filled with pollen.*

↑ *Following the spotted guidemarks, a common carder bumblebee,* Bombus pascuorum, *enters a foxglove* (Digitalis purpurea) *flower in England.*

species that nest underground, the queens fly along inspecting anything that resembles an old mouse hole or similar cavity. A number of species place the nest on the ground and cover it with a thatch of dry grass and moss.

First-Time Mother

The queen's first brood cell is made from wax secreted from glands in her own body and is stocked with a clump of up to a dozen eggs. The queen spends much of her time perched on top of the cell, keeping it warm and accelerating the development of her first brood. She also devotes some time to foraging for nectar, regurgitating the honey into a little storage pot that she builds of wax.

As the larvae grow, she builds a wax cell around each one. It will be removed to use elsewhere once the larvae have pupated and emerged as adults. The first workers are always tiny, sometimes too small even to leave the nest. However, they can help with domestic chores while the queen goes out foraging for food. She soon produces a further brood; and once the first batch of workers leaves the nest to take over the task of collecting food, she can stay and concentrate on laying eggs. The size of workers emerging from the brood cells gradually gets larger as they receive more generous food supplies as larvae. Nevertheless, they always remain smaller than the queen and are all females. They occasionally lay eggs, but these are quickly eaten by the queen, who reserves sole right to produce offspring.

The colony grows as the output of new workers exceeds the death of the old ones. The clumps of brood and storage cells are gradually extended in a haphazard arrangement typical of

⊖ *Having spent the winter months in hibernation, a queen early bumblebee,* **Bombus pratorum** *from Europe, stokes up with nectar from a springtime wildflower.*

bumblebees. As well as storing nectar in wax pots, some species also store pollen in old, disused larval cells. In these species the food supply for each larva is regurgitated through a hole in the cell wall bitten by a worker, who seals it up afterward. In other species the workers place food as and when it is needed in a pouch that they construct to one side of the larval cell. Bumblebee nests never attain the size seen in honeybees and rarely contain more than 400 workers at any one time, with around 100 being the usual figure.

↑ *The small garden bumblebee,* Bombus hortorum *from Europe, builds its nest in dense grass tussocks. Note the typically haphazard brood cells (occupied by larvae or pupae) and the storage cells containing honey.*

As the nest size increases in late summer, the queen is no longer able to eat all the eggs laid by the workers, and some of them develop into adults. They are all males, since the workers have never mated and so lay only haploid eggs. The queen goes on producing daughters, some of which will be treated to a special diet that will result in the emergence of new queens. Along with the males, they leave the nest to seek a mate. After mating, the males die, and the queens find a hibernation site, ready to start the process again in spring.

Sexual Roundabout

Sexual behavior in male bumblebees varies from species to species. In *Bombus nevadensis* from the United States the male has enlarged eyes. He uses them to constantly scan his territory, a conspicuous perch on an open mountain slope. He chases off rival males, sometimes engaging in aerial clashes that can injure the assailants. Females only rarely show up; but when they do, mating takes place on the wing.

In most species the males patrol a regular beat or circuit, stopping at distinct points to deposit a sweet scent from a gland in the mouthparts. The scents are specific for each species, which helps avoid confusion when several species are using the same circuit, as often happens. In such cases all the males move around the circuit in the same direction to avoid meeting. There is also a broad degree of height separation between species, and different species use the circuits at different times of the day. When virgin queens encounter the circuits, they investigate the scent-marked patches and mate with the first male to arrive.

Cuckoos in the Nest

Some species of bumblebees do not found their own nests but enter the nests of other species and act as cuckoos. Each species of cuckoo targets a specific host. For instance, in Europe *Bombus bohemicus* lays its eggs only in the nests of the common *B. lucorum*. Some cuckoo queens creep stealthily into the host nest and spend a day or two quietly absorbing its specific odor. This lulls the suspicions of the workers when the cuckoo finally emerges from cover and begins to lay eggs in cells that are about to be stocked with food. She does not kill the rightful queen, but eats her eggs whenever she comes across them, so that gradually more and more cuckoo males and females are produced.

The opposite tactic is used by certain other cuckoos. They rely on their powerful sting and thick skin to batter their way past any workers that get in the way, killing any that resist. The cuckoo's goal is to find and execute the rightful queen and take over the nest, leaving the

remaining workers no option but to rear male and female cuckoos until the nest finally expires through lack of a workforce. The cuckoo lifestyle is common in bees, being found in nearly one-fifth of all species.

Stingless Bees

The 300 or so species of stingless bees belonging to the subfamily Meliponinae are the smallest members of the Apidae. The smallest species is only 0.08 in (2 mm) long, and the largest only slightly exceeds the size of a honeybee. Most are black or reddish-brown, although some are yellow. All are restricted to the tropical zones, especially South America.

The nests are organized on a highly social basis and last for many years unless destroyed by predators, of which there are many. However, unlike most nests made by tropical wasps, the nests of stingless bees are usually immune to mass invasion by that scourge of the rain forest, the army ants. That is because their nests are usually situated deep inside hollow trees or termite nests. However, some attach a free-standing nest to branches. The sole entrance is formed by a narrow projecting tube that is smeared with a sticky coating of resin. The resin traps most insects on contact. If that fails, the bees plaster any intruders with a gluelike secretion that quickly gums up their legs. The

⬆ *A battalion of* Plebeia *species stingless bee workers forms a defensive throng on the tubelike entrance to their nest sited deep within a hollow tree in Brazil.*

⬇ *Several* Trigona fulviventris *stingless bees harvest sweet honeydew secreted by a cluster of adults and nymphs of the bug* Aethalion reticulatum *in Peru.*

nest itself is made of resin that is transported on the pollen baskets of the workers. Supplies are often harvested from resin oozing from the borings of beetle larvae in tree trunks. Back at the nest, the workers mix the resin with wax to form cerumen. The substance is used for making larval cells as well as slightly larger cells for storing pollen and honey. The nest's outer envelope consists of a durable substance called batumen, a blend of resin, wax, and other materials such as mud or animal droppings.

Some of the large species of stingless bees maintain an "exclusion zone" around the nest and attack anything that comes too close. In humans it is the head that is usually the focus of a massed attack by the enraged bees, which although unable to sting, have sharp jaws that can pierce human skin. Some species follow this up by dripping an irritant secretion from their

head glands into the wound, causing burning blisters that have earned the insects the name of "firebees." Most people just run when under attack, but it can be difficult to tear the bees out of one's hair since they will die rather than let go with their jaws. Some colonies are well able to expend a few workers in defense of their nest. In *Trigona* the nest may contain as many as 180,000 individuals, although a few hundred is more common in many species.

Raising the Brood

Stingless bees are unusual among highly social bees in using mass provisioning for their larval cells, much as in most solitary bees (and wasps). In the nurse bees that are in charge of feeding the larvae, the head gland is greatly enlarged and can produce large amounts of a jellylike substance similar to the royal jelly of honeybees. Several workers gather around a completed cell. They squirt it full of food, attracting the attention of the queen. She eats some of the food, along with an egg that is always laid by a worker. It is in that way that the queen gets much of her food, although she also feeds directly from the workers' mouths. She responds to her meal by laying her own egg in the open cell. The workers then seal the cell, enclosing the egg with the food that the larva needs to complete its development.

Production of males and new queens in most stingless bees is similar to the process in honeybees, except in *Melipona*, in which queens, workers, and males are reared in cells of the same size. Whether or not a larva will turn into a queen or a worker is probably determined genetically. New nests in stingless bees are founded by workers using supplies of cerumen and honey from the old nest. Once the group of pioneer workers has built a few brood cells and honey pots, a young virgin queen, along with a few workers, will forsake the old nest for the new. When the new queen has mated with one of a number of males (they hail from other nests and hover expectantly around the entrance of the new nest), she goes back inside and never emerges again.

243

Honeybees

There are seven species of honeybees, all included in the single genus *Apis*. Six of them are restricted to Asia, including the largest species, the giant oriental honeybee, *Apis dorsata*. The most widespread species is the western honeybee, often called just the honeybee, *Apis mellifera*. It is one of the most familiar of all insects, although *Eristalis* hover flies are often mistaken for it. The honeybee has been domesticated in hives for thousands of years and, although native only to Africa, the Middle East, and Europe, has in more recent times been introduced to the Americas, Australia, and New Zealand to act as a pollinator of crops and to provide honey. The honey produced in their nests (and also in smaller quantities in stingless bee nests) has been valued by humans since time immemorial. In some parts of the world people will take amazing risks in order to rob the bees of their supplies of the prized commodity.

The Economy of the Honeybee Nest

Native sites for honeybee nests are inside hollow trees and rock clefts. The giant oriental honeybee nests in a single, large, exposed comb attached high above the ground on the limbs of forest trees. Most common honeybees now nest inside artificial hives provided by beekeepers. Within the nest clusters of cells are used both to rear larvae and store honey. They are hung back to back on either side of a central plate of wax

 A beekeeper, wearing protective clothing, checks the condition of the honeycomb in the hive. Most honeybees now nest in artificial hives provided by beekeepers.

to form a comb, which is suspended from the nest roof. Each cell is hexagonal, since it is the most economic shape to use in an enclosed space. The cells are built of wax secreted by glands in the adult bee's abdomen.

All the labor within the nest is carried out by the workers, of which the nest may contain as many as 80,000. The sole duty for the queen, who is bigger than the workers, is to lay eggs. She does so with machinelike regularity, producing as many as 2,000 per day. During her six weeks of life every worker is capable of carrying out all the various tasks within the nest. In practice, jobs are allocated according to age. While she is still young (during the first three weeks), glands in the worker's abdomen that secrete wax and those in her head that produce royal jelly (a special food given to the larvae) are functioning in top gear. She therefore remains in the nest as a house bee, using her wax to build cells and doling out supplies of royal jelly to the larvae. She also receives nectar from incoming foragers. She "ripens" it by holding it in her jaws and exposing it to the air. It thickens via evaporation and can now be placed in a storage cell. Here the ripening process—which eventually produces honey—will continue, aided by other house bees who fan their wings to accelerate the evaporation process. Another duty for the young house bee is to feed the larvae in their open-fronted cells. During its life each larva will receive some 140 meals, after which it spins its silken cocoon. That stimulates the house bees to perform yet another task—capping the pupal cell with wax. New cells will also be needed to extend the size of the comb, while old cells require cleaning out. Sometimes they will be used again for rearing larvae, but more often for storing honey or

Worker honeybees throng on their comb, which, being built against a glass panel, reveals the larvae inside their wax cells.

A worker bee on a honeycomb—note the regular hexagonal shape of the open cells. All labor in the nest is carried out by workers.

supplies of pollen brought in by foragers. After about three weeks the house bee herself will become a forager, although in an emergency she is still capable of carrying out her duties in the nest.

Swarming in Honeybees

When a honeybee colony becomes too large, the queen starts to lose control over it. In the normal way she exerts her influence via a powerful pheromone, which is distributed among the workers. When the colony gets too

A still shot from the 1978 movie The Swarm. *However, in reality killer bees do not roam around looking for victims to attack.*

The Menace of "Killer Bees"

Killer bees are Africanized honeybees, *Apis mellifera scutellata*. They are a subspecies of honeybee that is the result of a crossbreeding experiment gone wrong.

In 1956 scientists in Brazil imported colonies of African honeybees with the intention of crossbreeding them with resident European honeybee populations to improve honey production. However, a number of queens—along with their workers—escaped. They have since spread northward, interbreeding with the local populations along the way, through South America into Mexico and the southern states of the United States. They first arrived in Texas in October 1990 and have since colonized New Mexico, Arizona, Nevada, and California.

The problem with Africanized honeybees is that they are far more aggressive than their European honeybee counterparts. Although their venom is no more potent than that of European honeybees, they are highly defensive and will attack perceived intruders much more readily and in far greater numbers. They react to disturbance much more quickly and will give chase over longer distances. Their alternative name of "killer bees" is deserved: Between 1988 and 1995 there were 175 reported fatalities from killer bee attacks in Mexico. The first reported death in the United States occurred in Harlingen, Texas, in July 1993. However, Africanized bees do not roam in swarms looking for victims to attack; the bees simply act in self-defense. Also, most serious attacks occur when the person is unable to get away quickly. Pets and livestock have most often been killed when they have been tied up and unable to escape.

⬆ *The queen honeybee*
(Apis mellifera) *is larger than the drones (males). The drones are themselves slightly larger than the workers, the queen's daughters.*

big for every worker to receive its daily pheromone ration, the workers prepare to split up the colony by initiating a swarm.

The first move must be to rear a number of new queens, and some of the workers start building special outsize queen cells. When the first of the virgin queens emerges, she stings all her sister queens to death in their cells. She then leaves the nest in order to mate. Shortly after her return the old queen flies out of the nest along with a large swarm of workers, leaving the young queen in charge of her old home. The old queen and her retinue then start a new nest in a fresh site.

Royal Diet

Larvae destined to be queens are fed a pure diet of royal jelly, more appropriately known as bee milk, since it is also fed to the workers. Bee milk is a highly nutritious food, being a mixture of secretions produced by two glands in the head. Larvae committed to developing into workers receive a weak mixture for the first few days, then just the thinner of the two secretions mixed with pollen for the rest of their development. The queen larvae get only the richest milk. Males (called drones) are reared simultaneously in cells with wider mouths than normal. The queen perceives the shape of the cell and lays an unfertilized (haploid) egg.

➡ *Somewhere in the middle of this swarm of honeybee workers* (Apis mellifera) *is the queen. She will found a new colony if a suitable nesting site can be located.*

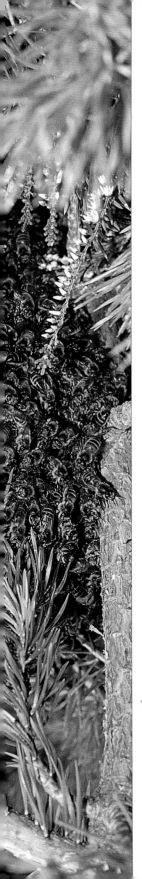

The Bee Dance

Worker honeybees that are allocated the job of foraging for nectar and pollen on flowers do not just leave the nest each morning and see what they can find. Instead, they wait in the nest until scout bees return from an exploratory trip to find the best sources of food that day. The scouts can communicate the exact location of the food (usually a patch of flowers or a flowering tree) using a remarkable "dance." It is performed on the vertical face of the comb and is a reenactment in mime of the trip that the scout has just made.

In the common honeybee, *Apis mellifera*, the dance is performed in the dark interior of the nest. A number of workers closely surround the performer and monitor her every move with their antennae. It is in *A. mellifera* that the "language" of dance is most advanced and informative. The performer is able to communicate not just the route to the food source and its exact position but also how good it is.

If the food lies within 80 feet (25 m) of the nest, the scout performs the "round dance," running several times in a circle with many changes of direction. The higher the concentration of sugar in the food, the higher the number of switches in direction. If the food source lies more than 330 feet (100 m) away, the bee performs a "waggle dance." She runs in two semicircles to form a figure eight, waggling her abdomen as she runs down the straight line that links the two halves of the figure. Distance is defined by the duration of the straight run and the frequency of waggles. A bee may also perform a mixture of the two "dances" for food lying in between the two distances. The direction and angle of the bee's dance represent the position of the food source in relation to the sun. The performer knows what the angle of the sun is at any one time during her dance, even within the darkness of the nest. Her internal clock compensates for the movement of the sun that takes place during her performance, which can last 30 minutes or so— enough time for the sun to move considerably from the position she memorized when she entered the nest. Food quality is probably communicated by the intensity of waggles and buzzes.

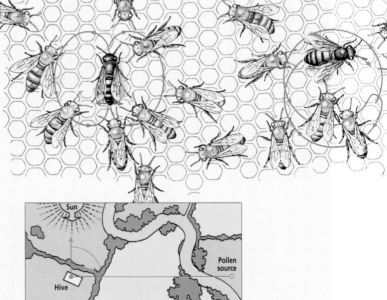

⬀ *The two general forms of honeybee dance: the "waggle dance" (left) and "round dance" (right).*

⬂ *The position of the food source as described in the waggle dance, viewed from the hive entrance.*

What Are Arachnids?

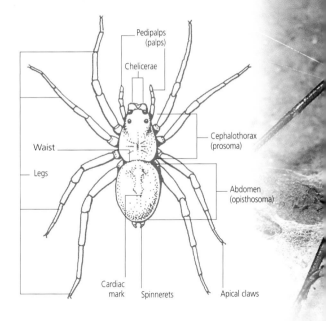

W ith over 75,000 known species the arachnids are a very successful class of animals, found widely in water and on land. The total given below is only provisional, since undoubtedly far more species are yet to be discovered and described, especially among the mites, where the number of unknown species probably runs into many thousands. Arachnids have conquered the earth comprehensively—there is probably no inhabitable region on the planet without its quota.

⊕ *Typical body plan of an arachnid. Unlike in insects, there are only two regions of the body rather than three, and normally eight legs instead of an insect's six.*

Common name Arachnids **Class** Arachnida

SUBCLASSES

Scorpiones	Scorpions
Pseudoscorpiones	Pseudoscorpions
Solifugae	Sun spiders
Palpigradi	Microwhip scorpions
Schizomida	Short-tailed whip scorpions
Uropygi	Tailed whip scorpions
Amblypygi	Tailless whip scorpions
Ricinulei	Hooded tick spiders
Opiliones	Daddy-longlegs
Acari	Mites and ticks
Aranae	Spiders

Number of species More than 75,000 (12,000+ U.S.)

Size From about 0.003 in (0.08 mm) to about 8 in (20 cm)

Key features Body of various colors, divided into 2 regions: the cephalothorax (prosoma) divided into 6 segments, and the abdomen (opisthosoma) divided into 12 segments; segmentation not normally visible at surface; cephalothorax with 6 pairs of appendages: chelicerae (1 pair), pincerlike or fanglike, used in subduing prey; pedipalps (1 pair), leglike or pincerlike; walking legs (4 pairs); unlike insects, arachnids do not have wings, antennae, or mandibles; metamorphosis absent—young arachnids resemble their parents

Diet Most arachnids are predators, the main exceptions being a few daddy-longlegs and numerous mites that feed partly or exclusively on plant materials; many mites and all ticks are parasites on larger animals

Habitat Most habitats where life can exist

Distribution Universal

Arachnids often have a major effect on their environment, none more so than the vast armies of microscopic mites that play a vital role in breaking down organic matter in the soil, recycling the nutrients, and making them available for reuse. Without this dedicated corps of refuse workers it is doubtful if life as we know it would be possible. On the downside, some mites can be serious pests of valuable cultivated plants and crops, while many mites and ticks can transmit serious diseases.

The Arachnid Body

Arachnids are built differently than insects, with which they are often confused. There are only two regions of the arachnid body, not three as in insects, and normally eight legs instead of an insect's six. The frontal section of the arachnid consists of a united head and thorax called a cephalothorax or prosoma. The rear half is the abdomen, or opisthosoma. In most arachnids the two halves of the body are joined by a waist. It can be narrow, as in spiders, or broad as in sun spiders. In pseudoscorpions, scorpions, ticks, mites, and daddy-longlegs the two halves are joined along their full width, and there is no waist at all.

⊕ *The arachnid division of the body into only two sections, the cephalothorax and abdomen, is clearly visible in the tailless whip scorpion,* Damon variegatus *(subclass Amblypygi), from tropical Africa.*

Arachnids do not have biting jawlike mandibles as in insects. Instead, they bear two pedipalps at the front end of the body. In scorpions they are modified into pincers for grasping and crushing prey. Pseudoscorpions have pincerlike pedipalps with hollow tips through which poison can be secreted. In many plant-feeding mites the pedipalps are devoted to silk production. In male spiders they are modified into organs for transferring sperm to the female's body. Some male spiders also use their pedipalps as signaling devices during courtship. Although arachnids lack antennae, some kinds—such as tailed and tailless whip scorpions—use their long front legs as antennalike sensory organs rather than for walking.

Breathing methods vary in the arachnids. In the smallest kinds, such as many mites, oxygen diffuses through the exoskeleton. In the larger and many of the smaller kinds breathing is via specialized book lungs or systems of internal tubes (tracheae). Book lungs are found in pairs on the underside of the abdomen and are flooded by air admitted through a slitlike pore (spiracle). Tracheae can occur in two versions. The sieve tracheae of ricinuleids, pseudoscorpions, and certain spiders spread outward from an air chamber supplied from the outside by a spiracle. In tube tracheae, found in mites, sun spiders, daddy-longlegs, and most spiders, there is little or no branching, and they may open directly via a spiracle or through a chamber. The oxygenated blood circulates through the body cavity in an "open" system, usually pumped by a simple tubular heart.

Most arachnids take food of animal origin, but a few daddy-longlegs and many mites take vegetable material. The majority of arachnids cannot swallow solid food and must dissolve all their meals with digestive juices. The juices are poured on the food, which can then be sucked up like soup, a process known as external digestion.

Sexual Arrangements

In most arachnids there are separate males and females; both sexes have a genital aperture on the underside of the abdomen. Females may receive sperm in liquid form or in tiny packets called spermatophores. In some cases the male lets the female collect the packets. In others he inserts them into her genital opening using various appendages. In spiders the male transfers liquid semen via his pedipalps (also called palps). Most arachnids lay eggs, but some—such as scorpions—give birth to live young.

African emperor
scorpion (*Pandinus
imperator*)

Common name Scorpions

Subclass   Scorpiones

Class   Arachnida

Number of species About 1,500 (about 75 U.S.)

Size   From about 1.6 in (4 cm) to about 8 in
                (20 cm)

Key features Body flattened, mostly brown, black, or
                yellowish, sometimes deep green; body broad
                at the front, tapering backward to a long,
                upwardly curved flexible tail bearing a hinged
                stinger at its tip; pedipalps modified into 2
                large pincerlike claws; a pair of comblike
                structures (pectines) trails down between the
                last pair of legs; eyes tiny, 2 in the center of
                the cephalothorax, 2–5 more on each side;
                breathing via book lungs

Habits   Mostly nocturnal, spending the day hidden in
                crevices, under stones or bark, or in burrows
                up to about 39 in (100 cm) deep; all species
                hunt other small animals; some species
                wander in search of prey, others sit and wait
                in ambush

Breeding   Courtship is complex and consists of a
                "dance" performed by male and female;
                females give birth to live young, which
                assemble on their mother's back and are
                carried around for some time; some species
                are parthenogenetic and produce young
                without first mating

Diet   Insects, other arachnids (especially scorpions),
                centipedes, millipedes, snails, frogs, toads,
                lizards, small snakes, birds, and small rodents

Habitat   Most common in deserts; also present in
                mountains, rain forests, gardens, in and
                around buildings, and on the seashore; a few
                blind species in caves

Distribution Worldwide, but mainly found in warmer
                tropical areas; only 1 species as far north as
                Alberta, Canada in North America; absent
                from northern Europe except as an accidental
                introduction in buildings

⊕ *One of the largest scorpions found in Africa, the African
emperor scorpion,* Pandinus imperator, *does not use its stinger
to kill prey, but as a last resort in defense. Body length up to
4 inches (10 cm).*

Scorpions

Scorpiones

*Because of the painful and sometimes fatal sting of
some species, scorpions are the most widely feared of
all arachnids. Yet for sheer deadliness they are closely
rivaled by certain Australian spiders.*

WITH THEIR DISTINCTIVE upturned tails and
lobsterlike claws, scorpions are the most easily
recognized of all arachnids. They lead secretive
lives and are rarely seen, although their habit of
creeping into crevices at daybreak can lead to
unpleasant encounters with humans. Campsites
and backyards are areas in which they may be
prevalent. Scorpions are an ancient group, and
fossils as old as 400 million years have been
found. They represent the oldest known
arachnids, yet they differ little from the living
scorpions we see today.

Although scorpions are present in a wide
range of habitats, deserts provide the greatest
diversity of scorpion species. The single richest
area is the Baja California region of Mexico. A
number of the larger scorpions make popular
pets. The trend has led to such intensive
overcollection of specimens from the wild that
they are now protected by international law
covering trade in threatened species. Part of
their popularity is due to their longevity—they
may live for 20 years or more.

Lethal Dose

The cephalothorax is covered by a broad, flat
carapace on which the tiny eyes are mounted.
The eyes give poor vision, scorpions being
creatures of touch rather than sight. The
segmented abdomen is long and fairly narrow.
It tapers off toward the upturned tail, which
makes up the last few segments. Unlike in
spiders, ticks, and mites, the segments of the
abdomen are clearly visible along its full length.
The join between the cephalothorax and
abdomen is broad and continuous, and there is
no hint of a "waist." The upturned tail ends in
a hinged stinger. It consists of a large, bulbous

⊕ *An elongate, rather
flattened body tipped by
a stinger mounted on a
long, upwardly curved
tail is typical of
scorpions, such as the*
Parabuthus capensis *from
southern Africa.*

portion containing a substantial dose of venom, and a thornlike hypodermic that injects the poison into the prey. The tail is held over to one side in species that live in narrow crevices and upward over the body in species that inhabit burrows. Stroking their way across the ground beneath the hind pair of legs there is a set of unique comblike organs called the pectines. They are thought to be highly sensitive vibration detectors, giving advance warning of the approach of prey or potential enemies. The males also use them to detect female pheromones.

Sensitive to Disturbance

The abundant hairs on the body and the long, thin hairlike trichobothria on the claws are also highly sensitive to disturbances in the air caused by prey. Movement across shifting sands is made easier for some of the desert species by having long, narrow "sandshoe" feet with fringes of hairs along the margins to spread the load. Some scorpions have stridulating mechanisms on various parts of the body that

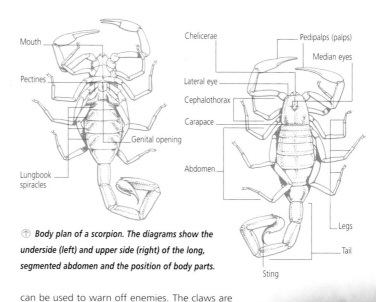

⬆ *Body plan of a scorpion. The diagrams show the underside (left) and upper side (right) of the long, segmented abdomen and the position of body parts.*

can be used to warn off enemies. The claws are held out to the front and vary in size. They can be slender and feeble tweezerlike structures or massively built "nutcrackers" that can splinter even the toughest beetle exoskeleton and pulverize the remains ready for digestion. Burrowing species also use the claws as shovels.

Nocturnal Hunters

Most scorpions emerge from their hideaways at night to hunt. They take a wide variety of prey, but especially other scorpions, often including juveniles of their own species. Some species hunt from home, merely sticking their heads and claws out of their burrrow or rock crevice and waiting for a meal to walk past. Despite their ability to administer a deadly or at least painful sting, scorpions have many enemies, some of which are immune to their venom. For some birds, snakes, and even rodents scorpions form a major part of the diet.

The majority of scorpions use their claws to catch, subdue, and pulverize their prey. The sting is rarely used, except in some of the smaller, lightly built species whose puny claws are incapable of dealing with vigorously struggling prey. The large-clawed species will also deploy their stings as a last resort if their victim refuses to give in. Armored insects such as darkling beetles present a more stubborn challenge, since they are often too tough to be overpowered by force alone. The scorpion must probe with its stinger until it finds a chink between the joints through which it can inject a fatal dose of venom. In the real giants of the scorpion world, such as the African emperor scorpion, *Pandinus imperator*, adults never seem to use their stingers to deal with prey, but the smaller juveniles often cannot cope without them. Using its pectines, a scorpion can detect the footsteps of approaching prey from a distance of around 18 inches (46 cm). Some species can snatch flying insects out of the air.

Scorpions are able to go without food for as long as a year. Their abstinence is possible because they have the lowest metabolic rate of any animal. They also rarely move far, so use little energy. When they catch a meal, it is often large, so they can build up enough reserves to last through lean times. Desert species can also glean all the water they need from their food. Their water loss is greatly reduced by a waxy coating on the body and by staying in the cool burrow during the hottest periods. The ability to extract most of the moisture from their droppings so that they are virtually dry is also a useful survival tool in an arid environment.

Courtship Dances

In scorpions the male has no means of directly transferring his spermatophore to the female. Instead, she has to pick it up, and it is the job of the male to guide her to the correct place. His method of directing her movements is known as the "dance of the scorpions." Standing face to face and grasping one another's chelicerae, the pair promenade back and forth. The male leads his partner until they pass over some suitable anchor point (such as a stick) to which he attaches his sperm packet (spermatophore). He then guides his partner across the spermatophore, whose protruding hooks catch in the female's genital aperture. The snagging hooks cause the packet to open, and the sperm transfers into the female's body. Some courtship dances last nearly 10 minutes and may cover a distance of several yards. Others are not really dances at all, and the male merely drags the female backward over the spermatophore. In some species there is a strange prelude to the proceedings in which the male and female stab each other repeatedly

→ *A Florida bark scorpion female, Centruroides gracilis, with babies on her back. They will remain there until their first molt, when they then disperse.*

Getting Stung

Every year thousands of people around the world are stung by scorpions. A few of the victims (mainly children and old people) die as a result. Only about 20 species of scorpions have a dangerous sting, the two most deadly species occurring in Mexico and North Africa.

In most species the effect is no worse than a bee sting. In others the pain is described as similar to holding the affected area in a raging inferno for the first 24 hours. After that the pain begins to subside. Antivenoms are now widely available for the most dangerous species and can usually be obtained in the countries where such stings are more likely to occur. Effective pain relief is also available.

with their stingers. The bizarre behavior appears to be a stimulant that is necessary for full sexual arousal. Further stinging may be needed to persuade the female to actually pick up the spermatophore. Some species engage in club fights with their tails, without actually stinging.

In some scorpions there are no such sexual skirmishes, since the females give birth to their young without first mating with a male. The process—known as parthenogenesis—is also found in certain insects.

Baby Carriers

Females give birth to between six and 105 live young after a remarkably long gestation period lasting seven to 12 months. In most species the emerging young are wrapped in a birth membrane that ruptures as they struggle free shortly after birth. The babies are generally miniature replicas of their parents. As they emerge, they crawl into a "brood basket"

formed by their mother's front legs before climbing up them and assembling on her back. Here they remain until shortly after their first molt, when they disperse. Delivery can take between one hour and three days, depending on species. Female emperor scorpions provide prey items for their babies in their early stages.

⊕ *Before mating, scorpions (here,* Vaejovis boreus) *engage in an elaborate dance in which the male seeks to maneuver the female over a spermatophore that he has dropped.*

253

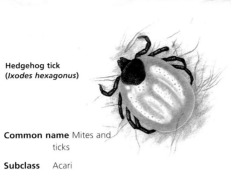

Hedgehog tick
(*Ixodes hexagonus*)

Common name Mites and ticks

Subclass Acari

Class Arachnida

Number of species About 45,000 (8,000+ U.S.)

Size Body length from about 0.003 in (0.08 mm) to about 0.6 in (15 mm)

Key features Body mainly black or brown, but many species red, green, or yellow; no division into cephalothorax and abdomen; pedipalps small, simple, and leglike; usually 4 pairs of walking legs; no tail or other appendages on abdomen; larvae have only 6 legs

Habits Many mites are free living in soil, on plants, or in both fresh and salt water; others develop within plants or on the bodies of animals; all ticks are parasitic on mammals, birds, and reptiles

Breeding Males may fight over access to females; sperm is transferred to the females by both direct and indirect methods; eggs hatch as 6-legged larvae, which molt to become 8-legged nymphs; females of many ticks lay several thousand eggs; ticks may need to use more than 1 kind of host in order to complete their life cycle

Diet Mites feed on all kinds of vegetable and animal materials; gall-forming mites are often restricted to a single genus or species of host plant; many mites take solid food; all ticks feed on blood

Habitat In soil, on plants, and on living animals in every conceivable type of habitat

Distribution Worldwide, including the deep seas and the polar regions; mites are probably the most ubiquitous of all animals

⊕ *As its common name suggests, the hedgehog tick, Ixodes* hexagonus, *from Europe is numerous on hedgehogs. A heavy infestation, particularly on young hedgehogs, can cause problems. Body length up to 0.3 inches (7 mm).*

Mites and Ticks

Acari

Mites are not only the most successful and widespread of all arachnids, but are among the most successful animals on earth. They are surpassed perhaps only by microorganisms such as bacteria.

THE 45,000 KNOWN SPECIES of Acari probably represent no more than one-twentieth of their true number. Mites can truly be said to have conquered planet earth, being at home not only in the kinds of conventional environments inhabited by other arachnids, but also occurring in such extreme habitats as the polar icecaps, deep water trenches in the oceans, hot springs, and at considerable depths in the soil. Mites also excel by their sheer numbers, with counts of over 1 million per square yard (800,000 per sq. m) being normal in the leaf litter of a typical temperate forest. These myriad individuals, belonging to as many as 200 different species, play a key role in natural decay by recycling nutrients back to the forest. Beetle mites (order Cryptostigmata) are the main soil inhabitants, feeding primarily on decaying plants.

At the other end of the scale a whole family of mites can develop inside the "ear" of a moth or within the tiny respiratory tube of a bee. Ticks and mites are also of enormous agricultural and medical significance as pests and parasites of plants and animals, and in the transmission of serious diseases to their hosts.

Life As a Parasite

Ticks feed exclusively on the blood of reptiles, birds, and mammals. They are generally much larger than most mites and therefore easier to observe. In hard ticks (Ixodidae) the tough, leathery body is more flattened than in mites. It is highly resistant to crushing, enabling the tick to survive such hazards as grooming by the host

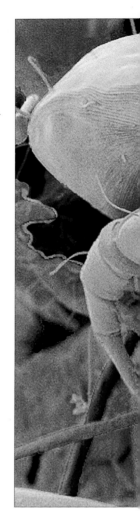

⊕ *A* Dermatophagoides *house-dust mite magnified to many times its normal size of 0.01 inches (0.3 mm). Every house contains millions of such mites, living in carpets, furniture, and bedding.*

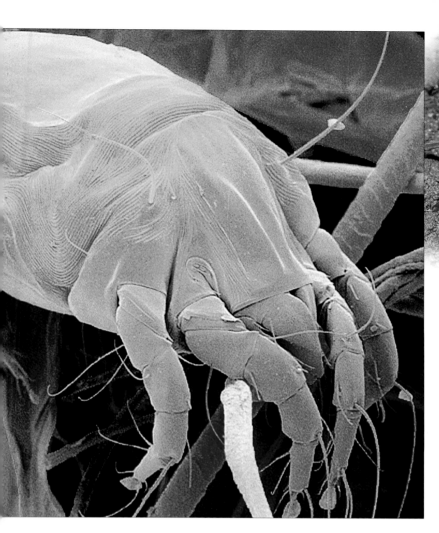

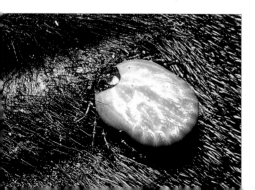

① *Large, furry velvet mites* (Trombidiidae) *inhabit deserts and savannas. They can often be seen wandering around after heavy rains.*

place. It can keep on gorging, often for several days, until completely bloated. At that point it dissolves its anchor-glue and falls off the host.

Eggs by the Thousand

Once a female's gargantuan blood meal has been transformed into eggs, she produces them in their thousands, then dies. The larvae that hatch have only six legs and are called seed ticks. They sit in wait on vegetation and climb onto a new host as it brushes past. The host is often a different species of animal than the one on which their mother fed. They then molt into eight-legged nymphs. The nymphs may seek out yet another type of host or stick with the original. The final stage is the adult. Every stage takes just a single huge meal from each host. The brown dog tick, *Rhipicephalus sanguineus*, is a typical hard tick and stays with a single host, the domestic dog, through all three life stages. *Ixodes kopsteini* from Indonesia is unusual in that the female does not deposit her eggs in soil but keeps them in her own body. When she dies, her tough outer skin acts as a protective case for the developing eggs.

or being crushed when a large, heavy host lies down or scratches against a tree. Although tough, the body is still capable of expanding like a balloon to several times its original size during a typical blowout feeding session. When engorged with blood, the body expands to nearly 1 inch (2.5 cm) long in some females. When feeding, the tick forces its sharp, beaklike mouthparts into the skin. The blood continues to flow freely without clotting because the tick's saliva contains an anticoagulant. In addition, the saliva usually incorporates a gluelike substance that fixes the tick firmly in

Soft ticks (Argasidae), such as the fowl tick, *Argas persicus*, are not so crush-proof. They live in the relative security of their host's burrow or nest and only spend a short time actually on the host. Their mouthparts are relatively weak, since they do not have to anchor the tick in place for days on end. Because their hosts are available for long, predictable periods, soft ticks are snack feeders, and meals often last just a few fairly risk-free minutes. Soft ticks undergo up to seven nymphal stages before becoming adults and take many small meals during each stage. Soft ticks can go without food for long periods. They can survive several years without feeding until a host becomes available.

Both hard and soft ticks find their hosts using indicators such as exhaled carbon dioxide, the heat generated by warm-blooded hosts, and vibrations caused by nearby movement.

Feeding on Females

Hard ticks normally mate only on the host's body. Males usually choose females that are actually filling up with blood. In some species the males never feed directly from the host, but act as parasites on their own females. In most species both sexes will feed from the host while mating. In the absence of a mate females will remain on the host for long periods and refrain from taking a full blood meal. Male ticks generally use their mouthparts to transfer a spermatophore into the female's genital aperture, a slow process that may take several hours. The female hard tick only ever needs to mate once: The number of sperm she receives (up to 120,000) is quite adequate for fertilizing the 10,000 or so eggs she will lay. Soft ticks mate many times, up to twice daily for some males, fertilizing just a few eggs each time.

Tiny Mites

Mites are generally far smaller than ticks, although red velvet mites about 0.4 inches (10 mm) in size can be seen walking around in deserts and grasslands after rains. Mites live in every kind of habitat, including both fresh water and the open sea, where they swim well by paddling with their legs. Many species are parasitic on animals, including the scabies mite, *Sarcoptes scabei*. Whole families of mites live on plants. The red spider mites (Tetranychidae) are often major pests. They are one of the few arachnids other than spiders to produce silk (from their pedipalps), using it to form extensive webbing that covers their host plants. They feed on the plant's juices by piercing it with their needlelike mouthparts. The damage they cause usually leads the leaf to wilt and die, often killing the whole plant. In spider mites there is an unusual disparity in numbers between the sexes, with females outnumbering males three to one.

Males seek out immature females and guard them. They often fight with other males for the privilege of being on hand when the female makes her final molt and becomes sexually receptive. In *Schizotetranychus celarius* from Asia males and females share a nest with their offspring and defend them against predatory mites, which are often killed if they attempt to invade the nest.

Mites of the family Eriophyidae only have four legs. They are known as gall mites because of the characteristic swellings they induce on their host plants. Although large numbers of galls may be present, the plant does not noticeably suffer, even from a heavy infestation.

⊕ *Swollen with blood after a meal, a female wood tick (genus Dermacentor) dwarfs an unfed companion. These ticks are carriers of Rocky Mountain spotted fever.*

Disease Carriers

Ticks transmit the widest range of diseases to humans and animals of all blood-sucking organisms. Human diseases include Rocky Mountain spotted fever, Lyme disease, and tick-bite fever. The most important of the mite-borne diseases is scrub typhus, transmitted by chiggers (or red bugs) in the family Trombiculidae. It is quite common in parts of tropical Asia and often fatal. The scabies or itch mite can cause severe inflammation on human skin, especially on the hands and wrists. House-dust mites may cause allergic respiratory reactions such as coughing and sneezing in people who are sensitive to them.

Hitching Rides

Many mites live permanently on their animal hosts, which also provide them with their sole source of food. Some mites seek out animals for transportation purposes. This form of hitchhiking is called phoresy. The behavior is usually seen in the penultimate nymphal stage, called the deutonymph. This stage is solely adapted for dispersal, and the nymph often has modified claws or special suckerlike organs for clinging to the transporter's body. Some species cement themselves firmly in place using anal fluid that hardens to form an anchor stalk. Large clusters are often seen attached to insects such as queen bumblebees, which are scarcely able to take off because of the extra weight they are carrying.

Some insects, especially dung beetles (Scarabaeidae) and carrion beetles (Silphidae), are often laden with a mixed cargo of mites. They include species actually living on the beetle, plus a range of hitchhikers.

About 100 species of hummingbird flower mites live solely on the pollen or nectar of flowers visited by hummingbirds. To move to a fresh flower, the mites scramble up the bill of a visiting bird and take up temporary lodging in its nasal cavity before disembarking.

↑ *A queen white-tailed bumblebee (*Bombus lucorum*) forages on heather while nymphs of the mite* Parasitellus fucorum *cluster on her thorax.*

Solpuga sp.

Common name Sun spiders (wind spiders, wind scorpions)

Subclass Solifugae

Class Arachnida

Number of species About 1,000 (about 120 U.S.)

Size From about 0.3 in (8 mm) to about 2.5 in (6.4 cm)

Key features Body very hairy, usually reddish-brown or yellowish; abdomen long, soft, and elongate-oval, with 10 conspicuous segments connected to the cephalothorax via a waistlike constriction; chelicerae large and pincerlike; 2 small eyes on the front edge of the cephalothorax; pedipalps long, slender, and unmodified

Habits Mainly desert living, usually nocturnal predators with a good bit of speed on their long legs; they hide during the day under stones, bark, or in burrows

Breeding Male seizes female without courtship and transfers sperm manually; females lay about 50 eggs in burrows in the ground and guard the eggs and babies until their first molt

Diet Insects, other arachnids (including scorpions), centipedes, small snakes, lizards, birds, and rodents

Habitat Mainly deserts and dry savannas

Distribution Over most of the warmer parts of the world, including southern Europe but excluding Australia; in North America mainly in the Southwest, but found as far north as southwestern Canada; single species from Florida is only one from eastern U.S.

⊕ *There are 25 different species of Solpuga in South Africa some of which are found in the Kruger National Park. The females dig burrows to lay their eggs. Body length up to 1.2 inches (3 cm).*

Sun Spiders

Solifugae

Their habit of living in sunny desert regions gives this group of hairy, large-jawed arachnids the name of sun spiders. Yet most species actually avoid the sun, being nocturnal.

WIND SPIDERS, THE ALTERNATIVE name for the Solifugae, comes from their ability to run like the wind on their long legs, making them by far the most fleet of foot of any arachnids. They also climb well, and in Africa a first encounter with one of the large resident species may be when it streaks up a leg, across the back of the head and down the other leg, the whole burst of activity being over in a matter of seconds.

Low-Slung Body

Sun spiders are built for running. They have a relatively streamlined, low-slung style of body carried on six long legs. The front legs are longer than the rest and are carried in the air. They are used as feelers, assisted by the long, slender, leglike pedipalps. On the hind legs there are tiny "T"-shaped organs that also serve a sensory function, probably assisted by the abundant hairs with which most species are clothed. The head is relatively large because of the pair of huge chelicerae that project forward between the single pair of tiny, and usually rather ineffective, eyes. Only in some day-active species are the eyes probably of much assistance in locating prey.

Active Hunters

All sun spiders are predators and hunt their prey actively, rather than sitting and waiting for a meal to walk past, as in many scorpions. As it hurries across the desert floor in a zigzag fashion, the sun spider constantly monitors its surroundings, using its sensitive front legs and

⊕ *The slender, hairy body with front legs held upward in a questing fashion are typical of solpugids such as this species from the African savannas.*

grind the victim's body, mashing it completely to a pulp before pouring on digestive fluids to dissolve the tissues.

Reproduction

Males are generally much smaller than the females, but have longer legs. There is no advance courtship—the male simply launches himself at the female and grabs her with his chelicerae. In most species he then spends some time nibbling his way gently down her back, gradually massaging away any objections she may have to the next step—insemination.

This varies from species to species. Usually the male deposits a droplet of semen on the ground, then picks it up in his chelicerae. He uses the chelicerae to tamp the semen into the female's genital aperture. *Metasolpuga picta* from the Namib Desert in southern Africa carries out its courtship in daytime, when the sand is hot enough to cook the semen droplet, so the male first deposits it on the female's relatively cool back before making the transfer. In a number of American species the male tips the female over so that he can make a direct body-to-body transfer, then turns around and uses his chelicerae to pack the seminal fluid home. Females generally dig nesting burrows in the ground and stand guard over their eggs and young until after their first molt, when they leave the nest and disperse.

palps. It is possibly the front legs and the palps that are responsible for the detection (probably by scent or vibrations) of crickets and other prey items concealed below ground, which are then dug out and eaten. Large sun spiders can easily deal with deadly scorpions as well as vertebrate prey such as lizards, mice, and small birds. Some species carry out their hunting in more predictable sites, such as around a termite nest where worker termites will be active or around a campfire that will attract insects. Some species climb trees in search of prey, assisted by special suckers on their feet, which function well even on glass surfaces.

Sun spiders do not have venom glands, which explains the outsize construction of their jaws. They are used independently to deal with prey, each jaw working against the other to

◉ A female sun spider of the genus Solpuga *extends her burrow. She loosens the earth with her chelicerae and pushes it clear of the tunnel.*

Mexican red-knee
tarantula
(*Brachypelma
smithi*)

Common name Tarantulas
(bird-eating spiders, baboon spiders,
whistling spiders)

Family	Theraphosidae
Suborder	Mygalomorphae
Order	Araneae
Subclass	Aranae
Class	Arachnida
Number of species	About 1,000 (about 30 U.S.)
Size	Body length from about 1 in (2.5 cm) to about 5 in (13 cm)
Key features	Large, abundantly hairy body; usually blackish or brownish, but sometimes bluish or purplish or boldly marked with orange, yellow, or white; 8 very small eyes forming a close group; legs thick and hairy, each with 2 claws at the tip and a tuft of hair on the underside; males longer legged than females and sometimes with brighter colors
Habits	Active at night, spending the day in burrows or in cavities in trees; hunting performed by touch and via sensory hairs; no web built; eyesight poor
Breeding	Males wander at night in search of females in their burrows; mating is brief, lasting only a minute or so; females not usually aggressive toward males; eggs laid in burrow or other cavity, sometimes carried around by the female; females are long-lived (20 years or more) and produce many broods
Diet	Mainly insects; also spiders, millipedes, sow bugs (woodlice), frogs, toads, lizards, small snakes (including rattlesnakes), and occasionally small birds or mice; long periods without food are not harmful
Habitat	Deserts, savannas, and forests, mainly at low elevations; often in houses in the tropics
Distribution	Mainly in warm areas; absent from Europe; U.S. species mostly in the southwestern deserts, absent from the southeastern U.S.

⬆ *The Mexican red knee tarantula, Brachypelma smithi, is found in the Pacific Coast regions of Mexico. Body length up to 2.4 inches (6 cm).*

Tarantulas Theraphosidae

For anyone suffering from arachnophobia, tarantulas, with their large, hairy bodies and long, thick legs, are the stuff of nightmares. Yet in fact most species are quite harmless.

TARANTULAS ARE OFTEN CALLED bird-eating spiders, although birds do not figure much in their diet. In Africa they are called baboon spiders, while their local name in Australia is whistling spiders, referring to the sounds they make by rubbing certain parts of the body together. Included here is the world's biggest spider, the goliath tarantula, *Theraphosa leblondi*, from the tropical rain forests of South America.

The leg span of the males can reach about 12 inches (30 cm). The tips of the legs are furnished with adhesive pads, making tarantulas good climbers, even sometimes on slippery vertical surfaces such as glass or metal. Burrow-living species seldom move far. They may spend their whole lives (maybe 20 years or more) in the same burrow, only emerging at night to hunt for prey a short distance from the entrance. Adult females molt regularly during their long lives, but males do not molt again once they are sexually mature.

Mostly Harmless

Prey is quickly crushed and mashed to a pulp by the powerful jaws. Although large, tarantulas are not generally a threat to humans, and the bite of most species (including all those from the United States) is no more painful than the sting from a wasp or bee. However, in some South American and African species the bite is toxic. In certain Australian species the bite produces pain all over the body, accompanied by vomiting and perspiring. Yet the patient soon recovers, and no deaths have been recorded. Many tarantulas are kept as pets and are increasingly being bred in captivity. They become very tame and are easily handled.

⊙ *Tarantulas are heavily built compared with other spiders, especially the legs, which are not only densely hairy but immensely thick as well. Aphonopelma seemannii, shown, is a favorite in the pet trade.*

throughout his courtship rituals. Male tarantulas die a short time after they have mated.

The female lays her eggs in her burrow, watching over the egg sac. She will sometimes carry it to the surface for the warm sunlight to help incubation, accelerating the development of the eggs. The baby spiderlings seldom move far from their nursery, setting up home under stones and logs nearby, although ballooning to faraway places has been observed in a few species. Some tropical species probably mature in just three to four years, but in most cases it is more likely to take seven to eight years.

Volley of Hairs

When alarmed, most tarantulas tilt backward and throw their front legs up, fangs bared, in a threatening stance. Some species back this up by buzzing or purring. If an attack occurs, many tarantulas can defend themselves by temporarily blinding their attacker. Sticking its abdomen up into the air, the spider rapidly vibrates its legs against a patch of fine hairs on top of the abdomen, tearing them off in large numbers and propelling them violently into the aggressor's face. The tips of the hairs are barbed and have a painful nettlelike action on human skin. The effect on delicate areas such as the mouth or eyes can be devastating. Some species will also shoot a powerful jet of unpleasant liquid into an opponent's face.

Hunting for a Mate

Female tarantulas seldom move far from their hideaway, usually a burrow in the ground, so the males have to wander in search of them after dark. On a warm night after rain the Arizona Desert can be crawling with males of the Arizona blond tarantula, *Aphonopelma chalcodes*, wandering around in their quest for females. The male recognizes the female's burrow by the smell and taste of her silk around the entrance, on which he taps out a message with his front legs to announce his arrival. The female rushes out and rears back on her hind legs as if about to plunge her widely bared fangs into her visitor. Instead, the male steps boldly forward and snags her gaping fangs behind a special spur on his front legs. That enables him to lever her body backward so that he can creep in underneath and insert his palps. In the Australian *Selenocosmia* whistling tarantulas, the male whistles continuously

⊕ Its entrance always open, the silk-lined burrow of the female Lyrognathus robustus goes deep inside a steep bank on a forested hillside in Malaysia.

Sydney funnel-web spider
(*Atrax robustus*)

Common name Funnel-web spiders

Family   Dipluridae

Suborder   Mygalomorphae

Order   Araneae

Subclass   Aranae

Class   Arachnida

Number of species About 250 (about 10 U.S.)

Size   Body length from about 0.1 in (3 mm) to about 2 in (5 cm)

Key features Easily recognized by the long, widely separated spinnerets, which can be half the length of the abdomen or more; body mainly brown or black, rather long and flat; 8 small eyes grouped closely together on a slightly raised tubercle

Habits   Web a broad, rather untidy sheet of dense, clothlike silk, often with a bluish tinge; usually placed among tree roots, in crevices in fallen trees, or among rocks; the spider waits in a tube set to one side of the web; some species can be aggressive and dangerous

Breeding   Males (which are only slightly smaller than females) leave their webs and wander in search of females at night; female usually lays eggs within the web's retreat, but in some species she carries them around with her

Diet   Insects, spiders, millipedes, worms, woodlice (sow bugs), and snails; larger funnel-web spiders can tackle frogs and lizards

Habitat   Woodlands, mainly among the mossy base of trees, but also among rocks or on tree trunks; some species found in gardens; several eyeless species live in caves

Distribution Mainly tropical and subtropical, but a few species in southern Europe (Spain) and North America

⊕ *The Sydney funnel-web spider,* Atrax robustus, *the most deadly spider in the world, burrows beneath logs and stones in cool places in eastern Australia. Body length up to 1.5 inches (4 cm).*

Funnel-Web Spiders

Dipluridae

Although most species are secretive and rarely seen, a single member of the family Dipluridae, *the Sydney funnel-web spider, has attracted extraordinary media attention because of its deadly bite.*

THE FAMILY DIPLURIDAE contains the most dangerous spider in the world—the Sydney funnel-web spider, *Atrax robustus*, from Australia. It has long fangs and enormous venom sacs compared with other spiders. The sacs are brimful of atraxotoxin, one of the most potent poisons known in the animal kingdom.

The concentration of atraxotoxin in the male Sydney funnel-web spider is six times as high as in the female, making any close encounter potentially hazardous. The males are also distressingly easy to provoke and will launch an attack of terrifying ferocity. At least 15 people have died after encounters with these amazingly tetchy creatures over the last 60 years. The riskiest time is when the males are moving around in search of females. Fortunately, an antidote to the toxin is now available by injection. Aggressive behavior tends to be common in the whole family, but only the Australian species are dangerously venomous.

⊕ *A male funnel-web spider,* Aname grandis, *bares his fangs while rearing up in a defensive posture.*

Mating and Motherhood

During mating, which takes place in the female's web, spurs on the male's front legs are used to grasp the base of the female's pedipalps or second pair of legs. *Ischnothele caudata* from Brazil is unique among all known members of the Mygalomorphae in its habit of caring for its babies after they have hatched. For the first five critical weeks of the spiderlings' lives their mother catches food for them and places it in the web. When her offspring are newborn, she shows the position of the meal by plucking on the silk with her legs and drumming against it with her palps.

Trap-Door Spiders

Trap-door spiders (Ctenizidae) lie in wait to ambush their prey. Here, a passing insect is about to be pulled through the hinged door.

Trap-door spiders (family Ctenizidae) look generally similar to funnel-web spiders, being mostly brown or black, but the male of the red-headed mouse spider, *Missulena insigne* from Australia, is bright blue and red. Trap-door spider males are often seen wandering around in search of females, which generally spend their whole lives inside their burrows. The burrows are usually deep in the ground, trap-door spiders being the most skilled tunnelers of all spiders. They are helped by having a specific digging tool—a rastellum—consisting of a rake of large spines down the edges of the chelicerae. The entrance is usually sealed with some kind of hinged door.

The spider waits just below the door, flinging it open when an insect walks past and dragging it inside. In some species the spider lifts the door ajar at night and sits with its legs slightly spread, ready to snap up passing prey. The door may be wafer thin and built mainly of silk, or it may be a "cork" door—a thick pluglike structure made of earth mixed with silk. In some tunnels there are doors to side branches within the nest as well as at the entrance. The spider is able to cling to its door with such force that it can be difficult to pry it open even with the aid of a knife. Most of the doors are well camouflaged, making them difficult to find.

Not all trap-door spiders build doors, so sometimes the entrance is left open. A few species surround the entrance with prey detectors consisting of a series of silk lines radiating like wheel spokes. They help give early warning of an insect's approach. In the twig-line spider, *Aganippe raphiduca* from Australia, the burrow is surrounded by a fan of twigs.

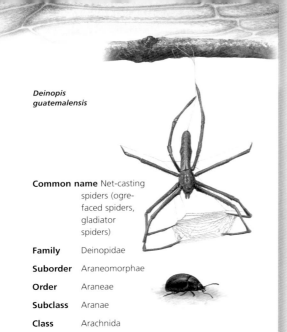

Deinopis guatemalensis

Common name Net-casting spiders (ogre-faced spiders, gladiator spiders)

Family Deinopidae

Suborder Araneomorphae

Order Araneae

Subclass Aranae

Class Arachnida

Number of species About 60 (1 U.S.)

Size Body length 0.5 in (13 mm) to 1.2 in (3 cm)

Key features Body long, slim, and twiglike, usually light brown; in *Deinopis* the small, flat face is almost entirely occupied by 2 huge staring eyes, below which are 2 tiny eyes (plus 4 more on top of the carapace, making 8 in all); in *Menneus* all the eyes are small

Habits Active at night, holding a tiny web in their front legs; the web is thrown over prey as it passes; during the day the spiders resemble twigs

Breeding Males are slightly smaller and more slender than females, with extremely long legs; female *Deinopis* constructs a globular egg sac suspended on a long silken line beneath a leaf; the finished sac is camouflaged with bits of leaf

Diet Various insects

Habitat On low trees and bushes in woods, rain forests, grasslands, and gardens; often common in built-up areas, sometimes on walls and fences

Distribution Mainly in warm areas, especially Australia; only a single species in North America (Florida); none in Europe

⊕ Deinopis guatemalensis, *a tropical species, hangs above its insect prey, preparing to drop its net over an unsuspecting bug. Body length up to 0.8 inches (20 mm).*

Net-Casting Spiders
Deinopidae

With their large forward-facing eyes deinopids are often called ogre-faced spiders. However, their other alternative name, gladiator spiders, is possibly more appropriate because of their net-casting accomplishments.

WHEN AT REST DURING THE DAY, the net-casting spiders often stretch out their long, slim bodies along a twig, making the spiders difficult to see. Two other spiders have similar habits, the *Tetragnatha* large-jawed orb weavers (Tetragnathidae) and *Tibellus* grass spiders (Thomisidae). In both the eyes are small, and their arrangement is different from any members of the Deinopidae. Some deinopid species hang among leaves during the day, resembling a small, branched twig.

The best chance of seeing one of the remarkable net-casting spiders is in the warmer regions of the world, especially Australia, which boasts no fewer than 14 species. Some can be quite common in suburban gardens. In most other parts of their range they are rare and difficult to locate, but they can be abundant in some South American rain forests. Searching at night with a flashlight when the spider is active is much more likely to yield results than looking for the static twiglike spiders in daytime. It is only under cover of darkness that a female may be seen making her egg sac, which she suspends from a leaf on a long silken line. The next day it may be difficult to find the sac, since it will have been camouflaged with bits of leaf.

Skillful Gladiators

As their common names of net-casting spiders and gladiator spiders would suggest, deinopids have a unique method of catching prey. The

pick the net up by its four corners. The structure is extremely elastic. The spider checks it by quickly yanking it out to its full extent, which is several times its original size.

Netting Prey

With its net ready, the spider settles down to wait, head downward and loosely suspended from its simple silk scaffold by its back legs. Until now the whole of its remarkable engineering feat has been accomplished by touch alone. Next, the huge, headlamplike eyes come into their own. Despite the dim light of the forest, an insect passing nearby will be lucky to escape unnoticed. Reacting with lightning-fast reflexes, the spider whips the net open to its maximum extent. It then sweeps it across the target, scooping it up in a helpless struggling mass. Meanwhile, the net collapses and envelops the prey in its sticky folds. The spider may then start feeding on the prey immediately. Otherwise it will bite it to quieten it down before removing it from the net and hanging it up for later consumption. The nets are usually too badly damaged for

whole process can be watched by the light of a flashlight an hour or two after sundown, when the spiders begin their night's work.

Hanging head downward from an open scaffold of threads, the spider first spins out a basic, rectangular framework of simple, dry silk. It then brings the cribellum into play, laying down zigzag bands of sticky whitish, hackled-band silk across the framework. The silk issuing from the cribellum is combed out by the calamistrum (row of bristles) on the back legs, which vibrates rapidly up and down like a shuttle as the silk is passed through it. The silk is positioned with great accuracy onto the framework. The finished net is about the size of a small postage stamp. The spider now turns around and uses its first two pairs of legs to

⊕ During the day some species of Deinopis align themselves along a twig where their sticklike bodies blend in perfectly.

reuse, so are bundled up and eaten. The process of making a new net can begin again, the whole procedure being repeated several times during the night if prey is abundant. In some species airborne prey is the main target, while in others the spider hangs poised with its net just above the ground and scoops up insects that walk beneath.

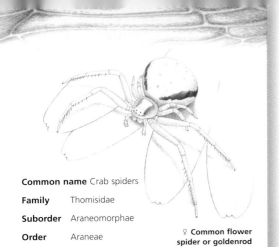

Common name Crab spiders

Family Thomisidae

Suborder Araneomorphae

Order Araneae

Subclass Aranae

Class Arachnida

♀ **Common flower spider or goldenrod spider (*Misumena vatia*)**

Number of species More than 2,000 (about 250 U.S.)

Size Body length from about 0.08 in (2 mm) to about 0.8 in (20 mm)

Key features Eight eyes, often on raised humps in 2 backwardly curving rows of 4 eyes each; body usually short and broad (but can be long and thin); back two pairs of legs often short and rather stumpy; front two pairs usually much longer and slimmer; each tarsus bears 2 claws; chelicerae lack teeth; venom usually very powerful

Habits Found on the ground, on leaves, or on flowers, usually remaining still for long periods in an ambush position; no silken webs built for catching prey; 1 species partially social

Breeding Males usually much smaller than females and normally a different color; mating generally takes place without any preceding courtship; during mating the male hangs upside down beneath the female, clinging to the underside of her abdomen; she may catch prey and feed while the male is thus occupied; females stand guard over their egg sacs, but often die before the babies hatch

Diet Most kinds of insects or other spiders

Habitat Almost anywhere: forests, grasslands, deserts, mountains, beaches, gardens, and houses

Distribution Worldwide, except in the very driest and coldest areas

⊕ *The common flower spider,* Misumena vatia, *awaits prey on a daisy. It is also found on goldenrod and other white or yellow flowers, giving it the alternative common name of goldenrod spider. Body length up to 0.4 inches (10 mm).*

Crab Spiders

Thomisidae

With more than 2,000 species described and many more remaining to be discovered, the Thomisidae *is one of the larger families of spiders. There are more than 200 species in North America.*

CRAB SPIDERS VARY IN SIZE from 0.08 inches (2 mm) in the smallest males, to 0.8 inches (20 mm) in the largest females. They are most closely related to the huntsman spiders (Sparassidae) and are generally one of the easiest families of spiders to recognize. Their fat, squat shape and chunky build are characteristic, although some species are exceptional in being longer and slimmer. The front two pairs of legs are noticeably long compared with the rear pair, which are used to anchor the spider firmly to the substrate when it is dealing with struggling prey. The overall impression is rather crablike, which is reinforced by the spiders' habit of moving forward, backward, or sideways with equal ease.

The eight eyes are small and arranged in a distinctive pattern. In the ambushing kinds of crab spiders vision is probably rather poor—it is doubtful if they can see more than an indistinct blur. Their feeble eyesight is no handicap; the spiders rely on touch for capturing their prey, which more or less blunders into their waiting clutches. Species that actively pursue their prey have much keener eyesight.

Ambushing Prey

Crab spiders do not construct silk snares for catching prey. They are mostly sit-and-wait predators, although a few kinds of *Philodromus* wander around in search of a meal. The stay-at-home species spend many hours sitting motionless with their long front legs held out crablike at either side. The legs snap closed in a pincer movement on any prey that comes within reach. Long, inward-facing hairs on the insides of the front legs help grasp the struggling prey and direct it rapidly toward the

⊕ *The numerous species of* Xysticus *in Europe and North America are small, brownish crab spiders, often found on flowers. Here,* X. cristatus *from Europe has caught a sawfly.*

fangs. Although small, the fangs are capable of delivering a bite that causes rapid death. Even a stout bumblebee is quickly overpowered by the exceptionally potent venom. Crab spiders take a wide variety of prey, especially flies and bees, but also moths, butterflies, bugs, and other insects. Some, such as the tropical antlike crab spiders (*Amyciaea* species), are specialists and prey solely on ants. Many such spiders also look remarkably like the ants they feed on.

Crab spiders do not have any teeth on the inner surfaces of their chelicerae. They cannot therefore mash up their prey during feeding to release the body fluids. Instead, crab spiders inject digestive fluid through a small hole made by the fangs in the prey's exterior skeleton. The dissolved body contents can then be sucked up like soup from a can, leaving a perfectly intact husk, deceptively lifelike yet completely drained. Unlike most web-building species, crab spiders do not store prey to meet future needs.

ⓝ *Some species of crab spiders not only prey exclusively on ants but also resemble them. Here, Amyciaea lineatipes from Thailand feeds on a weaver ant.*

As a result, they can only deal with one meal at a time—good news for any insect that stumbles on a crab spider busy feeding. Not only can the insect walk straight past the spider's face without arousing interest, it can walk back and forth over the spider's body in complete safety.

Different Homes

Some species of crab spiders live in a wide variety of situations from mountains, grasslands, and roadsides to vacant lots and gardens. The house crab spider, *Philodromus dispar*, can frequently be seen scampering across interior walls in both Europe and North America.

Many other kinds of crab spider are only found in rain forests, while others live under stones in deserts. A popular vantage point for a whole range of species is on flowers. The spiders may copy the color (mainly white, pink, or yellow). In the case of many brown species of *Xysticus* the spiders are happy to sit on any kind of flower. Certain species with a rather roughened, wrinkled body surface spend their lives on similarly rough-textured tree bark, while those that live on sand are speckled appropriately. A few kinds are green and catch their prey on leaves. *Heriaeus* from Europe is densely hairy and lives on hairy-leaved plants. The strangest place inhabited by any crab spiders is inside the pitchers of *Nepenthes* pitcher plants, the only place *Misumenops nepenthicola* from Asia ever calls home. The spider lurks just below the rim of the pitcher, attacking insects that are attracted to the liquid secreted by glands near the rim. Females attach their egg sacs to the inside walls of the pitcher.

The *Tibellus* grass spiders from Europe and North America have elongate, straw-colored bodies. They usually sit lengthwise on grasses or plant stems where they are notoriously hard to spot. Certain tropical crab spiders are masters of disguise. They survive by convincing their enemies that they are not really a spider at all, but a shiny blob of bird dropping. The behavior is not exclusive only to spiders. The long-horned beetle, *Aethomerus cretatus* from Brazil, avoids predators by taking on the color and shape of a bird dropping.

It has also been suggested that the spiders may copy the scent of a dropping in order to lure manure-loving flies to their death. Evidence for the theory is scarce, but in at least one instance a manure fly (Sepsidae) has been seen circling one of these spiders and showing a fair degree of interest in it.

⊙ **The Asian bird-dropping spider,** Phrynarachne tuberosa *from Nepal and India, is a species that mimics a bird dropping in order to evade predators.*

Midget Males

While there is often some variation in size between male and female spiders, with the females normally being larger, in some crab spiders the difference can be extreme. In the bizarre seven-spined crab spider, *Epicadus heterogaster* from Brazil, the large, knobby white female is dozens of times larger than the tiny, dark-brown male. Being such a midget does not seem to increase the male's risk of being eaten by his mate. In fact, the reverse seems to be true, and he is usually ignored. He can even wander over the female's body without provoking a reaction. Courtship appears to be absent, although the male may drum on the underside of the female's body with his palps, which possibly helps make her more receptive. A similar situation exists with many other crab spiders, such as *Misumena vatia*, although the difference in size between male and female is not always so extreme.

The problem of finding a mate in the first place may seem almost insoluble for such tiny males. The answer seems to be that in at least some (possibly all) species the females release pheromones that attract suitors directly to the correct spot. The chemical message avoids subjecting the relatively short-lived males to days of exhausting searching. It also ensures that they do not suffer a hostile reception from the female when they finally show up.

In the North American flower-living *Misumenopsis formosipes* the males stand guard over females that are shortly to undergo their final molt and become adults. It is crunch time for the females, since they have now attained the highly prized status of being sexually available virgins. Immature females are usually thin on the ground, so there is plenty of competition to find and keep them—males will fight to the death to hang on to a female they have "adopted." The victorious male usually capitalizes on his conquest by making a meal of the loser's corpse. The snack is a useful bonus given that standing on guard for lengthy periods beside a potential bride is hungry work. When rivals' corpses are unavailable, the male

⊙ *In* Xysticus cristatus *from Europe the male wraps the female's legs in a silken bridal veil before venturing in beneath her abdomen and inserting his palps.*

Bridal Veils

Although courtship in many crab spiders is absent, in certain species of *Xysticus* it occurs in rather an unusual form. In several species the male (who is about half the size of the female) lays down a swath of silk over the female's legs and the front half of her body. The silk forms what has become known as a bridal veil, the precise function of which is still open to debate. Its most obvious purpose would be to prevent the female from attacking the male while he is mating beneath her. Yet she is quickly able to shrug off her "bonds" once the male has mated and left, making this explanation less convincing. It is more likely that the silk of the bridal veil, being heavily saturated with the male's pheromones, serves to keep the female in a positive "mood" toward him throughout the period of close contact with her mate.

guardians stave off hunger and thirst by lapping nectar from the flowers on which they are sitting. They may also eat some of the pollen, an unusual habit for a spider.

Female Sentry Duty

Some female crab spiders place their egg sacs in the open on a plant. Others prefer a concealed location, such as within a curled leaf fastened with silk or in the dark recesses beneath a stone. The female generally stands on guard until she dies, which often occurs before the spiderlings hatch. During her period on sentry duty the female becomes noticeably shriveled, since she cannot feed unless an insect happens to come within reach. Despite all the mother's best efforts, several species of parasitic wasps regularly manage to sneak past her and lay their eggs within the egg sac. In *Diaea socialis* from Australia the female builds a nest within a leaf and lays her eggs in it. After her offspring hatch, they stay in the nest and extend it, working alongside her if she is still

alive, but otherwise working alone. When she dies, they stay on in their communal home.

The Common Flower Spider

Over a remarkably broad swath of the earth's temperate regions, from England to Japan in the east and Canada to Florida in the west, flower-visiting insects frequently run the gauntlet of attack by the common flower spider. *Misumena vatia* is known in the United States as the goldenrod spider because of its habit of sitting on flowers of that plant.

Although a number of other crab spiders also blend in perfectly with the flowers on which they wait in ambush, the common flower spider is by far the most widespread and successful species. Unlike most other crab spiders, in which the color of the body is fixed, the common flower spider enjoys a certain degree of flexibility: It has a limited but useful ability to switch its color to suit a particular

Female crab spiders, such as this *Xysticus cristatus* from Europe, generally stand guard over their egg sacs, although they often die before their offspring emerge.

background. White individuals generally rest on white flowers; but if they start to die off, and there is a yellow flower nearby, the spider will move across. At first the white spider shows up conspicuously against the yellow background, but over the next few days its whole body gradually becomes suffused with yellow until it finally blends in perfectly.

The change is reversible, and the spider can move home again, back to a white flower if it needs to. More than 85 percent of individuals will choose a matching background, either white or yellow. But such perfect camouflage, although useful, is not apparently absolutely necessary. Around 15 percent of individuals will perch on a nonmatching, contrastingly colored flower. Although they stand out against their background, they still seem to avoid being found and eaten by their enemies, and appear to enjoy reasonable success in catching insects. A yellow spider might therefore be seen sitting boldly on a purple flower with a bee hanging lifelessly from its jaws. If no flowers are available locally, the spider will simply sit on top of a leaf. Even in such an apparently unfavorable position it will capture at least some prey. The selection of suitable flowers does not happen by chance, but is almost certainly deliberate. A spider may even spot a bunch of white flowers high above its head and will somehow make its way up to them.

Experiments have shown that insects tend to avoid flowers on which something dark and contrasting is perched. So the flower spider's ability to match the color of its background really does seem to increase its harvest of nectar-seeking insects. Protection from enemies is another huge benefit of being difficult to see. Judging by the rarity with which the flower spider turns up in food offered to fledglings, birds are being fooled on a regular basis.

Formidable Predators

Not all enemies are so easily deceived: Even the most perfectly camouflaged spiders may fail to escape detection by the sophisticated sensory apparatus of female *Sceliphron* mud-dauber

⊙ *Main picture and inset: Female common flower spiders,* Misumena vatia, *wait in ambush for insects camouflaged against the colored petals of the flowers on which they sit. Above: A female heather spider,* Thomisus onustus, *is well camouflaged on a pink-spotted orchid.*

wasps. The nests of the formidable little hunters will often be crammed full of paralyzed female flower spiders providing a fresh food supply for the wasps' larvae. The males are too tiny and move around too much to get caught.

Subtle Camouflage

For all but the most expert of human eyes, picking out the flower spiders on their flowers is not an easy task. However, a bee or other insect sitting motionless on a flower for an abnormally long time could signify their presence. Closer inspection may reveal that the insect is not moving because its head has been pierced by the twin fangs of a female flower spider. The body remains intact and deceptively lifelike because its attacker, like all crab spiders, does not have teeth on its chelicerae, so cannot mash its prey into a pulp as many other spiders do. The flower spider is a valiant assailant and will tackle fat bumblebees and other stinging insects that are avoided by many larger spiders.

As in all crab spiders, the female flower spider stands guard over her egg sac, but usually dies before the babies hatch.

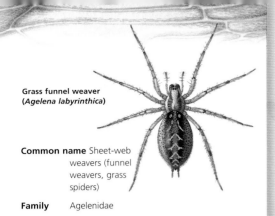

Grass funnel weaver
(*Agelena labyrinthica*)

Common name Sheet-web weavers (funnel weavers, grass spiders)

Family Agelenidae

Suborder Araneomorphae

Order Araneae

Subclass Aranae

Class Arachnida

Number of species About 800 (over 300 U.S.)

Size From about 0.08 in (2 mm) to about 0.8 in (20 mm)

Key features Longish, densely hairy, brown or blackish-brown body carried on long legs that are abundantly spiny and hairy; usually 8 eyes in 2 horizontal rows; some cave species eyeless; a pair of peglike spinnerets protrudes from abdomen tip and so is visible from above

Habits All species build a broad sheet web with a funnel at one side; shady corners and hollows are often favored sites; prey will be attacked both by day and after dark; some of the larger species often wander around houses at night; 2 species are social

Breeding Males and females about equal in size; males enter females' webs and announce their presence by tapping on the silk; in some species males and females cohabit for long periods in the female's web; eggs are laid beneath bark or stones, or within an exposed silken nest

Diet Insects of all types

Habitat Houses, cellars, barns, outhouses, mountains, woods, meadows, marshes, and roadsides; in dark corners or on low bushes and among grass or rocks

Distribution Worldwide but usually avoiding very dry areas and absent from the coldest zones; more common in temperate regions than in the tropics

⊕ *Agelena labyrinthica*, the grass funnel weaver, can be found among low vegetation and makes a sheet web with a tubular retreat. Body length up to 0.6 inches (15 mm).

Sheet-Web Weavers

Agelenidae

The Agelenidae includes some of the most familiar large, hairy, long-legged spiders to be found in houses in temperate areas, as well as many species that build their broad sheet webs in areas of remote wilderness.

MEMBERS OF THE AGELENIDAE are sometimes called funnel-web spiders. That name has been so widely applied to the notorious Sydney funnel-web spider, *Atrax robustus*—a member of the Dipluridae—that the name sheet-web weavers is now often being used for the Agelenidae.

Bad Press

It has been suggested that in many temperate parts of the world the common house or cellar spider, *Tegenaria domestica*, and its close relatives have been responsible more than any other spiders for giving the whole group a bad press. Depite being completely harmless, some people are afraid of these large spiders, with their long hairy legs and habit of scuttling rapidly across a bedroom floor. There are those who will not enter a room in which one of these spiders is known to be present. Originally a native of Europe, the house spider has been carried extensively around the world and is now found as widely apart as the northeastern United States, the Cape region of South Africa, and eastern Australia.

The typical agelenid web is usually a lifetime's work for its creator, gradually extended and elaborated to suit the spider's changing needs as it grows. The web consists of a broad sheet of nonsticky silk, often built near the ground, but also slung hammocklike on bushes, among rocks, and in shady corners in buildings. Despite the relatively large dimensions of the webs, their silk is remarkably transparent, and they are often only noticed when covered

with dew on a fall morning. Only then does their sheer abundance become evident, so that a neglected meadow in the eastern United States may be virtually covered in glistening webs of the common *Agelenopsis* species.

Death Trap

At one end the web tapers into a funnel that functions as the spider's lair. The more or less horizontal sheet does not in itself form the main means of trapping prey. It serves more as a safety net onto which the insects fall, having collided with the mass of criss-crossing lines above. The insect stumbles helplessly around in the sheet, completely out of its depth. Its feet plunge clumsily into the yielding surface like someone walking in deep snow. It is constantly snagged among the tangle of interlacing threads as it strives to drag itself toward the edge of the sheet and freedom.

The spider waiting at the mouth of its lair has no such problems crossing its web. It treats the sheet like a smooth surface as it hurtles out to the attack, always heading straight for the exact spot where the trapped insect is struggling. Certain more dangerous insects, such as large bumblebees, will probably receive the briefest of touches before the spider races

⊕ *The plump palps of this* Tegenaria duellica *house spider show that it is a male. It is pictured on its sheet web in the corner of an outhouse in England.*

⊕ *A female grass spider,* Agelenopsis aperta *from the United States, sitting in a characteristic pose at the mouth of the funnel that leads off her main horizontal sheet web.*

back to its lair. Here it waits for the bee to free itself from the web before cautiously returning to repair the damaged silk. Some individual *Tegenaria* are less easily intimidated than others. Rather than retreat from a bumblebee, they will bite it on a leg, whereupon the bee drops dead, instantly killed by the powerful poison. Once subdued, prey is carried back to the retreat for consumption in private.

Cohabiting in *Tegenaria*

Once they have reached sexual maturity, male agelenids, which are usually about the same size as the females, leave their home webs to search for a mate. In *Tegenaria* the male announces his arrival by tugging at the silk of the female's web with his first two pairs of legs and vibrating his abdomen. His movements transmit a code of pulsed tremors through the web, which are deciphered by the female as originating from a male of her own species. That stops her from rushing out to attack, as she would if she detected the random vibrations of a struggling insect. On approaching the female's funnel, the male adds a third element to his code by drumming on the silken mat with his pedipalps.

The chances are that after the brief introduction he will move in with the female and stay for some time as a lodger. Their relationship is not close, and they tend to take their meals separately, but they sometimes sleep close together in her retreat. Whenever the male senses a conflict of interest, such as when an insect arrives in the web, he reminds the female of who he is by resuming his abdominal vibrations so that he is not attacked by mistake.

In most species the eggs are laid close to the web, often underneath stones or peeling bark. The egg sacs are usually lens shaped, and in some species several may be produced in a single season. Bits of twig, flaking bark, and other detritus are often incorporated into the tough outer coat of the sac in order to camouflage it. The eggs usually overwinter inside the sac, sometimes with the corpse of the mother perched on top.

In the grass funnel weaver, *Agelena labyrinthica*, preparations for egg laying are far more elaborate. Heavily swollen with eggs, the female deserts the web in which she has grown up. She then begins to construct a large and complex nursery of dense, shining white silk attached to leaves or grasses. The sophisticated structure contains a series of passages that form a labyrinth, hence the spider's scientific name of *labyrinthica*. The mazelike brain twister presumably makes it more difficult for enemies such as parasitic wasps to find the eggs concealed within the twisting passages. Just in case, the mother remains on guard until the young have hatched, when she finally dies.

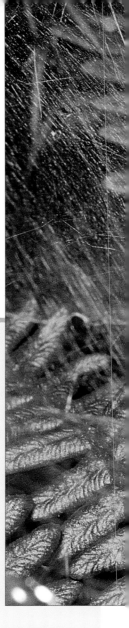

Females in a Trance

With the exception of *Tegenaria*, in most agelenids the two sexes spend only a brief time together. In the European grass funnel weaver the male seems to display little hesitation as he advances toward the female. Her lair is positioned inside the funnel to one side of the sheet web. Now and again he pauses to tap on the silk matting with his front feet, transmitting a species-specific identification message through the silk to the waiting female. If she has already mated, she will probably hurl herself across the web and try to drive him away. He is rarely so easily rebuffed and will probably stand his ground and spar with her in an open-jawed display of defiance. He may even establish who is the boss in the female's own web by driving her back toward her funnel.

With a virgin female the male has a significantly less stressful time. She will usually signal her sexual surrender by simply not reacting to him in such a cantankerous manner. Instead, she sits tight, adopting a submissive pose with her legs drawn inward. She is now quite literally a pushover, having entered a trancelike state that will not end until after the male has left her. She allows the male to grab one of her legs and to tow her just inside the mouth of her funnel, the favored place for mating.

Agelena Society

In *Agelena consociata* from the forests of West Africa egg laying, like all activities, is performed on a communal basis within huge shared webs. The nests contain thousands of individuals of both sexes and from every age group. *Agelena consociata* colonies can be described as true kibbutzim of the spider world. Work is shared out equally among all members. Even the males, which in many other social spiders tend to opt out of any housework within the nest, do their fair share around the home.

Eggs are deposited in communal chambers. They are well protected by a force of security guards consisting not only of adults but also of well-grown juveniles. The hatchlings and smaller juveniles huddle in large nursery zones to which food is delivered by adult females. A baby is supplied with food whether or not it is a blood relative of the female. That is probably because the females cannot recognize their own babies anyway in the prevailing muddle. Females also function as mobile soup kitchens, regurgitating liquid rations to the tinier babies.

⬆ *The grass funnel weaver,* Agelena labyrinthica *from Europe, favors the mouth of the funnel in the female's web for mating.*

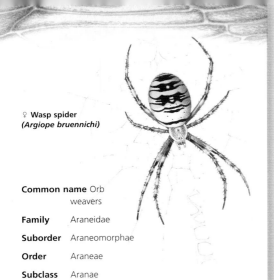

♀ **Wasp spider**
(Argiope bruennichi)

Common name Orb weavers

Family Araneidae

Suborder Araneomorphae

Order Araneae

Subclass Aranae

Class Arachnida

Number of species About 5,000 (about 200 U.S.)

Size Body length from about 0.08 in (2 mm) to about 1.8 in (4.5 cm)

Key features Body shape and color incredibly varied; can be smooth or spiny, oval or elongate, flattened or spherical, brown or brightly colored; 8 small eyes arranged in 2 horizontal rows of 4; third pair of legs always the shortest

Habits Most species build an orb web and sit in the center or in a retreat to one side; webs usually sited in low vegetation, sometimes in trees; webs sometimes communal; some species build a reduced web, swing a prey-catching "bola," or have no web at all and catch prey by sitting in wait like crab spiders

Breeding Males generally smaller than females, sometimes very much so; courtship usually consists of male vibrating threads of female's web; no courtship in some species with very small males; egg sacs usually placed among leaves or other vegetation, sometimes large and suspended like fruit

Diet Insects of all kinds

Habitat In every kind of terrestrial habitat; some species live in caves

Distribution Worldwide in habitable regions

↑ *Females of the wasp spider,* Argiope bruennichi, *have a quite unmistakable appearance, being large and strikingly colored. They build their extensive orb webs near ground level. Body length up to 0.9 inches (23 mm).*

Orb Weavers   Araneidae

Although renowned for the perfect structure of their orb webs, many members of the family Araneidae build reduced webs. Others have given up web building altogether and behave more like crab spiders.

THE CHANCES ARE THAT A perfect wagon-wheel style of orb web found sparkling in the sun on a dewy morning belongs to an araneid. A feat of construction and engineering, it is also unrivaled for its perfection and symmetry. Similar webs are fashioned by only a few related families, such as the Tetragnathidae and the unrelated feather-footed spiders (Uloboridae).

Varied Characteristics

Little can be said of orb weavers that even begins to sum up their incredibly varied characteristics. The most familiar of all web builders are probably certain species of *Araneus*, of which the garden spider—*A. diadematus*—is likely to be the best known. It is now fairly widespread in North America, having been introduced from its European home. In Europe it is the most common orb weaver in many regions. It is a typical *Araneus*, plump and rounded with fairly short legs, its body patterned in various shades of brown. Like many araneids, it usually sits on a leaf or in a lair to one side of the web, keeping in touch by holding one of the silken lines with a front leg. On warm days the garden spider will also wait for prey at the web's hub, but other species of *Araneus* appear never to do the same.

In *Argiope* the body is usually elegantly patterned with spots or stripes of silver or yellow. The attractive colors are generally on permanent display, since the spider sits in the center of its web at all times. Its way of arranging its legs is distinctive. They are frequently held together to form four pairs in the shape of a cross, giving the impression that only four legs are present, rather than eight.

→ *A juvenile silver argiope,* Argiope argentata, *sitting on its white disklike stabilimentum. The species is found from Florida to southern California and southward into South America.*

→ *The variable decoy spider,* Cyclosa insulana, *builds a variety of different styles of stabilimentum within its web. Here, the spider sits below its egg sacs.*

The spider can often be found sitting in a gap left in the center of the web's stabilimentum, a structure within the web made of zigzag bands of dense white silk. It usually positions itself with care, lining up the cross formed by its legs with the segments of the stabilimentum.

Mystery of the Stabilimentum

Stabilimenta are a typical feature of *Argiope* webs, although they vary in their structure. Until it is about half grown, the spider spends the day sitting on a disklike stabilimentum constructed of closely meshed white silk. When disturbed, the occupant flips onto the opposite side of the disk and hides. In the same way, it also uses the stabilimentum as a sunshade when the need arises. When about half grown, the spider switches to making a cross-shaped stabilimentum with a gap in the middle. The function of the stabilimentum, particularly the cross-shaped variety, is currently unknown: Several possible functions have been suggested, but none of them is very convincing.

The tiny *Cyclosa* decoy spiders always occupy a set position in their webs, one where

277

The bark spiders resemble crinkled dead leaves or swollen protrusions on bark. This is a female Caerostris mitralis *in the tropical rain forests of Madagascar.*

they are well hidden from predators. The web normally contains a stabilimentum of dense silk, which can be placed either vertically or in a spiral formation. A vertical stabilimentum normally incorporates the jumbled remains of former prey. In webs belonging to females it will also contain a few brownish egg sacs. A gap, exactly fitting the spider's body, is left in the middle of the stabilimentum. It is here that the spider sits—looking like just another piece of unpalatable rubbish. In a spiral stabilimentum the garbage dump lies at the center, where the spider lurks among its collection of former victims. Some species decorate the web with bits of dead leaf to make it even more confusing for an enemy.

In the *Arachnura* scorpion orb weavers the spider itself resembles a dead leaf and sits underneath a string of debris forming a vertical line down the middle of the web. The large, squat, lumpy bodies of the *Caerostris* bark spiders are remarkably similar to a bump on tree bark or a fallen dead leaf, depending on where the spider is sitting. *Carepalxis* species from Australia are expert at mimicking gum-nuts, the seed pods of *Eucalyptus* trees. A dark round patch positioned on top of the abdomen resembles the hole in the top of the nut.

Unusual Habits

Australia is rich in spiders with unusual habits, and none more so than the death's head spider, *Celaenia kinbergi*. As night falls, the dumpy-looking spider lures certain male moths to their death by giving off a pheromone that copies the scents released by the female moths. The deluded males flutter around the spider and are simply grabbed out of the air by its powerful front legs and eaten. The practice seems to be the ultimate simplification of the slightly more complicated methods used by *Mastophora* and other so-called bolas spiders. They attract male moths in the same way, but hook them out of the air, glued to the sticky blob of silk that is used to weight the end of the "fishing line." The spider swings the line around and around, and aims it with considerable accuracy at a passing moth before reeling it in to be eaten.

Spiny Spiders

The most bizarre araneids are the grotesque and short-legged *Gasteracantha* kite or spiny spiders and *Micrathena* thorn spiders. They are most common in the tropics, but are also found in the United States. Thorn spiders are restricted to the Americas, mostly in the tropics, but the arrow-shaped thorn spider, *Micrathena sagittata*, with its two stout red-tipped spines jutting upward from the apex of the abdomen, is common over most of the United States.

Kite spiders are found throughout the warmer parts of the world, but with few species in the Americas. Their webs, which are large in relation to the size of the spider, are often adorned near the center with a few tufts of fluffy white silk. They are frequently placed higher in trees than is typical for araneids. The spiders themselves often have a highly eccentric appearance, with long horns curving upward from the "shoulders" of the abdomen. In the bull's horn spider, *Gasteracantha arcuata* from Southeast Asia, the horns can be several times as long as the body. As in other kite spiders, there is also a set of shorter but much sharper spines along the rear of the abdomen. In most species the width of this is greater than its length, and the spines are hard and glossy.

Micrathena and *Gasteracantha* are among the most brightly colored araneids, often red and yellow or red and white. The classic warning colors seem to work in a conventional way to advertise the nasty taste of most of the spiders to potential predators. By contrast, some species are masters of disguise. The dainty thorn spider, *Micrathena gracilis* from the United States, resembles a speck of dead leaf.

The web of orb spiders has a dual function. It increases the effective hunting range of a static spider and slows down prey so that the spider has enough time to rush out and administer a bite before it escapes. The araneid orb web serves both purposes admirably. Its large size and sticky spiral threads, often allied to considerable strength, make it difficult even for large insects to escape before the spider has arrived. In the web's construction there is

⬆ *Although many species of kite spiders are furnished with abdominal thorns or horns, they are largest in the bull's horn spider, Gasteracantha arcuata from Asia.*

always a trade-off between strength and invisibility to prey. Thicker silk makes the web more conspicuous to insects. Some species have added modifications to the basic design of the orb web. In *Scoloderus cordatus* from Florida an enormous ladderlike section of mesh has been added above the orb, designed to knock the wings off moths as they flutter downward through the silk.

Diminishing Orbs

Despite the architectural perfection of the complete orb, some species only produce a part orb or have abandoned the orb web

altogether. In *Zygiella*—the missing-sector orb weavers—a few of the spirals have been made redundant, leaving a "v"-shaped gap bisected by a "signal" thread. In *Wixia ectypa* from the United States the beautiful orb is reduced further to just seven to eight radial spokes with a hub of untidy silk at the center. Any reduction in size without sacrificing capture rates must benefit the spider because, while it can recycle its web by eating the silk, feeding on the remains is impossible when a bird or mammal has blundered through it. Destruction of the web is a common disaster with the larger orbs; the less silk employed, the smaller the loss.

Once the struggles of a trapped insect have been detected by the waiting spider, it can react in one of two ways. In more "advanced" spiders, such as *Argiope*, the spider plays safe, throwing large amounts of silk onto the victim from a distance to bind it temporarily to the web. With its resistance subdued, the insect is rotated like a bobbin in the spider's back legs

The Only Aquatic Spider

The European water spider (*Argyroneta aquatica*) is the only spider that lives more or less permanently under water. It is the only member of the family Argyronetidae. Water spiders prey on a range of aquatic invertebrates, small fish, and tadpoles. They build a dome-shaped diving bell out of silk that they fill with air carried down from the surface. Spiders sit inside the bell with their legs hanging down into the water to sense passing prey. When submerged, they have a silvery appearance due to the air trapped on their hairy body surface.

⊕ *The water spider,* Argyroneta aquatica, *drags a minnow into its diving bell. The scientific name* Argyroneta *means "with a silvery net." The silvery net is the air bubble that enables the spider to breathe under the water.*

and completely swathed in silk. The spider then edges forward and administers the first bite to the unrecognizable blob that was an insect a few moments earlier. Smaller prey will be cut free from the web and carried back to the spider's retreat, while larger items are consumed where they lie. In less advanced species, such as thorn spiders, the initial tactics are reversed. Regardless of the type of prey, the spider treats it immediately to a lengthy bite. Only when any resistance has begun to fade does the process of wrapping begin. It is used mainly as a method of packaging rather than restraint.

For the *Arcys* triangle spiders from Australia the risk of losing a web is not a problem, since they do not make one. The brightly colored (generally red) spiders with their shiny and flattened triangular bodies wait in ambush on leaves, as in many crab spiders (Thomisidae). Also like crab spiders, the front legs are held out to the sides, and their inner edges are well armed with prey-retarding spines.

In all araneids the males are smaller than the females, but the degree of difference varies enormously. In genera such as *Mastophora*, *Gasteracantha*, *Herennia*, and *Argiope* the males are midgets compared with their mates. They are usually differently colored as well, often looking like a separate species. *Argiope* males can be seen hanging around near a female in her web, where they are accepted as guests for long periods and largely ignored.

Courtship by the tiny males is simple or entirely absent. In some species a certain

amount of leg quivering by the male as he approaches is all that the female seems to require. It is enough to make her angle her body sharply away from the web so that the male can slide onto her underside and insert his palps. In several species the male walks over the female, laying down a thin trail of silk across her body. This activity seems to stimulate her into arching her body outward for the male to creep in beneath.

Whatever the preliminaries to the act of copulation, the sequel in *Argiope* is often the same. While the male is busy inserting a palp, the female begins to wrap him in silk. If he is quick, he can break free and live to mate another day, perhaps after losing a leg or two.

In the ornate orb weaver, *Herennia ornatissima* from Asia, the tiny males have no such security problems during their contact with the much larger females. However, they still only ever manage to mate once because in this species the male's palps become mutilated as they are extracted from the female's body. With no further need for the now useless organs, the male simply bites them off. He then devotes the rest of his life to being a chaperone, sitting close by the female or even directly on her back, where he can prevent any rival males from gaining access to her for mating.

Sexual Sparring

In *Araneus* and its close relatives the males are only about 50 percent smaller than the females and often set up home with an immature female in her lair for a while. When she makes her last molt and becomes sexually receptive, her lodger can mate without too much trouble. That is the normal custom in the bank orb weaver, *Larinioides cornutus*, a common species in both Europe and North America. As in many araneids, the male conducts a vibratory courtship within the female's web designed to lure her onto a special mating thread that he has attached to her silken lines. Some fairly vigorous sparring seems to be part of the ritual in the species, but soon afterward the female seems ready to mate.

Later in the breeding season males of *Araneus* and related spiders usually face an uncompromisingly hostile reception from females who mated long ago and need peace and quiet to feed and lay their eggs. It is now that the males need pluck and doggedness. It is common to see a male *Araneus diadematus* driven back by the female's vicious lunges, only to find him climbing back into her web to try again.

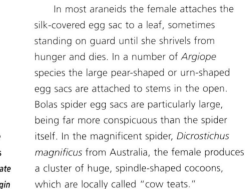

⊙ In many araneids the female attaches her egg sac to a leaf and then stands guard over it until she dies. This is the spiny flag spider, Alpaida cornuta, *from Costa Rica.*

⊙ While males of the garden spider, Araneus diadematus, *usually mate with newly molted virgin females, they will later engage in the risky courtship of a mated female (on right).*

In most araneids the female attaches the silk-covered egg sac to a leaf, sometimes standing on guard until she shrivels from hunger and dies. In a number of *Argiope* species the large pear-shaped or urn-shaped egg sacs are attached to stems in the open. Bolas spider egg sacs are particularly large, being far more conspicuous than the spider itself. In the magnificent spider, *Dicrostichus magnificus* from Australia, the female produces a cluster of huge, spindle-shaped cocoons, which are locally called "cow teats."

Golden Orb Weavers

Golden orb weavers of the family Nephilidae are the largest of all orb weavers. They are sometimes known as banana spiders because of the shape of the body, especially *Nephila clavipes*, the sole species found in the Americas. In the largest species, the Asian giant wood spider, *Nephila maculata*, the female's body can reach a length of 1.8 inches (4.5 cm), with a leg span of some 6 inches (15 cm). This species probably builds the biggest web of any spider, and the strong golden silk often spans forest streams. Most *Nephila* webs are occupied by squatters—*Argyrodes* dewdrop spiders. At first glance the lodgers look much like the *Nephila* males, which are minute brown pygmies only some 0.2 inches (5 mm) long. Several of these dwarf males may live temporarily in a female's web. They are so tiny that the females usually ignore them. In several species the male covers the female with a thin veil of silk before trying to insert his palps.

Glossary

Words in SMALL CAPITALS refer to other entries in the glossary.

Abdomen region of an INSECT'S body behind the THORAX, one of three body divisions consisting of up to 10 SEGMENTS in INSECTS

Antenna (pl. antennae) feelerlike sensory APPENDAGES mounted on the head

Anther the "male" pollen-bearing part of a flower

Appendage any limb or articulated outgrowth of the body such as ANTENNAE or wings

Aquatic living in water

Arachnid member of the CLASS Arachnida, including mites, spiders, and scorpions

Arthropod a "jointed-limbed" INVERTEBRATE with a hardened CUTICLE (EXOSKELETON): includes INSECTS, spiders, crustaceans

Bacterium (pl. bacteria) microscopic single-celled organisms with no nucleus in the cell

Biological control the use of natural PREDATORS, PARASITES, or disease organisms to reduce the numbers of a pest plant or animal

Book lungs in ARACHNIDS an air-filled space within the ABDOMEN containing blood-filled leaves stacked up like a book

Brood cell a specially prepared space or structure in the nests of some INSECTS in which food is stored, an egg is laid, and the LARVA completes its development

Camouflage pattern of colors designed to blend in with the background

Carnivore animal that eats meat

Carrion dead animal matter used as a food source by SCAVENGERS

Cephalothorax combined head and THORAX making up the front half of a spider's body

Cerci a pair of simple or SEGMENTED APPENDAGES at the rear end of the ABDOMEN, usually acting as sensory organs

Chafer a scarab beetle that feeds on leaves or flowers

Chitin protein that forms an important component of many INVERTEBRATE bodies, e.g., the INSECT EXOSKELETON

CITES an international conservation organization: Convention on International Trade in Endangered Species

Class biological grouping containing a number of related ORDERS

Cocoon silken case constructed by the LARVA in which the PUPA is formed

Commensal living in close association with another animal, not strictly parasitic, but may be damaging or disadvantageous to HOST in other ways. See PARASITE

Compound eye the eye typical of adult INSECTS, composed of numerous individual units (OMMATIDIA) that are marked on the surface by FACETS

Copulation the act of mating

Corbicula the pollen basket on the rear legs of some bees

Courtship preliminary activities that take place prior to mating and promote the coming together and correct identification of the two sexes

Cryptic coloration where the colors of an INSECT help it blend into its background; also referred to as CAMOUFLAGE coloration

Cuticle the external layer formed of CHITIN, which acts as an EXOSKELETON in INSECTS

Detritus an accumulation of tiny particles of dead or decomposing mateial

Dichromatism males and females have different colors and/or markings

Diurnal active during the hours of daylight

Elytron (pl. elytra) in most beetles the thickened leathery, often hard, front wing

Enzyme a chemical that acts as a catalyst in processes such as digestion

Epigyne specialized reproductive opening in most female spiders

Exoskeleton the tough outer covering of an INSECT'S body that forms its skeleton

External digestion digestion by REGURGITATING digestive fluids on to the food and sucking up the dissolved result

Facet the external surface of the individual unit (OMMATIDIUM) of a COMPOUND EYE

Family a biological grouping of genera (pl. of GENUS) more closely related to one another than any other grouping of genera and always ending in -idae, e.g., the mosquitoes belong to the family Culicidae

Femur the third SEGMENT of an INSECT'S leg

Fungus (pl. fungi) plantlike organisms that include yeasts and mushrooms. Many SPECIES are involved in the decay of wood

Gall an abnormal growth produced by a plant in response to the presence of an organism such as an INSECT egg. The gall increases in size as the INSECT LARVA inside feed on special "grazing" tissue lining the larval chamber

Genus (pl. genera) a group of SPECIES all more closely related to one another than to any other group of SPECIES

Halteres the club-shaped pair of hind wings in flies

Haploid eggs unfertilized eggs that produce only males

Hemolymph the name given to the blood of INSECTS and ARACHNIDS

Holoptic eyes where the two eyes meet along the top of the head and almost touch; most common in male flies of certain FAMILIES

Honeydew the sweet waste liquid produced by aphids and other plant bugs

Host the animal or plant with or on which another animal or plant lives and/or feeds. See PARASITE

Incomplete metamorphosis process of development in more primitive INSECTS that lack a PUPAL stage. The LARVA that develops from the egg resembles a miniature adult, and its wings develop externally

Insect a small INVERTEBRATE animal in the CLASS Insecta whose body is SEGMENTED (not always obviously so) and has a well-defined head, THORAX, and ABDOMEN, 3 pairs of legs, and usually 1 or 2 pairs of wings

Insemination internal fertilization of a female animal with sperm from a male

Instar the stage between molts of an INSECT. See MOLTING

Invertebrate animal lacking a backbone, as in worms, snails, INSECTS, etc.

IUCN International Union for the Conservation of Nature, responsible for assigning animals and plants to internationally agreed categories of rarity. See table on page 283

Johnston's organ a type of "ear" found near the base of the ANTENNA of certain INSECTS

Kleptoparasitism feeding from the food collected or caught by other species

Landmark a place or object at or around which INSECTS meet for the purpose of mating

Larva juvenile stage between egg and adult

Leaf miner a LARVA that burrows into a leaf and then eats the leaf cells

Lek a grouping of males trying to attract females for mating

Luminescent producing light

Mandibles the first pair of mouthparts situated on the head

Mate guarding a male keeping company with a female to prevent other males from mating with her

Maxillae the mouthparts immediately behind the MANDIBLES

Metamorphosis process of change by which one form develops into another—usually juvenile into adult

Metanotal gland a male structure that produces SECRETIONS attractive to female INSECTS

Microorganism single-celled organisms that can only be seen using a microscope

Mold the presence of a FUNGUS colony growing on the surface of another living organism

Molting shedding of the exterior skeleton, or EXOSKELETON (verb molt)

Nectar sugary secretion of flowers eaten by many adult INSECTS and converted into honey by some bees

Nocturnal active during the hours of darkness

Nymph a term for the LARVA of an INSECT whose wings develop externally, i.e., with INCOMPLETE METAMORPHOSIS

Ocellus (pl. ocelli) simple eye of an INSECT consisting externally of a single FACET

Ommatidium (pl. ommatidia) the long, cylindrical single unit of a COMPOUND EYE that acts as a light receptor

Opisthosoma ABDOMEN of ARACHNIDS

Order a biological grouping of FAMILIES more closely related to one another than to any other grouping of FAMILIES

Ovipositor the structure on female INSECTS through which eggs are laid (verb oviposit)

Oxidation a chemical reaction during which oxygen is used up

Palp SEGMENTED, fingerlike structure forming the mouthparts in INSECTS, used for touch or taste

Parasite organism that lives in or on the body of another (called the HOST) and feeds on it for at least part of its life cycle

Parthenogenesis production of young by a female without having first mated with a male

Patrolling mate location strategy in which males spend most of their time moving around in a constant search for females

Pectinate shaped like a comb, as in the ANTENNAE of some beetles and moths

Pheromone a chemical scent often used to attract or repel members of the opposite sex

Photosynthesis the formation of sugars and oxygen by green parts of plants when sunlight falls on them

Phylum a major group used in the classification of animals, consisting of one or more CLASSES

Planidium a LARVA, usually a PARASITE; after hatching from the egg, it actively searches for a HOST INSECT

Pollination transferring pollen from the ANTHERS to the STIGMA of a flower (usually from one flower to another, often on different plants) to effect fertilization

Polymorphism the existence, apart from the two sexes, of two or more distinctly different forms of the same SPECIES

Predator an animal that kills other animals for food

Proboscis tubelike feeding apparatus, common in INSECTS

Pronotum a protective shield covering the THORAX of an INSECT

Ptilinum balloonlike structure on the head of some flies that pumps up with blood and helps them force their way out of the pupal case. See PUPA

Pulvillus (pl. pulvilli) a pad on a fly's foot that helps it climb on smooth surfaces

Pupa (pl. pupae) the stage (usually static) that comes between the LARVA and the adult INSECT in those with complete METAMORPHOSIS

Puparium a covering that protects the PUPA beneath and is formed from the old LARVAL skin. It is present in some fly FAMILIES

Regurgitate to vomit up through the mouth

Rostrum the piercing mouthparts of a bug; it consists of an outer sheath with 2 pairs of sharp STYLETS inside

Saltatory made for jumping

Scavenger animal that feeds on dead material

Scutellum in bugs part of the PRONOTUM that extends backward over the ABDOMEN; it is normally shield shaped

Secretion a substance produced by a gland

Segment a section of a body part, such as the ABDOMEN, ANTENNA, or leg

Species a group of organisms that mate readily and produce healthy fertile offspring

Spermatophore a packet of sperm produced by male and delivered to female during courtship or mating

Spiracle an opening in the EXOSKELETON through which an INSECT breathes

Stabilimentum a dense ribbon of silk placed at certain positions in some spiders' webs

Stigma the "female" part of a flower that receives the pollen grains and on which they germinate

Stridulate to generate sound by rubbing one part of the body against another (noun stridulation)

Stylets sharp mouthparts modified for piercing skin or the surface of plants

Symbiont an organism that lives in close, mutually beneficial association with another, a process known as symbiosis (adj. symbiotic)

Tarsus (pl. tarsi) the series of small SEGMENTS making up the last and fifth region of the leg of INSECTS, the end bearing a pair of claws

Tegmen (pl. tegmina) the leathery forewings of the Orthoptera

Thorax the region of an INSECT's body behind the head and one of three bodily divisions. It bears the legs and the wings (where present)

Tibia (pl. tibiae) the fourth SEGMENT of an INSECT's leg, between the FEMUR and TARSUS

Tremulation vibrating or tapping the body against a surface to make a sound intended to attract members of the opposite sex

Trichobothria long fine hairs on spiders' legs used for detecting vibrations in the air

Warning colors bright, distinctive colors that warn an animal's enemies that it is not good to eat and should be left alone

IUCN CATEGORIES

EX **Extinct,** when there is no reasonable doubt that the last individual of the species has died.

EW **Extinct in the Wild,** when a species is known only to survive in captivity or as a naturalized population well outside the past range.

CR **Critically Endangered,** when a species is facing an extremely high risk of extinction in the wild in the immediate future.

EN **Endangered,** when a species is facing a very high risk of extinction in the wild in the near future.

VU **Vulnerable,** when a species is facing a high risk of extinction in the wild in the medium-term future.

LR **Lower Risk,** when a species has been evaluated and does not satisfy the criteria for CR, EN, or VU.

DD **Data Deficient,** when there is not enough information about a species to assess the risk of extinction.

NE **Not Evaluated,** species that have not been assessed by the IUCN criteria.

Further Reading

d'Abrera, B., *The Concise Atlas of Butterflies of the World*. London: Hill House Publishers, 2001.

Arnett, R. R. Jr., and Jacques, R. I. Jr., *Guide to Insects*. New York: Simon & Schuster, 1981.

Brooks, S., *Dragonflies* (Natural World Series). Washington, DC: Smithsonian Institution Press, 2003.

Dolling, W. R., *The Hemiptera*. Oxford: Oxford University Press, 1991.

Feltwell, J., *The Encyclopedia of Butterflies*. Poole, U.K: Blandford Press, 1993.

Foelix R. F., *Biology of Spiders*. Cambridge, MA: Harvard University Press, 1982.

Gauld, I., and Bolton, B. (eds.), *The Hymenoptera*. New York: Oxford University Press, 1988.

Gertsch, W. J., *American Spiders*. New York: van Nostrand Reinhold, 1979.

Gordon, D. G., *The Compleat Cockroach: A Comprehensive Guide to the Most Despised (And Least Understood) Creature on Earth*. Berkeley, CA: Ten Speed Press, 1996.

McGavin, G. C., *Bugs of the World*. New York: Facts On File Publications, 1993.

Michener, C. D., *The Bees of the World*. Baltimore, MD: Johns Hopkins University Press, 2000.

Milne, L., and Milne, M., *National Audubon Society Field Guide to North American Insects and Spiders*. New York: Alfred A. Knopf, 1998.

O'Toole, C. (ed), *The Encyclopedia of Insects*. Toronto: Firefly Books, 2002.

Preston-Mafham, K., *Grasshoppers and Mantids of the World*. London: Blandford Press, 1990.

Preston-Mafham, K., and Preston-Mafham, R., *The Natural History of Spiders*. London: Crowood Press,1996.

Pyle, R. M., *National Audubon Society Field Guide to North American Butterflies*. New York: Alfred A. Knopf, 1981.

Skinner, G. J., and Allen, G. W., *Ants* (Naturalists' Handbooks). Slough, U.K.: Richmond Publishing, 1996.

Spielman, A., and D'Antonio M., *Mosquito: A Natural History of Our Most Persistent and Deadly Foe*. New York: Hyperion, 2001.

White, R. E., *Peterson Field Guide to Beetles*. Boston, MA: Houghton Mifflin, 1983.

Winston, M. L., *The Biology of the Honeybee*. Cambridge, MA: Harvard University Press, 1987.

Useful Websites

http://animaldiversity.ummz.umich.edu/
University of Michigan Museum of Zoology animal diversity websites. Search for pictures and information about animals by class, family, and common name. Includes glossary

http://www.cedarcreek.umn.edu/insects/index.html
Cedar Creek Natural History Area of University of Minnesota has quite a lot of information about North American insects

http://www.earthlife.net/insects/
Provides a great deal of information on many insect groups

http://www.tolweb.org/tree
The Tree of Life is a collaborative web project produced by biologists from around the world. On more than 2,600 World Wide Web pages the Tree of Life provides information about the diversity of organisms on earth, their history, and characteristics. Each page contains information about one group of organisms

http://www.wcs.org
Website of the Wildlife Conservation Society

http://entomology.si.edu/
International Heteropterists' Society, for serious enthusiasts

http://www.coleoptera.org
Coleoptera website. For entomologists who work on beetles and others who are interested in insects

http://www.arachnology.org
The International Society of Arachnology home page leads to information on all sorts of arachnids, with links to other pages

http://www.nicksspiders.com/nicksspiders/namain.htm
Nick's Spiders, with lots of photographs, contains information on North American spiders

Index

Bold common names, e.g., **ants** indicate illustrated main entry. Bold page numbers, e.g., **200–217**, indicate the location of an illustrated main entry. Page numbers in parentheses, e.g., (34), indicate At-a-Glance boxes. Page numbers in italics, e.g., *16*, indicate illustrations of animals or topics not the subject of a main entry.

A

Acanthaspis 100
Acanthoclonia paradoxa 12
Acanthops falcataria 49
Acari **254–257**
Acrididae **60–67**
Acrophylla titan 26, 29
Adalia
    2-punctata 132–133,
    134–135
    10-punctata 132–133
Aeshna
    cyanea 16, *17, 22*
    juncea 25
Agathemera 30–31
Agelena labyrinthica 272,
    274, 275
Agelenidae **272–275**
Agelenopsis aperta 272
Aglais urticae 178–179
alates 204
Alloeostylus diaphanus 87
Alpaida cornuta 281
Amauris ochlea 183
Amblyomma 255
Amitermes meridionalis (34)
Amyciaea lineatipes 267
Anaea fabius 175
Aname grandis 262–263
Anartia amathea 180
Anisomorpha buprestoides
    26–27, 31
Anisoptera 16
Anisozygoptera 16
Anopheles (71)
Anthia hexasticta 124–125
Anthocoridae (99)
Anthonomus grandis (160)
anthrax 89
Anthribidae 154
ants 200–217
    alates 204
    army 214–215
    bullet *201*, 216–217
    cow-killer velvet 218–219
    Cremastocheilus beetles
        inhabiting ants' nests
        (150)
    defense, chemical 202
    driver 205
    green tree *208–209*
    harvester 212
    honeydew supplies (206)
    honeypot 212
    jet-black *207*
    leaf-cutting *204*, 210–211
    nests 204–207, 211–212
    plants and (206)
    red *209*
    scent trails (205)
    slave-making 209–210
    sociability 200
    tandem running (205)

ants (continued)
    termite-slaying 203
    velvet 218–219
    weaver 200–201,
        202–203, 212–213
    western harvester *212*
    white *see* termites
Apaturinae 176
Aphididae **116–121**
aphids 116–121, 135, *209*
    bean *118*
    cabbage *121*
    defense 119, 121
    feeding 116–117,
        118–119
    life cycle 117–118
    peach-potato *116*
    rose-root *119*
Aphis fabae 118
    breeding 117–118
Aphonopelma seemannii
    260–261
Apidae **236–247**
Apiomeris flaviventris 102
Apis
    mellifera 236, 246
    mellifera scutellata
        (245)
Apoderus coryli 159
apollos (swallowtail
    butterflies) **162–167**
Aptera fusca 40
Apterygota 8
arachnids 248–249
    anatomy 248–249
Araneidae **276–281**
Araneus diadematus
    280–281
Archeognatha 16
Arctia caja 190, *192*
Arctiidae **190–193**
Argiope
    argentata 276–277
    bruennichi 276
Argyroneta aquatica (280)
Arilus 104–105
Atrax robustus 262
Atta
    bisphaerica 211
    cephalotes 204, 210–211
Attelabus nitens 159
Atteva punctella 198

B

Baccha obscuripennis 79
backswimmers 90–93
Baroniinae 162–163
Battus philenor 164,
    166–167
bedbugs 98–99
bees
    and flowers (239)
    honeybees and
        relatives 236–247
    orchid 236–237
    stingless 236, 242–243
beetles
    bee 150–151
    betsy (bessbugs) (138)
    bombardier (124)
    chafer *see* chafers
    checkered 130–131
    diving 126–127
    dung 140–141, (142),
        145

beetles (continued)
    elephant 151, *152–153*
    European bee-wolf
        130–131
    fireflies 128–129
    flower 149–151
    Goliath 149–150, *151*
    ground 122–125
    Hercules *140*, 151
    hide (145)
    ladybug 120, **132–137**
    Neptune *150–151*
    patent-leather (bessbugs)
        (139)
    rhinoceros 151
    scarab 140–153
    stag 138–139
    Vedalia (134)
    water (diving) *126–127*
    see also weevils
bessbugs (139)
biological control *see* pest
    control
birdwings (swallowtail
    butterflies) **162–167**
    Queen Alexandra's *162*
Blattodea 8, **38–43**
Bombus
    hortorum 240–241
    lucorum 241
    pascuorum 239
    pratorum 240
    terrestris 238–239
Brachinus (124)
Brachycaudus cardui
    116–117
Brachyomus
    octotuberculatus 156
Brachypelma smithi 260
Brachytrupes orientalis 59
Brevicoryne brassicae 121
bubonic plague (55)
bugs
    assassin 100–105, *219*
    backswimmers
        90–93
    bedbugs 98–99
    burrower (112)
    capsid (plant) 94–97
    cone-nose *103*
    flower (99)
    giant shield (110)
    green capsid *94–95*
    leaf (plant) 94–97
    lightning (fireflies)
        128–129
    litter *42*
    Mexican bed *103*
    minute pirate (99)
    plant 94–97
    plataspid stink (109)
    red (chiggers) (256)
    shield (stink) **106–115**
    spider (97)
    stink 106–115
    wheel 104–105
    woundwort stink *113*
bumblebees (honeybees)
    236, 237–242
    buff-tailed 238–239
    carder *239*
    garden 240–241
    white-tailed *257*
butterflies
    African monarch *184*
    alfalfa 168

butterflies (continued)
    American monarch *182,*
        185
    Arachne checkerspots
        180–181
    artemesia swallowtail
        162–163
    brimstone 168–169
    brush-footed 174–181
    buckeye 176
    coolie 180
    green-lined charaxes
        174–175
    milkweed 182–185
    monarch (American) *184,*
        185
    painted lady *174–175*
    pipevine swallowtail
        166–167
    puddling *162–163*
    red admiral *174*
    silver emperor *177*
    swallowtail 162–167
    tiger swallowtail *167*
    whites *see* whites

C

Caerostris mitralis 278
Calopteryx splendens 19
Calosoma
    scrutator 123
    sycophanta 122
Calyptocephalus gratiosus
    129
Camponotus detritus
    202–203
Canthesancus gulo 100
Carabidae **122–125**
Catacanthus anchorago 106
caterpillars
    butterfly 208–209
    cinnabar moth *192–193*
    cloudless sulfur *170–171*
    danaid 182–183
    European puss moth *188*
    Euthalia 178
    gypsy moth (197)
    Lirimiris 188
    Naprepa 188
    notodontids 187–189
    orchard swallowtail
        164–165
    pipevine swallowtail *164*
    Prepona antimache 176
    red dagger wing *178–179*
    small tortoiseshell
        178–179
    swallowtail (165), *166*
    western tussock moth
        196
    yponomeutid
        198–199
Celaenia kinbergi (278)
Centruroides gracilis
    252–253
Ceramius tuberculifer 229
Ceratocoris cephalicus 109
Cerura vinula 188
chafers 146, *149*
    flower *149*
    pine *146*
Charaxes
    candiope 174–175
    subornatus 176
    rajahs 175–176

Chelorrhina polyphemus
    148–149
Chilocoris
    renipustlatus 136
cholera 89
Chorthippus brunneus
    60–61
Chrysops caecutiens 74, 76
Cicindela
Cimex lectularius 98, *98–99*
Cimicidae **98–99**
Circia 27
clegs (horseflies) **74–77**
Cleridae **130–131**
Cobanilla 194–195
Coccinella
    7-punctata 132, *134;*
    9-notata 132–133
Coccinellidae **132–137**
cockchafer, European *147*
cockroaches 38–43
    American *38, 39*
    giant burrowing 42
    lesser *39*
    reproduction 40–43
    wood *41*
Coenagrion puella 18–19,
    23
Coleoptera 8
Colias eurytheme 168
coloration, aposematic
    (warning) 13–14
Constrictotermes
    cyphergaster (34)
Cordulegaster boltonii 20
Corixidae (93)
Cotinus pyralis 128–129
cow killers 218
Cremastocheilus (150)
crickets 56–59
    ant-guest (59)
    black 56
    defense 59
    4-spotted tree *56–57*
    mating 56
    "singing" 56–57
Cryptocercidae 39–40
Ctenidae (263)
Ctenocephalides
    canis 52
    felis 52, *54–55*
Culicidae **68–71**
Culiseta annulata 68, 69, *71*
Curculio venosus 154
Curculionidae **154–161**
Cuterebra 85
Cyclommatus tarandus
    138–139
Cyclosa insulana 276–277
Cydnidae (112)
Cynipidae **220–221**
cytology (33)

D

Dactylotum 60–61
Damon variegatus 249
damselflies 16–25
    azure 18–19, *23*
    demoiselle 19
    reproduction 19–25
Danaidae **182–185**
Danaus
    chrysippus 166, 184
    plexippus 182, 184,
        185

Dasymutilla 218
  occidentalis 218–219
Deinopidae **264–265**
Deinopis 264–265, 265
  guatemalensis 264
Delias nigrina 169
Deraeocoris ruber 94, 96–97
Dermacentor 256
Dermaptera 8
Dermatophagoides 254–255
Dermolepida albohirtum 149
Diachlorus ferrugatus 77
diarrhea
  infantile 89
dichromatism, sexual 60
digestion, external 249
Dipluridae **262–263**
Diptera 8
diseases, from ticks and
  mites (256)
Dismorphia amphione 14
Dolichoderus 204
Dolichovespula media
  226–227
Dorylus nigricans 205
Doxocopa laure 177
dragonflies 16–25
  eastern amberwing *21*
  flame skimmer *16–17*
  4-spotted skimmer *24–25*
  golden-ringed *20*
  reproduction 19–25
  ruddy darter *20*
  southern hawker *16, 17,*
   22
Dynastes hercules 140
dysentery, bacterial 89
Dytiscidae **126–127**
Dytiscus marginalis 126,
  126–127, 127

E

Ectobius panzeri 39
Ectomocoris 219, (218)
Edessa rufomarginata
  106–107
Embioptera 8
Entimus granulatus 155
Ephemeroptera 8,
Eristalis
  nemorum 80
  tenax 78, 80
Euglossa 103
Eulyes amaena 101
Eumenes fenestralis 224
Eurota sericaria 192
Eurytides agesilaus 164
Euscyrtus bivittatus 58
Eustenogaster calyptodoma
  227
Euthalia 178
Extatosoma tiaratum 31
external digestion 249
eye diseases 89
Eysarcoris fabricii 113

F

false heads 188
filariasis (71)
fireflies 128–129
  eastern *128–129*
fleas 52–55
  cat 52, *54–55*
  and disease (55)

fleas (continued)
  dog 52
  human 53
  jumping ability (53)
  rabbit *52–53*, 54–55, (55)
  rat 55
flies
  black horsefly *76*
  "blinder" deerfly 77
  bot 84–85
  bulb 79, 80
  dark giant horsefly (eggs)
   76
  deerflies 74–77
  downlooker snipefly *75*
  drone *78*, 80
  elephant (horseflies)
   74–77
  face (houseflies) **86–89**
  flower (hover) **78–83**
  green colonel *73*
  horn (houseflies) **86–89**
  horseflies 74–77
  houseflies and relatives
   86–89
  hover 78–83
  long-horned general *72*
  noonday *86–87*
  nostril (bot) **84–85**
  snipe (75)
  soldier 72–73
  stable (houseflies) **86–89**
  3-spot horsefly *74*
  tsetse (89)
  warble 84–85
flight, insects (14)
Formica rufa 209
Formicidae **200–217**
Furcula bifida 186

G

Gasteracantha arcuata 279
gladiators (49)
Glossina mortisans 89
gnats 68–71
Gnophaela vermiculata 191
Goliathus druryi 151
Gonepteryx rhamni 168–169
Graphium antiphates
  162–163
grasshoppers 60–67
  bladder 65–66
  eastern lubber *64–65*, 65
  elegant *63*
  feeding 63
  gaudy 66
  gold-horned lubber *64*
  lubber 64–65
  mating 63–64
  painted *60–61*
  short-horned 60
  "singing" 63–64
  toad 65
Gryllidae **56–59**
Gryllus bimaculatus 56
Gymnopleurus aenescens
  144

H

hepatitis B virus 99
Hexodon latissimum
  140–141
Hippodamia convergens
  136–137

Hiranetis braconiformis
  102–103
Homalopteryx laminata 38
honeybees and
  relatives 236–247
  honeybee dance (247)
  nests 244–245
honeydew (208)
hornets, giant 223
Hospitalotermes 36–37
Hypoderma
  bovis 84
  lineatum 84–85
Hystrichopsylla schefferi 53

I

Icerya purchasi (134)
infant deaths
  gaudy grasshoppers and
   66
  houseflies and 89
Insecta 8
insects 8–15
  body plan 9–10
  development stages 9
  flight (14)
  gender differences 12
  metamorphosis 8–9
  mimicry in 13–14
  protective resemblance 13
Isoptera 8, **32–37**
Ixodes hexagonus 254

J

Jezebels (whites) **168–173**
Junonia coenia 177

K

kleptoparasitism 85

L

lady beetles (ladybugs)
  132–137
ladybirds (ladybugs)
  132–137
ladybugs 132–137
  convergent *136–137*
  7-spot *132*
Lamarckiana 65
Lampyridae **128–129**
Lampyris noctiluca 128
Lasius fuliginosus 207
leaf insects 26–31
Lepidoptera 8, *8–9*
Libellula
  quadrimaculata 24–25
  saturata 16–17
Libyaspis coccinelloides 109
lice 50–51
  body (51)
  crab 50–51
  dog 50
  head 50
  on humans (51)
Lirimiris 188
locusts 60, (62)
louse *see* lice
Lucanidae **138–139**
Lucanus cervus 12, 138
luminous insects 128–129
Lygocoris pabulinus 94–95
Lygus rugulipennis 94

Lymantria
  dispar (197)
  monacha 194
Lymantriidae **194–197**
Lyme disease (256)
Lyramorpha 110–111
Lyrognathus robustus 261

M

Macraspis lucida 144
Macropanesthia rhinoceros
  42
Macrosiphum cholodkovskyi
  119
Macrotermes 37
Maculolachnus submacula
  119
malaxation 230
Manomera tenuescens
  26–27
mantids 44–49
mantis, praying (mantids)
  44–49
Mantis religiosa 44
Mantodea 8, **44–49**
Mantophasmatodea (49)
Marpesia petreus 178–179
Mecoptera 8
Mecopus torquis 157
Megaloptera 8
Megasoma elephas 152–153
Meliponinae 242
Melolontha melolontha 15,
  147
Mesembrina meridiana
  86–87
Messor 200
Metasyrphus luniger 82–83
methyl palmitate 227
Micrathena sagittata 279
Milesia crabroniformis 78
mimicry
  Batesian 14
  by bugs 95
  by butterflies 14,
   165–167, 180
  by cockroaches 38
  by flies 81–82
  in insects 13–15
  by mantids 49
  by moths 186–188
  Müllerian 14
Miridae **94–97**
Miris striatus 95
Mischocyttarus
  immarginatus 227
Misumena vatia 266,
  270–271
mites 254–257
  animal hosts 257
  diseases (256)
  house-dust 254–255,
   (256)
  scabies (256)
  size 256
  velvet *255*
mosquitoes 68–71
  blood feeding 70, (71)
  disease and (71)
  egg-laying 68–70
  feeding 68, 71
  ring-legged *68, 69, 71*
moths
  ailanthus webworm *198*
  angle-shades *12–13*

moths (continued)
  black arches 194
  ermine 198–199
  fairy 198–199, (199)
  garden tiger (great tiger)
   190, 192
  great tiger *190, 192*
  gypsy (197)
  poplar kitten *186*
  processionary (189)
  tiger 190–193
  tussock 194–197
  yucca (199)
  see also caterpillars
Musca domesticus 86, 88
Muscidae **86–89**
Mutillidae **218–219**
myxomatosis 52, (55)
Myzus persicae 116

N

nagana (89)
Naprepa 188
Nasutitermes 32
  corniger 36
  ephratae 35
Necrosia 12
Nematopogon
  swanmerdamella
  198–199
Neptunides polychromus
  150–151
Neuroptera 8
Neuroterus
  numismalis 221
  quercus-baccarum 220
Nisitrus 59
Noroma nigrolunata 195
Notodontidae **186–189**
Notonecta glauca 90,
  90–91, 91, 92
Notonectidae **90–93**
Nymphalidae **174–181**
Nymphalinae 176–179

O

Odonata 8, **16–25**
Odontomyia viridula 73
Odontotaenius disjunctus
  139
Odontotermes obesus
  32–33
Oecanthus quadripunctatus
  56–57
Oecophylla
  longinoda 40–41
  smaragdina 202,
   208–209, 212–213,
   214
Oedipoda miniata 60
Oestridae **84–85**
Oncomeris flavicornis 110
Oplomus dichrous 108
orange-tips (whites)
  168–173
Orgyia vetusta 196
Ornithoptera alexandrae
  162, *162*
Orthoptera 8
osmeterium *164–165*, (165),
  166
Otiorhynchus singularis 160
ovoviviparity 125
Oxythyrea funesta 149

P

Pachycondyla commutata 203
Pandinus imperator 250
Papilio 9
 aegeus 164
 glaucus 167
 machaon 162–163
Papilionidae **162–167**
Papilioninae 163–166
Parabuthus 18–19
 capensis 250–251
Paraponera clavata 201, 216–217
Parasitellus fucorum 257
Parasphendale agrionina 45
Parcoblatta 41
Parnasiinae 164
parthenogenesis
 in beetles 157
 in bugs 117
 in walkingsticks 29
 in scorpions 253
Passalidae (139)
Pediculus
 humanus (51)
 humanus capitis 51
Pentatomidae **106–115**
Periplaneta americana 38, 39
Perithemis tenera 21
Peromatus 106–107, 114–115
pest control (biological control)
 by ants 219
 by bugs 108–110
 by ladybugs (134)
 by weevils 160
Phalera sundana 187
phasma, great brown 26
Phasmatodea 8, **26–31**
Phelypera distigma 158–159
pheromones 11–12, 203, (205), (225), 229, 233, 235, 245–246
Philipomyia 74–75
Phlogophora meticulosa 12–13
Phoebis sennae 170–171
phoresy 257
Phrynarachne tuberosa 268
Phthiraptera 8, **50–51**
Phthirus pubis 50–51
Phyllium 28–29
Phymateus 66–67
Phytonomus nigrirostris 154
Pieridae **168–173**
Pieris
 brassicae 170–171
 rapae (170)
Pisilus tipuliformis 104
plague, bubonic (55)
plain tiger 184–185
plants
 and ants (206)
Plataspidae (109)
Plebeia 242
Plecoptera 8
Pogonomyrmex occidentalis 212
Poladrys minuta 180–181
Polistes
 cinerascens 233
 fastidiosus 228–229

Polistes (continued)
 instabilis 222–223, 230–231
Polybia occidentalis 226–227
polymorphism 13
polyphenism 13
Polyphylla fullo 146
Polyspilota aeruginosa 47, 46–47
praying mantis **44–49**
Prepona antimache 176
prominents 186–189
 coxcomb 186–187
 defense 188–189
provisioning
 mass 226
 progressive 226
Pseudocreobotra ocellata 48–49
Pseudomops 40–41
Pseudomyrmex ferruginea 206
Psocoptera 8
Pterostichus madidus 123
Pterygota 8
Ptilodon capucina 186–187
puddling 162–163
Pulex irritans 53

R

Ranzovius (97)
 contubernalis (97)
Raphidioptera 8
Reduviidae **100–105**
reflex bleeding 136
Rhagionidae (75)
Rhagio scolopaceus 75
Rhicnogryllus lepidus 57
Rhigus horridus 160–161
Rhinastus latesternus 154–155
Rhingia campestris 78–79, 80
Rhinocoris tristis 104
Rhodagastria 191
Rocky Mountain spotted fever 256 (256)
Rodalia cardinalis (134)
Romalea microptera 64
Rosema 186

S

Scarabaeidae **140–153**
Scorpiones **250–253**
scorpions **250–253**
 African emperor 250
 anatomy 250–251
 body 251
 Florida bark 252–253
 mating 252–253
 stings (252)
 tailless whip 249
 wind (sun spiders) **258–259**
scrub typhus (256)
sedge darner 25
Sehirus bicolor 112–113
sexual dichromatism 60
Sibine see *Acharia*
Siphonaptera 8, **52–55**
sleeping sickness (89)
Solifugae **258–259**
Solpuga 258
Someticus bohemani 125

sperm competition 22
spiders
 aquatic (280)
 arrow-shaped thorn 279
 Asian bird-dropping 268
 banana (281)
 bark 278
 bird-eating (tarantulas) **260–261**
 bull's horn 279
 crab 266–271
 death's head (278)
 decoy 276–277
 European water (280)
 flower 269–270, *270–271*
 funnel-web 262–263
 garden 280–281
 gladiator (net-casting) **264–265**
 goldenrod 269–270
 grass (sheet-web weavers) **272–275**
 house 273
 net-casting 264–265
 ogre-faced (net-casting) **264–265**
 spiny 278–279
 spiny flag 281
 sun **258–259**
 trap-door (263)
 wasp 276
 wind (sun) **258–259**
 see also tarantulas; weavers
Spilopsyllus cuniculi 52–53
stabilimenta 277–278
Stagmatoptera septrionalis 46–47
Stelopolybia pallipes 232
stick insects (walkingsticks) **26–31**
 giant 29
 titan 26
Stratiomyidae **72–73**
Stratiomys
 longicornis 73
 potamida 72–73
Strepsiptera 8
sulfurs (whites) **168–173**
 mass migration 172
 orange 168
 ultraviolet markings 171
swordtails (swallowtail butterflies) **162–167**
 fivebar 162–163
Sympetrum sanguineum 20
Symphoromyia (75)
Syrphidae **78–83**

T

Tabanidae **74–77**
tabanids **74–77**
 blood feeding 77
 feeding 77
 larvae 77
 mating 74–76
Tabanus
 atratus 76
 sudeticus 76
 trimaculatus 74
Taeniopoda auricornis 64
tarantulas 260–261
 Mexican red-knee 260
Tegenaria duellica 273
termitaria (34)

termites 32–37, 200, 201
 colonies 33–35
 compass (34)
 defense (37)
 feeding 35–36
 fungus gardens (34), 35, 37
 nasute soldier 32
 nests (34)
 western subterranean 32–33
Tessaratomidae (110)
Thanasimus formicarius 130
Theraphosidae **260–261**
Thomisidae **266–271**
Thysanoptera 8
Thysanura 8
tick-bite fever (256)
ticks 254–257
 diseases (256)
 hard 255
 hedgehog 254
 wood 256
timemas 26, (29)
Toxorhynchites moctezuma 70
Trachelophorus giraffa 157
Triatoma sanguisuga 103
Triatominae (103)
Trichius fasciatus 150–151
Trichodectes canis 50
Trichodes
 apiarius 130–131
 ornatus bonnevillensis 131
Trichoptera 8
Trigona fulviventris 242–243
Troginae (145)
trophallaxis (202), 216, 230
trophic eggs 201–202
tumblebugs 140, 142
typhoid 89
Tyria jacobaeae 192–193

V

Vaejovis boreas 253
Vanessa
 atalanta 174
 cardui 174–175
Vespa crabro 223
Vespidae **222–235**
Vespula
 germanica 234–235
 vulgaris 68, 73
virgin birth *see* parthenogenesis
viviparity 99
Volucella bombylans 81

W

walkingsticks 26–31
 defense 30–31
 giant thorny 31
 Macleay's specter 31
 slender-bodied 26–27
 2-striped 26–27
wasps
 feeding (233)
 fig (221)
 gall 220–221
 German 234–235
 hornets 223
 mason 224
 mass provisioning 226

wasps (continued)
 nectar-gathering 229
 nest cooling (229)
 nest defense 235
 nests 226–229
 paper (social) **222–235**
 potter (social) 222, 224–226
 progressive provisioning 226
 social 222–235
 yellow jacket 226–227, 232–233
 water boatmen (backswimmers) **90–93**
 lesser (93)
waterbug 38
weavers
 funnel (sheet-web) **272–275**
 grass funnel 275
 orb 276–281
 sheet-web **272–275**
weevils **154–161**
 acorn 154
 big-foot *154–155*
 boll (160)
 clay-colored 160
 cloverleaf 154
 destructive habits 159–160, (160)
 eight-humped 156
 fungus 159
 giraffe-necked 156–157
 hazel leaf-rolling 159
 larvae 159
 oak leaf-rolling 159
 pest control 160
 reactions to danger 160
 reproduction 155–159
 rough-backed emerald 155
 twelve-spined 160–161
 zygopine 157
whites 168–173
 cabbage whites (170)
Wyeomyia 70

X

Xysticus cristatus 266–267, 268–269

Y

Yponomeuta padella 198–199
Yponomeutidae **198–199**

Z

Zonocerus elegans 63
Zoraptera 8
Zygoptera 16

Picture credits